AIR RESOUR

→ AKVOS.
SOKOLSCKI
323-5025

The
HANDBOOK *of* ENVIRONMENTAL COMPLIANCE *in* ONTARIO

Second Edition

John-David Phyper

Brett Ibbotson

McGraw-Hill Ryerson
Toronto   Montreal

The Handbook of Environmental Compliance in Ontario
Second Edition

Second edition published in 1994

First published in 1991 by
McGraw-Hill Ryerson Limited
300 Water Street
Whitby, Ontario, Canada
L1N 9B6

Publisher: Donald S. Broad

Canadian Cataloguing in Publication Data

Phyper, John David
        The handbook of environmental compliance in Ontario

2nd ed.
ISBN 0-07-551557-1

1. Environmental law – Ontario.   I. Ibbotson, Brett.
II. Title

KE0717.P59 1994   344.713′046   C94-930558-8
KF3775.P59 1994

This publication is designed to provide accurate and authoritative information on the subject matter covered. It is sold with the understanding that neither the authors nor the publisher is engaged in rendering legal, accounting, or other professional advice.

Editorial services provided by Word Guild, Toronto

This book was printed and bound in the United States using acid-free paper.

TABLE OF CONTENTS

LIST OF FIGURES

LIST OF TABLES

Preface

IN THE PREFACE TO THE FIRST edition, we stated that the *Handbook* had been written to assist people responsible for ensuring that businesses and industrial activities in Ontario comply with environmental regulations and requirements — individuals who, whether they look after a small shop or direct the environmental affairs of a large corporation, have a personal stake in the environmental management of those companies.

Since its publication in 1991, we have received comments from many environmental managers and engineers, and we also have been pleasantly surprised to hear from lawyers, students, regulators, teachers, and consultants. Their comments have been overwhelmingly positive, and we are grateful for the support and encouragement.

We expected that the changing nature of environmental management would make it necessary to revise parts of the *Handbook* after a few years. This edition incorporates numerous changes that have occurred in regulations, technologies, and expectations since 1991.

Not anticipated were some of the broad administrative changes that have taken place in the last two years:

- the combining of the Ministries of Environment and Energy
- the wholesale reorganization that is occurring at the Ministry of Environment and Energy
- the much publicized and anticipated Clean Air Program being withdrawn and eventually replaced by the proposed Air Management Strategy which, in turn, was abandoned
- the coming into effect of the revised and amended version of the Environmental Protection Act and other statutes

With the combining of the two ministries, we employ the acronym MOEE when referring to the Ministry itself and in references to documents released in 1993. However, we have retained the MOE acronym when referencing publications published by the Ministry when it was the Ministry of the Environment.

The new organizational structure of the MOEE is based on function rather than environmental media. As a result, the Air Resources Branch, Water Resources Branch, Waste Management Branch, and Hazardous Contaminants Coordination Branch will cease to exist. In their place are branches in the Environmental Sciences and Standards Division with titles that reflect a "multi-media" approach:

- The Science and Technology Branch will assess the impact of contaminants on ecosystems and humans, identify priorities for environmental action, and develop technological approaches to solving environmental problems.
- The Standards Development Branch will develop environmental standards and guidelines, and coordinate the management of pesticides.
- The Program Development and Support Branch will develop regulations and programs that protect human health and the environment with special emphasis on pollution prevention, provide a "one window" contact for municipalities and industry, and provide advice on interpreting gaps in policies.
- The Environmental Monitoring and Reporting Branch will conduct environmental monitoring, report on the state of the environment, and coordinate data management systems.
- The Laboratory Services Branch will provide analytical capabilities.
- The Environmental Bill of Rights (EBR) Office will facilitate implementation of the EBR and establish the electronic registry that will provide public access to environmentally significant proposals and decisons.

We have tried to avoid referring to specific former branches except in situations where a branch played a role in the development of a specific document, policy, or guideline.

Although the latest revision of the Environmental Protection Act largely involved changes to the designations (numbers) assigned to parts, sections, and regulations, the changes can be confusing to people who were familiar with the former designations that had been used for several years. The correct citation is the *Environmental Protection Act, R.S.O. 1990, c. E.19 as amended;* however, we prefer to use the simpler and less daunting EPA, and we make similar simplifications when referring to various regulations. Similar revisions were made to the *Occupational Health and Safety Act, R.S.O. 1990, c. 0.1.* and its associated regulations. Table P.1 is a guide to the new designations for some of the parts, sections, and regulations referenced in the *Handbook.*

In April 1994, the MOEE released a document titled *Manual of Guidelines and Procedures.* This manual will be available in electronic format on the INTERNET system.

Although it has been necessary to make substantial changes to the *Handbook*, we have tried to remain true to its original goal of providing information succinctly and directly that responds to the following questions:

- What are the applicable environmental regulations and requirements for a specific situation?
- What should be monitored, measured, or tested to evaluate compliance?
- What methods are there for achieving compliance?
- What are the penalties for not complying?
- Are things likely to change in the near future? If so, how?

The material in this book is based on the experience and opinions of the authors, as well as written information available at the time that the book was being prepared. Every effort has been made to ensure that the information is current and reflects the latest developments in environmental management. The authors welcome suggestions for ways to improve the application of the *Handbook* both in the field and in the classroom.

Table P.1
SELECTED REVISED REGULATIONS OF ONTARIO

Regulation Name	Former Designation(s)	New Designation
Regulations Made under the Environmental Protection Act		
Ambient Air Quality Criteria	Reg. 296	Reg. 337
Air Pollution - General	Reg. 308	Reg. 346
Mobile PCB Destruction Facilities	Reg. 148/86	Reg. 352
Ozone-Depleting Substances - General	Reg. 394/89, 518/90	Reg. 356
Spills	Reg. 618/85	Reg. 360
Waste Management - General	Reg. 309	Reg. 347
Waste Management - PCBs	Reg. 11/82	Reg. 362
Regulations Made under the Gasoline Handling Act		
General	Reg. 439	Reg. 521/93
Regulations Made under the Occupational Health and Safety Act		
Asbestos	Reg. 570/82 plus several amendments	Reg. 837
Asbestos in Construction Projects and in Buildings and Repair Operations	Reg. 654/85, 510/92	Reg. 838

To Christine and my family
for their love and support
J.-D.P.

To my parents for their unfailing support
and to Debra for her patience and encouragement
B.G.I.

Acknowledgments

THIS *HANDBOOK* REPRESENTS THE efforts of more than the two authors. During its preparation and even before, many others shared information, expertise, and opinions.

To ensure that the material contained in the *Handbook* has been presented properly and is current, draft versions of chapters were reviewed by individuals who are active in that particular area of environmental management. All of the following people freely gave of their time and ideas, and the authors express their indebtedness to each.

Mr. G. Craig, Director, Toxicology, Beak Consultants

Mr. P. Dunn, Manager, Waste Management, Environmental Services Dept., Regional Municipality of Hamilton-Wentworth

Mr. D. Hopper, Principal, Angus Environmental Limited

Mr. D. Inkley, Utilities, Stelco Inc.

Mr. L. Kende, Supervisor, Noise Assessment, Ontario Ministry of Environment and Energy, Approvals Branch

Mr. R. Lall, Ontario Ministry of Environment and Energy, Central Region

Dr. D. Mackay, Professor of Chemical Engineering, University of Toronto

Mr. J. McDougall, Environmental Engineer, Phyper & Associates Limited

Mr. B. Powers, Senior Environmental Scientist, Angus Environmental Limited

Ms. C. Sefton, Counsel, Williams & Shier

Mr. E. Villeneuve, Manager, Environmental Auditing, Noranda Inc.

Mr. G. Zikovitz, Head, Spills Action Centre, Ontario Ministry of Environment and Energy

1.0

The Changing Nature of Environmental Management

DURING THE PAST FEW DECADES, there have been several occasions when there were indications that major changes were about to occur in our attitudes and actions toward the environment. The 1960s brought attention to environmental indifference and neglect. By the early 1970s, several major pieces of environmental legislation were being enacted and environmental agencies were being established. But this movement seemed to lose some of its momentum in the mid-'70s and early '80s, perhaps because most individuals and companies did not yet perceive an immediate stake in proper environmental management. The 1990s have seen environmental issues come back into prominence. This latest surge, however, promises to be distinctly different from earlier efforts. For several reasons, including those outlined below, it has become increasingly difficult to dismiss, ignore, or circumvent the latest tide of change that is occurring to the nature of environmental management.

Environmental regulations are becoming more comprehensive in virtually all aspects of sampling, analysis, and interpretation. More and more regulations outline how samples are to be gathered, the numbers of samples to be collected, how they should be analyzed, which parameters should be measured, and the frequency with which the results must be reported.

Environmental regulations are becoming more stringent. Not only do regulations address more parameters than ever before, but the acceptable concentrations of many parameters continue to become more protective of the environment. This is partially the result of continuing advances in analytical techniques which allow smaller and smaller quantities of substances to be measured. It also is influenced by the resistance that any effort to reduce stringency would face, even if less stringent objectives are warranted or supported by scientific information.

Environmental regulations are becoming more complex as they address more aspects of environmental management (such as those noted above), but also due to the participation of more agencies. Laws to protect the environment can be passed by all three levels of government in Canada.

1

Federal responsibilities for environmental legislation include environmental management at federal facilities (such as airports and international harbours), transportation (other than on roads within provinces), discharges that may be deleterious to fish, the import and export of goods and wastes, and issues deemed to be in the national interest such as the proper management of special materials (such as polychlorinated biphenyls). The Canadian Environmental Protection Act (CEPA) covers the registration of new chemicals and will be used to set regulations to control chemicals on the Priority Substance List.

Provincial jurisdiction includes emissions to air, discharges to water, waste management, and intraprovincial road transportation. Federal regulations can be used by provincial agencies if province-specific regulations have not been passed, but Ontario has issued regulations for many environmental situations. The environmental legislation that has been enacted and proposed over the last few years in Ontario has put it at the forefront of environmental regulation. Keeping pace with the changes has become a major challenge. Table 1.1 lists many of the major pieces of environmental legislation in Ontario and the corresponding federal acts.

Municipal governments can impose environmental requirements on activities within their jurisdictions or on those who use their facilities. Many municipalities in Ontario have established noise and sewer-use by-laws. An increasing number of municipalities are becoming involved with the siting and operating of solid waste management facilities. Some have established environmental protection offices or departments which investigate situations of concern. Municipal agencies often act in a cooperative and/or support role to provincial agencies.

Environmental agencies are becoming more resolute in identifying and prosecuting offenders. Provincial legislation such as the Environmental Statute Amendment Act of 1988 provides provincial representatives with greater powers of search and seizure of information and records, and greater authority to prosecute those who do not comply. The Investigations and Enforcement Branch, which investigates polluters, and the Legal Services Branch, which prosecutes environmental offenders, clearly illustrate the intention of the Ontario Ministry of Environment and Energy (MOEE) to hold offenders accountable for their actions. Fines for environmental offences in 1992 totalled $3.6 million, a 33% increase over 1991, and a 500% increase since 1985/86.

The liabilities and penalties for non-compliance have greatly increased. New legislation squarely places responsibility not only on corporations and organizations, but also on their officers and managers. Both federal and provincial legislation makes the officers of a company who participate, authorize, or acquiesce to an offence, guilty of the offence and liable for punishment. Stiff fines and jail terms can be imposed. Sentences handed down during 1992 by Ontario courts included the longest jail term in Canadian history and the single largest fine in Ontario.

Reliance on the traditional command-and-control approaches is diminishing. Since the mid-1980s, programs have been initiated in Ontario that emphasize pollution prevention rather than control. A key component in the current provincial agenda is the Pollution Prevention Pledge Program. The program invites industrial facilities to develop pollution reduction goals more stringent than those required by regulations and to attain those goals through planning, commitment, and achievement. Through this program, the MOEE hopes to reduce the release of persistent, toxic, and bioaccumulative chemicals by 50% by the year 2000. At the heart of the program is the belief that actions taken to eliminate or reduce the creation of pollutants at the source can produce environmental as well as economic benefits. It also recognizes that the traditional approach of investing equipment and capital in pollution control technology has been too costly and often ineffective.

Public attitudes and expectations are changing. While the regulatory framework is undergoing massive change, those changes may become secondary to the sweeping changes in attitude among individuals that are now beginning to influence the marketplace and reach into corporate boardrooms. Changes in broadly held attitudes and expectations will have the greatest impact on how environmental management strategies and policies evolve.

Corporate attitudes and expectations are changing. It is not important to determine which came first: the recent awakening of environmental awareness or the new vigour of environmental policy-making. What is important is that they support one another. In response to growing concern about the environment, the increased costs of non-compliance, and the increased liabilities, several companies are taking the lead in environmental protection. The "greening" of the boardroom is under way and spreading quickly. Many companies are beginning to realize that pollution is bad for business and that sound environmental management can protect and enhance the value of physical assets as well as corporate reputations.

Companies that do not have acceptable environmental records will struggle for credibility with the public. Each company will have to wrestle with what is the most appropriate way for it to respond to the changes that are occurring. One component of corporate response could be to adopt principles such as those listed in Table 1.2 which are based on the CERES Principles (formerly the "Valdez Principles"). These form a code of ethics that would require a company to curb pollution, reduce waste, offer compensation for environmental damage, and report every year about their operations with respect to the environment.

Given all of these changes, how can this book help? *The Handbook of Environmental Compliance in Ontario* is intended to serve as a guide that plant managers, environmental engineers, advisors, and students can consult to understand regulatory requirements, the way(s) to achieve compliance, and the liabilities posed by various types of operations and activities. Each chapter addresses a different facet of environmental management in terms of current and proposed legislation, obtaining approvals and permits, methods used to assess compliance, sampling and modelling techniques, penalties and liabilities, and reporting requirements.

Chapter 2/ Air Quality and Atmospheric Emissions presents current regulatory requirements as defined by the Environmental Protection Act (EPA) and Regulation 346. As the regulatory philosophy evolves from one of command-and-control to pollution prevention, broad changes are beginning to be made to the framework of regulatory requirements that address air quality issues and atmospheric emissions.

Chapter 3/ Water Quality and Liquid Discharges focuses on the Municipal, Industrial Strategy for Abatement (MISA) program being implemented in Ontario. MISA is "technology driven" and requires that dischargers install the best available technology that is economically achievable. Eventually it will be applied to all direct and indirect liquid dischargers including those to storm and sanitary sewers. The stated objective of MISA is the virtual elimination of persistent toxic substances from Ontario discharges.

Chapter 4/ Waste Management and Transportation presents the requirements of EPA Regulation 347. The regulation sets out a comprehensive system for monitoring hazardous and liquid industrial wastes from point of generation to ultimate disposal. The chapter also provides information on the provincial and federal statutes that describe the requirements for packing, labelling, etc. of dangerous goods, including wastes, during transportation.

Chapter 5/ Assessing and Remediating Contaminated Property addresses the environmental issues that arise whenever contaminated properties are being considered for sale or redevelopment. Like most jurisdictions, Ontario is faced with the difficult task of insuring that contaminated properties are adequately cleaned up prior to rezoning, re-use, or redevelopment. Recent guidelines on the decommissioning/clean-up of contaminated sites are discussed along with steps to conduct a pre-purchase assessment or inspection. In addition to the guidelines, other pertinent statutes and restrictions under common law and contract law are presented.

Chapter 6/ Noise and Vibration are defined as contaminants under the EPA. The regulation of noise for the most part, however, is managed through municipal by-laws which in turn are influenced by the MOEE Model Municipal Noise Control By-Law. A brief overview of the noise guidelines in Ontario is presented.

Chapter 7/ Special Materials addresses polychlorinated biphenyls (PCBs), one of the most regulated groups of chemicals in Canada. There are both provincial and federal regulations that govern the use, storage, handling, transportation, and disposal of such special materials. This chapter also presents the regulatory requirements for managing materials that contain asbestos.

Chapter 8/ Enforcement addresses this key part of environmental regulation. In Ontario, the Investigation and Enforcement Branch of the MOEE investigates and makes recommendations regarding appropriate legal remedies against pollution and polluters, as well as supplies information in support of prosecutions. The chapter discusses the various levels of government response to violations and describes both corporate and individual responses to site visits and interviews. Liabilities and penalties under various acts and regulations are summarized.

Chapter 9/ Environmental Fate is a primer to understanding the behaviour of chemicals in the environment which can be a valuable aid to managing the production, storage, handling, transportation, and disposal of chemicals. Information is presented on key environmental parameters, partition coefficients, reaction rates, and transport and transformation processes.

Chapter 10/ Environmental Audits illustrates how audits are increasingly being incorporated into environmental management programs. Recent changes in regulatory requirements further emphasize the need for well-planned audits. This chapter discusses the objectives and potential applications for various types of audits and addresses the issue of confidentiality.

Chapter 11/ Risk Assessment and Management demonstrates how these have become essential to identifying potential sources of risk. Different approaches to risk assessment and the situations where risk assessment can be applied are presented.

Chapter 12/ Emergency Planning and Spills describes the types of procedures that need to be in place to respond to unscheduled releases of materials. In Ontario, Part X of the EPA outlines the responsibilities and requirements for the notification and restoration following a spill. The chapter discusses the legal requirements following a spill, and spill prevention. In addition, the use of Best Management Practice (BMP) plans are discussed.

Chapter 13/ The Role of Toxicity Testing in Environmental Management describes how toxicity testing techniques are incorporated into the regulation of liquid effluents and their potential role in evaluating soils. The different types of toxicity tests (acute and chronic) are described as is the potential role of Toxicity Reduction Evaluations.

Table 1.1
SUMMARY OF MAJOR ONTARIO AND FEDERAL
ENVIRONMENTAL ACTS

Ontario Acts
- Environmental Protection Act (EPA)
- Dangerous Goods Transportation Act (DGTA)
- Ontario Water Resources Act (OWRA)
- Energy Act
- Gasoline Handling Act (GHA)
- Environmental Assessment Act (EAA)
- Environmental Statute Amendment Act
- Pesticides Act
- Planning Act
- Conservation Authorities Act
- Municipal Act

Federal Acts
- Canadian Environmental Protection Act (CEPA)
- Transportation of Dangerous Goods Act (TDGA)
- Fisheries Act
- Canadian Water Act (CWA)
- Arctic Water Pollution Prevention Act
- Northern Inland Waters Act
- International River Improvement Act (IRIA)

Table 1.2
ENVIRONMENTAL PRINCIPLES FOR CORPORATIONS

---

1. Protection of the Biosphere
Minimize and strive to eliminate the release of any substance that may damage the environment or its inhabitants. Safeguard wildlife habitat and open spaces while preserving biodiversity. Minimize contributions to global concerns such as the greenhouse effect, depletion of the ozone layer, and acid rain.

2. Sustainable Use of Natural Resources
Use natural resources such as water, soils, and forests in ways that are sustainable. Conserve nonrenewable natural resources through efficient use and careful planning.

3. Reduction and Disposal of Waste
Minimize the creation of waste, especially hazardous waste. Wherever possible recycle materials. Dispose wastes safely and responsibly.

4. Efficient Use of Energy
Invest in improved energy efficiency and conservation. Maximize the energy efficiency of products and services.

5. Risk Reduction
Minimize the environmental, health, and safety risks to employees and local communities by employing safe technologies and operating procedures, and by being constantly prepared for emergencies.

6. Market Safe Products and Services
Offer products or services that minimize adverse environmental impacts. Inform consumers of the environmental benefits and/or impacts of products or services.

7. Damage Compensation
Take responsibility for harm caused to the environment. Be prepared to restore the environment and compensate persons who are adversely affected.

8. Disclosure
Disclose incidents that cause environmental harm or pose undue hazards to employees and to the public. Disclose potential environmental, health, or safety hazards posed by operations. Do not take action against employees

who report any condition that creates a danger to the environment or poses health and safety hazards.

9. Environmental Directors and Managers

Appoint at least one senior officer who is qualified to represent environmental interests. Have that officer report directly to the chief executive officer. Commit resources to implement these principles and report on a regular basis as to their implementation.

10. Assessment and Annual Audit

Make public an annual evaluation of progress in implementing these principles and in complying with all applicable laws and regulations.

11. Incorporate the Importance of Environmental Management into Corporate Attitudes

Recognize that environmental management is not something to be avoided or dismissed. Realize that proper environmental management can protect and enhance physical assets and corporate reputations.

2.0

Air Quality and Atmospheric Emissions

2.1 OVERVIEW

As recently as the 1970s, air quality concerns tended to be local in nature and were often limited to gases such as carbon monoxide, sulphur dioxide, or nitrogen oxides, dust, and a few metals. Today's concerns are just as likely to focus on regional "airsheds," the transboundary migration of substances, or global issues such as acidic precipitation and ozone depletion. Frequently, the substances being studied are those emitted in trace amounts.

In Canada, the control of air pollution sources is largely a provincial responsibility, and Ontario has a relatively comprehensive package of regulations, policies, standards, and guidelines in place. Sections 2.2 and 2.3 describe the provincial and federal regulations, respectively. Section 2.4 outlines the current process followed by the Ministry of Environment and Energy (MOEE) for issuing approvals to emission sources. Section 2.5 describes techniques that can be used to monitor concentrations of substances in emissions and ambient air. Mathematical models which can be used to estimate air quality are presented in Section 2.6. The requirements to provide information about sources of air emissions to the MOEE are outlined in Section 2.7.

Many of the aspects of air quality management in Ontario described in Sections 2.4 through 2.7 are entering a transitional phase as current practices become updated, augmented, or replaced in response to the proposed regulatory reforms outlined in Section 2.8. The MOEE has proposed an Air Management Strategy (AMS) to reform and improve the control and regulation of stationary and mobile sources. The proposed strategy represents a fundamental shift in philosophy towards greater emphasis on control at source and pollution prevention.

2.2   PROVINCIAL REGULATIONS

2.2.1 Environmental Protection Act

The Environmental Protection Act (EPA), originally promulgated in 1971, is directed toward the protection and conservation of the natural environment. While much of the original text does not specifically address air quality or atmospheric emissions, those aspects of environmental management are included in the broad intent and general language of the EPA. For example, Section 9(1) states that no person shall construct, alter, extend, or replace anything or alter the production rate of any process that may discharge a contaminant into any part of the natural environment, except water, without a Certificate of Approval. There are several exceptions including routine maintenance, heating equipment, and noise- and vibration-emitting equipment in facilities housing not more than three families. Section 2.4 provides additional information on obtaining approvals.

Section 14(1) requires that no person shall discharge a contaminant or cause or permit the discharge of a contaminant into the natural environment that causes or is likely to cause an adverse effect. Section 1(1) defines **adverse effect** as:

- impairment of the natural environment for any use that can be made of it
- injury or damage to property or plant or animal life
- harm or material discomfort to any person
- an adverse effect on the health of any person
- impairment of the safety of any person
- rendering any property or plant or animal life unfit for use by man
- loss of enjoyment of normal use of property
- interference with the normal conduct of business

Obviously, several of these types of adverse effects can be caused by emissions to the atmosphere or the way(s) that emissions can affect air quality. For example, the loss of enjoyment of normal use of property can include nuisances such as odour and dust.

Other parts of the EPA can apply to air quality issues under certain conditions. For example, Part VI deals with ozone-depleting substances. It has prohibited, since 1 July 1989, the transport, storage, use or display of anything which contains an ozone-depleting substance, with the exception of prescription drugs.

Part X of the EPA deals with spills of pollutants. Section 92 states that every person having control of a pollutant shall immediately notify a range of authorities should a spill occur. Section 93 of the EPA requires that the responsible party do everything practicable to prevent, reduce, or ameliorate the effect and to restore the natural environment. Part X also deals with clean-up orders and issues regarding compensation. (Refer to Chapter 12 for additional information.)

2.2.2 Regulation 346

Air quality and atmospheric emissions are addressed specifically in Regulation 346 which was promulgated under the EPA. The regulation consists of a General Section, Schedule 1 which lists various prescribed air quality concentrations, and an Appendix that describes various air pollutant atmospheric dispersion algorithms (equations). The fundamental philosophy that guides Regulation 346 is that if there is sufficient dilution of pollutants in the atmosphere, then the overall impact will be acceptable.

Sections 1 through 4 of the General Section provide the definitions to be used in the regulation, set forth several exceptions, and describe the Air Pollution Index (API). There is an allowance for curtailing operations of sources of air emissions when the API reaches certain levels.

Section 5 forbids a person from causing or permitting the concentration of a contaminant to exceed the values set in Schedule 1 at prescribed locations called **points of impingement.**

Section 6 requires that no person shall cause or permit to be caused the emission of any air contaminant to the extent or degree as may:

- cause discomfort to persons
- cause loss of enjoyment of normal use of property
- interfere with normal conduct of business
- cause damage to property

There is some redundancy and inconsistency between the requirements of Section 6 of Regulation 346 and those of Section 14 of the EPA.

Section 7 describes a visible emissions chart and limits visible emissions observations to provincial officers trained by the MOEE.

Section 8 limits the opacity of allowable emissions depending on the type of fuel used. If the fuel source is liquid, then the opacity limit is <20%; if the fuel source is solid, then the opacity limit is <40% at the point of emission for a period of not more than four minutes in the aggregate in any 30-minute period. In recent years, the number of sources being cited for violations of visible emissions has increased steadily with "tickets" being issued by provincial officers.

Section 9 provides that the Ministry shall be notified forthwith when any emissions in excess of those permitted occur.

Section 10 prohibits the burning of materials other than that for which the burner was designed and at greater than design rates.

Section 11 contains specific prohibitions related to construction and sand and gravel extraction operations.

Section 12 limits incinerator emissions to 100 ppm total hydrocarbons (expressed as methane).

Section 13 prohibits persons from storing, handling, or transporting, any solid, liquid, or gaseous material or substance in such manner that an air contaminant is released.

The **Appendix of Regulation 346** presents algorithms which may be used to calculate half-hour, point-of-impingement (POI) concentrations. Different algorithms are identified for various configurations of emission sources, receptor locations, and wake effects of adjacent buildings. The algorithms and input parameters are described in Section 2.6.5.

The POI can be loosely defined as the nearest, off-property point where the level of air pollution is of interest. The regulation includes a number of drawings which provide some guidance in determining the location of the POI. There are three basic modelling procedures included in the regulation:

- "Short Circuit"
- Virtual Source
- Tall Stack

The exact model to be applied in each case depends on the relationship of the source of emission to the building it is released from, and on the relationship between the source of emission and the POI.

Schedule 1 of Regulation 346 contains the half-hour, POI standards for approximately 100 substances. In August 1991, the MOEE published the most recent version of the *Summary of Point of Impingement Standards, Ambient Air Quality Criteria (AAQCS), and Approvals Screening Levels (ASLs)*. A full list of published standards and criteria are presented in Table 2.1.

The MOEE has changed the classification system so that all previous "guidelines," "provisional guidelines," "tentative standards," and "interim standards" are now classified as Interim Standards (IS). The MOEE has also proposed a new type of criterion called Approvals Screening Level (ASL). An ASL is a POI concentration that can be used to allow the approval of a small number of sources. For a POI number to be reclassified from an ASL to a standard, it must be reviewed by the MOEE Advisory Group on Environmental Standards. The ASL classification will be used by the MOEE to deal with chemicals not covered by Standards or Interim Standards.

The MOEE has identified several deficiencies in the current version of Regulation 346 (MOE, 1987). For example, the overall approach is one that allows dilution to be a means of managing emissions while not encouraging the control of emissions at source. There is no opportunity for direct public participation in setting standards or the process of issuing Certificates of Approval (C of A). There is no provision for a C of A to be reviewed or to expire. The science of air dispersion modelling has also advanced considerably since Regulation 346 was first issued. Some of the specific deficiencies in the current modelling approach include the inability to address multiple sources, long-range transport and deposition, very short-term effects, very long-term effects, and synergistic effects of pollutants.

2.2.3 Other Provincial Regulations

Several regulations have been passed to control air emissions from specific processes, and types of industries, industrial sectors, or equipment in Ontario. These include:

- Regulation 14/86: Mobile PCB Destruction Facilities
- Regulation 77/92: Ground Source Heat Pump
- Regulation 271/91: Gasoline Volatility
- Regulation 295: Air Contaminants from Ferrous Foundries
- Regulation 297: Asphalt Paving Plants
- Regulation 311: Motor Vehicles
- Regulation 338: Emissions from Boilers
- Regulation 349: Hot Mix Asphalt Facilities
- Regulation 350: Lambton Industry Meteorological Alert
- Regulation 355: Ontario Hydro
- Regulation 356: Ozone-Depleting Substances
- Regulation 361: Sulphur Content of Fuel
- Regulation 660/85: Inco Sudbury Smelter Complex
- Regulation 661/85: Falconbridge Smelter Complex
- Regulation 663/85: Algoma Sinter Operations
- Regulation 751: Emissions of Pesticides

2.2.4 MOEE Policies and Guidelines

The MOEE has published the following policies and guidelines related to air emissions:

Policy 01-01: Combustion in Incinerators

Policy 01-03: Air Pollution Control on Incinerators

Policy 01-04: Operation of the Air Pollution Index and the Air Quality Index

Policy 01-05: Crematoria

Policy 05-01: Cement Industry Guidelines

Policy 05-02: Compliance

Guideline: *Interim Design and Review Guidelines for Wood-Fired Combusters*, Approvals Branch, August 30th, 1990

2.2.5 Occupational Health and Safety Act

Section 132(2)(b) and 132(3) of the Ontario Health and Safety Act should be reviewed prior to placing an emission point near a fresh air intake vent:

132(2): The replacement air shall,

(b) be free from contamination with any hazardous dust, vapour, smoke, fume, mist or gas

132(3): The discharge of air from any exhaust system shall be in such a manner so as to prevent the return of contaminants to any work place

2.3 FEDERAL REGULATIONS

2.3.1 Canadian Environmental Protection Act

Prior to 1988, the Clean Air Act was the only piece of federal legislation to cover air pollution. In 1988, the Clean Air Act, the Environmental Contaminants Act, and the Ocean Dumping Control Act were consolidated into the Canadian Environmental Protection Act (CEPA). The key elements of CEPA that are relevant to air quality and atmospheric emissions include:

- provisions to control all aspects of the life cycle of toxic substances including development, manufacturing, storage, transportation, use, and disposal
- the regulation of fuels and components of fuels
- the regulation of emissions from federal departments, boards, agencies, and Crown corporations
- provisions to create guidelines and environmentally safe codes of practice
- provisions to control sources of air pollution in Canada where a violation of international agreement would otherwise result

Section 34 of CEPA provides for regulating substances specified in the List of Toxic Substances in Schedule 1 of CEPA. Schedule 1 also states that the control of atmospheric releases is the most appropriate approach to regulating asbestos (mines and mills), lead (secondary lead smelters), mercury (chloro-alkali mercury plants), and vinyl chloride (vinyl chloride and polyvinyl chloride plants).

While the main responsibility to control air pollution sources is a provincial jurisdiction, the federal government can establish ambient air quality objectives and encourage provinces to adopt them as binding standards.

2.3.2 Management Plan for Nitrogen Oxides and Volatile
Organic Compounds

Environment Canada developed a Management Plan for Nitrogen Oxides (NO_x) and Volatile Organic Compounds (VOCs) to identify domestic environmental protection requirements and to ensure that Canada fulfilled its international obligations. The objective of the plan is to reduce the one hour ambient air concentration for ozone to below 82 ppb (0.16 mg/m^3) across Canada. Both NO_x and VOCs are precursors to ozone formation. Elements of the industrial and regional specific initiatives of the plan include:

- energy conservation measures
- industrial source control
- product modifications

The Management Plan has been designed to be flexible enough so that parts of the plan may be replaced with equivalent provincial legislation. However, at present there are no regulations governing the release of NO_x and VOCs.

2.3.3 Ozone-Depleting Substances

The federal government of Canada has developed three regulations to control the manufacture, importation and sale of Ozone-Depleting Substances. The Ozone-Depleting Substances Regulations No. 1, 2, and 3 regulate chlorofluorocarbons, certain bromofluorocarbons and products containing chlorofluorocarbons.

Regulation No. 1 outlines control limits for the manufacture, export, and import of bulk chlorofluorocarbons. In addition, Schedule III of the regulation lists the information that importers, exporters, and manufacturers must maintain; Schedule II lists information that Environment Canada requires on a quarterly basis. Regulation No. 2 outlines similar measures for the manufacture, import, and export of certain bromofluorocarbons.

Regulation No. 3 restricts the sale, manufacture, or import of pressurized containers containing 10 kg or less of chlorofluorocarbons and packaging material for food or beverages that is made of plastic foam in which a chlorofluorocarbon was used as the foaming agent. Exemptions to the restrictions include products used in the human and animal healthcare fields.

Provincial Regulation 356 reiterates the federal legislation regarding pressurized containers containing chlorofluorocarbons. The regulation also details restrictions on the manufacture of flexible polyurethane foam and various rigid insulation foams listed in Section 25 of the regulation. The restrictions include the percentage content of the chlorofluorocarbon in the product and the schedule for its reduction.

2.4 OBTAINING APPROVALS FOR EMISSIONS

Section 9(1) of the EPA requires that a Certificate of Approval be obtained by any person who intends to:

- construct, alter, extend or replace any plant, structure, equipment, apparatus, mechanism or thing that may discharge or from which may be discharged a contaminant into any part of the natural environment other than water; or
- alter the process or rate of production with the result that a contaminant may be discharged into any part of the natural environment other than water or the rate or manner of discharge of a contaminant into any part of the natural environment other than water may be altered.

It is important to remember that having and complying with the terms and conditions of a C of A does not exclude the possibility of being prosecuted. For example, a C of A might describe maximum emission rates of specific chemicals. The rates could be met, but if the emission still causes odours or other adverse effects, the emitter may not be in compliance.

As a result of amendments to the EPA that have been passed over the years, sources which have existed unchanged since 30 June 1988 do not require Certificates of Approval.

Section 9(2) requires that an applicant for a C of A provide whatever information is required by the MOEE to assess the emission source properly. The application must include:

- the name of the owner and operator of the source
- a complete description of the process generating the contaminant including a process flow sheet, operating schedule, production data, and raw materials
- a description of the systems, if any, to be used to reduce emissions
- an emission inventory for all contaminants which could be discharged to the atmosphere
- surrounding land use and points of impingement
- general information concerning toxic materials, waste storage and noise
- an assessment of the compliance with Regulation 346

Section 9(3) identifies several exemptions from the requirement to obtain a C of A:

a) routine maintenance carried out on any plant, structure, equipment, apparatus, mechanism or thing
b) equipment for the combustion of fuel, other than waste incinerators, in buildings or structures designed for the housing of not more than three families
c) any equipment, apparatus, mechanism or thing in or used in connection with a building or structure designed for the housing of not more than three families where the only contaminant produced by such equipment, apparatus, mechanism or thing is sound or vibration

d) any plant, structure, equipment, apparatus, mechanism or thing that may be a source of contaminant of a class exempted from the regulation

e) any plant, structure, equipment, apparatus, mechanism or thing used in agriculture

f) any motor or motor vehicle that is subject to the provisions of EPA, Part III

Additional exemptions are also provided in Regulation 346, Section 3. These include fuel-burning equipment for comfort heating (with less than 1.5 million BTU/hr heat input), equipment for the preparation of food in a domestic residence, equipment for construction/maintenance of a highway, and source of visible light radiation intended for the purpose of advertising.

Section 9(6) is an important but often overlooked part of the EPA. It allows a proponent (the owner and/or operator of a source) to make changes to a system without obtaining a C of A or an amendment to an existing C of A by notifying the MOEE director. The section only applies when the changes will result in a decrease of emissions and insufficient time is available to obtain the C of A or amendment.

As of October 1992, a processing and handling fee is payable upon submission of an application for a C of A. The fee provisions are contained in Ontario Regulation 503/92. The fee is 2% of the cost of the pollution device, with a minimum of $50 and a maximum of $100,000. A pollution control device is defined as anything which reduces or controls the discharge of pollutants or conveys or emits a pollutant. Included in the cost estimate are labour, materials and the market value of any required buildings. Excluded in the costs are land, engineering and consulting services, already existing or approved things, and this fee and all taxes.

The Approvals Branch of the MOEE has begun an effort to streamline the approvals process. The stated goal of the branch is to process applications with a 30-day average turnaround, and a 60-day maximum, from the time a complete application is received. Any approval that will take longer than 30 days to process is brought to the attention of the director of the Approvals Branch. The improvement is being accomplished with a program of staff training and a detailed reviewer's manual.

The MOEE *Guide for Applying for Certificates of Approval-Air* (September, 1992) uses the following headings to describe the information that a proponent should provide in a C of A application:

- abstract of the proposal
- general description of the proposal
- data sheets
- process flow diagram

- process step(s) and/or unit(s)
- operating conditions, process streams, and flow rates
- stacks, vents, contaminant emission information
- contaminant emission summary table
- supporting information for contaminant emissions
- existing sources of contaminants
- dispersion calculations
- site, plot, roof, and elevation plans
- supporting information for the assessment of noise and vibration emissions

Applicants are encouraged to complete dispersion modelling to determine the point-of-impingement concentrations of contaminants (refer to sections 2.2.2 and 2.6.5).

Most delays in processing C of A applications result from incomplete or confusing information. It is important to completely and accurately respond to the information requirements of the Approvals Branch accurately and completely. This is particularly true in cases where unusual or new and innovative processes or control systems are proposed, or where difficult or contentious pollutants could potentially be emitted.

2.5   MONITORING AND SURVEYS

2.5.1 Monitoring Objectives

Monitoring of air emissions or ambient air quality may be needed or advisable for various reasons. Routine monitoring may be a requirement of a control order, C of A, or other directive. An emitter may monitor as part of an internal environmental management program. Special or one-time efforts may be undertaken to investigate specific conditions. Whatever the reason, it is vital that the individuals who collect samples — whether for regulatory purposes or as part of an internal sampling program — be properly trained, follow acceptable protocols, and have samples analyzed using techniques with appropriate detection limits. The cost of air sampling programs and the potential impact of the results on evaluations of compliance or decisions to change control technology do not allow for a haphazard approach.

2.5.2 Source Testing Technologies and Frequency

There are two broad types of emission testing: continuous emission monitoring and campaign or compliance testing. Continuous emission monitoring (CEM) involves the real time or near real time measurement of the concentration of a pollutant in an emission stream, and the simultaneous measurement of flow rate parameters.

Instrumentation to measure concentration in real time in industrial environments is limited to a small range of pollutants: opacity, nitrogen oxide, sulphur dioxide, total hydrocarbons, carbon monoxide, carbon dioxide, hydrogen sulphide, and some organic compounds. CEM systems are very complex and expensive to operate and maintain, and therefore are used only on the largest or more contentious sources.

Campaign or compliance testing refers to test programs carried out over one or two days to monitor emissions from an operating facility.

The protocols for source testing are lengthy and comprehensive. Table 2.2 presents a partial list of references for pertinent testing protocols. The MOEE Source Testing Code (Version 2) describes the currently preferred methodologies. These include:

Method 1: location of sampling site and sampling points.

Method 2: determination of stack gas velocity and volumetric flow rate.

Method 3: determination of molecular weight of dry stack gas.

Method 4: determination of moisture content of stack gases.

Method 5: determination of particulate matter emissions from stationary sources.

There are several techniques that can be used to sample emission points such as stacks and exhausts. Particulate matter is sampled using isokinetic sample trains. Many organic compounds are sampled using non-isokinetic sample trains that include appropriate absorption solutions or adsorbents. Metals may be present in several forms simultaneously (adsorbed to particles, as vapours, as fumes) and therefore should be sampled using a combination of isokinetic and adsorbents. Dioxins, furans, and trace organic compounds are usually sampled using a modified, particulate matter sampling train.

Isokinetic sampling involves matching the sampling velocity with the gas velocity through alterations in the volumetric flow rate of the sample and the probe nozzle diameter (Sparks, 1984).

Emissions from many combustion processes are now believed to be sources of dioxins and furans. Because of concerns about the potential human health effects and environmental distribution of these compounds, considerable attention is being directed at quantifying and reducing combustion emissions. If the MOEE suspects that dioxins and furans may be formed during an industrial process, especially one involving high temperatures, a dioxin and furan sampling program may be required.

2.5.3 Visible Emissions

Many emissions are visible due to the presence of liquid sprays or mists, solid particles, or coloured gases. Sections 8(1) and 8(2) of Regulation 346 describe how the acceptability of a visible emission is determined based on its opacity (the degree to which it obstructs the passage of light):

(1) Subject to subsection (2), no person shall cause or permit to be caused a visible emission that obstructs the passage of light to a degree greater than 20% at the point of emission for a period of not more than four minutes in the aggregate in any 30-minute period.

(2) A visible emission from a source of combustion employing solid fuel may obstruct the passage of light to a degree greater than 20% but no greater than 40% at the point of emission for a period of not more than four minutes in the aggregate in any 30-minute period.

Opacity is the most commonly used parameter for evaluating emissions from stationary sources. The most common way of determining the opacity of visible emissions is through the observations of certified observers.

The MOEE has offered courses to certify visible emissions observers. The classroom instruction component of the training addresses types of sources, legislation, and the roles of factors such as sun angle, plume angle, and point of observation. Individuals are familiarized with plumes of various colours and opacities. A certificate, valid for six months, is awarded if a sufficient number of randomly selected emissions are properly evaluated during a test at the end of the course. The document entitled *Visible Emissions Identification* is used as the manual for certifying observers (MOE, 1982).

While non-MOEE staff can be certified as visible emissions observers, the current version of Regulation 346 only recognizes observations made by trained provincial officers during the course of enforcement procedures if the results are to be used to assess compliance in a legal context. Such observations must be made in accordance with Section 7(3) of Regulation 346.

In recent years, the number of sources being cited for violations of visible emissions has increased steadily. It is frequently the offence described on **tickets** issued by provincial officers (see Section 8.5). Three key parameters used to assess visible emissions are duration of emission, opacity, and the type of fuel involved (if relevant). At facilities where opacity is a concern, on-line meters can be installed which continuously record the opacity of the emission stream as it passes through a stack.

2.5.4 Ambient Air Sampling

Ambient air monitoring may be undertaken by regulatory agencies to evaluate general conditions, establish the concentrations typically present at a location, identify trends in air quality, and identify regional differences or similarities. Ambient air monitoring can also be used to collect data for enforcement purposes. The MOEE maintains a network of air monitoring stations at locations across the province for monitoring concentrations of various parameters including gases such as sulphur dioxide, suspended particulate matter and its constituents such as lead, and dust-fall. Environment Canada maintains the National Air Pollution Surveillance (NAPS) network.

Ambient air quality surveys also can be undertaken prior to a source becoming operational and the data subsequently used to evaluate the effects that the source has on local air quality.

At industrial facilities, ambient air monitoring may be undertaken to assess the potential off-site migration that could occur in the event of a spill or unscheduled release. Such information can be valuable during an emergency response situation.

In most instances, ambient air concentrations are relatively low compared to concentrations in emission sources. The preferred sampling method is to draw air through a loop, cell, or reaction chamber where the concentration(s) is measured and the result is available within a few moments of taking the sample. If such "real-time" analysis is impractical, there are several other approaches that can be employed:

- whole air samples can be pumped into bags or containers often made of special plastics that are later transported to a laboratory.
- air can be passed through a filter which traps particles. The filter can be weighed to determine the mass of material collected or the filter can be dissolved and the residue analyzed.
- air can be passed through a trap that is maintained at a relatively low temperature. The condensed material that collects in the trap can be analyzed.
- air can be bubbled through a liquid medium or passed through a packed bed of charcoal granules, synthetic material, or a polyurethane plug to absorb gaseous compounds.

2.5.5 Odours

Two approaches are used in the assessment of odour. One is to monitor individual substances being emitted and compare their concentrations to odour thresholds. The other is to consider the odour potential of an entire emission. The latter is determined by an odour panel, a group of trained people who smell samples to determine if an odour is discernible. Typically, a series of dilutions are created by mixing samples of the emission with odour-free air. A positive response is produced when 50% or more of the members of the panel can detect an odour in a sample. The findings of an odour panel can be used to describe the total number of odour units associated with an emission.

While the term "odour threshold" implies that detection occurs at a specific concentration, detectability, in fact, is highly variable. An individual's sensitivity can be influenced by many factors and, as a result, odour thresholds may be reported as specific values, ranges, or as geometric averages and standard deviations.

Table 2.3 presents a list of odour thresholds for selected chemicals. The odour thresholds for some compounds such as hydrogen sulfide are extremely low. As much as 50% of the public's complaints to the MOEE are associated with odour.

2.5.6 The Need for Quality Assurance and Quality Control

A rigorous Quality Assurance/Quality Control (QA/QC) program is an essential part of any air quality and emission testing effort. The following aspects of sample collection, handling, and analysis should be addressed in a QA/QC program:

- sampling procedures (including the cleaning of equipment between sampling efforts)
- calibration of field equipment
- chain-of-custody procedures for samples
- standard reference methods for laboratory standard solutions
- method blank samples and method blank samples spiked with a standard solution be included during the course of an analytical run
- assessments of precision, accuracy, and completeness

2.5.7 Emission Surveys

As part of broader environmental initiatives, primarily aimed at the reduction or elimination of toxic discharges and pollution prevention, a range of surveys and inventories has recently appeared. These include the MOEE Air Emission Inventory and the National Pollutant Release Inventory (NPRI). The latter includes releases to air, water, and waste streams. These two surveys require industries to provide considerable detail about their facilities, processes, and emissions to government regulators. Much of this information could make its way into the public domain and it could also be available to government officials to assist with prosecutions. For these reasons, accuracy, completeness, and consistency are essential.

Ontario Air Emissions Inventory

In March 1992, MOEE and Environment Canada sent letters to approximately 2,000 industries located within 50 miles of the Great Lakes, requesting data about 1990 and 1991 air emissions. Environment Canada also indicated its intent to audit completed inventories for completeness and accuracy.

The inventories are being used by the MOEE to update the province-wide emission information database. Environment Canada is using the inventories to implement domestic pollution control programs and to meet international obligations for the reporting of national emissions.

Information required prior to filling out the questionnaire includes:

- map and/or drawing of the facility
- list of exhaust stacks/vents
- list of fuel combustion equipment
- annual fuel consumption for each fuel type
- process flow charts and production quantities
- solvent usage and type (if >1,000L per year)
- bulk storage (if >10,000L)
- list of fugitive emission sources
- list of related internal environmental reports

The emission survey consists of nine forms and detailed descriptions of the information being sought:

Form 1   Company Description
Form 2   Stack Information
Form 3   Combustion Equipment
Form 4   Fuel Consumption
Form 5   Process (one for each emitting process)
Form 6   Solvent Usage
Form 7   Bulk Storage
Form 8   Fugitive Emission
Form 9   Internal Studies

It is anticipated that companies will be required to update these emission inventories on a semi-regular basis. The requirement for the compilation of emission inventories on a regular basis will be included in federal-provincial and international air quality agreements.

National Pollutant Release Inventory (NPRI)

Included in the Federal Green Plan was a provision for the the compilation of an inventory of all emissions of toxic and persistent substances into the Canadian environment. The first reporting year was 1993, with reports due by June 1994.

Under the authority of the Canadian Environmental Protection Act, the federal Minister of the Environment will, each year, request any facility that uses or processes 10 tonnes or more annually of a substance on the NPRI list, in a concentration greater than 1%, and whose employees collectively work 20,000 or more person-hours a year, to report. The report format and reporting procedures are similar to United States SARA Title 313, Form R, procedures and forms. Environment Canada will provide an electronic version of the forms which can be used to generate the reports and for electronic submission of data.

The reports will be entered into a database which will be accessible by the public. Environment Canada will also prepare a printed report each year which will summarize the largest emitters, by location, by material emitted, by industry, etc. The information used to generate the inventory will be auditable material under CEPA and must be kept on file at the facility and be available to Environment Canada inspectors for at least three years.

2.6 MODELLING

2.6.1 Overview

Mathematical models can be used to predict how atmosphere pollutants behave and the concentrations that result at specific times and locations. Over the last two decades, the sophistication of such models has grown rapidly. Many of the latest models attempt to address various factors that influence atmospheric dispersion such as atmospheric stability, irregular or complex terrain, multiple-emission sources, local building wake effects, and short-term events.

Regulation 346 identifies several relatively simple models which may be used to estimate concentrations at specific points of impingement (POI). The result of such calculations can be a key element in decisions for issuing or denying a C of A.

All but the simplest models take into account atmospheric stability, which represents the turbulence of the transporting wind and its ability to disperse emitted materials (Bowne, 1984). Stability categories can be semi-quantitatively specified in terms of wind speed, incoming solar radiation during the day, and cloud cover during the night (Pasquill and Smith, 1983):

Surface Wind Speed (m/s)	DAY Incoming Solar Radiation Strong	Moderate	Slight	NIGHT Thinly Overcast or ≥4/8 low cloud	≤3/8 cloud
<2	A	A-B	B	—	—
2-3	A-B	B	C	E	F
3-5	B	B-C	C	D	E
5-6	C	C-D	D	D	D
>6	C	D	D	D	D

Stability is least for Class A and highest for Class F. The neutral class (D) is assumed to occur for overcast conditions during day or night.

2.6.2 Gaussian Plume Models

Gaussian plume models are one way of estimating airborne concentrations of pollutants in the vicinity of a source. Downwind concentrations are calculated based on the height of release, the emission rate, exit velocity and temperature from the source, wind speed, and general atmospheric conditions. This type of model assumes that the plume will spread both laterally and vertically. The concentrations of a substance in such a plume are described in mathematical terms as having a "normal" or Gaussian distribution. Gaussian plume models are generally considered to be capable of predicting annual average concentrations at a point of exposure within a factor of two to four for pollutants released continuously over flat terrain (Cohrssen and Covello, 1989). More complex conditions contribute to greater uncertainty in predictions.

2.6.3 Long-Range Transport Models

Long-range atmospheric transport models attempt to predict pollutant concentrations over geographical regions as large as entire continents. Trajectories that released pollutants might follow are computed based on historical wind data from weather stations within the region. Generally, these models are thought to predict annual average concentrations within a factor of three to five (Cohrssen and Covello, 1989).

2.6.4 Puff Models

Puff models are based on the same principles as Gaussian models, but they are used to simulate the transport of emissions after episodic or short-duration releases, such as explosions or accidental releases (Cohrssen and Covello, 1989).

2.6.5 Regulation 346 Algorithms

The algorithms identified in Regulation 346 are based on Gaussian plume dispersion models. The configuration of the building on which the emission point is located and the adjacent buildings determines which of the algorithms is most appropriate for specific situations. To assist in the selection of the appropriate algorithm, figures are provided in Regulation 346 that illustrate various configurations of stack and building heights and location of adjacent buildings. Four different scenarios are described:

Scenario 1   Receptor is located within 5 m of the source and the emission is caught in either the wake of the building or an adjacent building (i.e. less than 100 m).

Scenario 2   Receptor is located greater than 5 m from the source and the emission is caught in either the wake of the building or an adjacent building (i.e. less than 100 m).

Scenario 3   Receptor is located greater than 5 m from the source and the emission is not being caught by the wake of the building or an adjacent building (i.e. less than 100 m).

Scenario 4   Multiple sources: worst-case concentrations from aforementioned sections for a receptor are to be added together.

Scenarios 2 and 3 implicitly use atmospheric stability classes C and D in the modelling.

Various parameters may be needed to use the algorithms. These can include stack height, emission exit velocity and temperature, emission rate of the pollutant, and the distance and height of closest receptor.

Software for dispersion modelling may be requested from the MOEE, 125 Resources Road, Rexdale, Ontario, M4V 1K6 (Tel. 416-235-5772 or

416-235-5764). The applicant will be required to supply three blank diskettes.

2.6.6 U.S. EPA Models

The U.S. EPA has recommended atmospheric dispersion models in its *Guidelines on Air Quality Models* (U.S. EPA, 1980). Some of these models may be better suited to evaluating some conditions than the algorithms stipulated in Regulation 346; however, permission from the MOEE should be obtained prior to using the models for assessment of compliance.

RAM Gaussian Plume Multiple-Source Air Quality Model – A steady-state model for estimating concentrations of stable pollutants for average times of an hour to a day from point and area sources.

Industrial Source Complex Models (ISC) – Both a short-term and a long-term version of this Gaussian plume dispersion model are available. The models account for settling, dry deposition of particles, and down-wash. In addition, the models can handle area, line or volume sources. Limited adjustment can be made for terrain.

Multiple-Point Gaussian Dispersion Algorithm with Terrain Adjustment (MPTER) – A multiple-point source algorithm with terrain adjustment. It is useful for estimating air concentrations of nonreactive pollutants.

Single-Source Model (CRSTER) – A steady-state Gaussian plume model that is applicable to rural or urban areas and uneven terrain. The model is able to determine the maximum concentration for certain averaging times and can also determine the meteorological conditions that caused the maximum concentration. This is the basic model used by the U.S. EPA for evaluating single-point sources.

Valley Model – The model considers the worst-case impact in complex terrain. It is comprised of a modified Gaussian plume model which assumes that the horizontal crosswind distribution has a uniform rather than a normal distribution and has special algorithms for situations where a plume impacts elevated terrain.

2.7 REPORTING REQUIREMENTS

2.7.1 General Requirements

Section 13 of the EPA requires that every person who discharges into the natural environment or who is responsible for a source that discharges to the environment any contaminant in an amount, concentration, or level in excess of that prescribed by the regulations shall forthwith notify the Ministry. Accordingly, anyone who emits a substance into the atmosphere in concentrations that exceed the conditions of an order or C of A must notify the MOEE.

Reporting requirements may become more frequent and entail more detail under the proposed air management programs (see Section 2.8).

2.7.2 Incident Reporting

An "incident" is defined in the EPA as the discharge of a contaminant into the environment out of the normal course of events that is likely to cause an adverse effect. There are several sections of the EPA that impose requirements to notify various parties when an incident occurs. Some sections are somewhat generic in nature. For example, Section 15(1) of the EPA requires that every person who discharges a contaminant or causes or permits the discharge of a contaminant into the natural environment out of the normal course of events that causes or is likely to cause an adverse effect shall forthwith notify the Ministry.

Similarly, Section 92(1) of Part X requires every person having control of a pollutant that is spilled and every person who spills or causes or permits a spill of a pollutant that causes or is likely to cause an adverse effect shall forthwith notify the following persons of the spill, of the circumstances thereof, and of the action that the person has taken or intends to take with respect to the MOEE, the municipality or the regional municipality where the spill occurred, and the owner of the pollutant. Additional information on incident reporting requirements is provided in Section 12.2

More specific to air quality concerns is Section 9 of Regulation 346 which requires notification where a failure to operate in the normal manner or a change in operating conditions occurs, or a shutdown of the source or part thereof is made for some purpose, results in the emission of air contaminants that exceeds the POI concentrations specified in Schedule 1 or exceeds any of the criteria specified in Sections 6 or 8 of Regulation 346 (see Section 2.2.2). Under such circumstances, the owner or operator of the source of air pollution shall immediately notify a provincial officer and provide details of such failures, change or shutdown. A written account shall be provided as soon as practicable.

A provincial officer may authorize, in writing, the continuance of such operation for a reasonable period of time given the circumstances and may impose upon the owner or operator such terms and conditions for continued operation as the officer considers necessary.

2.8 PROPOSED PROGRAMS

2.8.1 Overview

The MOEE has proposed several regulatory programs to address air contaminants. These programs included the Clean Air Program (CAP) – August 1990; the Stationary Source Control Program (SSCP) – fall of 1992; and the Air Management Strategy (AMS) – spring of 1993. All of these programs proposed a broad rewriting of the entire air pollution legislation and all procedures and criteria used.

The MOEE commissioned a series of studies which evaluated the economic and administrative impact of CAP. Rapid implementation of CAP was deemed too costly and it was subsequently placed on hold.

The SSCP proposed that the "solution to pollutants is prevention." It was modified to become the AMS by including nonstationary sources. The AMS proposed the philosophy that pollution prevention was preferable to dilution or control.

It appears that none of the CAP, SSCP, or AMS will proceed in their entirety. Instead, various parts of each will gradually be placed onto the regulatory agenda. The components most likely to be included in new regulations in the near term are:

- the use of the CAP models to assess compliance
- the development of *de minimis* levels of sources for which appraisals will not be required
- the development of "Permit-by-Rule" regulations for common groups of air pollution sources (e.g. combustion appliances)
- the proposal that called for greater public participation in the process by which Certificates of Approval are issued has been initiated in the new Environmental Bill of Rights, while the proposal for source registration has already been included in the provincial emission survey and federal NPRI program
- the use of time limited and renewable Certificates of Approval

2.8.2 Clean Air Program

In November 1987 and August 1990, the MOEE released discussion papers on the proposed Clean Air Program. Three philosophical points formed the basis of CAP:

- the primary means of controlling emissions should be at the source rather than allowing their dilution in the air
- emissions of toxic pollutants should be virtually eliminated
- the atmosphere should not be used as a disposal facility for pollutants

By requiring that emissions be controlled at source, CAP was to eliminate the use of dispersion as a way of dealing with air pollution. It would have also eliminated the option of using tall stacks as a means of complying with air quality criteria.

Under CAP, the level of control was to be a function of the "environmental hazard" posed by the substance being emitted. This twinning of the level of control to the level of concern is illustrated in the following CAP terms:

Level 1 Contaminants in this level present a high degree of environmental hazard (i.e. they are persistent or tend to bio-accumulate in the environment). Known and probable human carcinogens likely will be included in Level 1. Control is aimed at virtually eliminating emissions of Level 1 substances.

Level 2 Contaminants in this level are of moderate concern. They may affect distant receptors via long-range transport and/or transformation in the atmosphere. Control is aimed at minimizing emissions to the extent feasible.

Level 3 Contaminants in this level are of moderate concern but because of nuisance effects, controls are required to levels well below those at which health effects could occur. Control is aimed at providing reasonable abatement to avoid nuisances.

The MOEE developed a ranking system for assessing the relative environmental hazard of chemical contaminants. The scoring system dealt only with individual contaminants on the basis of health effects on human beings and animals, and damage to vegetation.

Other proposed components of the CAP program included:

- establishing methodologies that can be used to determine appropriate control requirements
- setting Air Quality Standards (AQS)
- source registration
- a two-phased approval process
- adopting an airshed approach and new mathematical models

Establishing Control Requirements

Rather than setting emission limits for types of emission sources, the proposed approach under CAP was for the MOEE to outline a methodology for evaluating control technologies. The methodology would focus on the types of data that need to be gathered and the way(s) that the data should be used to determine control requirements. A proponent would then follow the methodology to identify the appropriate control requirement for a specific source. A draft working document entitled *Guidelines for Determining Level 1 Controls* was issued (Smith, 1990).

Sources of Level 1 substances were to require a Level 1 Control Limit Evaluation. The methodology was described by the MOEE as a "top-down analysis" in that the most stringent control requirements must be considered first. The methodology consists of four steps:

Step 1   Identification of Control Alternatives
Step 2   Effectiveness Ranking of Control Alternatives
Step 3   Evaluation of Control Alternatives
Step 4   Impact Analysis of Control Alternatives

Step 1 requires the review of technically feasible alternatives to identify the control technology that will provide the **Lowest Achievable Emission Rate** (LAER). The alternatives explored should go beyond simply reviewing existing controls for the source category in question. The types of controls to be assessed should include existing control technology; technically feasible alternatives; innovative control technology; use of production processes, fuels and other raw materials which are inherently less polluting; and specific design or operational parameters.

Once the appropriate control options have been compiled, **Step 2** involves ranking them in order of control effectiveness and presented in a submission in the ranked order with the most effective option at the top. Accompanying each option should be a description of control efficiencies, expected emissions, and environmental impacts or benefits.

Step 3 involves assessing the technical feasibility and potential for significant adverse impacts on environmental media other than air, or significant adverse secondary impacts on air quality associated with a particular technology. The cost of achieving the control technology will *not* be included in the assessment.

In **Step 4**, the potential environmental impact associated with each control alternative is assessed. Both beneficial and adverse impacts should be discussed and quantified wherever possible. As the goal of the program is the virtual elimination of toxic emissions, the MOEE has stated that the argument for accepting a less stringent control technology of an insignificant air quality impact will not be accepted.

This approach, which excludes cost and implicitly imposes an acceptable level of risk through the Small Source Exemption Limit (described below), was challenged by numerous emitters.

In some instances, there may be compelling reasons for not instituting LAER control requirements. For such situations and for sources of Level 2 or 3 substances, two other levels of control requirement are available:

Best Available Control Technology - Economically Achievable (BACT-EA) will be the emission rate achieved by the best control technology generally available, taking into account economic and other factors. A proponent's evaluation should examine options that are more stringent and less stringent and determine the incremental financial aspects of each option and possibly other aspects (such as energy consumption).

A **New Source Performance Standard** (NSPS) will be the emission rate associated with the minimum level of control demonstrated as acceptable at similar sources. Regional and industrial economic factors were to be included in the evaluation.

For certain levels of emissions, it may be impractical to require stringent control. Hence, guidelines were being developed for assessing a *de minimis* level of emission below which control is not required. This **Small Source Exemption Limit** (SSEL) may take one of several forms:

1. An emission cap which defines an emission limit per unit time (kg/year)
2. A concentration limit, where the *de minimis* level is defined on the basis of a contaminant concentration in the stack being less than the standard or on some reasonable factor times the standard
3. A combination of 1 and 2

Air Quality Standards

Under CAP, it was intended that Air Quality Standards would be established. AQS values would represent the ultimate impact or change in air quality that is acceptable. If a source threatens to violate the AQS in an airshed, it would have needed to implement more stringent controls or be located elsewhere. Draft AQS values were issued in the initial CAP discussion paper (MOE, 1987).

Source Registration

Under CAP, a source registration system analogous to the U.S. EPA Superfund Reauthorization and Recovery Act (SARA) Title III was considered. The purpose of the program was to identify and quantify, on an annual basis, stationary sources of releases of **specified substances** into the environment. All emission sources greater than a prescribed *de minimis* level were to be required to register with the MOEE. Accurate quantification of the emission were to be only be required at facilities that are relatively large emitters. As indicated in Subsection 2.5.7, the MOEE initiated an emission survey in 1992. The information, along with the federal NPRI, fulfils the request for information stated in the CAP.

Approvals

Under CAP, it was proposed that approvals process be broken into two parts. The first concerned approvals for construction, and the second the Certificates of Approval to operate. Certificates to operate would be renewed on a five- to 10-year cycle. Approvals were to possibly specify stack sampling and ambient air monitoring requirements. The emphasis of CAP was to be on self-monitoring with the MOEE auditing the results.

Modelling

As part of the "airshed" management approach, the MOE new dispersion models were proposed under CAP. All contributing sources within a specified area would be modelled to assess their contribution on the overall airshed.

The models were to be used to screen approval applications. It was intended that a proponent must demonstrate compliance of the entire airshed (including the proposed source after accounting for mandated control equipment) with the air quality standards.

As described in Section 2.6, the algorithms described in Regulation 346 are relatively simple, Gaussian plume models. They were developed to compare sources but not to predict concentrations of contaminants downwind. The proposed models for use in CAP included a worst-case meteorology source assessment program, multiple-source gas dispersion program and associated programs, and special air dispersion models.

It is anticipated that the algorithms proposed in the worst-case and multiple-source models, and in one of the special air dispersion models (shoreline fumigation model), will be employed in future air management programs.

The **worst-case meteorology program** is a screening model designed for the quick computation of the meteorological conditions that produce the highest ground level concentration for a given source. The model generates its own possible meteorological conditions and hence input is limited to information on the stack such as its diameter and the emission rate. The model seeks the maximum concentration(s) for each atmospheric stability class considered and the source type. The stability classes cover convective, neutral, stable, and transition conditions. The model is only for single-source emissions.

The **multiple source gas dispersion model**, also called the "gas model," allows the calculation of the downwind concentration from several sources of emissions at a given set of receptors for a given set of meteorological parameters. Hourly meteorological data are required to run this model.

The advection of cooler, stable air from a large water body over relatively warmer, unstable air over land may result in the formation of a Thermal Inversion Boundary Layer (TIBL). Exhaust plumes which are released into the stable air near the shoreline and transported inland by the lake-breeze may become entrained in the unstable TIBL. The rapid mixing of the plume once it intersects the TIBL is referred to as "continuous fumigation." Such a situation may persist for up to several hours during which receptors may experience high pollutant concentrations. The **shoreline fumigation model** (Misra, 1980) was proposed for studying those types of situations.

Sources located in **complex terrain** or near significant topographic features require individual treatment. The MOEE identified two criteria for classifying sources in complex terrain (MOE, 1987):

1) The release height of the contaminant is less than two times the maximum terrain height. The maximum terrain height is defined as the difference between the highest height level (including tree tops) and the lowest height level within a distance of 20 times the stack height.

2) The gradient of terrain height with distance from the source must be greater than one-fifth (1/5). Gently sloping terrain would not be considered to be sufficiently complex to recommend physical modelling.

Three options are available for evaluating sources in complex terrain: physical modelling, ambient air monitoring, or modifying the worst-case model. Physical modelling may involve wind tunnels or water tanks using a scaled-down version of the source and terrain features. Ambient air monitoring would involve a comprehensive field study at the proposed site. Such a field study would include measurements of the local meteorological and pollutant dispersion characteristics at several locations around the source.

To predict the ground level concentrations using the worst-case model for a complex terrain, the following conservative modifications should be made:

- Use a reduced plume height (recommended to equal one-half the centreline plume height calculated for flat terrain). The flat terrain plume height would be calculated as the sum of the stack height and plume rise.
- Calculate the ground level concentrations at the height of the varying terrain for the nearest receptor.
- Use maximum receptor distance equal to 100 times the stack height.

Pollutant dispersion from sources located on or near a building(s) may be influenced by the changes in air flow caused by the building(s). The degree to which dispersion is affected depends on meteorological conditions and the relative proximity of the source to the building(s). **Building wake algorithms** were presented in MOE, 1987.

Interpretation of Model Results

Under CAP, the results of modelling will be used to divide emissions sources into two groups (MOE, 1987). **Type A** sources or groups of sources are those which are predicted to have little effect on ambient air concentrations of a contaminant, even under worst-case conditions. Such sources contribute less than 30% of the AQS. No further modelling is required unless there are special circumstances.

Type B sources or source complexes produce emissions resulting in concentrations greater than 30% of the air quality standard. If the modelling results indicate that contaminant emissions may result in the AQS being exceeded, two scenarios may occur. If the source complexes are located in a region where a relatively uniform background concentration for the contaminant exists, no further modelling is required unless special circumstances indicate otherwise when the maximum contribution plus the maximum uniform background is less than the AQS.

If the source complexes are located in a region with a non-uniform background due to other sources, more detailed modelling would be required. The modelling must take into account the contributions of all sources in the area. If needed, physical modelling in wind tunnels may also have to be conducted.

If the results of modelling lead to the conclusion that there will be non-attainment of the air quality standards, the source emissions will have to be reduced to appropriate levels or the source may need to be relocated.

Non-Attainment Areas

In areas where modelling or monitoring of local air quality fails to meet the standards, further abatement action on the source(s) emitting the contaminant of concern will be instituted through the Control Order mechanism. New sources that would emit a substance already at levels that exceed air quality standards may not be allowed into the area.

Where several sources contribute to non-attainment, an approach similar to the MOEE Remedial Action Plans (RAP), currently used for areas of unacceptable water quality, may be employed.

2.8.3 Air Management Strategy

The Air Management Strategy (AMS) was introduced in the spring of 1993. The philosophy underlying the AMS is one of pollution prevention, not dilution or control. The MOEE intended to use a broader spectrum of approaches to controlling emissions from stationary sources. The four main elements of this strategy were:

- Elimination of the Most Toxic Chemicals
- Improved Air Quality Standards and Dispersion Models
- Emissions Reductions
- Residual Impact Studies

The AMS program was abandoned because of insufficient resources. The assessment of new dispersion models is ongoing, however, through a joint government industry technical committee.

2.9   SUMMARY

Legislation concerning air quality and atmospheric emissions has not changed in Ontario for several years. Recently proposed programs include the Clean Air Program (CAP) – August 1990; the Stationary Source Control Program (SSCP) – fall of 1992; and the Air Management Strategy (AMS) – spring of 1993. CAP was deemed too costly, SSCP was abandoned because it did not address nonstationary sources, and AMS was abandoned because of insufficient resources within the MOEE. Nevertheless, these proposed programs do illustrate a philosophical evolution at the MOEE from dilution to pollution control equipment to pollution prevention.

The MOEE has identified deficiencies in the mathematical models used to assess emissions in Regulation 346. The MOEE has initiated a joint government-industry technical committee to review proposed air dispersion models and their potential roles.

While broad program changes have not come about, some aspects of air quality management have changed appreciably in the last few years. The filing and review of applications for Certificates of Approval have become better defined. However, this has been accomplished by a processing and handling fee.

Both the MOEE and Environment Canada have shown renewed interest in collecting emission data from industries. The assembled information will be used to update databases of emissions.

REFERENCES

Bowne, N.E. 1984. "Atmospheric Dispersion." In *Handbook of Air Pollution Technology*. S. Calvert and H.M. Englund, eds. Toronto: John Wiley and Sons.

Clayton, G., and F. Clayton. 1981. "Patty's Industrial Hygiene and Toxicology." Toronto: John Wiley and Sons: 3387.

Cohrssen, J.J., and V.T. Covello. 1989. "Risk Analysis: A Guide to Principles and Methods for Analyzing Health and Environmental Risks." Office of the President of the United States. ISBN 0-934213-20-8.

Fazzalari, F. 1978. "Compilation of Odour and Taste Threshold Values Data." American Society for Testing and Materials, DS 48A.

Leonardos, G. 1984. "Odour Sampling and Analysis." In *Handbook of Air Pollution Technology*.

Misra, P.K. 1980. "Dispersion From Tall Stacks into a Shore Line Environment." *Atmos. Env.* 14: 396-400.

Ontario Ministry of the Environment (MOE). May 1982. *Visible Emission Identification*. Second edition.

Ontario Ministry of the Environment (MOE). November 1987. "Stopping Air Pollution at Its Source: CAP, Clean Air Program."

Ontario Ministry of the Environment (MOE). August 1990. *CAP – Stopping Air Pollution at Its Source*. Draft Regulation.

Ontario Ministry of the Environment (MOE). August 1991. *Summary of Point-of-Impingement Standards, Ambient Air Quality Criteria (AAQCs), and Approval Screening Levels (ASLs)*. Air Resources Branch.

Ontario Ministry of the Environment and Energy (MOEE). September 1992. *Guide for Applying for Certificates of Approval – Air*.

Pasquill, F., and F.B. Smith. 1983. "Atmospheric Diffusion." Third edition. Chichesten: Ellis Horwood Ltd. ISBN 0-85312-587-2.

Smith, K.E. 1990. "Determining State of the Art Emission Controls for Regulatory Purposes." Presented at the Annual Spring Conference of the Air and Waste Management Association – Ontario Section. 22 to 24 April, Toronto.

Sparks, L.E. 1984. "Particulate Sampling and Analysis." In *Handbook of Air Pollution Technology*.

Stahl, W.H. 1973. "Compilation of Odor and Taste Threshold Values Data." American Society for Testing and Materials (ASTM), Data Series DS48, Philadelphia, PA.

U.S. Environmental Protection Agency. 1980. *Guideline on Air Quality Models*. OAQPS Guideline Series. Research Triangle Park, NC.

Table 2.1

AMBIENT AIR QUALITY CRITERIA AND POINT-OF-IMPINGEMENT LIMITS FOR AIR CONTAMINANTS

Contaminant Name	Contaminant Code or CAS No.	Point-of-Impingement Standard			Ambient Air Quality Criteria (AAQC)			
		Half Hour Point-of-Impingement Limit (µg/m3)	Point-of-Impingement Limiting Effect	Status	Annual (µg/m3)	24 Hour (µg/m3)	One Hour (µg/m3)	10 Minute (µg/m3)
Acetic Acid	64-19-7	2500	Odour	S		2500		
Acetone	67-64-1	48000	Odour	S		48000		
Acetophenone	98-86-2	625	Odour	IS			1167	850
Acetylene	74-86-2	56000	Odour	S		56000		
Acrolein	107-02-8	28	Health	IS		23.5		
Acrylamide	79-06-1	45	Health	S		15		
Acrylonitrile	107-13-1	300	Health	IS		100		
Alkyltoluene sulphonamide, n-				IS		120		
Aluminum oxide	1344-28-1	100		IS		120		
Ammonia	7664-41-7	3600	Odour	S		3600		
Ammonium chloride	12125-02-9	100		IS		120		
Amyl acetate, iso-	128-92-8					53200		
Amyl acetate, n-	628-63-7					53200		
Amyl acetate, secondary	626-38-0					66500		
Antimony and compounds	7440-36-0	75	Health	S		25		
Arsenic and compounds	7440-38-2	1	Health	IS		0.3		
Arsine	7784-42-1	10	Health	S		5		
Asbestos (fibers > 5 cm in length)	1332-21-4		Health	IS		0.04	fibers/cm3	
Asbestos (total)	1332-21-4			IS				
Barium - total water soluble	7440-39-3	5	Health	S		10		
Benzene	71-43-2	30	Health	CARC				
Benzo(a)pyrene - single source	50-32-8		Health	IS	0.00022	0.0011		
Benzo(a)pyrene, all sources	50-32-8	0.0033			0.0003			
Benzothiazole	95-16-9	200	Health	IS		70		
Benzoyl chloride	98-88-4	350	Health	IS		125		
Beryllium and compounds	7440-41-7	0.03	Health	S		0.01		

Point-of-Impingement Standard | **Ambient Air Quality Criteria (AAQC)**

Contaminant Name	Contaminant Code or CAS No.	Half Hour Point-of-Impingement Limit (µg/m3)	Point-of-Impingement Limiting Effect	Status	Annual (µg/m3)	24 Hour (µg/m3)	One Hour (µg/m3)	10 Minute (µg/m3)
Biphenyl	92-52-4	60	Odour	IS			60	
Borax	1303-96-4	100	Health	IS		33		
Boric acid	10043-35-3	100	Health	IS		33		
Boron	7440-42-8	100		S		120		
Boron tribromide	10294-33-4	100	Corrosion	S		35		
Boron trichloride	10294-34-5	100	Corrosion	S		35		
Boron trifluoride	7637-07-2	5		S		2		
Bromacil	314-40-9	30	Health	IS		10		
Bromine	7726-95-6	70	Health	S		20		
Bromochlorodifluoromethane (Halon 1211)	75-63-8	see Bill 218-CFCs						
Bromotrifluoromethane (Halon 1301)		see Bill 218-CFCs						
Butanol, iso-	78-83-1	1940	Odour	IS		655	15000	2640
Butanol, n-	71-36-3	2278	Odour	IS		770	15000	3100
Butanol, tertiary	75-65-0			UD		303000		
Butanone, 2- (Methyl ethyl ketone)	78-93-3	31000	Odour	S			31000	
Butyl acetate, n-	123-86-4	735	Odour	IS		248	15000	1000
Butyl acrylate	141-32-2	100		IS		120		
Butyl stearate	123-95-5	100		IS		120		
Cadmium and compounds	7440-43-9	5	Health	S		2		
Calcium carbide	75-20-7	20	Corrosion	IS		10		
Calcium cyanide (as total salt)	592-01-8	100		IS		120		
Calcium hydroxide	1305-62-0	27	Corrosion	S		13.5		
Calcium oxide	1305-78-8	20	Corrosion	S		10		
Captan	133-06-2	75	Health	IS		25		
Carbon black	1333-86-4	25	Soiling	S		10		
Carbon disulphide	75-15-0	330	Odour	S		330		

Contaminant Name	Contaminant Code or CAS No.	Point-of-Impingement Standard			Ambient Air Quality Criteria (AAQC)			
		Half Hour Point-of-Impingement Limit (µg/m3)	Point-of-Impingement Limiting Effect	Status	Annual (µg/m3)	24 Hour (µg/m3)	One Hour (µg/m3)	10 Minute (µg/m3)
Carbon monoxide	630-08-0	6000	Health	S		15700 (8 hour avg.)	36200	
Carbon tetrachloride	56-23-5	1800	Health	IS		600		
Chloramben	133-90-4	100	Health	IS		120		
Chlordane	57-74-9	15	Health	IS		5		
Chlorinated dibenzo-p-dioxins (CDDs) ** D/F PCDD		0.00045	Health	IS	0.0003			
Chlorine	7782-50-5	300	Health	S		150		
Chlorine dioxide	10049-04-4	85	Health	S		30		
Chlorodifluoromethane (Freon 22)	75-45-6	1050000	Health	IS		350000		
Chloroform	67-66-3	1500	Health	IS		500		
Chloropentafluoroethane (CFC-115)	76-15-3	see Bill 218-CFCs						
Chromium-di-, tri- and hexavalent forms	7440-47-3	5	Health	IS		1.5		
Citric acid	77-92-9	100	Particulate	IS		120	300	
Coal tar pitch volatiles - soluble fraction	8007-45-2	3	Health	IS	0.2	1		
Cobalt	7440-48-4	0.3	Health	S		0.1		
Copper	7440-50-8	100	Health	S		50		
Cresols	1319-77-3	230	Health	S		75		
Cyanogen chloride	506-77-4	15	Health	IS		12		
Cyclo sol 63	CYCLO SOL	25000	Health	IS		5000		
Cyclohexane	110-82-7	300000	Health	IS		100000		
Dalopon sodium salt	127-20-8	100	Health	IS		50		
Decaborane	17702-41-9	50	Health	S		25		
Decane, n-	124-18-5			UD				
Decene, 1-	872-05-9	180000	Health	IS		60000	60000	
Detergent enzyme (Subtilisin)	1395-21-7	0.2	Health	IS		0.06		
Diacetone alchohol	123-42-2	990	Odour	IS		335		1350

Contaminant Name	Contaminant Code or CAS No.	Half Hour Point-of-Impingement Limit (µg/m3)	Point-of-Impingement Limiting Effect	Status	Annual (µg/m3)	24 Hour (µg/m3)	One Hour (µg/m3)	10 Minute (µg/m3)
Diazinon	333-41-5	9	Health	IS		3		
Diborane	19287-45-7	20	Health	S		10		
Dibromotetrafluoroethane (Halon 2402)	124-73-2	see Bill 218-CFCs						
Dibutyl amine	111-92-2			UD			2645	
Dibutyl phthalate (DBP)	84-74-2	100	Health	IS		50		
Dibutyltin dilaurate	77-58-7	100	Health	IS		30		
Dicapryl phthalate	131-15-7	100		S		120		
Dichloro-1,1,2,2,-tetrafluoro ethane, 1,1-(Freon 114)	1320-37-2	2100000	Health	IS		700000		
Dichlorobenzene, ortho-	95-50-1	37000	Health	IS			30500	
Dichlorobenzidene, 3,3-	91-94-1			CARC				
Diethyl amine	109-89-7			UD			2910	
Diethyl phthalate (DEP)	84-66-2	100	Health	IS		125		
Diethylene glycol monobutyl ether	112-34-5					65		
Diethylene glycol monobutyl ether acetate	124-17-4					85		
Diethylene glycol monoethyl ether	111-90-0	800	Odour	IS		273		1100
Diethylene glycol monoethyl ether acetate	112-12-5					1800		
Diethylhexyl phthalate (DEHP)	117-81-7	100	Health	IS		50		
Difluorodichloromethane (Freon 12)	75-71-8	1500000	Health	IS		500000	see Bill 218-CFCs	
Dihexyl phthalate (DHP)	84-75-3	100	Health	IS		50		
Diisobutyl ketone	108-83-8	470	Odour	IS		3500		
Dimethyl acetamide, n,n-	127-19-5	900	Health	IS		300		
Dimethyl amine	124-40-3			UD			1840	
Dimethyl disulphide	624-92-0	40	Odour	S			40	
Dimethyl ether	115-10-6	2100	Odour	IS		2100		
Dimethyl methylphosphonate	756-79-6					875		649

		Point-of-Impingement Standard			Ambient Air Quality Criteria (AAQC)			
Contaminant Name	Contaminant Code or CAS No.	Half Hour Point-of-Impingement Limit (µg/m3)	Point-of-Impingement Limiting Effect	Status	Annual (µg/m3)	24 Hour (µg/m3)	One Hour (µg/m3)	10 Minute (µg/m3)
Dimethyl phthalate (DMP)	131-11-3	100	Health	IS		125		
Dimethyl sulphide	75-18-3	30	Odour	S			30	
Dimethyl- 1,3-diamino propane, n,n-	109-55-7	60	Health	IS		20		
Dioctyl phthalate	117-84-0	100	Health	S		120		
Dioxane	123-91-1			UD		3500		
Dioxolane-1,3	646-06-0	30	Health	IS		10		
Diphenylamine	122-39-4	50	Health	IS		17.5		
Diquat dibromide - respirable	85-00-7	0.096	Health	IS		0.032		
Diquat dibromide - total in ambient air	85-00-7	0.48	Health	IS		0.16		
Dodecyl benzene sulphonic acid	1886-81-3	100	Health	IS		120		
Dodine	24391-00-3	30	Health	IS		10		
Droperidol	548-73-2	3	Health	IS		1		
Dustfall		8000 (ug/m2)	Soiling	S	4.6 g/m2 + 7 g/m2 (annual) (30 day)			
Ethanol (Ethyl alcohol)	64-17-5	19000	Odour	IS			19000	
Ethyl acetate	141-78-6	19000	Odour	S			19000	
Ethyl acrylate	140-88-5	4.5	Odour	S			4.5	
Ethyl benzene	100-41-4	4000	Odour	S			4000	
Ethyl ether	60-29-7	30000	Odour	IS		30000		
Ethyl hexanol, 2-	104-76-7	600	Odour	IS			600	
Ethyl-3-ethoxy propionate	763-69-9	147	Odour	IS		50		200
Ethylanthroquinone, 2-	84-51-5	30	Odour	IS		10		
Ethylene	74-85-1	160	Health	IS		40		
Ethylene dichloride	107-06-2	1200	Health	IS		400		
Ethylene glycol	107-21-1			IS		12700		
Ethylene glycol butyl ether (Butyl cellosolve)	111-76-2	350	Odour	IS		2400		500

Contaminant Name	Contaminant Code or CAS No.	Point-of-Impingement Standard			Ambient Air Quality Criteria (AAQC)			
		Half Hour Point-of-Impingement Limit (µg/m3)	Point-of-Impingement Limiting Effect	Status	Annual (µg/m3)	24 Hour (µg/m3)	One Hour (µg/m3)	10 Minute (µg/m3)
Ethylene glycol butyl ether acetate (Butyl cello.ace)	112-07-2	500	Odour	IS		3250		700
Ethylene glycol dinitrate	628-96-6	10	Health	IS		3		
Ethylene glycol ethyl ether (Cellosolve)	110-80-5	800	Odour	IS		380		1100
Ethylene glycol ethyl ether acetate (Cellosolve ace.)	111-15-9	220	Odour	IS		540		300
Ethylene glycol monohexyl ether	112-25-4					2500		
Ethylene oxide	75-21-8	15	Health	IS		5		
Ethylenediaminetetra acetic acid	60-00-4	100		IS		120		
Fentanyl citrate	990-73-8	0.06	Health	IS		0.02		
Ferric oxide	1309-37-1	75	Soiling	S		25		
Fluoridation - as total fluorides, total GS	7664-39-3				40 µg/100cm2/30 day			
Fluoridation - as total fluorides, total NM	7664-39-3				80 µg/100cm2/30 day			
Fluorides (as HF) - gaseous - growing season GS	7664-39-3				0.34 µg/m3/30 day			
Fluorides (as HF) - gaseous - growing season GS		4.3	Vegetation	IS				
Fluorides (as HF) - total, growing season GS	7664-39-3	8.6	Vegetation	IS				
Fluorides (as HF) - total, growing season GS	7664-39-3				0.69 µg/m3/30 day			
Fluorides (as HF)- total, non-growing season NM	7664-39-3	17.2	Vegetation	IS		3.44		
Fluorides (as HF)- total, non-growing season NM	7664-39-3				1.38 µg/m3/30 day			
Fluorides in dry forage-dry weight	7664-39-3				35 ppm/30 day avg. * 80 ppm/30 day avg. ** 60 ppm/60 day avg. ***			
Fluorinert 3M-FC-70	FLUORINERT	100		IS		120		

		Point-of-Impingement Standard			Ambient Air Quality Criteria (AAQC)			
Contaminant Name	Contaminant Code or CAS No.	Half Hour Point-of-Impingement Limit (µg/m3)	Point-of-Impingement Limiting Effect	Status	Annual (µg/m3)	24 Hour (µg/m3)	One Hour (µg/m3)	10 Minute (µg/m3)
Fluorotrichloromethane (CFC-11)	75-69-4	see Bill 218-CFCs						
Formaldehyde	50-00-0	65	Odour	S			65	
Formic acid	64-18-6	1500	Health	S		500		
Furfural	98-01-1	1000	Odour	S			1000	
Furfuryl alcohol	98-00-0	3000	Health	S		1000		
Gasoline	8006-61-9			UD				
Glutaraldehyde	111-30-8	42	Health	IS		14	35	
Haloperidol	52-86-8	0.3	Health	IS		0.1		
Hexachlorocyclopentadiene	77-47-4	6	Health	IS		2		
Hexamethyl disilazane	999-97-3	5	Health	IS		2		
Hexamethylene diisocyanate monomer	822-06-0	1.5	Health	IS		0.5		
Hexamethylene diisocynate trimer	4035-89-6	3	Health	IS		1		
Hexane	110-54-3	35000	Health	IS		12000	12000	
Hexylene glycol	107-41-5	14400	Health	IS				
Hydrogen bromide	10035-10-6	800	Health	IS			668	
Hydrogen chloride	7647-01-0	100	Corrosion	S		40		
Hydrogen cyanide	74-90-8	1150	Health	S		575		
Hydrogen peroxide	7722-84-1	90	Health	IS		30	30	
Hydrogen sulphide	7783-06-4	30	Odour	S				
Iron-metallic	15438-31-0	10	Soiling	S		4		
Isobutyl acetate	110-19-0	1220	Odour	IS		412		1660
Isopropyl acetate	108-21-4	1470	Odour	IS		500		2000
Isopropyl benzene	98-82-8	100	Odour	IS			100	

Point-of-Impingement Standard / **Ambient Air Quality Criteria (AAQC)**

Contaminant Name	Contaminant Code or CAS No.	Half Hour Point-of-Impingement Limit (µg/m3)	Point-of-Impingement Limiting Effect	Status	Annual (µg/m3)	24 Hour (µg/m3)	One Hour (µg/m3)	10 Minute (µg/m3)
Lead	7439-92-1	10	Health	S	3 µ/m3/30 day +			
Lead - single sample	7439-92-1				2 µ/m3/30 day ++			
Lead in dustfall	7439-92-1				0.1 g/m2/30 day			
Lindane (Hexachlorocyclohexane)	58-89-9	15	Health	IS		5		
Lithium - other than hydrides	7439-93-2	60	Health	S		20		
Lithium hydrides	7580-67-8	7.5	Health	S		2.5		
Magnesium oxide	1309-48-4	100		S		120		
Malathion	121-75-5	100		IS		120		
Maleic anhydride	108-31-6	100	Health	IS		30		
Manganese compounds (as Mn) - including permanganates	7439-96-5	7.5	Health	IS		2.5		
Mercaptans (as Methyl mercaptan) - total	74-93-1	20	Odour	S			20	
Mercaptobenzothiazole disulphide	120-78-5	100		IS		120		
Mercury	7439-97-6	5	Health	S		2		
Mercury (as Hg) - alkyl compounds	7439-97-6	1.5	Health	IS		0.5		
Metaldehyde (Acetaldehyde tetramer)	108-62-3	100		IS		120		
Methacrylic acid	79-41-4	2000	Odour	IS		2000		
Methane diphenyl diisocyanate	101-68-8	3	Health	IS		1		
Methanol (Methyl alcohol, Wood alcohol)	67-56-1	84000	Health	IS		28000		
Methoxychlor	72-43-5	100		IS		120		
Methyl acrylate	96-33-3	4	Odour	S			4	
Methyl bromide	74-83-9	4000	Health	IS		1350		
Methyl chloride	74-87-3	20000	Health	IS		7000		
Methyl ethyl ketone (2-Butanone)	78-93-3	31000	Odour	S			31000	
Methyl ethyl ketone peroxide	1338-23-4	250	Health	IS		80		
Methyl isobutyl ketone	108-10-1	1200	Odour	IS		1200	200	

Contaminant Name	Contaminant Code or CAS No.	Point-of-Impingement Standard — Half Hour Point-of-Impingement Limit (µg/m3)	Point-of-Impingement Limiting Effect	Status	Ambient Air Quality Criteria (AAQC) — Annual (µg/m3)	24 Hour (µg/m3)	One Hour (µg/m3)	10 Minute (µg/m3)
Methyl mercapto aniline	2987-53-3			UD				
Methyl methacrylate	80-62-6	860	Odour	S		860		
Methyl salicylate	119-36-8	300	Health	IS		100		
Methyl styrene, alpha	98-83-9			UD				
Methyl-2-hexanone, 5-	110-12-3	460	Odour	IS		160	24000	
Methyl-2-pyrrolidone, n-	872-50-4			UD			40000	630
Methyl-n-amyl ketone	110-43-0			UD		4600		
Methylal	109-87-5	18000	Health	IS		6200		
Methylcyclopentadienyl manganese tricarbonyl (MMT)	12108-13-3	30	Health	IS		10		
Methylene chloride	75-09-2	5300	Health	IS		1765		
Methylene dianiline	101-77-9	30	Health	IS		10		
Methylene-bis-2-chloroaniline, 4,4-	101-14-4	30	Health	IS		10		
Miconazole nitrate	22832-87-7	15	Health	IS		5		
Milk powder	MILK POWDER	20	Soiling	S		20		
Mineral spirits		30000	Odour	IS		10000		
Molybdenum	7439-98-7	100		IS		120		
Monochlorobenzene	108-90-7	4200	Health	IS		25	3500	4500
Monomethyl amine	74-89-5	25	Odour	S		22.5		50
Naphthalene	91-20-3	36	Odour	IS		100		
Naphthol, alpha-	90-15-3	100	Health	IS		2		
Nickel	7440-02-0	5	Vegetation	S		0.5		
Nickel carbonyl	13463-39-3	1.5	Health	S		35		
Nitric acid	7697-37-2	100	Corrosion	S		120		
Nitrilotriacetic acid	18662-53-8	100		S				

Contaminant Name	Contaminant Code or CAS No.	Half Hour Point-of-Impingement Limit (µg/m3)	Point-of-Impingement Limiting Effect	Status	Annual (µg/m3)	24 Hour (µg/m3)	One Hour (µg/m3)	10 Minute (µg/m3)
Nitrogen oxides (as Nitrogen dioxide)	10102-44-0	500	Health	S		200	400	
Nitroglycerin	55-63-0	10	Health	IS		3		
Nitrosodiethylamine, n-	55-18-5			CARC				
Nitrosodimethylamine, n-	62-75-9			CARC				
Nitrous oxide	10024-97-2	27000	Health	IS		9000		61800
Octane	111-65-9	45400	Odour	IS		15300		
Octene, 1-	25377-83-7	150000	Health	IS		50000		
Oleic acid	112-80-1	6	Health	IS			5	
Oxalic acid	144-62-7	75	Health	IS		25		
Ozone	10028-15-6	200	Health	S			165	
Palladium - water soluble compounds	7657-10-1	30	Health	IS		10		
Paraquat dichloride - respirable	1910-42-5	0.009	Health	IS		0.003		
Paraquat dichloride - total in ambient air	1910-42-5	0.045	Health	IS		0.015		
Penicillin	1406-05-9	0.3	Health	IS		0.1		
Pentaborane	19624-22-7	3	Health	S		1		
Pentachlorophenol	87-86-5	60	Health	IS		20		
Perchloroethylene	127-18-4	10000	Health	IS		4000		
Phenol	108-95-2	100	Health	S		100		
Phosgene	75-44-5	130	Health	S		45		
Phosphine	7803-51-2	30	Health	S		10		
Phosphoric acid (as P205)	7664-38-2	100	Health	S		120		
Phosphorus oxychloride	10025-87-3	40	Health	IS		12		
Phosphorus pentachloride	10026-13-8	30	Health	IS		10		
Phthalic anhydride	85-44-9	100		S		120		
Pimozide	2062-78-4	3	Health	IS		1		
Platinum - water soluble compounds	7440-06-4	0.6	Health	IS		0.2		

Contaminant Name	Contaminant Code or CAS No.	Half Hour Point-of-Impingement Limit (μg/m3)	Point-of-Impingement Limiting Effect	Status	Annual (μg/m3)	24 Hour (μg/m3)	One Hour (μg/m3)	10 Minute (μg/m3)
Polybutene-1-sulphone		100		IS		120		
Polychlorinated biphenyls (PCBs)	1336-36-3	0.45	Health	IS	0.035	0.15		
Polychloroprene	25267-15-6	100		IS		500		
Potassium cyanide	151-50-8	100		IS		120		
Potassium hydroxide	1310-58-3	28	Corrosion	IS		14		
Potassium nitrate	7757-79-1	100		IS		120		
Propanol, iso- (Isopropyl alcohol, Isopropanol)	67-63-0	24000	Odour	IS		24000		
Propanol, n- (Propyl alcohol)	71-23-8	48000	Health	IS		16000		
Propionaldehyde	123-38-6	7	Odour	IS		2.5		10
Proprionic acid	79-09-4	100	Odour	IS			100	
Proprionic anhydride (as Proprionic acid)	123-62-6	100	Odour	IS			100	
Propylene dichloride	78-87-5	2400	Odour	S		2400		
Propylene glycol	57-55-6	100	Health	IS		120		
Propylene glycol methyl ether	107-98-2	89000	Odour	IS		30000		121000
Propylene glycol monomethyl ether acetate	108-65-6	5000	Odour	IS		5000		
Propylene oxide	75-56-9	13500	Health	IS		4500		
Pyridine	110-86-1	60	Odour	IS		150		
Selenium	7782-49-2	20	Health	IS		10		
Silane	7803-62-5	450	Health	IS		150		80
Silica- respirable, under 10 μm aerodynamic diameter	7631-86-9	15	Health	IS		5		
Silver	7440-22-4	3	Health	S		1		
Sodium bisulphite	7631-90-5	100		IS		120		
Sodium chlorate	7775-09-9	18	Health	IS		6		
Sodium chlorite	7758-19-2	60	Health	IS		20		
Sodium cyanide	143-33-9	100		IS		120		

Contaminant Name	Contaminant Code or CAS No.	Point-of-Impingement Standard		Status	Ambient Air Quality Criteria (AAQC)			
		Half Hour Point-of-Impingement Limit (µg/m3)	Point-of-Impingement Limiting Effect		Annual (µg/m3)	24 Hour (µg/m3)	One Hour (µg/m3)	10 Minute (µg/m3)
Sodium hydroxide	1310-73-2	20	Corrosion	IS		10		
Stannous chloride (as Sn)	7772-99-8	30	Health	IS		10		
Strontium	7440-24-6	100		IS		120		
Strontium carbonate	1633-05-2	100		IS		120		
Strontium hydroxide	18480-07-4	100		IS		120		
Strontium oxide	1314-11-0	100		IS		120		
Styrene	100-42-5	400	Odour	S		400		
Sulphamic acid	5329-14-6	100		IS		120		
Sulphur dioxide	7446-09-5	830	Health	S	55	275	690	
Sulphur hexafluoride	2551-62-4	1800000	Health	IS		600000		
Sulphuric acid	7664-93-9	100	Corrosion	S		35		
Suspended particulate matter - under 44 µm aero. diam	TSP	100	Visibility	S	60++	120		
Talc - fibrous	14807-96-6	5	Health	IS		2		
Tellurium - excluding hydrogen telluride	13494-80-9	30	Health	S		10		
Tetrabutylurea	4559-86-8	30	Health	IS		10		
Tetrahydrofuran	109-99-9	93000	Odour	S		93000		
Tetramethyl thiuram disulphide	137-26-8	30	Health	IS		10		
Thiourea	62-56-6	60	Health	IS		20		
Tin	7440-31-5	30	Health	S		10		
Titanium	7440-32-6	100		S		120		
Tolmetin sodium	35711-34-3	15	Health	S		5		
Toluene	108-88-3	2000	Odour	S		2000		
Toluene diisocyanate	584-84-9	1	Health	S		0.5		
Total reduced sulphur (as Hydrogen sulphide)	TRS	40	Odour	IS			40	
Trichlorobenzene, 1,2,4-	120-82-1	100		IS		400		

Contaminant Name	Contaminant Code or CAS No.	Point-of-Impingement Standard Half Hour Point-of-Impingement Limit (µg/m3)	Point-of-Impingement Limiting Effect	Status	Ambient Air Quality Criteria (AAQC) Annual (µg/m3)	24 Hour (µg/m3)	One Hour (µg/m3)	10 Minute (µg/m3)
Trichloroethane, 1,1,1- (Methyl chloroform)	71-55-6	3500000	Health	S		115000		
Trichloroethylene	79-01-6	85000	Health	S		28000		
Trichlorofluoromethane	75-69-4	18000	Health	IS		6000		
Trichlorotrifluoroethane (CFC-113)	76-13-1	see Bill 218-CFCs						
Trifluorotrichloroethane	76-13-1	2400000	Health	S		800000		
Trimethyl amine	75-50-3	0.5	Odour	IS			0.5	
Trimethyl benzene, 1,2,4-	95-63-6	500	Odour	IS		1000		
Trimethylol propane	77-99-6	100	Health	IS		1250		
Tripropyltin methacrylate		3	Health	IS		1		
Vanadium	7440-62-2	5	Health	S	0.2	2		
Vinyl chloride	75-01-4	3	Health	IS		1		
Vinylidene chloride (1,1-Dichloroethene)	75-35-4	70	Health	IS		35		
Varfarin	81-81-2	30	Health	IS		10		
Whey powder	WHEY POWDER	100		IS		120		
Xylenes	1330-20-7	2300	Odour	S		2300		
Zinc	7440-66-6	100		S		120		
Zinc chloride	7646-85-7	12	Health	IS		10		

Notes

avg.   8-hour average for carbon monoxide based on high background levels from automobiles
*   average monthly results for growing season
**   average results of any single month
***   average of 2 consecutive months
GS   Growing Season May 1 – September 30 – NE & NW Regions
   April 1 – September 30 – other regions
NM   Non-growing season October 1 – March 31

+ arithmetic mean   ++ geometric mean
S = Air Quality Standard   IS = Interim Standard
CARC = Carcinogen,   UD = Under Development, or odour threshold review.
Irr = Irritant
D/F = dioxins & furans
A = AAQC chemicals listed in Regulation 296 under the Environmental Protection Act

Table 2.2
PARTIAL LIST OF SAMPLING PROTOCOLS

---

1) Ontario Ministry of the Environment. 1980. "Source Testing Code (Version 2)." Report No. ARB-66-80, November.

2) Canadian Standards Association. 1986. "Method for the Continuous Measurement of Oxygen, Carbon Dioxide, Carbon Monoxide, Sulphur Dioxide and Oxides of Nitrogen in Enclosed Combustion Flue Gas Streams." CSA Report No. CAN/CSA-A223.2 M86, September.

3) Federal Register. 1977. "EPA Standard Methods for Source Emitted Gaseous Pollutants: SO2, NOx, H2SO4 and SO2." Standards for New Source Performance Standards under Title 40, Part 60, Vol. 42, Number 160.

4) Federal Register. 1980. "EPA Standard Methods for Source Emitted Gaseous Pollutants: Hydrogen Fluoride." Standards for New Source Performance Standards under Title 40, Part 60, Vol. 45, Number 121.

5) Federal Register. 1973. "EPA Standard Methods for Source-Emitted Gaseous Hazardous Air Pollutants: Mercury." National Emission Standards for Hazardous Air Pollutants, Title 40, Part 61, Vol. 38, Number 66.

6) Federal Register. 1976. "EPA Standard Methods for Source-Emitted Gaseous Hazardous Air Pollutants: Vinyl Chloride." National Emission Standards for Hazardous Air Pollutants, Title 40, Part 61, Vol. 41, Number 205.

7) U.S. Environmental Protection Agency. 1977. "Measurement of Polycyclic Organic Materials and Other Hazardous Organic Compounds in Stack Gases - State of the Art." EPA Report 600/2-77-202, October.

8) American Society of Mechanical Engineers. 1984. "ASME Draft Protocol for the Determination of Chlorinated Organic Compounds in Stack Emissions." Draft Report No. 4, October.

9) U.S. Environmental Protection Agency. 1984. "Protocol for the Collection and Analysis of Volatile POHCs Using VOST." EPA Report 600/8-84-007, March.

Table 2.3
ODOUR RECOGNITION THRESHOLDS

Chemical	Recognition Odour Threshold (ppm)	Reference
acetone	100.0	(1)
acrolein	0.21	(1)
ammonia	47.0	(1)
benzene	4.7	(1)
cellosolve	0.550	(2)
cellosolve acetate	0.14	(2)
cyclohexanone	0.120	(2)
hydrogen sulfide	0.00047	(1)
methyl isobutyl ketone (MIBK)	0.28	(2)
nitrobenzene	0.0047	(1)
n-butanol	1.0	(2)
phenol	0.047	(3)
toluene	5.0	(2)
trichloroethylene	21.4	(1)
V.M. and P. naphtha	0.86	(4)

References:
1 - Leonardos, 1989
2 - Fazzalari, 1978
3 - Stahl, 1973
4 - Clayton and Clayton, 1981

Table 2.4
PROPOSED INTERIM LIST OF LEVEL 1 CONTAMINANTS

acrylonitrile
4-aminobiphenyl
arsenic
asbestos
benzene
benzidine
beryllium
bis(chloromethyl) ether
cadmium
carbon tetrachloride
chloroform
chloromethyl methyl ether
chromium
diethylsulfate
dimethyl sulfate
dimethylcarbomoyl chloride
epichlorohydrin
ethylene dibromide
ethylene oxide

formaldehyde
hexachlorobenzene
lead
N-methyl-N-nitrosourea
4,4'-methylenebis (2-chloroaniline)
2-naphthylamine
nickel
nickel carbonyl
N-nitrosodimethylamine
perchloroethylene
polychlorinated biphenyls
polychlorinated dibenzo
    dioxins/furans
polycyclic aromatic hydrocarbons
propylene oxide
silica (respirable)
styrene oxide
vinyl bromide
vinyl chloride

Reference: MOE, 1990

3.0

Water Quality and Liquid Discharges

3.1 OVERVIEW

All three levels of government — federal, provincial, municipal — are involved in water quality management and the regulation of liquid discharges in Ontario. Regulatory requirements are laid out in a relatively comprehensive combination of acts, regulations, policies, guidelines, and by-laws; however, legislation governing water discharges in Ontario is currently undergoing significant change at the federal and provincial levels.

New federal legislation under the Fisheries Act and the Canadian Environmental Protection Act (CEPA) has recently been passed for discharges from pulp and paper facilities. It is anticipated that regulations for other industrial sectors will follow. The federal government has also recently introduced a program of "Pollution Prevention" to move industry to voluntarily reduce contaminant levels by upstream modifications to the process or through the substitution of raw materials.

In Ontario, the Municipal and Industrial Strategy for Abatement (MISA) program applies to nine industrial sectors, but eventually will apply to all types of industrial dischargers and municipal wastewater treatment facilities. The ultimate goal of the program is the virtual elimination of persistent, toxic contaminants from all discharges into Ontario waterways.

Sections 3.2 and 3.3 of this chapter describe the current provincial legislation. Sections 3.4 and 3.5 outline federal and municipal requirements, respectively. The process for receiving approvals to discharge liquid effluents is described in Section 3.6. Monitoring and reporting requirements are outlined in Sections 3.7 and 3.8, respectively.

3.2 PROVINCIAL REGULATIONS AND GUIDELINES (EXCLUDING MISA)

3.2.1 Ontario Water Resources Act

The Ontario Water Resources Act (OWRA) contains a general prohibition against the discharge of any material into water. Section 30(1) requires that "every person that discharges or causes or permits the discharge of any material of any kind into or in any water or on any shore or bank thereof or into or in any place that may **impair** the quality of the water of any waters is guilty of an offence."

Section 28 of the OWRA indicates that the quality of water shall be deemed to be impaired if any material (or any derivative of such material) is discharged or deposited and causes or may cause injury to any person, animal, bird, or other living thing as a result of the use or consumption of any plant, fish, or other living matter or thing in the water or in the soil in contact with the water.

Under Section 33(2)(a), it is an offence to place, discharge, or allow to remain within an area defined as a source of public water supply, any material that may impair the quality of the water.

3.2.2 Environmental Protection Act

As noted in Section 2.2.1, the Environmental Protection Act (EPA) is broadly directed toward the protection and conservation of the natural environment. Much of the original text does not specifically mention water quality or liquid discharges, but the broad scope of this legislation encompasses water quality and aquatic environments.

Subsection 14(1) states that no person shall discharge a contaminant or cause or permit the discharge of a contaminant into the natural environment that causes or is likely to cause an **adverse effect.** While the EPA definition of "adverse effect" includes many components (see Section 2.2.1), some that are most appropriate in the context of water management include:

- impairment of the quality of the natural environment for any use that can be made of it
- injury or damage to property or to plant or animal life
- an adverse effect on the health of a person
- loss of enjoyment of normal use of property
- interference with the normal conduct of business

Other sections of the EPA address water quality indirectly. For example, Part IV deals with the discharge of waste upon or over ice.

Despite its initial orientation toward the total natural environment, the EPA has become a cornerstone in the control of liquid discharges because it holds all of legislation for the MISA program. Due to its importance and complexity, the MISA program is addressed separately in Section 3.3.

3.2.3 Water Quality Guidelines, Policies, and Objectives

Several MOEE publications describe water quality guidelines, policies, and objectives for various types of water and aquatic environments. Such guidelines, policies, and objectives are not legally enforceable but are often used to evaluate water quality in Ontario. Components of the guidelines, policies, and specific objectives, however, are legally enforceable when incorporated in a certificate of approval or order. Table 3.1 presents a list of MOEE policies. Note that "sewage works" refers to any works for the collection, production, treatment, storage, supply, and distribution of water or any part of any such works.

Provisions for the protection and enhancement of ambient water quality are outlined in the document entitled *Water Management: Goals, Policies, Objectives, and Implementation Procedures* (MOE, 1992a). Also referred to as the "Blue Book," it contains several MOEE policy statements concerning water quality management and the **Provincial Water Quality Objectives** (PWQO).

The PWQO include narrative and numerical criteria designed for the protection of aquatic life and recreation in and on the water. The PWQO represent a desirable level of water quality that the MOEE strives to maintain in surface waters of the province. They cover conventional parameters, radioactive material, metals, turbidity, and a few industrial organic compounds (see Table 3.2).

In June 1991, the MOEE released a document entitled *Provincial Water Quality Objectives and Guidelines.* The document lists additional PWQO, proposed PWQO, **Provincial Water Quality Guidelines** (PWQG), and proposed PWQG. A significant amount of the PWQG are for organics (see Table 3.2). The term proposed indicates that the objective or guideline is undergoing external peer review.

The PWQO values are based on the scientific rationale described in *Rationale for the Establishment of Ontario's Provincial Water Quality Objectives* (MOE, 1984) and *Ontario's Water Quality Objectives Development Process* (MOE, 1989). The most recent rationale considers data for acute and chronic toxicity, bioaccumulation and mutagenicity, and persistence. Also considered is information concerning fate, physical/chemical properties, taste, odour, tainting of fish, impacts on wildlife, recreation (bathing and aesthetics), sediment quality, and the standards of other agencies.

In addition to the PWQO, the "Blue Book" uses the terms **zero tolerance** and **undefined tolerance limits** to describe some substances (also listed in Table 3.5). Substances with zero tolerance are those that can bioaccumulate or concentrate in the aquatic environment to levels which are harmful or lethal to organisms. It is the intent of the MOEE to prohibit any new discharges of these substances and to reduce all existing releases to the lowest practicable levels. The MOEE has developed PWQO or PWQG for most of these chemicals which are to be used to assess existing discharges.

Several substances on the "Blue Book's" list of undefined tolerance limits have subsequently had PWQO or PWQG developed (see Table 3.2).

The "Blue Book" also addresses the concept of **mixing zones** noting that it is not practical to treat all effluents to the extent that they comply with the PWQO values at the point of release or discharge. Therefore, some volume of water must be provided for dilution or modification of the effluent before the objectives can be met. While it is permissible to exceed PWQO values within a mixing zone, the effluent can not be immediately lethal to swimming organisms that are not able to evade the zone. It is possible for an effluent to be toxic but be avoidable. For example, fish can detect and avoid zones of very low pH if given the opportunity to do so. The mixing zone mainly represents a loss of habitat, but it must not be allowed to become an area where aquatic life is killed or seriously damaged.

A third key MOEE publication that identifies water quality objectives is the document entitled *Ontario Drinking Water Objectives* (MOE, 1984b). As the title indicates, this document addresses drinking water quality as compared to the "Blue Book" which addresses ambient water quality. The MOEE currently has three categories of **drinking water quality objectives**.

The term **Maximum Acceptable Concentration** (MAC) describes limits applied to substances above which there are known or suspected adverse health effects. Drinking water supplies should not exceed MAC limits continuously.

The term **Interim Maximum Acceptable Concentration** (IMAC) describes limits for substances of current concern with known chronic effects in mammals and for which MAC values have not been established. A substance detected at a concentration above its IMAC signals the need for more sampling and investigation. The requirement for corrective action is made on a case-by-case basis.

The term **Maximum Desirable Concentration** (MDC) is used for limits on substances which, when present at concentrations above the limits, are either aesthetically objectionable to an appreciable number of consumers or may interfere with good water quality control practices. The MDC should not be exceeded whenever a more suitable supply or treatment process is or can be made available at a reasonable cost.

Table 3.5 lists numerical values assigned to all three types of drinking water quality objectives.

3.2.4 Banned and Phase-Out Chemicals

In June 1991, the Ontario Ministry of the Environment's Hazardous Contaminants Branch and Water Resources Branch were directed to establish a list a candidate substances to be considered for banning, phasing out, or use/release reductions. The results of this effort include (i) a process for selecting substances; (ii) primary and secondary lists of substances for consideration; (iii) a review of the data on loadings of the Primary List substances to receiving waters from industrial and municipal direct point source discharges; (iv) a hazard evaluation of industrial and municipal effluents monitored under MISA; and (v) a review of the receiving water impacts, including sediment and biota impacts, attributable to point and non-point source inputs of substances on the Primary List.

The Primary List of Candidate Substances for Bans or Phase-Outs (see Table 3.6) is a list of substances present in or discharged to Ontario surface waters which most of the approximately 800 substances assessed are inherently hazardous due to their persistence in water or sediment, potential to bioaccumulate, and toxicity. It is recommended that these substances be given first priority in considering candidate substances for banning, phasing out, or use/release reduction.

3.3 MUNICIPAL, INDUSTRIAL STRATEGY FOR ABATEMENT (MISA) PROGRAM

3.3.1 Goals and Objectives

The MISA program is a major initiative by the MOEE to reduce water pollution from industrial and municipal discharges. The overall objective of the program is the **virtual elimination of persistent, toxic contaminants from all discharges** into Ontario waterways. MISA regulations are issued under the EPA.

During its initiation, the program was directed toward the following goals:
- identify and measure toxic substances in discharges
- increase emphasis on control technology
- augment and expand the existing water quality impact approach
- strengthen enforcement mechanisms

In 1992, the MOEE shifted the goals of MISA toward pollution prevention and reduction in the multi-media transfer of pollutants. The MOEE requires pollution prevention be incorporated into the design of all new or upgraded water and sewage works prior to the design of pollution control equipment. The MOEE also requires an assessment of the impact of residual wastes and by-products on the whole environment including air, land, and water during the design of water and sewage works. Removal of a pollutant from one media with direct transfer to another media is discouraged.

3.3.2 Direct Dischargers

The MISA program divides all dischargers into two broad categories. One includes industries and municipal treatment plants that discharge effluents directly into surface waters. Such **direct dischargers** currently are defined as including the municipal sector and the following nine industrial sectors:

Petroleum refining	Industrial minerals
Organic chemicals	Electric power generation
Iron and steel	Metal mining and refining
Pulp and paper	Metal casting manufacturers
Inorganic chemicals	

The MISA program for direct discharges can be subdivided into the following three phases: Phase I – Monitoring Regulation; Phase II – Effluent Limit Regulation; and Phase III – Abatement and Enforcement. Phase I has been completed for these sectors. Most industrial sectors are currently completing Phase II, while a few have initiated Phase III.

3.3.3 Phase I: Monitoring Regulation

Phase I of MISA was directed towards monitoring the chemicals that are present in effluents. Phase I consists of two regulations. The first was the General Regulation (Regulation 695/88 as amended by Regulation 533/89) which applied to all sectors. It addressed various aspects of monitoring such as analytical procedures, sampling protocols, reporting requirements, and flow measurement.

The sample collection and analyses section of this regulation has been referenced on new Certificates of Approval for both MISA and non-MISA dischargers.

The second regulatory component consisted of the sector-specific effluent regulations. For example, Regulation 321/89 applied to the Iron and Steel Sector. Sector-specific regulations defined the discharge streams to be sampled, types of discharge, the parameters to be analyzed, and the frequency of sampling.

The following is a brief summary of terminology developed during Phase I and carried over into MISA Phases II and III and other government programs (e.g. Certificates of Approval).

Types of Discharges

Eight types of discharge streams were identified in the sector-specific regulations:

Process effluent – discharged water that comes into contact by design with an industrial process.

Cooling water – a discharge used to remove heat that is not intended to come into contact with process material.

Combined effluent (the term appeared in sector-specific regulations and in the General Regulation) – an effluent that results from the intentional combination of process effluent with one or more of cooling water, storm water, and waste disposal site effluent.

Storm water – runoff from a storm event or thaw discharged from a developed area or a plant. *Storm event* – a rainfall or series of rainfalls on an operating day that exceeds five millimetres. *Thaw* – the melting of snow or ice sufficient to create an effluent stream at the plant.

Waste disposal site effluent and **storage site effluent** – any liquids and associated materials collected from a waste disposal site or storage area for discharge to a surface watercourse.

Any process effluent, waste disposal site effluent, or storage site effluent had to be monitored prior to being discharged to a surface watercourse after any final treatment, and upstream of any significant contaminant masking or significant dilution by any other effluent.

Emergency overflow – a diversion of effluent that causes the effluent to by-pass a sampling point ordinarily used for that effluent.

Final effluent (as used in the regulation for the iron and steel sector) – a discharge that contains process effluent and one or more of cooling water, storm water and waste disposal site effluent.

Parameters to be Analyzed

Effluents were monitored for five broad groups of parameters during Phase I:

- conventional parameters (such as ammonia, cyanide, and pH)
- organic parameters (such as benzene and toluene)
- PCBs and dioxins
- characterization/open characterization
- acute toxicity testing

A detailed list of parameters and the **Analytical Test Groups** (ATGs) to which parameters were assigned are presented in Table 3.7.

Characterization referred to the analysis of samples to identify and quantify all of the parameters in Table 3.7, except those in ATGs 28a, 28b and 29. Additional exceptions were granted for a sector if specific chemicals are not purchased or manufactured by that sector. *Open characterization* referred to the analysis of samples to identify and quantify ATGs 16, 17, 19, 20 and 23 and to identify and approximately quantify ATGs 28a, 28b and 29.

Phase I also involved the performing of acute toxicity tests using rainbow trout (*Salmo gairdneri*) and/or the water flea (*Daphnia magna*).

Chapter 13 presents a detailed discussion of toxicity testing and interpretation of toxicity test results.

Sample Handling and Analysis

Phase I was relatively explicit in terms of how samples were to be gathered and analyzed, and the results reported. The MISA regulation specifies sample/laboratory containers, sample type (grab versus composite), material to be used in the sampler, minimum sample volumes, maximum sample storage time, sample preservatives, method detection limits, flow accuracies, quality assurance/quality control procedures, instrument measurement method principles, data storage and reporting procedures, and the retention time of records.

The method detection limit (MDL) was the minimum concentration of a parameter in laboratory grade water necessary to infer its presence with a confidence greater than 99%. It can be used to compare laboratories in terms of achieving a level of detection. The MDL should not be confused with the minimum detection limit that a laboratory can achieve. The minimum detection limit can vary from sample to sample depending upon the presence or absence of substances that interfere with analytical techniques (i.e. the "matrix" effect) and/or the ability of the laboratory to prepare a sample for analysis.

Reporting Requirements

At different times during Phase I, various types of monitoring reports were submitted. The information required for the initial report included plot plans indicating the location of samplers and flow measuring devices, descriptions of operations, descriptions of flow instrumentation and samplers, the accuracy of flow devices, and analytical documentation. It was the responsibility of the discharger to inform the MOE of all changes in the information submitted in the initial report.

Calibration reports, intended sampling date reports, and reports of the method used to estimate/measure storm water volumes were due prior to the commencement of monitoring. The calibration report had to show that the devices being used to measure or estimate flow are within the accuracies specified by the regulation (see Section 3.7.7).

During Phase I, it was also necessary to submit sampling reports that describe the date, duration, and cause of each sampling effort, toxicity testing reports when those types of investigations are undertaken, and equipment malfunction/problem reports when conditions or events interfere with fulfilling the requirements of the regulation (together with a description of remedial action).

Analytical test data reports, which included flow and in some cases precipitation data, were submitted during the course of the monitoring program at time periods specified by the regulation. The data had to be entered into a computer data base provided by the MOE. Both a floppy disk and a hard copy were submitted to the MOE. The data bases used are the **MISA** Data Entry System (MIDES) and the **Tox**icity **Data** entry system (TOXDATA). User manuals for each data system were provided by the MOE.

3.3.4 Phase II: Effluent Limit Regulation Development

The objective of Phase II is to establish allowable concentrations of substances in effluents. These effluent limit regulations are based upon MISA monitoring data and an evaluation of whatever constitutes the best available technology that is economically achievable. The limits are developed by sector-specific Joint Technical Committees (JTC) that include representatives from both the MOEE and industry.

The process for calculating effluent limits comprises:

- subcategorization of the plant or process
- selection of parameters for potential treatment
- evaluation of technology
- an economic analysis of the best available technology
- calculation of effluent limits

Difficulties were encountered initially with the aforementioned process and subsequently deviations on a sector-by-sector basis were performed.

Selection of Parameters

Prior to initiating the process for parameter selection, an attempt is made to classify each plant/process within a sector into a homogeneous group to ensure that plant sites or facilities with similar characteristics are treated uniformly in terms of limits.

The approach proposed for parameter selection divides parameters into two primary categories:

Category A – bioaccumulative toxic substances

Category B – other toxic substances (not bioaccumulative)

Category B includes conventional and non-conventional parameters. A bioaccumulative toxic substance is defined as a toxic substance with a bioconcentration factor (BCF) greater than 1,000 or the octanol-water partition coefficient (K_{OW}) greater than 10,000.

Parameters in Category A are carried further into the process automatically, regardless of their concentration or frequency of detection in plant effluents. Whether parameters in Category B are carried forward depended upon the frequency at which the parameter is found above the appropriate PWQO or PWQG value.

Selection of Best Available Technology

Each JTC attempted to consider at least four best achievable technology (BAT) options for economic analysis. The BAT options include the demonstrated and combined technologies which best advance the sector or sub-sector towards the realization of the goals, policies, and objectives of the MISA activity. Selection of BAT options are based on the following factors:

- at least one BAT option should produce an effluent which is non-lethal to fish
- at least one BAT option that produces an effluent which is non-lethal to Daphnia magna
- if there is no BAT option, the Best Practicable Technology   (BPT) identified by the U.S. EPA for the sector or sub-sector in question
- the BAT option that utilizes the best technology currently in use in Ontario in the sector or sub-sector in question
- at least one BAT option that consists of any technologies or combinations of technologies which advance the sector or sub-sector towards the goals, policies, and objectives prescribed by MISA

The fifth factor includes the technology which may provide optimal water conservation, maximum reduction in priority and/or conventional pollutants, minimum impact on other media (atmosphere and land), and maximum use of the 3 Rs (see Section 4.9). In most cases, each of the proposed BAT categories did overlap.

Economic Analysis

In most cases a technical cost evaluation of each BAT identified in the previous step is performed. The cost of the technology would then be evaluated in terms of affordability by the sector. Affordability is assessed on a sector or sub-sector basis using economic and financial indicators and tests. Financial indicators included total debt/total assets for solvency, return on assets for profitability, and current ratio for liquidity. The particular method used is selected by each sector's JTC.

The economic analysis provided decision-makers with the potential economic and financial consequences of different BAT options, including the distribution of these effects on sectors and groups in Ontario. The final outcome of the assessment was the selection of Best Available Technology Economically Achievable (BATEA).

BATEA does not mean that a specific technology must be employed, but rather that the quality of the discharge must be equivalent to the what BATEA can achieve. Several approaches may be capable of achieving the effluent associated with BATEA. These include changes in manufacturing processes, substitution of chemicals used in processes, the recycling of waste by-products, and end-of-pipe treatment.

Limits

The negotiated control parameters are divided into two groups:

1 A short list of parameters that will have a daily maximum limit and monthly average limits based on 30-day measurements and four weekly measurements.

2 The remaining parameters would only have a daily maximum limit to be monitored on a quarterly basis.

Effluent Limits Regulations

In general terms, the MISA Sector Effluent Limits Regulations consist of the following sections:

Part I   – General
Part II   – Sampling Points
Part III   – Calculation of Loadings
Part IV   – Parameter and Lethality Limits
Part V   – Monitoring
Part VI   – Effluent Volume
Part VII   – Storm Water Control Study
Part VIII – Records and Reports
Part IX   – Commencement and Revocation Provisions

In the following section, key components of the MISA sector **effluent limits regulations** are discussed. Note that sector-specific regulations may be slightly different and that compliance with this regulation does not limit or reduce a discharger's obligation under an approval, order, direction, or other instrument issued under any act.

Assessment Parameters – Parameters for which there is no limit, but must be monitored according to the regulation.

Limited Parameter – Parameter for which a limit is specified in the regulation.

Sample Points – Sampling points must be established for each process effluent and cooling water effluent stream so that the plant loadings accurately reflect the level of discharge of each limited parameter and assessment parameter from the plant. A discharger is not allowed to permit process effluent to be discharged from their plant except through a process effluent stream on which there is a sampling point that is used for sampling in accordance with the regulation.

Calculation of Loading – If the actual analytical result is $\geq 1/10$ the Method Detection Limit, then the analytical result must be employed. If the actual analytical result is $< 1/10$ the MDL, then the value "zero" must be employed. Monthly average loadings are to be calculated using the arithmetic mean of the daily loadings.

Sample Collection – The MOEE publication *Protocol for the Sampling and Analysis of Industry/Municipal Wastewater,* dated July 1993, must be used. Daily samples are to be collected during an operating day (in some circumstances it may be any period of 24 consecutive hours, while in others cases they must be collected between 7:00 a.m. and 10:00 a.m.), weekly samples are not to be collected within four days of each other (all process samples must be collected on the same day), and quarterly samples are not to be collected within 45 days after the previous weekly sample. Process effluent and cooling water do not have to be collected, however, if there is no industrial processing going on at the plant.

In some cases, the regulations require on-line analysis for the measurement of pH during each operating day.

Duplicates, travelling blanks, and travelling spiked blanks are required at different frequencies as part of the Quality Assurance/Quality Control (QA/QC) program.

The effluent regulation requires acute lethality testing using *Daphnia magna* and rainbow trout. Lethality tests shall be carried out as a single concentration test using 100% effluent. A period of 15 days is required between the collection of toxicity samples.

In addition to the acute lethality testing, dischargers may be required to perform chronic toxicity testing using ceriodaphnia and fathead minnow. The chronic test involving ceriodaphnia is a seven-day reproduction inhibition and survivability test. The fathead minnow test is a seven-day growth inhibition test. (See Chapter 13 for additional information about aquatic toxicity.)

Parameter Limits – The discharger is responsible for ensuring that each daily and monthly process effluent plant loading for each parameter does not exceed the values specified in the regulation. Each discharger must also control the quality of each process effluent to ensure that the pH value of any sample collected at a process effluent sampling point is within 6.0 - 9.5.

Lethality Limits – The quality of each process effluent monitoring stream and each cooling water effluent monitoring stream shall not result in a mortality of more than 50% of the test organisms (*Daphnia magna* and rainbow trout) in 100% effluent (i.e. a toxic discharge).

If toxicity tests indicate non-toxic conditions for 12 consecutive months, the frequency of testing can be reduced to quarterly. The frequency goes back to monthly, however, if any of the quarterly results indicate that the discharge is toxic.

Flow Measurement – Flow measurement devices must provide for an accuracy of within ± 15% for process effluents and ±20% for cooling water effluents.

Storm Water – The goal of storm water control is to reduce contaminant loading to the maximum extent practicable and to ensure that storm water discharges are not acutely lethal. Storm water is defined as rain water runoff, snow melt, surface runoff, and natural drainage from a plant site.

MISA Effluent Limits Regulations do not set limits for storm water discharges, but instead require a Storm Water Control Study (SWCS). Key components of the SWCS include:

- record-keeping and reporting to determine quantity and quality of storm water discharges
- identifying sources of storm water contamination

- identifying the need to control based on nature of problem(s)
- evaluating prevention and control measures
- identifying preferred prevention and control measures
- implementing control measures

Figure 3.2 presents the requirements and schedule for a SWCS. Additional information on SWCS can be obtained from the MOEE publication entitled *Protocol for Conducting a Storm Water Control Study* (MOEE, 1993b).

Record-Keeping – Records of all monitoring for limits (concentration and loading), toxicity, flow, and quality control stipulated by the regulation must be stored in an electronic format acceptable to the MOEE director. The discharger must also keep records of all problems or malfunctions related to sampling, chemical analyses, on-line analysis for pH measurement, lethality tests, flow measurement, or other problems encountered that interfere with fulfilling the requirements of the regulation. The duration and course of each malfunction along with a description of any remedial action taken must also be kept.

Public – On or before the first day of June in each year, the discharger must prepare a report relating to the previous calender year and include summaries of:

- plant loadings
- monitoring data
- exceedances
- incidents where sample points were by-passed

These reports must be available to any person at the plant and a copy must be sent to the MOEE director.

Reporting – A discharger must notify the director, during normal business hours and as soon as the results are available, if a daily plant loading or monthly average plant loading exceeds the limit, or if the lethality limits are exceeded.

Information must be submitted quarterly in an electronic format acceptable to the MOEE director along with a hard copy signed by the direct discharger no later than 45 days after the end of the quarter.

3.3.5 Phase III: Abatement and Enforcement

Once an effluent limit regulation is in place, there are several mechanisms that will alert the MOEE to violations:

1 Dischargers are required to notify the MOEE of violations
2 The MOEE will screen submitted monitoring data
3 The MOEE will evaluate data collected during inspections

MOEE responses to a violation may include the issuing a Notification of Violation to the discharger. A notice can request an explanation of reason(s) for the violation and a remedy for the problem. If the MOEE makes a written abatement request for action to reduce, prevent or eliminate pollution, a reasonable time to comply will be specified. Additional information on MOEE responses is provided in Chapter 8.

Another MOEE response option is to issue Control Orders (under either the EPA or the OWRA). Control Orders can require specified abatement actions to be accomplished within a given schedule.

3.3.6 Indirect Dischargers

Under MISA, restrictions will be developed for the amounts and concentrations of persistent or toxic contaminants discharged from municipal sewage treatment plants (STPs), analogous to those for the other nine industrial sectors.

The MOEE, in conjunction with municipalities, is developing a MISA sewer-use control program which will require municipalities to limit the toxic waste put into municipal sewer systems by industries (the "indirect dischargers"). The following activities are being considered: model sewer-use by-laws; monitoring of wastewater treatment plants; monitoring of significant industrial dischargers by municipality; development of local limits for selected parameters; and development of industrial sector pretreatment limits. The local limits will reflect the capacity and degree of treatment available at the treatment plant that receives the discharge and the assimilative capacity of the receiving water body.

The MOEE is proposing that the municipalities monitor significant industrial dischargers by collecting one 24-hour composite sample. The sample will be analyzed for most of the parameters on the MISA Effluent Monitoring Priority Pollutant List (EMPPL). Information on estimated contaminant loading collected during this monitoring will be used by the municipalities to develop local limits.

3.3.7 Recommendations for Complying with MISA

Eventually all liquid effluents, direct and indirect, will be affected by the MISA program. The following are some suggestions for successfully implementing the MISA program:

- start early to organize a MISA team and ensure that members are properly trained
- at larger facilities, consider dedicating a person to MISA operations and coordination
- consider automatic sampling equipment
- establish a 24-hour on-call sampling crew or obtain a service contract with a reputable company
- provide back-up for all activities including sampler personnel, flow measurement equipment, automatic samplers, and the laboratory

- carefully review the abilities of both internal and external laboratories to meet MISA requirements; include protocol in contract
- integrate MISA monitoring into routine sampling operations
- establish computerized database from the storage and assessment of data
- perform in-house audits of the monitoring program to ensure that proper protocols are being followed for sampling, analysis, data recording, and reporting
- develop internal limits (flags) which are below regulatory limits to identify problems before non-complying values occur
- perform statistical assessment of monitoring data to identify trends and correlations between parameters
- prepare written operating procedures for all wastewater treatment equipment and perform internal performance monitoring using indicator parameters (see Section 3.7)

3.4 FEDERAL REGULATIONS

3.4.1 Relationship with Province

Historically, a Federal/Ontario Environmental Accord was in place which obliged the province to enforce, and be accountable for compliance and reporting on federal requirements in Ontario. This Environmental Accord has expired, however, and a new agreement has not been reached between the federal government and the MOEE.

3.4.2 Canadian Environmental Protection Act

Section 34(1) of the Canadian Environmental Protection Act (CEPA) allows for the regulation of releases of toxic substances (as defined in Schedule 1) in terms of:

- quantity or concentration
- places or areas where the substance may be released
- the commercial or processing activity which gives rise to the release of the substance
- the manner and conditions which the substance may be released into the environment, either alone or in combination with any other substance
- the circumstances or conditions under which the minister may, for the proper administration of this Act, modify any requirement for sampling, analysis, testing, measurement or monitoring, or the methods and procedures for conducting any required sampling, analysis, tests, measurements or monitoring

The CEPA also covers the concentration of nutrients in products. Subsection 50(2) prohibits the manufacture for use or sale in Canada or import of any cleaning agent or water conditioner that has nutrient concentrations above those specified by regulations made under the Act. Part VI of the Act addresses ocean dumping, conditions and terms of dumping permits, dumping to avert danger, and the granting of permits to dump.

Under CEPA, National Effluent Regulations have been promulgated for the pulp and paper sector. The **Pulp and Paper Mill Defoamer and Wood Chip Regulations** specifically address defoamers used at pulp and paper mills in Canada. The regulation restricts the content of dibenzofurans and dibenzo-para-dioxins in defoamers that are manufactured, imported, offered for sale, or sold for use in Canadian mills. Reporting requirements include quarterly reports for any person who manufactures, imports, offers for sale or sells defoamers for use in mills in Canada. In addition, five years' transaction records of all defoamer products must be maintained by anyone who maufactures, imports, offers for sale or sells defoamers for use in mills in Canada.

The Pulp and Paper Mill Effluent Chlorinated Dioxins and Furans Regulations require that all pulp and paper mills in Canada shall not discharge into the environment any final effluent that contains measurable concentrations of 2,3,7,8-tetrachlorodibenzo-paradioxins or 2,3,7,8-tetrachlorodibenzofurans.

The ban took effect on 1 July 1992. However, if an operator indicated 60 days prior to the effective date a plan to eliminate the discharge of 2,3,7,8-tetrachlorodibenzo-para-dioxins or 2,3,7,8-tetracholorodibenzofurans, that operator had until 1 January 1994. The regulations list the required sampling protocols and schedules for mill operators.

3.4.3 Fisheries Act

Section 14 of the Fisheries Act forbids the depositing (or permitting the deposit) of a **deleterious substance** in any type of waters frequented by fish or in any other place under circumstances where the substance could enter the water. A deleterious substance is defined by the Act as:

- any substance that, if added to water, would degrade or alter the quality of that water so that it is rendered harmful to fish; and
- any water that contains a substance in which quantity or concentration would, if added to water, degrade the quality of the water and, therefore, cause harm to fish.

Chapter 13 presents additional information on federal requirements concerning aquatic toxicity testing.

Site Specific Pulp and Paper Effluent Regulations have been promulgated under the Fisheries Act. The regulations apply to all pulp and paper mills discharging effluent to receiving water and to off-site treatment facilities which treat effluent discharged by pulp and paper mills where the quantity of biochemical oxygen demanding matter (measured as BOD) is higher than 5,000 kg per day, or represents more than 20% of the total quantity of BOD from all sources treated by the off-site facility.

Every three years, all mills will be required to provide Environment Canada with an interpretative report and supporting data on an Environmental Effects Monitoring (EEM) study to be conducted in accordance with requirements published by Environment Canada. These studies will provide information as to whether discharges of deleterious substances in water frequented by fish have altered, disrupted, or destroyed fish habitat. As a result, EEM will provide information to evaluate the need for further control measures by evaluating the effectiveness of existing control measures and by assessing changes in the receiving environment.

Similar regulations are anticipated for the metal mining industry.

3.4.4 Pollution Prevention Program

In 1990, the federal government held consultations with the public that formed the basis for actions identified in Canada's Green Plan. As a result of this consultation, the Green Plan included a component dedicated to the prevention of pollution. The $25 million Great Lakes/St. Lawrence Pollution Prevention Initiative was announced in March 1991. The Pollution Prevention Initiative is a program dedicated to involving all of society in the source reduction of toxic pollutants. The program also includes a bilateral partnership with the United States.

The Great Lakes Pollution Prevention Initiative comprises three program areas: the Binational Lake Superior Program, Sectoral Programs, and the Great Lakes Pollution Prevention Centre. The first Sectoral Program was the Automotive Pollution Prevention Program (APPP), a bilateral Canada/ U.S. effort directed at the voluntary reduction in toxic substance use, generation, or release.

The Canadian Automotive Manufacturing Pollution Prevention Project is a component of the APPP and involves the federal Department of Environment, the Ontario Ministry of Environment and Energy, and the participating member companies of the Motor Vehicle Manufacturers' Association (MVMA). A similar project is underway in the U.S.

The goal of the MVMA Project is to produce a verifiable reduction of persistent toxic substances as well as other environmental contaminants (toxic substances) used, generated, or released by the participating member companies of the Canadian MVMA.

3.5 MUNICIPAL REQUIREMENTS

3.5.1 Overview

The quality and quantity of water discharged to a municipal sewer system (i.e. indirect discharge) is regulated by the municipality or the Ontario Clean Water Agency (OCWA). The OCWA recently assumed responsibility of 346 water and sewage plants from the MOEE. The discharge from the municipal system (i.e. direct discharge) is regulated by the MOEE.

Most municipalities in Ontario have passed by-laws which control discharges to sewers (sanitary, combined, and storm). In 1988, the MOEE developed a Model Sewer-Use By-law to provide a uniform basis to regulating sanitary, combined, and storm sewers across Ontario. Many municipalities, cities, and towns have incorporated the MOEE model by-laws into their own by-laws.

In the following sections the various components of the MOEE model sewer-use by-law are discussed. If assessing a discharge to a municipal system, it is imperative that a copy of the most recent sewer-use by-law for that municipality be obtained as the majority will differ slightly from the MOEE Model Sewer-Use By-Law.

3.5.2 Discharges to Sanitary and Combined Sewers

Municipal sewer-use by-laws usually include numerical limits for some parameters and prohibitions for selected types of material and waste. Table 3.8 presents the allowable concentrations stipulated in the MOEE sewer-use by-law for discharges to sanitary and combined sewers. The by-law expressly prohibits dilution to achieve those limits.

In 1989, the Municipality of Metropolitan Toronto issued its own sewer-use by-law (By-law 153-89). The range for pH in the Metropolitan Toronto is 6 - 10.5, whereas the MOE by-law specifies 5.5 - 9.5.

Several materials are not allowed in any amount into sanitary/combined sewers. These include:

fuels	severely toxic material
PCBs	waste radioactive material
pesticides	

Exemptions include PCB material if the owner/operator has a Certificate of Approval which expressly allows the discharge, or the owner/operator has approval from the municipality, or the concentration is less than 5 μg/L of PCBs. The discharge of radioactive materials is allowed if it is in accordance with a licence from the Atomic Energy Control Board.

The by-law also uses the term "wastes" to identify materials prohibited from being discharged to sewers. These wastes are defined according to the same definitions used in Regulation 347 under the EPA (see Section 4.3) and include:

acute hazardous waste chemicals   pathological wastes
hazardous industrial wastes   PCB wastes
hazardous waste chemicals   reactive waste
ignitable wastes

Exemptions are allowed for the discharge of pathological waste if it has been decontaminated prior to discharge and the owner/operator has a C of A from the MOEE, or permission from the municipality.

Water that does not originate from a municipality (e.g. lake water) may be discharged to the municipality system if the municipality is provided with information on the amount of water and its source. The municipality may require the discharger to enter into a water surcharge agreement (refer to Subsection 3.5.4). In some municipalities, however, storm water is not allowed into the sanitary sewer system regardless of any surcharge agreements. Dischargers to the municipal sewer system need to keep aware of all by-law requirements.

3.5.3 Discharges to Storm Sewers

Table 3.9 presents the allowable limits for discharges to storm sewers as declared in the MOEE sewer by-law and the Metropolitan Toronto sewer by-law. In addition, water containing dyes or colouring material which discolour the water or produce a visible sheen are not allowed. The limits only apply to storm water runoff from industrial process areas.

There are several exemptions to the MOEE limits. Cooling water is allowed if the owner/operator has a C of A from the MOEE, or written approval from the director, or approval from the municipality.

Exemptions can be obtained for total suspended solids (TSS), dyes and colouring, oil and grease, visible sheens, and metal concentrations if the discharger has a C of A issued under the EPA or the OWRA, or has a Best Management Practice (BMP) plan which has been approved by the municipality.

BMP plans should address ancillary sources of water from material storage areas, loading and unloading areas, plant site runoff, in-plant transfer, process and material handling areas, and sludge and hazardous waste disposal areas. A detailed discussion of BMP plans is presented in Section 12.7.

Discharges to storm sewers cannot include:

- automotive or machine oils/greases
- fuels
- paints or organic solvents
- PCBs
- pesticides
- severely toxic material
- waste disposal site leachate

• waste radioactive materials

There are no provisions for exemptions for these wastes.

3.5.4. Surveys, Programs, and Agreements

Waste Survey – All companies listed in Schedule B of the Industrial Sectors of the Model Sewer-Use By-Law may be required to submit a **waste survey report** to the local municipality if they discharge to a sanitary, combined, or storm sewer. The waste survey report should identify sources of water, average flow rates (sanitary, non-contact cooling water, contact cooling water, process water or other), and pollutant information (known and present, suspected to be present, known absent, suspected absent, or expected concentrations of pollutants).

Completed reports are to be reviewed by the municipality to determine which industries might be major dischargers to the sewer and to assess their impact on the sewage treatment processes. Depending on the quantities and characteristics of its discharges, a discharger may be required to enter into any one of several types of agreements with the municipality.

Agreements and Programs – If a discharge to a sewer exceeds by-law limits and the discharger believes that this will continue to be the case, the discharger may be able to enter into an **overstrength agreement** with the municipality whereby the municipality is paid to treat the discharge. Overstrength agreements can only apply to the following parameters and only if the excess capacity exists at the municipal wastewater treatment plant:

• biochemical oxygen demand (BOD)
• phenolics
• total suspended solids (TSS)
• phosphorus
• total Kjeldahl nitrogen (TKN)
• solvent extractable matter

The payment schedule is based on the excess amount of material being deposited to the sewer. For example, a municipality might impose a surcharge of 28 cents per kg of excess BOD in a discharge. Payment typically is made quarterly and based upon the actual flow rate times a concentration specified in the overstrength agreement. Rebates may be possible provided that there is sufficient data to support such a claim. Most overstrength agreements require the installation of a flow-measuring device.

For parameters that can not be covered by an overstrength agreement, a compliance program may need to be established. A compliance program allows for a period of grace while action is being taken to reduce contaminant levels.

A compliance program specifies parameter limits that are not to be exceeded while the program is in effect. A compliance program also can specify activities to be undertaken. These may include retaining an engineer, source characterization, treatability studies, start-up of a treatment system, or alteration in the process.

If non-municipal source water is discharged to a sanitary or combined sewer, a discharger may be required to enter into a **water surcharge agreement.** This agreement offsets the cost of treating the water which is normally incurred as a surcharge on the purchase of water from a municpality. Credits may be available against the surcharge if municipality source water is treated and discharged directly to a water body or if employed in the finished product.

3.6 OBTAINING APPROVALS FOR DISCHARGES

3.6.1 Direct Discharge

The MOEE document entitled *Guide For Applying for Approval of Municipal and Private Water and Sewage Works* (MOE, 1992b) describes the process of applying for a C of A. Most of the following text is derived from that document.

Requirements – Prior to the establishment, extension, or change in sewage works, a C of A as per Section 52, water works, and 53, sewage works (formerly section 23 and 24) of the OWRA must be obtained. Sections 53(1) and (5) of the OWRA require that:

(1)   No person shall establish, alter, extend or replace new or existing sewage works except under and in accordance with an approval granted by the Director,

(2)   No person shall use or operate sewage works for which an approval is required under Subsection(1) unless the required approval has been granted and complied with.

According to Section 53(6) the above requirement to obtain an approval does not apply:

(a)   to a sewage works from which sewage is not to drain or be discharged directly or indirectly into a ditch, drain or storm sewer or a well, lake, river, pond, spring, stream, reservoir or other water or watercourse

(b)   to a privately-owned sewage works designed for the partial treatment of sewage that is to drain or be discharged into a sanitary sewer

(c)   to a privately-owned sewage works serving only five or fewer private residences

(d)   to a sewage works the main purpose of which is to drain agricultural lands

(e) to a drainage works under the Drainage Act, the Cemeteries Act, the Public Transportation and Highway Improvement Act or the Railways Act

(f) to such sewage works as may be exempted by regulations made under this Act,

but this section does apply to a sewage works for the distribution of sewage on the surface of the ground for the purpose of disposing of the sewage.

Section 53(6)(a) essentially excludes sewage systems having a subsurface disposal and all associated collection works from the requirements of approval under Section 53 of the OWRA. Such works would, however, require approval under Part VIII of the EPA. Similarly, other works that are exempted form OWRA may require approval under other legislation.

Failure to comply with these requirements is considered to be a violation of the OWRA and therefore subject to penalties as specified in that Act.

Approval Process – The following are the key steps in obtaining a C of A:

• Pre-submission consultation with MOEE provides an opportunity to define objectives for the project, discuss approval requirements and identify public concerns.

• Two copies of application forms plus supporting documentation must be submitted to MOEE. One copy must be sent to the director of Approvals Branch with fee (where applicable), and the second copy to local MOEE office.

• The MOEE will review the proposal to assess whether the works comply with relevant Ministry guidelines and policies.

The following steps are performed by the MOEE as part of its review:

• Upon receipt of the submission, the application is entered into a computer data base by administration staff. The application is then forwarded to the appropriate unit and assigned to a Review Engineer.

• The Review Engineer conducts a short initial screening and review to determine if there are any gross errors or omissions of information. **Incomplete applications are returned to the proponent.**

• When the application is accepted for review, the proponent is sent an acknowledgment letter specifying a Ministry reference file number, anticipated processing time, and the Review Engineer's name and telephone number.

• The Review Engineer performs a review of the application to assess whether the details are complete; the proposal complies with all Ministry acts, regulations, policies, objectives and guidelines; the design reflects sound environmental engineering principles; adequate controls and contingencies are provided to facilitate the proper operation of the works; the estimated fee has been calculated in accordance with the impending regulation.

- The Review Engineer may also request input to the review from the District Office, Technical Assessment Section of the appropriate Regional Office or other branches of the Ministry.

The review leads to one or more of the following:

    i)   a request for additional information

    ii)   a request for design changes and revised fee estimate

    iii) a draft approval recommended to the director

    iv) a draft notice of denial recommended to the director

- Requests for additional information and design changes are communicated in writing to the proponent with a deadline for response. Failure to respond will result in the assumption that the proponent no longer wishes to proceed with the application and the application will be returned.
- A public hearing under Section 54 or 55 of the OWRA may be required prior to the issuance of an approval under the Act. Pursuant to Section 7 of the OWRA, when the Environmental Assessment Board holds a public hearing, it shall serve notice of its decision resulting from the hearing, and the director shall implement this decision. Should a public hearing be required, the fee submitted with the application will be refunded. In these circumstances the fee will be required only when the certificate is ready to be issued. An invoice will be sent to the proponent.
- Upon recommendation of the Review Engineer, when satisfied, the director (Approvals Branch) will grant approval by signing a certificate of approval. If a C of A already exists for the proposal, it may be amended to include the new works.

According to section 53(4), if it is in public interest to do so, the director may:

a) refuse to grant the approval

b) grant the approval on such terms and conditions as the director considers necessary

c) impose new terms and conditions to the approval

d) alter the terms and conditions of the approval

e) revoke or suspend the approval

However, should the director decide to do any of the above, Section 100 of the OWRA requires that the director provide written notice of intentions with reasons. This notice may be appealed to the Environmental Appeal Board provided that the appeal is filed within 15 days of receipt of the notice.

Upon granting of the director's approval, the applicant may then proceed to construct and operate the works. A copy of the C of A should be attached to the application (it is usually referenced) and a copy of the conditions should be attached to the piece of equipment for which it applies.

Costs – As of the 1st of October 1992, the MOEE began charging fees for approvals for commercial, industrial, and private sector undertakings. In accordance with the impending regulation, the fee for an approval under Sections 52 and 53 OWRA for the establishment of new sewage and water works or the extension, alteration, or replacement of existing sewage and water works is 2% of the estimated cost of the new works or 2% of the estimated cost of the extension, alteration, or replacement of existing works. The fee may be not less than $50 and not more than $100,000.

The fee is based upon the costs of equipment, labour, materials, and other construction costs including buildings necessary for the proper functioning of the subject matter, but does not include costs for land, engineering services, taxes, and costs of any pollution control facilities for which permit or approval is applied for under other sections of OWRA or EPA and for which appropriate fees have been or will be paid. For applications not involving any costs, the flat fee of $50 will be applied.

To comply with the new goals of the MOEE, the proposal or upgrade to the sewage works should include in its design pollution prevention concepts and mitigation of multi-media transfer. The removal of a pollutant from one media with direct transfer to another media is discouraged.

The MOEE currently takes a firm stand when the construction of facilities begins before a C of A is issued. There are cases of construction being stopped by the owner so as to not jeopardize a pending C of A, and of the MOEE refusing to issue a C of A for completed facilities. The supplying of utility services to a site, such as those covered by a Municipal Building Permit, do not seem to be of a concern to the MOEE; however, the regional MOEE office should be contacted.

Timing – In the past, submissions took three to six months before a C of A was obtained. The MOEE, in conjunction with industry, has revised the system significantly reducing the time. A typical approval may now take from six weeks to three months.

The expected processing time goals for applications include:

i) Applications which arrive with complete documentation, and with environmental impact information, effluent criteria, hydrogeological criteria or raw water quality analysis which have been accepted/endorsed by the Regional Ministry Office during pre-submission consultation are likely to be processed within four weeks.

ii) Applications which arrive with complete documentation, but with environmental impact information, effluent criteria, hydrological criteria or raw water quality analysis which have not been accepted/endorsed by the Regional Ministry Office will be processed. However, the review time will be as long as necessary.

Note: It is expected that where the proponent initiates pre-submission consultations, this situation will not occur except under emergency conditions.

iii) Applications for which a public consultation/hearing is required will be processed. However, the review time will be as long as necessary.

iv) Applications which arrive without environmental impact information, effluent criteria, hydrological criteria or raw water quality analysis where required will be returned to the applicant.

v) All other incomplete applications will be returned to the applicant.

A complete application of approval consists of a completed and signed application form and all relevant supporting information as specified in the application form and in this document.

It is in a discharger's best interest to make sure that an application is submitted at the earliest possible stage of a project, and that the application provides sufficient information for its evaluation.

3.6.2 Local Municipalities

Permission from the local municipality must be obtained prior to establishing new sewer connections, but not for new or modified sewage treatment systems or discharges. However, most municipalities require a discharger to complete and submit a waste survey report (subsection 3.5.4.) They also require that the report be updated and resubmitted whenever changes are made to the quality or quantity of a discharge.

3.6.3 Permit to Take Water

Section 34 of the OWRA requires that "No person shall take more than a total of 50,000 litres of water in a day" from ground and/or surface waters without a permit issued by the director.

An application to the Regional Technical Assessment Section is required to receive a permit to take water. Examples of information that must be included with the application include a design brief, a hydrology reprint, a construction reprint, and water quality analysis.

3.7 MONITORING

3.7.1 Monitoring Requirements

As described in previous sections of this chapter, monitoring requirements may be imposed on a facility by various acts and regulations including MISA (either as a direct and/or indirect discharger), the federal

Fisheries Act and CEPA, MOEE Certificate of Approvals, control orders, clean-up orders, overstrength agreement, and compliance agreement monitoring with a municipality.

In addition to the monitoring that is imposed upon it by regulatory agencies, a facility may perform in-house monitoring for various reasons:
- assess compliance
- operate a wastewater treatment facility
- obtain a rebate for an overstrength agreement
- source assessment of elevated contaminants levels
- Toxicity Reduction Evaluation (see Chapter 13)
- assess the effects of an incident
- determine net loadings
- assess "background" conditions prior to constructing a facility

In some cases, the procedures used for sampling and analysis may be different for the non-regulated monitoring compared to those of regulated monitoring programs. For example, higher method detection limits (MDL) may be suitable for an in-house program to track down the source of a substance in a wastewater stream compared to measurements in final effluent.

3.7.2 Chemical Quality Parameters of Interest

The chemicals present in an effluent or discharge stream are influenced by various factors that include the use of the water (e.g. non-contact versus contact cooling water), the source of the water (e.g. river water versus lake water), whether chemical additives such as chlorine or algicides are used, pre- and final treatment, and whether sources include ground water inflow or runoff.

Table 3.7 presents the Analytical Test Groups (ATGs) of the MISA program. In addition to the MISA parameters, the following parameters may need to be analyzed, especially when assessing the operations of a wastewater treatment system or considering the possible re-use of an effluent stream:
- alkalinity and acidity
- biochemical oxygen demand (BOD)
- chemical oxygen demand (COD)
- chlorine and chloride*
- cyanide (free)
- dissolved gases: oxygen, hydrogen sulphide, etc.
- fluoride*
- iron*
- sulphate
- temperature
- oil and grease

The asterisks denote parameters that MISA may require for some industrial sectors: iron for the Iron and Steel Sector, and chloride and fluoride for the Industrial Minerals Sector.

Biochemical Oxygen Demand (BOD) is the amount of molecular oxygen required to stabilize the decomposable matter present in a water by aerobic biochemical action. Because the complete stabilization of a given waste may take too long, a standard laboratory BOD test has been developed which incubates the material for a period of five days at 20°C. The results of a BOD$_5$ test are often used to assess the efficiency of both municipal and industrial biological treatment plants and the appropriateness of the wastewater.

Chemical Oxygen Demand (COD) measures the non-biodegradable as well as the ultimate biodegradable organic compounds in terms of oxygen consumption to stabilize the decomposition.

3.7.3 Surrogate Parameters

There are many situations where it is sufficient or appropriate to use surrogate parameters to assess effluent or water quality. Most surrogate parameters provide information that is similar to the parameters or conditions that are of actual concern. For example, an effluent might be analyzed for total phenols when, in fact, it is a specific phenolic compound that is of interest.

Most surrogates are used because the sample requirements are simpler, or the samples require less time or expense to analyze than the compound of interest. Some surrogates lack the sensitivity of specific compounds, but this may not be a limitation for assessing certain situations.

Surrogates should be used only after a correlation between it and the parameter of concern has been developed. For example, some effluents have shown a strong correlation between absorbed metals and TSS. In such cases, TSS can be used to monitor a discharge stream on a frequent basis and specific metals analyzed only if a pre-defined TSS concentration is exceeded.

Another example is the COD test which is more reproducible and less time consuming than a BOD test; however, the COD/BOD correlation is such that it is normally only a qualitative value. A change in the ratio of biodegradable to non-biodegradable organic compounds affects the correlation (WPCF and ASCE, 1982).

The analysis of organic parameters is relatively expensive when compared to conventional parameters and many of the surrogate parameters deal with organic compounds. For example, total oil and grease, dissolved organic carbon, total organic carbon, total halogens, or total phenols can be monitored on a regular basis with the provision for analyzing specific compounds if a threshold concentration is exceeded.

For some groups of organic compounds, specific members can be used as either as indicators of the possible presence of other group members or may become recognized as the compounds of greatest potential concern and therefore the prime objective of frequent monitoring. For example, benzene may be the only non-halogenated volatile compound of concern in an effluent. Similarly, benzo(a)pyrene can be used for other polyaromatic hydrocarbons. While large cost savings can be realized, such selections are best based on substantial supporting data.

3.7.4 Sample Collection and Preservation Methods

Prior to the collection of samples, the MOEE *Protocol for the Sampling and Analyses of Industrial/Municipal Wastewater* (MOEE, 1993a) should be reviewed. This document provides detailed information on accepted methods of sample collection and preservation.

Prior to the introduction of the MISA monitoring program, the most common form of sampling was **grab sampling**. It is still widely used when only a few samples are required. The MISA monitoring program requires that grab samples be taken for five ATGs: 15 – Sulphide, 16 – halogenated volatiles, 17 – non-halogenated volatiles, 18 – water soluble volatiles, and 28a – open characterization for volatiles.

One weakness of grab samples is that the samples may only be indicative of effluent quality at the time that the sample is collected. To improve the representativeness of effluent sampling efforts, automatic samplers or on-line analyzers can be used.

Automatic samplers can operate in one of two modes: collecting and combining equal volume sub-samples at equal time intervals, or collecting and combining samples which are flow proportional. The benefits of these types of devices are that the manpower commitment is reduced and the data represents a truer mean of the concentration of the discharge stream as more sub-samples can be collected.

On-line analyzers have been available for many years but only recently have capabilities been extended beyond conventional parameters such as pH and conductivity. On-line analyzers are now available that continuously analyze effluents for organic compounds. On-line effluent analyzers for benzene, toluene, and xylene are used by some industries in Sarnia.

A relatively complex continuous monitoring system has been providing continuous analysis of volatile organic compounds in the St. Clair River for several years. The equipment was installed by a local environmental association of 15 chemical and oil refining companies along the St. Clair River that are part of the industrial complex at Sarnia. The monitoring equipment has detection limits in the low ppb range for eight target compounds. Valid data capture typically averages greater than 90%. The system is used to alert association members to spills as they occur, thus allowing the company to contain the spill immediately and take remedial action. Depending upon the chemicals to be analyzed in a sample, preservatives should be added to either the sample container or laboratory container to ensure a concentration which is representative of the discharge quality. The chemicals that are used to preserve samples sometimes are categorized as either pre-preservatives or preservatives. **Pre-preservatives** are added to the sample container before the sample itself. For example, a pre-preservative should be used if an automatic sampler is being to collect samples which will be analyzed for ATG 2 – cyanide, or 14 – phenols. **Preservatives** are added after the sample has been collected in the sample container. Table 3.10 lists the preservatives for all of the MISA monitoring parameters.

3.7.5 Analytical Methods

Table 3.7 presents the analytical protocols and method detection limits for each of the MISA Analytical Test Groups. Additional information of analytical techniques is provided in the MISA General Effluent Monitoring Regulation (Regulation 695/88 as amended by Regulation 533/89) and the MOEE *Protocol for the Sampling and Analyses of Industrial/Municipal Wastewater* (MOEE, 1993a).

Various other sources are available that describe analytical protocols. One of long standing is *Standard Methods* which is revised and reissued every few years (APHA, AWWA, WPCF, 1985).

3.7.6 Quality Assurance and Quality Control

It is essential that an effective Quality Assurance/Quality Control (QA/QC) program be implemented with all monitoring programs. It assures the controllability, accountability, and retractability of the work being performed.

A good QA/QC program involves close supervision and surveillance of all field operations, documentation, and review of sampling procedures, and the assurance that appropriate laboratory analysis techniques are employed.

The QC program should ensure that data are generated within known limits of accuracy and precision. This involves the application of method detection limits and travelling blank samples, and the collection of replicate samples and duplicate samples.

The MISA program has several requirements concerning QA/QC:
- an MDL must be calculated for each parameter
- "standard reference materials" must be employed to ensure that the laboratory standard solutions be validated
- reasonable control limits must be developed for the analyses of method blank samples

- during the course of an analytical run for specified ATGs, a replicate sample, a method blank sample, and a method blank sample spiked with a standard solution must be included
- travelling blanks and travelling spiked blanks must be used
- replicate and duplicate samples must be provided

A **replicate sample** refers to one of at least two samples removed from a single sample container in a manner that minimizes the difference between the samples. A **duplicate sample** is similar, but means one of two samples collected at a sampling point.

3.7.7 Flow Measurement/Estimation Methods

Flow systems are assigned to two basic categories: flow in closed channels and flow in open channels. **Closed channel flow** is defined as flow in completely filled pressure conduits (pipes). Pressure conduits are usually used for fresh water lines or for industrial processes, and flow through these is often measured by some type of device inserted into the line. Measuring devices for closed channel flow include the venturi meter, flow nozzle, orifice meter, magnetic flow meter, and pitot tube flow meter.

Open channel flow is defined as flow in any channel in which the liquid flow with a free surface. Examples are runoff ditches, canals, flumes, and other uncovered conduits. Certain closed channels, such as sewers and tunnels when flowing partially full, and not under pressure are classified as open channels. There are numerous methods of determining the rate of flow in an open channel.

Timed Gravimetric – Collection of the entire contents of the flow during a fixed length of time.

Dilution – The flow rate is measured by determining the degree of dilution of an added tracer solution in the flowing water.

Velocity – The flow rate is calculated by determining the mean flow velocity across a cross-section and multiplying this rate by the width of the channel at this point and the measured liquid level. The latter is measured by a second device. The sophistication of this type of system and accuracy has improved considerably in recent years.

Hydraulic Structure – Some type of hydraulic structure such as a weir is introduced into the flow stream. The function of the hydraulic structure (primary device) is to produce a flow that is characterized by known relationship (usually nonlinear) between a liquid level measurement (head) at some location and the flow rate of the stream.

Slope-Hydraulic Radius Area – Measurements of water surface slope, cross-sectional area, and wetted perimeter over a length of uniform section channel are used to determine the flow rate, utilizing a resistance equation such as the Manning formula. The flow channel itself serves as the primary device.

The MISA monitoring regulations specify the accuracies by which various types of flows must be measured or estimated:

Combined and Process Subcategory Effluent – The MOEE has proposed that combined effluent streams be continuously monitored with an overall flow device accuracy of ±15% as part of MISA's Effluent Limits Regulation.

Cooling Water – An accuracy of ±20% of the actual flow has been proposed by the MOEE as part of MISA's Effluent Limits Regulation.

Other Types of Effluents – Flow device accuracy for other types of discharges (e.g. storm water and waste disposal site effluents) is usually ± 20%. Most industrial sectors do not require flow measurement for storm water discharges or waste disposal site effluent. Instead, the duration and volume of these discharges may be estimated or measured.

Note that the accuracy of the primary devices may be determined by either calibration or certification reports. A certification report must certify that the primary flow device was installed according to international standards.

Flow measurement is a key element in the determination of the mass loading of a particular chemical. As such, it has become an integral part of the MISA program and municipal overstrength agreements.

In the next few years, flow measurement may take on even greater importance as water conservation is promoted by the Ontario Ministry of Natural Resources and the MOEE. Surcharges on the use of water may come to play a larger role in water conservation policy.

3.8 REPORTING REQUIREMENTS

3.8.1 Reporting Monitoring Data

Many of the monitoring programs described in this chapter require the timely reporting of data. The actual reporting requirements are a function of the particular monitoring program.

Reports can vary from a letter containing a few analytical results to computer disks containing electronic information for the MIDES or TOX-DATA systems, and associated hard copy for the MISA monitoring system.

It is in a discharger's interest, regardless of reporting requirements, to begin compiling a computerized environmental data base. The data base should assist in the generation of reports, performing error checks, and allow for easier assessment of past trends in contaminant loadings and overall compliance.

3.8.2 Incident Reporting

As defined by the EPA, an incident is the discharge of a contaminant into the environment out of the normal course of events that is likely to cause an adverse effect. Section 15(1) of the EPA states that every person who discharges a contaminant or causes or permits the discharge of a contaminant into the natural environmental out of the normal course of events that causes or is likely to cause an adverse effect shall forthwith notify the Ministry.

Section 92(1) requires that every person having control of a pollutant that is spilled and every person who spills or causes or permits a spill of a pollutant that causes or is likely to cause an adverse effect shall forthwith notify the following persons of the spill, of the circumstances, and of the action that the person has taken or intends to take with respect to:

- the MOEE
- the municipality or, if the spill occurred within the boundaries of a regional municipality, the regional municipality within the boundaries of which the spill occurred
- where the person is not the owner of the pollutant and knows or is able to ascertain readily the identity of the owner of the pollutant, that person must inform the owner of the pollutant
- where the person is not the person having control of the pollutant and knows or is able to ascertain readily the identity of the person having control of the pollutant, that person must inform the person who has control of the pollutant

Section 30(2) of the OWRA also deals with incident reporting in that every person that discharges or causes or permits the discharge of any material of any kind, and such discharge is not in the normal course of events, or from whose control material of any kind escapes into or in any waters or on any shore or bank thereof or into or in any place that may impair the quality of the water of any waters, shall forthwith notify the minister of the discharge or escape, as the case may be.

If a toxic substance (as defined by Schedule 1) is released into the environment in contravention of the CEPA, then Section 36 of the CEPA requires that a person who owns or has charge of a substance immediately before its initial release or its likely initial release into the environment, or who causes or contributes to the initial release or increases the likelihood of the initial release, must report the incident as soon as possible in the circumstances and make a reasonable effort to notify any member of the public who may be adversely affected by the release or likely release.

Additional incident reporting requirements are described in Chapter 12.

3.9 SUMMARY

The prime pieces of legislation that govern direct discharges in Ontario are the provincial EPA and OWRA and the federal Fisheries Act and

CEPA. In addition to site or sector-specific limits imposed by legislation, numerical ambient water quality objectives and guidelines are available from the MOEE.

The provincial MISA program currently addresses direct dischargers from several industrial sectors. Over time this program will be expanded to other industrial sectors and indirect dischargers. MISA clearly places the responsibility for rigorous monitoring, effluent control, and reporting on the owners and/or operators of facilities that discharge effluents. The overall objective of the MISA program is the virtual elimination of persistent, toxic contaminants from all discharges into Ontario waterways.

Currently, indirect dischargers are regulated by the local municipality or the Ontario Clean Water Agency if the latter operates the municipal sewer treatment plant. Most municipalities have by-laws which stipulate allowable concentrations and prohibit specified materials and waste from being discharged.

REFERENCES

American Public Health Association (APHA), American Water Works Association (AWWA), Water Pollution Control Federation (WPCF). 1985. *Standard Methods for the Examination of Water and Wastewater.* Sixteenth edition.

Municipality of Metropolitan Toronto. November 1989. "By-Law 153-89."

Ontario Ministry of the Environment (MOE). 1984a. *Rationale for the Establishment of Ontario's Provincial Water Quality Objectives.*

Ontario Ministry of the Environment (MOE). 1984b. *Ontario Drinking Water Objectives.* Revised 1983.

Ontario Ministry of the Environment (MOE). 1988. *Model Sewer-Use By-Law.* ISBN O-7729-4419-9.

Ontario Ministry of the Environment (MOE). May 1989. *Ontario's Water Quality Objective Development Process.* Draft, Aquatic Criteria Development Committee.

Ontario Ministry of the Environment (MOE). July 1991. *Provincial Water Quality Objectives and Guidelines.*

Ontario Ministry of the Environment (MOE). 1992a. *Water Management Goals, Policies, Objectives, and Implementation Procedures of the Ministry of the Environment.* Revised. (Blue Book).

Ontario Ministry of the Environment (MOE). September 1992b. *Guide for for Applying for Approval of Municipal and Private Water and Sewage Works.*

Ontario Ministry of Environment and Energy (MOEE). July 1993a. *Protocol for the Sampling and Analyses of Industry/Municipal Wastewater.*

Ontario Ministry of Environment and Energy (MOEE). January 1993b. *Protocol for Conducting a Storm Water Control Study.*

Water Pollution Control Federation (WPCF) and American Society of Civil Engineers (ASCE). 1982. "Wastewater Treatment Plant Design." WPCF Manual of Practice No. 8 and ASCE Manual on Engineering Practice No. 36.

Table 3.1
MOEE POLICIES RELATED TO WATER QUALITY

02-03   **Financial Assurance** – Guidelines are provided for the calculation of financial assurance required.

07-05   **Guidelines for Compatibility between Sewage Treatment Facilities and Sensitive Land Uses** – This policy is intended to minimize the effect of odours emanating from municipal and private sewage treatment works on sensitive adjacent land uses.

08-01   **Levels of Treatment for Municipal and Private Sewage Treatment Works Discharging to Surface Waters** – This policy describes the levels of treatment that the Ministry requires at municipal and private sewage treatment works discharging to surface waters.

08-02   **Statement of Policy to Govern the Separation of Sewers and Watermains** – Sewage works, including sanitary sewers, sanitary forcemains, storm sewers, storm forcemains and all appurtenances and fittings thereto, and watermains located parallel to each other, should be constructed in separate trenches maintaining a clear horizontal separation distance of 2.5 m.

08-03   **Minimize Accepted Level of Servicing for Municipally and Privately Owned Communal Systems** – This policy describes the minimum recommended level of servicing for municipally owned communal water and sewage systems in the Province of Ontario.

08-04   **Policy to Govern the Provision and Operation of Phosphorus Removal Facilities at Municipal, Institutional and Private Sewage Treatment Works** – This policy describes the requirements for the provision and operation of phosphorus removal facilities on a drainage basin basis. The policy states that certain drainage basins in the province require phosphorus removal down to 1.0 mg/L total phosphorus in the effluent.

08-06   **Policy to Govern Sampling and Analysis Requirements for Municipal and Private Sewage Treatment Works** – This policy describes the minimum sampling and analysis requirements of the Ministry for Municipal and Private Sewage Works. The purpose of this requirement is to assess the works performance and compliance with effluent requirements.

It should be noted, however, that conditions imposing monitoring and sampling in a Certificate of Approval under section 52 and 53 of the OWRA will govern monitoring of performance and compliance for any specific works.

12-02 **Construction Prior to Approval** – Sewage or water works constructed without the approval of the Director contravene section 52 or 53 of the OWRA.

12-03 **Approval of Expansion to Previously Constructed and Unapproved Facilities** – This policy relates to expansion or additions to sewage and water works constructed prior to the passage of the OWRA.

15-01 **Water Management — Goals, Policies, Objectives and Implementation Procedures of the Ministry of the Environment** – This policy, often referred to as the "Blue Book," ensures the effective management of the province's water resources. It also establishes specific receiving water criteria (i.e. PWQO – Provincial Water Quality Objectives) for many pollutants.

15-02 **Surface Water Quality Management Deviation from "Policy 2"** – This policy elaborates on the Ministry practice concerning deviations from Surface Water Quality Management "Policy 2" as outlined in Policy 15-01. Deviation from "Policy 2" refers to instances where in areas with water quality not meeting Provincial Water Quality Objectives, it is not possible, (for reasons specified) to prevent further degradation of existing water quality.

15-03 **Provincial Water Quality Objectives for Radionuclides and Total Dissolved Solids** – The policy outlines principles associated with these parameters.

15-06 **Drinking Water Quality: Ontario Drinking Water Objectives (ODWO)** – This policy deals with the protection and enhancement of drinking water quality as described in the Ministry document entitled "Ontario Drinking Water Objectives."

15-08 **Incorporation of the Reasonable Use Concept into Groundwater Management Activities** – This policy establishes the basis for determining the reasonable use of ground water on property adjacent to sources of contaminants.

15-10   **The Resolution of Groundwater Interference Problems** – Policy is intended to facilitate the implementation of MOEE Policy 15-01. The policy covers the implementation and timing of Ministry response to complaints about contaminated water supplies.

15-13   **Potable Water Storage Structures** – This policy establishes the requirement for the provision of covers for structures used for the storage of potable water.

15-14   **Treatment Requirements for Municipal and Communal Water Works Using Surface Water Sources** – This policy describes the treatment that the Ministry requires at municipal and communal water works using surface water as a raw water supply.

15-15   **Treatment Requirements for Municipal and Communal Water Works Using Groundwater Sources** – This policy describes the treatment that the Ministry will require at municipal and communal water works using ground sources for raw water supply.

Table 3.2
PROVINCIAL WATER QUALITY OBJECTIVES AND GUIDELINES

Substance	CAS	PWQO/G Status	Value (µg/L)
1,1,2,2-tetrachloroethane	79345	PWQG	70
1,1,2-trichloroethane	79005	PWQG	800
1,1-dichloroethane	75343	PWQG	200
1,1-dichloroethylene	75354	PWQG	40
1,2,3,4-tetrachlorobenzene	634662	PWQO	0.1
1,2,3,5 tetrachlorobenzene	634902	PWQO	0.1
1,2,3-trichlorobenzene	87616	PWQO	0.9
1,2,4,5-tetrachlorobenzene	95943	PWQO	0.15
1,2,4-trichlorobenzene	120821	PWQO	0.5
1,2-dichlorobenzene	95501	PWQO	2.5
1,2-dichloroethane	107062	PWQG	100
1,3,5-trichlorobenzene	108703	PWQO	0.65
1,3-dichlorobenzene	541731	PWQO	2.5
1,3-dimethylnaphthalene	N/A	Proposed PWQG	0.09
1,4-dichlorobenzene	106467	PWQO	4
1-methylnaphthalene	90120	Proposed PWQG	2
2-methylnaphthalene	91576	Proposed PWQG	2
2,3,7,8-tetrachlorodibenzo-p-dioxin	1746016	Proposed PWQG	0.02 pg/L
2,3,7,8-tetrachlorodibenzo-p-furan	51207139	Proposed PWQG	0.2 pg/L
2,4-D (BEE)	1928456	PWQO	4
2,4-dimethylphenol	105679	Proposed PWQG	10.5
2,4-dinitrotoluene	121142	Proposed PWQG	4
2,6-dimethylnaphthalene	N/A	Proposed PWQG	0.02
2,6-dimethylphenol	576261	Proposed PWQG	8.4
2,6-dinitrotoluene	606202	Proposed PWQG	3
2-methylnaphthalene	91576	Proposed PWQG	2
2-nitrophenol	88755	Proposed PWQG	0.5
3,4-dimethylphenol	95658	Proposed PWQG	17.5
3-nitrophenol	N/A	Proposed PWQG	22
4,6-dinitro-o-cresol	534521	Proposed PWQG	0.2
4-nitrophenol	100027	Proposed PWQG	48
abietic acid	514103	PWQG (e)	(a), (c)
Aldrin/Dieldrin	309002	PWQO	0.001
alkalinity	N/A	PWQO	no decrease > 25%
aluminum	7429905	PWQG	(a)
ammonia (unionized)	7664417	PWQO	20
aniline	62533	Proposed PWQG	2
antimony	7440360	Proposed PWQG	7

Substance	CAS	PWQO/G Status	Value (µg/L)
Aroclor 1016	12674-11-2	PWQO (e)	(e)
Aroclor 1221	11104-28-2	PWQO (e)	(e)
Aroclor 1232	11141-16-5	PWQO (e)	(e)
Aroclor 1242	53469-21-9	PWQO (e)	(c)
Aroclor 1248	12672-29-6	PWQO (e)	(c)
Aroclor 1254	11097-69-1	PWQO (e)	(c)
Aroclor 1260	11096-82-5	PWQO (e)	(e)
arsenic	7440382	PWQO	100
benzene	71432	Proposed PWQG	100
beryllium	7440417	PWQO	(a)
bis (2-ethylhexyl) phthalate	117817	PWQO (b)	(b)
cadmium	7440439	PWQO	0.2
cadmium (revised)	7440439	Proposed PWQO	(a)
Chlordane	57749	PWQO	0.06
chlorine	7782505	PWQO	2
chlorobenzene (monochlorobenzene)	108907	PWQO	15
chromium	7440473	PWQO	100
cobalt	7440484	Proposed PWQG	0.4
copper	7440508	PWQO	5
copper (revised)	7440508	Proposed PWQO	(a)
m- cresol	108-39-4	Proposed PWQG	1
o- cresol	95-48-7	Proposed PWQG	1
p- cresol	106-44-5	Proposed PWQG	1
cyanide (free)	57125	PWQO	5
Dalapon	75990	PWQO	110
DDT & metabolites	50293	PWQO	0.003
dehydroabietic acid (DHA)	1740198	PWQG	(a)
dibutylphthalate	84742	PWQO (c)	(c)
di-n-butyltin	683181	Proposed PWQG	0.08
di-n-octylphthalate	117840	PWQO	(d)
Diazinon	333415	PWQO	0.08
dibutylphthalate	84742	PWQO	4
Dicamba	N/A	PWQO	200
dichlorophenols (applies to all 10 isomers)		PWQO	0.2
diethylhexylphthalate	117817	PWQO	0.6
diethylphthalate (DEP)	84662	PWQO	(d)
dimethylphthalate	131113	PWQO	(d)
Diquat	2764729	PWQO	0.5
dissolved gases	N/A	PWQO	< 110% sat. value
dissolved oxygen	N/A	PWQO	(a)
Diuron	330541	PWQO	1.6
Dursban	2921882	PWQO	0.001
Endosulphan	115297	PWQO	0.003
Endrin	72208	PWQO	0.002

Substance	CAS	PWQO/G Status	Value (µg/L)
ethylbenzene	100414	Proposed PWQG	8
Fenthion	55389	PWQO	0.006
Guthion	86500	PWQO	0.005
Heptachlor & Heptachlor epoxide	76448	PWQO	0.001
hexachlorobenzene	118741	PWQO	0.0065
hexachlorobutadiene	87683	Proposed PWQG	0.07
hexachloroethane	67721	Proposed PWQG	0.5
hydrogen sulphide	7783064	PWQO	2
iron	7439896	PWQO	300
isopimaric acid	5835267	PWQG (e)	(a), (c)
lead	7439921	PWQO	(a)
lead (revised)	7439921	Proposed PWQO	(a)
levopimaric acid	79549	PWQG (e)	(a), (e)
Lindane (gamma - 1,2,3,4,5,6-hexachlorocyclohexane)	58899	PWQO	0.01
m-dinitrobenzene	N/A	Proposed PWQG	1
m-xylene	108383	Proposed PWQG	2
Malathion	121755	PWQO	0.1
mercury	7439976	PWQO	0.2
Methoxychlor	74435	PWQO	0.04
Mirex	2385855	PWQO	0.001
molybdenum	7439987	Proposed PWQG	10
monochlorophenols (applies to all 3 isomers)	25167800	PWQO	7
neoabietic acid	471772	PWQG (j)	(a), (j)
nickel	7440020	PWQO	25
nitrobenzene	98953	Proposed PWQG	0.02
o-chlorophenol (2-chlorophenol)	95578	PWQO	(d)
o-dinitrobenzene	N/A	Proposed PWQG	1
o-xylene	95476	Proposed PWQG	40
oil & grease	N/A	PWQO	(a)
p-dinitrobenzene	N/A	Proposed PWQG	2
p-xylene	106423	Proposed PWQG	30
palustric acid	1945535	PWQG (e)	(a), (c)
Parathion	56382	PWQO	0.008
pentachlorobenzene	608935	PWQO	0.03
pentachlorophenol	87865	PWQO	0.5
pH	N/A	PWQO	6.5-8.5
phenol (monohydroxybenzene)	108952	Proposed PWQG	5
phenols	N/A	PWQO	1
phosphorus, total	77231401	PWQG	(a)
phthalates, other	various	PWQO	0.2
pimaric acid	127275	PWQG (c)	(a), (e)
polychlorinated biphenyl	(PCBs -Total) various	PWQO	0.001
Pyrethrum	800347	PWQO	(a)
radionuclides	various	PWQO	(a)

Substance	CAS	PWQO/G Status	Value (µg/L)
resin acids, total	various	PWQG (e)	(a)
sandaracopimaric acid	N/A	PWQG (j)	(a), (e)
selenium	7782492	PWQO	100
silver	7440224	PWQO	0.1
Simazine	122349	PWQO	10
strontium	7440246	Proposed PWQG	7
styrene	100425	Proposed PWQG	4
swimming and bathing	N/A	PWQO	(a)
temperature	N/A	PWQO	(a)
tetrachloroethylene	127184	Proposed PWQG	50
tetrachlorophenols (applies to all 6 isomers)	108703	PWQO	18
tetraethyl lead	78002	Proposed PWQG	0.0007
tetramethyl lead	75741	Proposed PWQG	0.006
thallium	7440280	Proposed PWQG	0.3
toluene	108883	Proposed PWQG	0.8
Toxaphene	N/A	PWQO	0.008
trans- 1,2-Dichloroethylene	156605	Proposed PWQG	200
tributyltin	various	Proposed PWQG	0.00004
trichloroethylene	79016	PWQG	20
triethyl lead	78002	Proposed PWQG	0.4
triethyltin	994310	Proposed PWQG	0.01
triphenyltin	76879	Proposed PWQG	0.001
turbidity	N/A	PWQO	(a)
vanadium	7440622	Proposed PWQG	7
zinc	7440666	PWQO	30
zinc (revised)	7440666	Proposed PWQO	20

Legend
(a) PWQO/G is either a narrative, or dependent on pH, alkalinity, or hardness; see Blue Book Table 1 and footnotes below
(b) PWQO is for DIMETHYLHEXYLPHTHALATE (0.6 µg/L)
(c) PWQO is for DIBUTYLPHTHALATE (4.0 µg/L)
(d) PWQO is for OTHER PHTHALATES (0.2 µg/L)
(e) PWQO/G is available for total PCBs, for total resin acids and for DHA, but not other individual isomers
(f) CAS numbers are CIS–156592; trans – 156605
PWQG = Provincial Water Quality Guideline
PWQO = Provincial Water Quality Objective

Reference: MOEE, 1994.

Footnote 1: Aluminum, Phosphorus and Resin Acid Guidelines

PARAMETER	PROVINCIAL WATER QUALITY GUIDELINE
Aluminum, Inorganic Monomeric	0.015 mg/L, at pH 4.5 to 5.5 measured in clay-free samples
Aluminum, Acid Soluble Inorganic	< 10% increase above avg. background at pH>5.5-6.5 in clay-free samples
Aluminum, Total	0.075 mg/L at pH 6.5-9.0 measured in clay-free samples
Dehydroabietic Acid	see footnote 1
Resin Acids, Total	see footnote 1
Phosphorus, Total	To avoid nuisance algae concentration in lakes, total P should not exceed 20 µg/L
	To protect against aesthetic deterioration in lakes, total P should not exceed 10 µg/L
	To avoid excess plant growth in rivers & streams, total P should not exceed 30 µg/L

Footnote 2: Proposed Metal PWQO/G

Substance	Hardness (mg/L)	Proposed PWQO/G (µg/L)
Cadmium	0 - 100	0.15
	> 100	0.45
Copper	0 - 20	1
	> 20	5
Lead	0 - 30	1
	30 - 80	3
	> 80	5

Footnote 3: Total resin acids and DHA are pH dependent as shown below:

Receiving water pH	DHA (µg/L)	Total Resin Acids (µg/L)
5	1	1
5.5	2	3
6	2	4
6.5	4	9
7	8	25
7.5	12	45
8	13	52
8.5	14	60
9	14	62

Table 3.3
SCHEDULE 1—ANALYTICAL TEST GROUP NUMBERS AND PARAMETERS

#	ANALYTICAL TEST GROUP NAME	PARAMETERS
1	Chemical Oxygen Demand	Chemical oxygen demand (COD)
2	Total cyanide	Total cyanide
3	Hydrogen ion (pH)	Hydrogen ion (pH)
4a	Nitrogen	Ammonia plus Ammonium Total Kjeldahl nitrogen
4b	Nitrogen	Nitrate + Nitrite
5a	Organic carbon	Dissolved organic carbon (DOC)
5b	Organic carbon	Total organic carbon (TOC)
6	Total phosphorus	Total phosphorus
7	Specific conductance	Specific conductance
8	Suspended solids	Total suspended solids (TSS) Volatile suspended solids (VSS)
9	Total metals	Aluminum Beryllium Cadmium Chromium Cobalt Copper Lead Molybdenum Nickel Silver Thallium Vanadium Zinc
10	Hydrides	Antimony Arsenic Selenium
11	Chromium (Hexavalent)	Chromium (Hexavalent) (NOTE 1)
12	Mercury	Mercury
13	Total alkyl lead	Tetra-alkyl lead (NOTE 2) Tri-alkyl lead (NOTE 2)

ANALYTICAL TEST GROUP		PARAMETERS
#	NAME	
14	Phenolics (4AAP)	Phenolics (4AAP)
15	Sulphide	Sulphide
16	Volatiles, Halogenated	1,1,2,2-Tetrachloroethane
		1,1,2-Trichloroethane
		1,1-Dichloroethane
		1,1-Dichloroethylene
		1,2-Dichlorobenzene
		1,2-Dichloroethane (Ethylene dichloride)
		1,2-Dichloropropane
		1,3-Dichlorobenzene
		1,4-Dichlorobenzene
		Bromoform
		Bromomethane
		Carbon tetrachloride
		Chlorobenzene
		Chloroform
		Chloromethane
		Cis-1,3-Dichloropropylene
		Dibromochloromethane
		Ethylene dibromide
		Methylene chloride
		Tetrachloroethylene (Perchloroethylene)
		Trans-1,2-Dichloroethylene
		Trans-1,3-Dichloropropylene
		Trichloroethylene
		Trichlorofluoromethane
		Vinyl chloride (Chloroethylene)
17	Volatiles, Non-Halogenated	Benzene
		Ethylbenzene
		Styrene
		Toluene
		o-Xylene
		m-Xylene and p-Xylene (NOTE 3)
18	Volatiles, Water Soluble	Acrolein
		Acrylonitrile

ANALYTICAL TEST GROUP		PARAMETERS
#	NAME	
1 9	Extractables, Base Neutral	Acenaphthene
		5-nitro Acenaphthene
		Acenaphthylene
		Anthracene
		Benz(a)anthracene
		Benzo(a)pyrene
		Benzo(b)fluoranthene
		Benzo(g,h,i)perylene
		Benzo(k)fluoranthene
		Camphene
		1-Chloronaphthalene
		2-Chloronaphthalene
		Chrysene
		Dibenz(a,h)anthracene
		Fluoranthene
		Fluorene
		Indeno(1,2,3-cd)pyrene
		Indole
		1-Methylnaphthalene
		2-Methylnaphthalene
		Naphthalene
		Perylene
		Phenanthrene
		Pyrene
		Benzylbutylphthalate
		Bis(2-ethylhexyl)phthalate
		Di-n-butylphthalate
		4-Bromophenyl phenyl ether
		4-Chlorophenyl phenyl ether
		Bis(2-chloroisopropyl)ether
		Bis(2-chloroethyl)ether
		2,4-Dinitrotoluene
		2,6-Dinitrotoluene
		Bis(2-chloroethoxy)methane
		Diphenylamine (NOTE 4)
		N-Nitrosodiphenylamine (NOTE 4)
		N-Nitrosodi-n-propylamine

ANALYTICAL TEST GROUP		PARAMETERS
#	NAME	
20	Extractables, Acid (Phenolics)	2,3,4,5-Tetrachlorophenol
		2,3,4,6-Tetrachlorophenol
		2,3,5,6-Tetrachlorophenol
		2,3,4-Trichlorophenol
		2,3,5-Trichlorophenol
		2,4,5-Trichlorophenol
		2,4,6-Trichlorophenol
		2,4-Dimethylphenol
		2,4-Dinitrophenol
		2,4-Dichlorophenol
		2,6-Dichlorophenol
		4,6-Dinitro-o-cresol
		2-Chlorophenol
		4-Chloro-3-methylphenol
		4-Nitrophenol
		m-Cresol
		o-Cresol
		p-Cresol
		Pentachlorophenol
		Phenol
21	Extractables, Phenoxy Acid Herbicides	
22	Extractables, Organochlorine Pesticides	
23	Extractables, Neutral -Chlorinated	1,2,3,4-Tetrachlorobenzene
		1,2,3,5-Tetrachlorobenzene
		1,2,4,5-Tetrachlorobenzene
		1,2,3-Trichlorobenzene
		1,2,4-Trichlorobenzene
		2,4,5-Trichlorotoluene
		Hexachlorobenzene
		Hexachlorobutadiene
		Hexachlorocyclopentadiene
		Hexachloroethane
		Octachlorostyrene
		Pentachlorobenzene

ANALYTICAL TEST GROUP NAME		PARAMETERS
24	Chlorinated Dibenzo-p-dioxins and Dibenzofurans	2,3,7,8-Tetrachlorodibenzo-p-dioxin
		Octachlorodibenzo-p-dioxin
		Octachlorodibenzofuran
		Total heptachlorinated dibenzo-p-dioxins
		Total heptachlorinated dibenzofurans
		Total hexachlorinated dibenzo-p-dioxins
		Total hexachlorinated dibenzofurans
		Total pentachlorinated dibenzo-p-dioxins
		Total pentachlorinated dibenzofurans
		Total tetrachlorinated dibenzo-p-dioxins
		Total tetrachlorinated dibenzofurans
25	Solvent Extractables	Oil and grease
26	Fatty and Resin Acids	
27	Polychlorinated Biphenyls (PCBs) (Total)	PCBs (Total)
28a	Open Characterization - Volatiles	
28b	Open Characterization - Extractables	
29	Open Characterization - Elemental	Aluminum
		Antimony
		Arsenic
		Barium
		Beryllium
		Bismuth
		Boron
		Cadmium
		Calcium
		Cerium
		Cesium
		Chromium
		Cobalt
		Copper
		Dysprosium
		Erbium
		Europium
		Gadolinium
		Gallium
		Germanium
		Gold
		Hafnium
		Holmium
		Indium

ANALYTICAL TEST GROUP NAME		PARAMETERS
29	Open Characterization - Elemental (continued)	Iridium
		Iron
		Lanthanum
		Lead
		Lithium
		Lutetium
		Magnesium
		Manganese
		Mercury
		Molybdenum
		Neodymium
		Nickel
		Niobium
		Osmium
		Palladium
		Phosphorus
		Platinum
		Potassium
		Praseodymium
		Rhenium
		Rhodium
		Rubidium
		Ruthenium
		Samarium
		Scandium
		Selenium
		Silicon
		Silver
		Sodium
		Strontium
		Sulfur
		Tantalum
		Tellurium
		Terbium
		Thallium
		Thorium
		Thulium
		Tin
		Titanium
		Tungsten
		Uranium

ANALYTICAL TEST GROUP NAME		PARAMETERS
29	Open Characterization - Elemental (continued)	Vanadium
		Ytterbium
		Yttrium
		Zinc
		Zirconium

NOTE 1: Analyze for hexavalent chromium only if total chromium is greater than 1.0 milligrams per litre.

NOTE 2: Analyze for alkyl leads only if total lead is greater than 1.0 milligrams per litre.

NOTE 3: m-Xylene and p-Xylene often co-elute in the analysis. A single combined result may be reported as m-Xylene.

NOTE 4: Diphenylamine & N-Nitrosodiphenylamine often co-elute in the Gas Chromatography/Mass Spectrometry (GC/MS) analysis. A single combined result may be reported as Diphenylamine.

Table 3.4
SUBSTANCES WITH ZERO OR UNDEFINED TOLERANCE LIMITS

I) Substances with Zero Tolerance Limits
Mercury
DDT and metabolites
Polychorinated Biphenyl (PCB)
Polybrominated Biphenyl (PBB)
Dechlorane (Mirex)

II) Substances with Undefined Tolerance Limits
Metals:

Aluminum	Manganese
Antimony	Molybdenum
Barium	Strontium
Boron	Thallium
Cesium	Tin
Cobalt	Vanadium

Organic Compounds:

Acrylonitrile	Furfural
Alkyl Amines	Haloforms
Aryl Amines	Mercaptans
Aryl Chlorides	Nitrosamines
Aryl Sulfonic Acids	Nitro Aromatics
Azo & Diazo Compounds	Phenols and Derivatives
Benzene & Aliphatic Derivatives	Polycyclic Aromatic

Hydrocarbons:

Carbon Tetrachloride	Quinoline
Chlorinated Ethylenes	Styrene
Chlorophenols	Sulphonates

Pesticides:

Bayer '73	Alochlor (Lasso)
Benomyl (Benilate)	Amitrole
Dichlorobenil	Atrazine
Disulfoton (Disyston)	Cutrine
Kelthane (Dicofol)	Cyanazine
Methyl Parathion	Glyphosate
Naled (Dibrom)	Paraquat
Rotenone	Trifluralin (Treflan)
PMA and TFM	2,4,5-T

Table 3.5
DRINKING WATER QUALITY OBJECTIVES

Parameter	MAC (mg/L)	IMAC (mg/L)	AO (mg/L)
Alachor		0.005	
Aldicarb	0.009		
Aldrin + Dieldrin	0.0007		
Arsenic		0.025	
Atrazine		0.06	
Azinphos-methyl	0.02		
Barium	1.0		
Bendiocarb	0.04		
Benzene	0.005		
Benzo(a)pyrene	0.00001		
Boron		5.0	
Bromoxynil		0.005	
Cadmium	0.005		
Carbaryl	0.09		
Carbofuran	0.09		
Carbon Tetrachloride	0.005		
Chlordane	0.007		
Chlorpyrifos	0.09		
Chromium	0.05		
Cyanazine		0.01	
Cyanide	0.2		
Diazinon	0.02		
Dicamba	0.12		
1,2-Dichlorobenzene	0.2		0.003
1,4-Dichlorobenzene	0.005		0.001
Dichlorodiphenyltrichloroethane (DDT)+ metabolites	0.03		
1,2-Dichloroethane		0.005	
Dichloromethane	0.05		
2,4-Dichlorophenol	0.9		0.0003
2,4-Dichlorophenoxy acetic acid (2,4-D)	0.1	0.1	
Diclofop-methyl	0.009		
Dimethoate		0.02	
Dinoseb	0.01		
Dioxin and Furan		0.000000015 (a)	
Diquat	0.07		
Diuron	0.15		
Fluoride	(b)		
Glyphosate		0.28	
Heptachlor + Heptachlor Epoxide	0.003		
Lead	0.01 (c)		
Lindane	0.004		
Malathion	0.19		
Mercury	0.001		
Methoxychlor	0.9		
Metolachlor		0.05	
Metribuzin	0.08		
Monochlorobenzene	0.08		

Parameter	MAC (mg/L)	IMAC (mg/L)	AO (mg/L)
Nitrate (N)	10.0 (d)		
Nitrite (N)	1.0 (d)		
Nitrate + Nitrite (N)	10.0 (d)		
Nitrilotriacetic Acid	0.4		
Nitrosodimethylamine (NDMA)		0.000009	
Paraquat		0.01	
Parathion	0.05		
Pentachlorophenol	0.06		0.03
Phorate		0.002	
Picloram		0.19	
Polychlorinated Biphenyl		0.003	
Prometryne		0.001	
Selenium	0.01		
Simazine		0.01	
Temephos		0.28	
Terbufos		0.001	
2,3,4,6-Tetrachlorophenol	0.10		0.001
Triallate	0.23		
Trichloroethylene	0.05		
2,4,6-Trichlorophenol	0.005		0.002
2,4,5-Trichlorophenoxy acetic acid (2,4,5-T)	0.28		0.02
Trifluralin		0.045	
Trihalomethanes	0.35 (e)		
Turbidity	(f)		(f)
Uranium	0.10		
Vinyl Chloride	0.002		

MAC　—　Maximum Acceptable Concentration
IMAC　—　Interim Maximum Acceptable Concentration
AO　　—　Aesthetic Objective
NTU　—　Nephelometric Turbidity Unit
mg/L　—　milligrams per litre
pg/L　—　picograms per litre

a)　Total toxic equivalents when compared with 2,3,7,8-TCDD (tetrachlorodibenzo-p-dioxin)
b)　The MAC for naturally occurring fluoride in drinking water is 2.4 mg/L. A MAC of 1.5 mg/L was established to ensure that when fluoride is added to drinking water, the concentration (1.2 +/– 0.2 mg/L) is maintained such that the population obtains optimal benefit in the prevention of dental caries yet not develop mottling of teeth or skeletal fluorosis.
c)　This objective applies to water at the point of consumption. Since lead is a component in some plumbing systems, first flush water may contain higher concentrations of lead than water that has been flushed for five minutes. Faucets, therefore, should be thoroughly flushed before water is taken for consumption.
d)　Where nitrate and nitrite are present, the total of the two should not exceed 10 mg/L.
e)　The term trihalomethanes includes chloroform, bromoform, bromodichloromethane and chlorodibromomethane. Their total concentration should not exceed 0.35 mg/L at anytime.
f)　A MAC for turbidity of 1 NTU in drinking water leaving the treatment plant was established to ensure the efficiency of the disinfection process. Treatment processes can result in increased turbidity in the distribution system. To ensure that the aesthetic quality is not degraded, an aesthetic objective for turbidity at the free flowing outlet of the ultimate consumer has been set at 5 NTU.

Reference: MOEE, 1994.

Table 3.6
PRIMARY LIST OF CANDIDATE SUBSTANCES FOR BANS OR PHASE-OUTS

- anthracene
- arsenic
- benzo[a]pyrene
- benzo[ghi]perylene
- ben[a]anthracene
- DDT (+DDD & DDE)
- 1,4-dichlorobenzene
- 3,3-dichorobenzidine
- dieldrin
- hexachlorobenzene
- alpha-hexachlorocyclohexane (a-HCH)
- gamma-hexachlorocyclohexane (y-HCH)
- mercury
- mirex
- pentachlorophenol
- perylene
- phenanthrene
- polycholorinated biphenyls (PCBs)
- polychlorinated dibenzo(p)dioxins and -furans (PCDD/Fs)
- toxaphene
- tributyl tin

Table 3.7
SCHEDULE 3, PART A—ANALYTICAL PRINCIPLES AND ANALYTICAL METHOD DETECTION LIMITS

Column 1 ANALYTICAL TEST GROUP #	Column 2 PARAMETERS CONVENTIONAL AND METAL PARAMETERS	Column 3 SAMPLE PREPARATION METHOD PRINCIPLES	Column 4 INSTRUMENTAL MEASUREMENT METHOD PRINCIPLES	Column 5 ALTERNATE INSTRUMENTAL MEASUREMENT METHOD PRINCIPLES	Column 6 ANALYTICAL METHOD DETECTION LIMITS mg/L
1	Chemical oxygen demand (COD)	Preparation for measurement system as appropriate followed by reflux or oven digestion at 150°C in presence of oxidizing reagents	Back titration or Colourimetric measurement of trivalent chromium (Cr III)	N/A	10
2	Total cyanide	Acid distillation	Ion Chromatography or Colourimetry or Specific Ion Electrode or Titration	Polarography via the method of standard addition in the presence of suitable electrolyte	0.005
3	Hydrogen ion (pH)	Preparation for measurement system as appropriate	pH electrode and pH meter	N/A	N/A
4a	Ammonia plus Ammonium	Preparation for measurement system as appropriate eg. distillation	Colourimetry or Specific Ion Electrode or Titration or Ion Chromatography	N/A	0.25 as Nitrogen
	Total Kjeldahl nitrogen	Preparation for measurement system as appropriate followed by Kjeldahl digestion procedure	Colourimetry or Specific Ion Electrode or Titration or Ion Chromatography	N/A	0.5 as Nitrogen
4b	Nitrate + Nitrite	Preparation for measurement system as appropriate	Colourimetry or Ion Chromatography	N/A	0.25 as Nitrogen

Column 1 ANALYTICAL TEST GROUP #	Column 2 PARAMETERS CONVENTIONAL AND METAL PARAMETERS	Column 3 SAMPLE PREPARATION METHOD PRINCIPLES	Column 4 INSTRUMENTAL MEASUREMENT METHOD PRINCIPLES	Column 5 ALTERNATE INSTRUMENTAL MEASUREMENT METHOD PRINCIPLES	Column 6 ANALYTICAL METHOD DETECTION LIMITS mg/L
5a	Dissolved organic carbon (DOC)	Preparation for measurement system as appropriate followed by filtration through glass fibre filter, retention size approximately 2 micrometers	Quantitative conversion of carbon to carbon dioxide (CO_2) by one of: i) Ultra violet persulphate digestion or ii) combustion at >800°C with a catalyst or iii) combustion at >1100°C, catalyst optional followed by infrared or colourimetric detection. DOC may be determined directly using a sample free of inorganic carbon or as the difference between total carbon and inorganic carbon.	N/A	0.5 as Carbon

Column 1 ANALYTICAL TEST GROUP #	Column 2 PARAMETERS CONVENTIONAL AND METAL PARAMETERS	Column 3 SAMPLE PREPARATION METHOD PRINCIPLES	Column 4 INSTRUMENTAL MEASUREMENT METHOD PRINCIPLES	Column 5 ALTERNATE INSTRUMENTAL MEASUREMENT METHOD PRINCIPLES	Column 6 ANALYTICAL METHOD DETECTION LIMITS mg/L
5b	Total organic carbon (TOC)	Preparation for measurement system as appropriate. Particulates must be reduced in size sufficiently to ensure effective processing by the measurement system. Particulates may be separated from the liquid with subsequent exclusive analysis of both phases.	Quantitative conversion of carbon to carbon dioxide (CO2) by one of: i) Ultra violet persulphate digestion or ii) combustion at >800°C with a catalyst or iii) combustion at >1100°C, catalyst optional followed by infrared or colourimetric detection. TOC may be determined directly using a sample free of inorganic carbon or as the difference between total carbon and inorganic carbon or by appropriate combination of the results from the analysis of the sample phases.	N / A	5 as Carbon
6	Total phosphorus	Preparation for measurement system as appropriate followed by perchloric acid digestion or a mixture of nitric acid to sulphuric acid (HNO3/H2SO4) at a ratio of 5:1 or a Kjeldahl equivalent mixture.	Colourimetry or Inductively Coupled Plasma - Atomic Emission Spectrometry	N / A	0.1 as Phosphorus

Column 1 ANALYTICAL TEST GROUP #	Column 2 PARAMETERS CONVENTIONAL AND METAL PARAMETERS	Column 3 SAMPLE PREPARATION METHOD PRINCIPLES	Column 4 INSTRUMENTAL MEASUREMENT METHOD PRINCIPLES	Column 5 ALTERNATE INSTRUMENTAL MEASUREMENT METHOD PRINCIPLES	Column 6 ANALYTICAL METHOD DETECTION LIMITS mg/L
7	Specific conductance	Preparation for measurement system as appropriate	Conductivity meter and cell	N/A	5 µS/cm
8	Total suspended solids (TSS)	Preparation for measurement system as appropriate	Filtration - particle retention of glass fibre filter < or = 2 micrometres followed by drying of filter and particulates at 103°C ± 3°C and gravimetry	N/A	5
	Volatile Suspended solids (VSS)	Perform TSS analysis	Ignite filter at 550°C for 4 hr. or until filter weight remains constant.	N/A	10
9	Aluminum Beryllium Cadmium Chromium Cobalt Copper Lead Molybdenum Nickel Silver Thallium Vanadium Zinc	Nitric evaporation or aqua regia digestion	Atomic absorption spectrometry and/or Emission Spectrometry - Inductively Coupled Plasma (ICP) or Direct Current Argon Plasma Spectrometry (DCP)	See Analytical Test Group 2	0.03 0.01 0.002 0.02 0.02 0.01 0.03 0.02 0.02 0.03 0.03 0.03 0.01

Column 1 ANALYTICAL TEST GROUP #	Column 2 PARAMETERS CONVENTIONAL AND METAL PARAMETERS	Column 3 SAMPLE PREPARATION METHOD PRINCIPLES	Column 4 INSTRUMENTAL MEASUREMENT METHOD PRINCIPLES	Column 5 ALTERNATE INSTRUMENTAL MEASUREMENT METHOD PRINCIPLES	Column 6 ANALYTICAL METHOD DETECTION LIMITS mg/L
10	Antimony Arsenic Selenium	Acid Digestion	Hydride Generation Atomic Absorption	See Analytical Test Group 2	0.005 0.005 0.005
11	Chromium (Hexavalent) (Analyze for hexavalent chromium only if total chromium >1.0mg/L)	i) None ii) Solvent extraction	i) Colourimetry ii) Atomic absorption	See Analytical Test Group 2	0.01
12	Mercury	Oxidative acid digestion	Cold vapour atomic absorption	N/A	0.0001
13	Tetra-alkyl lead Tri-alkyl lead (-inorganic ligand) (Analyze for alkyl leads only if total lead is >1.0mg/L)	i) Liquid/liquid extraction ii) Derivatization	i) Colourimetry using Dithiozone reagent or Atomic absorption ii) Gas Liquid Chromatography	N/A	0.002 0.002
14	Phenolics (4AAP)	Preparation for measurement system as appropriate followed by distillation from acidified (pH <4) sample	Colourimetry of buffered sample or Colourimetry of chloroform extract	N/A	0.002
15	Sulphide	Filtration and dissolution of precipitate	Methylene blue colourimetry or Specific Ion Electrode or ion chromatography	See Analytical Test Group 2	0.02

Column 1 ANALYTICAL TEST GROUP #	Column 2 PARAMETERS ORGANIC PARAMETERS	Column 3 SAMPLE PREPARATION METHOD PRINCIPLES	Column 4 INSTRUMENTAL MEASUREMENT METHOD PRINCIPLES	Column 5 ALTERNATE INSTRUMENTAL MEASUREMENT METHOD PRINCIPLES	Column 6 ANALYTICAL METHOD DETECTION LIMITS FOR STANDARDS IN REAGENT WATER µg/L
16	1,1,2,2-Tetrachloroethane	Purge and trap	Gas Chromatography/ Mass Spectrometry (GC/MS) Capillary column	Gas Chromatography/ Electron Capture or Hall Single capillary column	1.0
	1,1,2-Trichloroethane				1.0
	1,1-Dichloroethane				1.0
	1,1-Dichloroethylene				1.0
	1,2-Dichlorobenzene				1.0
	1,2-Dichloroethane (Ethylene dichloride)				1.0
	1,2-Dichloropropane				1.0
	1,3-Dichlorobenzene				1.0
	1,4-Dichlorobenzene				1.0
	Bromoform				ND*
	Bromomethane				1.0
	Carbon tetrachloride				1.0
	Chlorobenzene				1.0
	Chloroform				ND*
	Chloromethane				1.0
	Cis-1,3-Dichloropropylene				1.0
	Dibromochloromethane				1.0
	Ethylene dibromide				1.0
	Methylene chloride				1.0
	Tetrachloroethylene (Perchloroethylene)				1.0
	Trans-1,2-Dichloroethylene				1.0
	Trans-1,3-Dichloropropylene				1.0
	Trichloroethylene				1.0
	Trichlorofluoromethane				ND*
	Vinyl chloride (Chloroethylene)				ND*

Column 1 ANALYTICAL TEST GROUP #	Column 2 PARAMETERS ORGANIC PARAMETERS	Column 3 SAMPLE PREPARATION METHOD PRINCIPLES	Column 4 INSTRUMENTAL MEASUREMENT METHOD PRINCIPLES	Column 5 ALTERNATE INSTRUMENTAL MEASUREMENT METHOD PRINCIPLES	Column 6 ANALYTICAL METHOD DETECTION LIMITS FOR STANDARDS IN REAGENT WATER µg/L
17	Benzene	Purge and trap	Gas Chromatography/ Mass Spectometry (GC/MS) Capillary column	Gas Chromatography Flame Ionization or Photo Ionization Single capillary column	10*
	Ethylbenzene				10*
	Styrene				10*
	Toluene				10*
	o-Xylene				10*
	m-Xylene/p-Xylene (NOTE 1)				10*
18	Acrolein	Purge and trap	Gas Chromatography/ Mass Spectrometry (GC/MS) Capillary column	Gas Chromatography Electron Capture/Hall & Flame Ionization/ Photo Ionization Single capillary column	ND*
	Acrylonitrile				ND*

Column 1 ANALYTICAL TEST GROUP #	Column 2 PARAMETERS ORGANIC PARAMETERS	Column 3 SAMPLE PREPARATION METHOD PRINCIPLES	Column 4 INSTRUMENTAL MEASUREMENT METHOD PRINCIPLES	Column 5 ALTERNATE INSTRUMENTAL MEASUREMENT METHOD PRINCIPLES	Column 6 ANALYTICAL METHOD DETECTION LIMITS FOR STANDARDS IN REAGENT WATER µg/L
19	Acenaphthene	Liquid/liquid extraction	Gas Chromatography/ Mass Spectrometry (GC/MS) Capillary column	High Performance Liquid Chromatography Ultra Violet or Fluorescence Detection	10*
	5-nitro Acenaphthene				10*
	Acenaphthylene				10*
	Anthracene				10*
	Benz(a)anthracene				10*
	Benzo(a)pyrene				10*
	Benzo(b)fluoranthene				10*
	Benzo(g,h,i)perylene				10*
	Benzo(k)fluoranthene				10*
	Camphene				10*
	1-Chloronaphthalene				10*
	2-Chloronaphthalene				10*
	Chrysene				10*
	Dibenz(a,h)anthracene				10*
	Fluoranthene				10*
	Fluorene				10*
	Indeno(1,2,3-cd)pyrene				10*
	Indole				ND*
	1-Methyl naphthalene				10*
	2-Methyl naphthalene				10*
	Naphthalene				10*
	Perylene				10*
	Phenanthrene				10*
	Pyrene				10*

Column 1 ANALYTICAL TEST GROUP #	Column 2 PARAMETERS ORGANIC PARAMETERS	Column 3 SAMPLE PREPARATION METHOD PRINCIPLES	Column 4 INSTRUMENTAL MEASUREMENT METHOD PRINCIPLES	Column 5 ALTERNATE INSTRUMENTAL MEASUREMENT METHOD PRINCIPLES	Column 6 ANALYTICAL METHOD DETECTION LIMITS FOR STANDARDS IN REAGENT WATER µg/L
19 cont'd	Benzylbutylphthalate	Liquid/liquid extraction	Gas Chromatography/ Mass Spectrometry (GC/MS) Capillary column	N/A	1 0 *
	Bis(2-ethylhexyl)phthalate				1 0 *
	Di-n-butylphthalate				1 0 *·
	4-Bromophenyl phenyl ether				1 0 *
	4-Chlorophenyl phenyl ether				1 0 *
	Bis(2-chloroisopropyl)ether				1 0 *
	Bis(2-chloroethyl)ether				1 0 *
	2,4-Dinitrotoluene				1 0 *
	2,6-Dinitrotoluene				1 0 *
	Bis(2-chloroethoxy)methane				1 0 *
	Diphenylamine (NOTE 2)				1 0 *
	N-Nitrosodiphenylamine (NOTE 2)				1 0 *
	N-Nitrosodi-n-propylamine				1 0 *

Column 1 ANALYTICAL TEST GROUP #	Column 2 PARAMETERS ORGANIC PARAMETERS	Column 3 SAMPLE PREPARATION METHOD PRINCIPLES	Column 4 INSTRUMENTAL MEASUREMENT METHOD PRINCIPLES	Column 5 ALTERNATE INSTRUMENTAL MEASUREMENT METHOD PRINCIPLES	Column 6 ANALYTICAL METHOD DETECTION LIMITS FOR STANDARDS IN REAGENT WATER μg/L
20	2,3,4,5-Tetrachlorophenol	Liquid/liquid extraction pH adjusted to <2 Derivatization, if appropriate Cleanup	Gas Chromatography/ Mass Spectrometry (GC/MS) Capillary column	N/A	10*
	2,3,4,6-Tetrachlorophenol				10*
	2,3,5,6-Tetrachlorophenol				10*
	2,3,4-Trichlorophenol				10*
	2,3,5-Trichlorophenol				10*
	2,4,5-Trichlorophenol				10*
	2,4,6-Trichlorophenol				10*
	2,4-Dimethylphenol				10*
	2,4-Dinitrophenol				10*
	2,4-Dichlorophenol				10*
	2,6-Dichlorophenol				10*
	4,6-Dinitro-o-cresol				10*
	2-Chlorophenol				10*
	4-Chloro-3-methylphenol				10*
	4-Nitrophenol				10*
	m-Cresol				10*
	o-Cresol				10*
	p-Cresol				10*
	Pentachlorophenol				10*
	Phenol				10*
21	Extractables, Phenoxy Acid Herbicides	N/A	N/A	N/A	N/A
22	Extractables, Organochlorine Pesticides	N/A	N/A	N/A	N/A

Column 1 ANALYTICAL TEST GROUP #	Column 2 PARAMETERS ORGANIC PARAMETERS	Column 3 SAMPLE PREPARATION METHOD PRINCIPLES	Column 4 INSTRUMENTAL MEASUREMENT METHOD PRINCIPLES	Column 5 ALTERNATE INSTRUMENTAL MEASUREMENT METHOD PRINCIPLES	Column 6 ANALYTICAL METHOD DETECTION LIMITS FOR STANDARDS IN REAGENT WATER µg/L
23	1,2,3,4-Tetrachlorobenzene	Liquid/liquid extraction Neutral pH Cleanup if necessary	Gas Liquid Chromatography Electron capture Dual capillary or Gas Chromatography/ Mass Spectroscopy (GC/MS) Capillary column	N/A	0.01
	1,2,3,5-Tetrachlorobenzene				0.01
	1,2,4,5-Tetrachlorobenzene				0.01
	1,2,3-Trichlorobenzene				0.01
	1,2,4-Trichlorobenzene				0.01
	2,4,5-Trichlorotoluene				0.01
	Hexachlorobenzene				0.01
	Hexachlorobutadiene				0.01
	Hexachlorocyclopentadiene				0.01
	Hexachloroethane				0.01
	Octachlorostyrene				0.01
	Pentachlorobenzene				0.01
24	2,3,7,8-Tetrachlorodibenzo-p-dioxin	Liquid/liquid extraction and cleanup or if TSS >15mg/L filter sample, extract solids by Soxhlet using toluene, extract filtrate normally, combine both extracts	Gas Chromatography/ Mass Spectroscopy (GC/MS) Capillary column	N/A	0.0003
	Octachlorodibenzo-p-dioxin				0.0003
	Octachlorodibenzofuran				0.0003
	Total heptachlorinated dibenzo-p-dioxins				0.0003
	Total heptachlorinated dibenzofurans				0.0003
	Total hexachlorinated dibenzo-p-dioxins				0.0003
	Total hexachlorinated dibenzofurans				0.0003
	Total pentachlorinated dibenzo-p-dioxins				0.0003
	Total pentachlorinated dibenzofurans				0.0003
	Total tetrachlorinated dibenzo-p-dioxins				0.0003
	Total tetrachlorinated dibenzofurans				0.0003

Column 1 ANALYTICAL TEST GROUP NUMBER	Column 2 PARAMETERS ORGANIC AND INORGANIC PARAMETERS	Column 3 SAMPLE PREPARATION METHOD PRINCIPLES	Column 4 INSTRUMENTAL MEASUREMENT METHOD PRINCIPLES	Column 5 ALTERNATE INSTRUMENTAL MEASUREMENT METHOD PRINCIPLES	Column 6 ANALYTICAL METHOD DETECTION LIMITS FOR STANDARDS IN REAGENT WATER µg/L
25	Oil and Grease	Acidify with a mineral acid to approximately pH 2. Liquid/liquid extraction plus solvent rinsings of sample containers	Gravimetric	N/A	1000
26	Fatty and Resin Acids	N/A	N/A	N/A	N/A
27	Polychlorinated Biphenyls (PCBs) (identify Aroclors present & total concentration)	Liquid/liquid extraction Neutral pH Cleanup if necessary	Gas Liquid Chromatography Electron capture Single capillary column or Gas Chromatography/Mass Spectroscopy (GC/MS) Capillary column Report as PCB Aroclors	N/A	0.1

NOTE 1: m-Xylene and p-Xylene often co-elute in the analysis. A single combined result may be reported as m-Xylene.

NOTE 2: Diphenylamine & N-Nitrosodiphenylamine often co-elute in the Gas Chromatography/Mass Spectrometry (GC/MS) analysis. A single combined result may be reported as Diphenylamine.

Column 1 ANALYTICAL TEST GROUP NUMBER	Column 2 PARAMETERS ORGANIC AND INORGANIC PARAMETERS	Column 3 SAMPLE PREPARATION METHOD PRINCIPLES	Column 4 INSTRUMENTAL MEASUREMENT METHOD PRINCIPLES	Column 5 ALTERNATE INSTRUMENTAL MEASUREMENT METHOD PRINCIPLES	Column 6 LIMIT OF CHARACTERIZATION µg/L
28a	Open Characterization - Volatiles	Purge and trap	Gas Chromatography/ Mass Spectroscopy (GC/MS)	N/A	10* against 1,3-Dichlorobutane
28b	Open Characterization - Extractables	Liquid/liquid extraction Neutral pH followed by Liquid/liquid extraction pH <2 Derivatization of acidic extract optional Cleanup optional	Gas Chromatography/ Mass Spectroscopy (GC/MS)	N/A	10* against D10 Phenanthrene
29	Aluminum	Nitric evaporation or aqua regia digestion	Atomic absorption spectrometry and/or Emission Spectrometry - Inductively Coupled Plasma (ICP) or Direct Current Argon Plasma Spectrometry (DCP) or Inductively Coupled Plasma/Mass Spectroscopy (ICP/MS)	N/A	50*
	Antimony				50*
	Arsenic				50*
	Barium				50*
	Beryllium				50*
	Bismuth				50*
	Boron				50*
	Cadmium				50*
	Calcium				50*
	Cerium				50*
	Cesium				50*
	Chromium				50*
	Cobalt				50*
	Copper				50*
	Dysprosium				50*
	Erbium				50*
	Europium				50*
	Gadolinium				50*

Column 1 ANALYTICAL TEST GROUP NUMBER	Column 2 PARAMETERS ORGANIC AND INORGANIC PARAMETERS	Column 3 SAMPLE PREPARATION METHOD PRINCIPLES	Column 4 INSTRUMENTAL MEASUREMENT METHOD PRINCIPLES	Column 5 ALTERNATE INSTRUMENTAL MEASUREMENT METHOD PRINCIPLES	Column 6 LIMIT OF CHARACTERIZATION µg/L
2 9 (continued)	Gallium	Nitric evaporation or aqua regia digestion	Atomic absorption spectrometry and/or Emission Spectrometry - Inductively Coupled Plasma (ICP) or Direct Current Argon Plasma Spectrometry (DCP) or Inductively Coupled Plasma/Mass Spectroscopy (ICP/MS)	N/A	5 0 *
	Germanium				5 0 *
	Gold				5 0 *
	Hafnium				5 0 *
	Holmium				5 0 *
	Indium				5 0 *
	Iridium				5 0 *
	Iron				5 0 *
	Lanthanum				5 0 *
	Lead				5 0 *
	Lithium				5 0 *
	Lutetium				5 0 *
	Magnesium				5 0 *
	Manganese				5 0 *
	Mercury				5 0 *
	Molybdenum				5 0 *
	Neodymium				5 0 *
	Nickel				5 0 *
	Niobium				5 0 *
	Osmium				5 0 *
	Palladium				5 0 *
	Phosphorus				5 0 *
	Platinum				5 0 *
	Potassium				5 0 *
	Praseodymium				5 0 *
	Rhenium				5 0 *
	Rhodium				5 0 *
	Rubidium				5 0 *
	Ruthenium				5 0 *
	Samarium				5 0 *

Column 1 ANALYTICAL TEST GROUP NUMBER	Column 2 PARAMETERS ORGANIC AND INORGANIC PARAMETERS	Column 3 SAMPLE PREPARATION METHOD PRINCIPLES	Column 4 INSTRUMENTAL MEASUREMENT METHOD PRINCIPLES	Column 5 ALTERNATE INSTRUMENTAL MEASUREMENT METHOD PRINCIPLES	Column 6 LIMIT OF CHARACTERIZATION µg/L
29 (continued)	Scandium	Nitric evaporation or aqua regia digestion	Atomic absorption spectrometry and/or Emission Spectrometry Inductively Coupled Plasma (ICP) or Direct Current Argon Plasma Spectrometry (DCP) or Inductively Coupled Plasma/Mass Spectroscopy (ICP/MS)	N/A	50*
	Selenium				50*
	Silicon				50*
	Silver				50*
	Sodium				50*
	Strontium				50*
	Sulfur				50*
	Tantalum				50*
	Tellurium				50*
	Terbium				50*
	Thallium				50*
	Thorium				50*
	Thulium				50*
	Tin				50*
	Titanium				50*
	Tungsten				50*
	Uranium				50*
	Vanadium				50*
	Ytterbium				50*
	Yttrium				50*
	Zinc				50*
	Zirconium				50*

* Value above which all organic compounds or elements must be identified and their approximate concentration determined in open characterization analyses as per the publications cited in subsection 4(4).

Table 3.8
LIMITS ON DISCHARGES TO SANITARY AND COMBINED SEWERS

Parameter	*Limit*
Temperature	< 65 °C
pH*	5.5 to 9.5
Total Suspended Solids	350 mg/L
Biological Oxygen Demand	300 mg/L
Phenolic Compounds	1 mg/L
Total Kjeldahl Nitrogen	100 mg/L
Oil and Grease (mineral)	15 mg/L
Oil and Grease (animal/veg.)	50 mg/L
Total Cyanides	2 mg/L
Chlorides	1500 mg/L
Fluorides	10 mg/L
Sulfates	1500 mg/L
Phosphorus	10 mg/L
Aluminum	50 mg/L
Iron	50 mg/L
Antimony	5 mg/L
Arsenic	1 mg/L
Bismuth	5 mg/L
Cadmium	1 mg/L
Chromium	5 mg/L
Cobalt	5 mg/L
Copper	3 mg/L
Lead	5 mg/L
Manganese	5 mg/L
Mercury	0.1 mg/L
Molybdenum	5 mg/L
Nickel	3 mg/L
Selenium	5 mg/L
Silver	5 mg/L
Tin	5 mg/L
Titanium	5 mg/L
Vanadium	5 mg/L
Zinc	3 mg/L

Notes

* All limits are the same in the MOE and Metro Toronto by-laws except for pH. The Metro Toronto limit for pH is 6.0 to 10.5.

References: MOE, 1988; Metropolitan Toronto, 1989

Table 3.9
LIMITS ON DISCHARGES TO STORM SEWERS

Parameter	MOE Limit	Metro Limit (if different)
Temperature	< 40 °C	
pH	6.0 to 9.0	
Total Suspended Solids	15 mg/L	
Biological Oxygen Demand	Not set	15 mg/L
Oil and Grease	Not set	No sheen
Cadmium	1 µg/L	
Chromium	200 µg/L	
Copper	10 µg/L	
Lead	50 µg/L	
Mercury	1 µg/L	
Nickel	50 µg/L	
Zinc	50 µg/L	
Fecal Coliform	200 per 100 mL	

References: MOE, 1988; Metropolitan Toronto, 1989

Table 3.10
SAMPLE PRESERVATIVES

Parameter ATG	Sample Preservative
1*, 4a, 5a, 5b and 6	Add sulphuric acid after sampling to lower pH to 2 but not < 1.5
2	Add sodium hydroxide (cyanide free) to raise pH to 12
3, 4b, 7, 8, 10** 11, 13, 19, 20, 23, 24, 25, 26, 27, 28a, 28b, chloride, sulphate and fluoride	None
9, 10**, 29 iron	Add nitric acid (containing < 1mg/L of all analytes) to lower pH to <2.
12	Add 1 to 2 mL of nitric acid per 250 mL sample followed by at least 0.5 mL of potassium dichromate solution to produce definite yellow colour.
14	Add sulphuric acid solution prior to sampling to lower pH to 2 but not <1.5: diluted acid may be used. Or, prior to sampling, add 1 mL of solution containing 3N phosphoric acid and 0.5 g/L copper sulphate pentahydrate per 250 mL sample.
15	Add 0.5 mL 2N zinc acetate solution per 250 mL sample followed dropwise by 5% sodium carbonate or 5% sodium hydroxide to pH 10.
16, 17 and 18	Only for samples containing residual chlorine. Prior to sampling add 80 mg sodium thiosulphate per 1 L. Store in the dark.

Notes
* * No preservative may be added but the maximum storage time is reduced from 28 days to four
* ** Can be either none or same as for metals if to be analyzed from same sample

Figure 3.1
PROPOSED PROCESS FOR DETERMINING EFFLUENT LIMITS

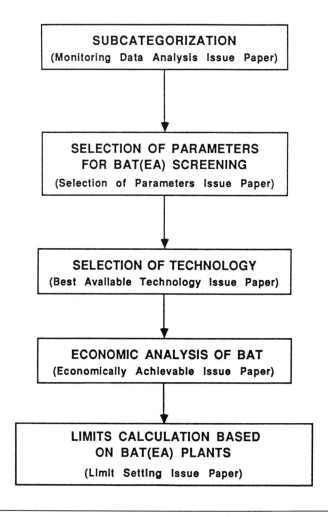

Figure 3.2
REQUIREMENTS FOR A STORM WATER
CONTROL STUDY

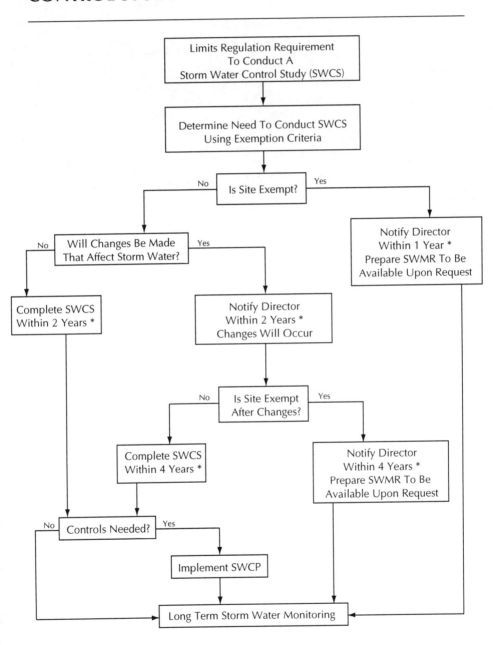

* Time From Promulgation of Regulation

4.0

Waste Management and Transportation

4.1 OVERVIEW

Relative to other aspects of environmental management, the generation, handling, and disposal of waste materials are regulated extensively by both provincial and federal statutes. Part V of the Ontario Environmental Protection Act (EPA) and the associated regulations, notably Regulation 347, established several waste classes and categories and set out the responsibilities of waste generators, waste management system operators, and waste transporters. They also set out the requirements for obtaining approvals to operate waste management systems and describe a comprehensive manifest system for tracking wastes from their point of generation to their recycling or disposal.

For the purpose of transportation, some types of wastes are considered to be "dangerous goods." The transportation of such materials on roads within the province falls under the requirements of the Ontario Dangerous Goods Transportation Act (DGTA). It is strongly patterned after its federal counterpart, the Transport of Dangerous Goods Act (TDGA), which pertains to marine, air, rail, and interprovincial and international road transportation.

The major piece of federal legislation that influences waste management is the Canadian Environmental Protection Act (CEPA) which includes provisions for the control of all aspects of the life cycle of toxic substances including their importation, transport, distribution, and ultimate disposal as waste. Elements of the CEPA related to waste management include:

- authority to regulate waste handling and disposal practices of federal departments, boards, agencies, and Crown corporations
- provisions to create guidelines and codes for environmentally sound practices as well as objectives setting desirable levels of environmental quality

127

- authority to regulate the export and import of hazardous wastes entering into, leaving, or passing through Canada
- provisions to issue permits to control dumping at sea from ships, barges, aircraft, and man-made structures (excluding normal discharges from off-shore facilities involved in the exploration for, exploitation, and processing of sea-bed mineral resources)

4.2 DEFINITIONS AND CLASSIFICATIONS

4.2.1 Defining Waste

While several regulations define specific types of waste (for example, Ontario Regulation 362 defines PCB waste), Section 25 in Part V of the EPA provides the basic definition of **waste** which includes "ashes, garbage, refuse, domestic waste, industrial waste, or municipal waste and such materials as are designated in the regulations." Specifically identified as waste in Regulation 347 are materials as diverse as dust suppressant, inert fill, rock fill, mine tailings, processed organic waste, waste-derived fuel, used tires that have not be refurbished, woodwaste, and refrigerant waste.

While the courts have interpreted "waste" to be materials thrown aside or discarded as worthless, the MOEE has determined that some materials with value need to be considered as waste and therefore subject to the requirements of the EPA and Regulation 347. These include (MOE, 1985):

- materials that are sold for heating value or otherwise being re-used, recycled, or reclaimed
- all products and by-products from waste transfer, bulking, treatment, or processing facilities
- oil recovered from oily water treatment facilities as well as blended or bulked waste solvents destined for disposal or recycle, and
- commercial chemical products or by-products, including those that are off-specification or that have exceeded their expiry date

Conversely, some types of waste materials are **exempted** from the requirements of Part V for one or more of the following reasons:

- they are regulated by other statutes (examples include agricultural wastes, hauled sewage, and dead animals)
- they are generally perceived to be innocuous (examples are rock fill and "clean" soil from an excavation)
- they are recyclable

Recyclable materials are considered to be raw materials and as such are exempted from the provisions of Regulation 347. Section 1 defines recyclable material as waste transferred by a generator and destined for a site where:

- it will be wholly utilized in an ongoing agricultural, commercial, manufacturing, or industrial process
- it will be processed principally for functions other than waste management and in ways that do not involve combustion or land application of waste, and
- it will be promptly packaged for retail sale or offered for retail sale to meet a realistic market demand

Again, Regulation 347 specifies a few exceptions to the definition. For example, recyclable materials do not include used, shredded, or chipped tires. Hazardous Wastes or Liquid Industrial Wastes (see Section 4.2.2) are considered to be recyclable materials only if transported directly from a generator to a recycler.

The question as to whether or not a process is being used for waste management can be determined by reviewing its viability if the waste were not available. Processes or operations that are not viable without the incoming waste are deemed to be in the business of waste management.

According to the definitions in Regulation 347, by-products or intermediates from traditional refining operations, such as mineral or metal recovery, are recyclable materials. For example, sludges from an electrolytic recovery process for metals which are subsequently processed to remove precious metals, such as silver or gold, are not considered wastes.

There are also **small quantity exemptions** (SQE) for several of the waste categories.

4.2.2 Classifying Wastes

In Ontario, all waste materials (except those that are exempted or defined as recyclable materials) must be classified using a system outlined in Regulation 347 and illustrated in Figure 4.1. Two broad classes of waste are used by the MOEE that require special precautions because the wastes can pose unusual hazards: **subject waste** and **registerable waste**. Table 4.1 presents examples of materials in each class.

The subject waste class includes hazardous waste and liquid industrial waste. In turn, **Hazardous Waste** is divided into the following 10 categories. Regardless of the category, all hazardous wastes (except when generated in amounts less than the SQEs noted below) must be registered with the MOEE. The categories are listed below according to a hierarchy that can be followed sequentially to determine the priority of classification and identify the **primary** classification of the waste. Once the primary classification is determined, the letter which represents this classification (e.g. "S" for severely toxic wastes) is added to the three-digit waste class number which is provided in Appendix 2 of Regulation 347 so that an appropriate **waste class** can be determined. (An example is shown in Figure 4.3.)

1 A waste that contains any of the substances listed in Schedule 3 of Regulation 347 at a concentration greater than 1 ppm is characterized as being **Severely Toxic (S)**. Examples include pesticides such as 2,4,5-T and pentachlorophenol. There is no SQE for such wastes. Empty containers and inner liners are considered to be hazardous waste.

2 A waste that contains any part of the human body, including tissues and bodily fluids, but excluding fluids, extracted teeth, hair, nail clippings and the like which are non-infectious; any part of the carcass of an animal infected with a communicable disease or suspected by a licensed veterinarian to be infected; or non-anatomical waste infected with communicable disease is characterized as **Pathological (P)**. There is no SQE for such wastes. Empty containers and liners are also hazardous unless they have been incinerated, autoclaved, or otherwise sterilized to make them non-infectious.

3 A waste that is defined to be a PCB waste according to Regulation 362 is characterized as a **PCB Waste (D)**. Generally, PCB wastes contain PCBs at concentrations greater than 50 ppm by weight. The only SQE is for electrical capacitors that have never contained more than 1 kg of PCBs. These types of capacitors do not need to be registered. (See Chapter 7 for additional details.)

4 & Any commercial products or manufacturing intermediates that are
5 off-specification or otherwise unacceptable for use and that contain any of the substances listed in Schedules 2(A) or 2(B) of Regulation 347 are characterized as being either **Acute Hazardous Waste Chemical (A)** or **Hazardous Waste Chemical (B)**. This includes materials such as pharmaceutical or pesticide waste products that contain active ingredients from Schedules 2(A) or 2(B). Active ingredients are constituents that have been included in a formulated product for an intended effect.

   The SQE for waste listed in Schedule 2(A) is 1 kg of waste per month. Containers with a capacity greater than 20 litres, and that contained the Schedule 2(A) material, are considered to be hazardous unless triple-rinsed using an appropriate solvent. Inner liners weighing more than 10 kg that contained Schedule 2(A) products are also considered hazardous unless they have been triple-rinsed using an appropriate solvent.

   The SQE for waste listed in Schedule 2(B) is 5 kg of waste per month. Empty containers and inner liners are not considered hazardous.

6 Any industrial waste stream that is generated from a process listed in Schedule 1 of Regulation 347 is characterized as being **Hazardous Industrial Waste (H)**. There is a SQE of 5 kg per

month. Empty containers and inner liners are not hazardous. The "heel" rule (i.e. if less than 1 inch (2.54 cm) of material remains) is used to determine if a container is empty.

7 A waste that meets the Regulation 347 definition for ignitability is characterized as being **Ignitable Waste (I)**. The following criteria are used to determine if a waste should be categorized as ignitable:

- it is a liquid with a flash point less than 61°C (e.g. ethanol or gasoline)
- it is a solid capable, under standard temperature and pressure, of causing fire due to friction, absorption of moisture, or spontaneous chemical changes and, when ignited, burns so vigorously and persistently that is creates a hazard (e.g. charcoal)
- it is an ignitable compressed gas having a critical temperature less than 50°C or an absolute vapour pressure greater than 294 kPa at 50°C, or exerts an absolute pressure, in the cylinder, packaging tube or tank in which it is contained, greater than 275 ± 1 kPa at 21.1°C or 717 ± kPa at 54.4°C, and are ignitable at normal atmospheric pressure when in a mixture of 13% or less by volume with air, or have a flammability range of at least 12 (e.g. methane, butane, and propane)
- it is an oxidizing substance which readily yield oxygen to stimulate, or contribute to, the combustion of other materials (e.g. chlorates, permanganate, and nitrates)

There is an SQE of 5 kg per month. Empty containers and inner liners are not hazardous.

8 A waste that meets the Regulation 347 definition for corrosivity is characterized as being Corrosive Waste (C). The following criteria are used to determine if a waste should be categorized as corrosive:

- it is aqueous and has a pH less than or equal to 2.0 or greater than 12.5
- it is a liquid and corrodes steel (SAE 1020) at a rate greater than 6.35 millimetres per year at a test temperature of 55°C using the National Association of Corrosion Engineers test method TM-01-69

There is an SQE of 5 kg per month. Empty containers and inner liners are not hazardous.

9 A waste that meets the Regulation 347 definition for reactivity is characterized as being **Reactive Waste (R)**. The following criteria are used to determine if a waste should be categorized as corrosive:

- it is normally unstable and readily undergoes violent change without detonating
- it reacts violently with water
- it forms potentially explosive mixtures with water
- when mixed with water it generates toxic gases, vapours, or fumes

in a quantity sufficient to present danger to human health or the environment

- it is a cyanide- or sulphide-bearing waste which, when exposed to pH conditions between 2.0 and 12.5, can generate toxic gases, vapours, or fumes in an quantity sufficient to present danger to human health or the environment
- it is capable of detonation or explosive reaction if it is subjected to a strong initiating source or if heated under confinement
- it is readily capable of detonation or explosive decomposition or reaction at standard temperature and pressure
- it is a Class 1 explosive as defined by the TDGA (see Schedule II, List I of the TDGA)

There is an SQE of 5 kg per month. Empty containers and inner liners are not hazardous.

10 Any waste that produces a leachate which contains any of the substances at concentration greater than 100 times the concentrations listed in Schedule 4 of Regulation 347 (see Table 4.2) is characterized as being **Leachate Toxic (L)**. There is a SQE of 5 kg per month. Empty containers and liners are not hazardous.

In addition, waste from plants that produce coal tar should be treated as hazardous waste (Waste Class 222H). For any soils and sediments contaminated with benzo[a]pyrene (B[a]P), the following guidelines have been developed (MOE, 1989):

- if the concentration of B[a]P in leachate is above 1 ppb, then the material is classified as hazardous (Waste Class 222T)
- if the concentration of B[a]P in the leachate is 1.0 ppb or less, but greater than 0.1 ppb, then the material is classified as non-hazardous but registerable waste, provided it passes the Slump Test described in Regulation 347 (Waste Class 222N)
- if the concentration of B[a]P in the leachate is 0.1 ppb or less, but greater than 0.01 ppb, then the contaminated material is classified as non-hazardous solid waste, provided it passes the Slump Test, and
- if the concentration of B[a]P in the leachate is 0.01 ppb or less, then the material does not have to be removed from the site

The second type of subject waste is a **Liquid Industrial Waste** (L). This class applies to a waste if it meets none of the criteria for hazardous waste and is a liquid as defined by the Slump Test. It is broadly defined to include any liquid waste or sludge from industrial, commercial, manufacturing, research, or experimental activities. The following wastes are exempted from this waste class:

- hauled sewage
- waste from the operation of a water works subject to the Ontario Water Resources Act

- waste that is produced in any month in an amount less than 25 L or otherwise accumulated in an amount less than 25 L
- waste directly discharged from a waste generation facility into a sewage system subject to the Ontario Water Resources Act
- waste from a food packing, processing, and preparation operations including wineries and cheese-making facilities
- drilling fluids and produced waters associated with oil and gas exploration, development, and production
- processed organic waste
- asbestos waste

A waste is classified as a **Registerable Waste** (N) if it produces a leachate that contains any of the substances at concentration between 10 and 100 times the concentrations listed in Schedule 4 of Regulation 347 (see Table 4.2). The SQE is 25 kg of waste per month. While generators of Registerable Wastes must be registered as such with the MOEE (see Section 4.3), the wastes are not subject to the handling and disposal requirements placed on subject wastes.

Waste materials that have insufficient concentrations of substances to be classified as Registerable Wastes, but which nevertheless are wastes as defined by the EPA or Regulation 347, are referred to as **non-registerable wastes**. Generators do not need to register with the MOEE and the wastes are not subject to the handling and disposal requirements placed on Registerable Wastes.

4.2.3 Materials that Are Difficult to Classify

Although the waste classification system described in Section 4.2.2 works well for most wastes, there are some materials for which the existing definitions do not provide a clear indication as to whether they are wastes or how they should be managed. An example is contaminated soil. It is well known that there are many properties where soils might be classified as registerable or subject wastes if subjected to the leachate test described in Regulation 347. If these materials were deemed to be wastes while in the ground, it could follow that the properties would need to be classified as waste disposal sites (according to the definition of "waste disposal site" provided in Section 25 of the EPA). It also has been argued that such soils become waste only upon being excavated or otherwise worked. Under such a scenario, the re-use of treated soil as fill could be construed as creating a waste disposal site (since the soil, even though it had been treated, would still be waste). These uncertainties have hindered clean-up efforts at some sites in Ontario (see Chapter 5).

Similar difficulties can arise when dealing with mildly contaminated soil. The presence of contaminants could be interpreted to mean that the soil that does not strictly conform to the definition of "inert fill," or that it should not be considered to be an "innocuous waste" (refer to Section 4.2.1). That rationale has been used to classify mildly contaminated soil as non-registerable waste and has resulted in large quantities of soils being disposed at landfill sites in recent years. Faced with capacity limitations at landfill sites, some municipalities, particularly in the Greater Toronto Area, have restricted or banned the disposal of soils.

In August 1992, the MOEE issued a proposed policy for managing various types of **excess materials** including excavated soil and rock (MOE, 1992). In effect, the proposed policy is an attempt to clarify how to manage materials that occupy the "grey area" between Registerable Waste and exempt waste or inert fill. The policy describes a method for classifying excess materials and expectations of how materials in each classification would be managed. One of the objectives of the policy is to reduce the strain that soil disposal has placed on municipal landfill sites. As of September 1993, no confirmation had been announced as to the adoption of the proposed policy. (See Section 5.3.3 for further discussion of the policy.)

4.3 RESPONSIBILITIES OF WASTE GENERATORS

Section 1 of the EPA defines the term "person responsible" as the owner or the person in occupation or having charge, management, or control of a source of contaminant. In Part V, this concept is expanded and divided into three types of responsible persons: "waste generators"; "owners" of waste management facilities or disposal sites; and "operators" of systems or sites. (Responsibilities of the latter two are discussed in Section 4.4.)

Generators include operators of commercial and manufacturing facilities that produce waste as well as operators of waste transfer, bulking, treatment, or processing facilities that forward materials off-site for subsequent management.

Generators are responsible for the wastes they generate until the wastes are delivered to a an approved disposal site. At that point, the owners or operators of the disposal site become responsible for the wastes. This provides generators with some protection from long-term liabilities associated with disposal.

Every generator of subject or registerable wastes in amounts greater than the SQEs described in Section 4.2 must complete a Generator Registration Report. The report must be filed with the MOEE and a Generator Registration Number obtained. It is an offence to store, dispose, and transport subject waste unless a Generator Registration Number has been obtained. Out-of-province waste generators that transport or dispose of subject waste in Ontario must also register with the MOEE.

Figure 4.2 presents a Generator Registration Report. Part 1 requires information as to the company's name and address, and a company official and position. Consultants who act on behalf of the company cannot sign the report. Part 2 requires a description of the waste, the generating process, and the quantity of waste. In addition, information on the primary and secondary characteristics of the waste, and the laboratory that analyzed the waste may also be required. Part 3 of the report covers some waste management aspects, notably the intended receiver and carriers.

Some of the information provided in a Generator Registration Report is accessible to the public. The MOEE maintains the Public Information Database which provides information on the type of waste, the volumes generated, and the generator's name and address.

Any changes to processes or the types of wastes that are generated must be reported to the MOEE in writing. Regulation 347 also requires that waste generators must notify the MOEE if subject wastes in quantities greater than the appropriate SQEs are stored on property for longer than three months. This necessitates some type of waste inventory system to track the duration of waste storage. Such systems should be reviewed during environmental audits (see Chapter 10).

The generator of a waste is responsible for ensuring that the disposal site receiving the waste has the appropriate Certificates of Approval. Generators often ask for a copy of the C of A or the certificate number prior to entering into an agreement with a disposal site operator.

While a waste is being transported, both the generator of the waste and the carrier of the material are liable should there be an incident involving the material. Generators can make it a contractual condition that ownership of the waste is transferred when the carrier picks up the material.

If the disposal site refuses to receive a waste, the carrier can take the waste back to the generator. The generator is legally required to accept the material back. If the waste is returned to the generator, the generator is then classified as a receiver and must follow the appropriate procedures (see Section 4.5.4).

Registration is not required in anticipation of wastes that may be generated through spills. Emergency registration procedures are available for spill situations.

4.4 MANAGING WASTES

4.4.1 Definitions

Part V of the EPA refers to waste management facilities as either being **waste disposal sites** or **waste management systems**. Disposal sites include any land where waste is deposited, disposed, handled, stored, transferred, treated, or processed plus any operation or equipment used in connection with those activities. Disposal sites include landfilling sites, incineration sites, transfer stations, packing and baling sites, dumps, used tire sites, and organic soil conditioning sites. Waste management systems include any facilities or equipment used to collect, handle, transport, store, process, or dispose of waste and may include one or more disposal sites.

Section 42 of Part V outlines several conditions that apply to the transfer of responsibility for disposal of a waste from a waste generator to the owner or operator of a disposal facility or transfer station:

(1) The ownership of waste that is accepted at a waste disposal site by the operator of the site is transferred to the operator upon acceptance.

(2) Where waste is deposited but not accepted at a waste disposal site, the ownership of the waste shall be deemed to be transferred to the operator of the site immediately before the waste is deposited.

(3) Subsections (1) and (2) apply only in respect of a waste disposal site for which a C of A or a provisional C of A is in force.

(4) Subsection (1) applies only in the absence of a contract to the contrary.

(5) Subsections (1) and (4) do not relieve any person from liability except liability as owner of a waste that is delivered to and accepted by the operator of a waste disposal site in accordance with law including an applicable C of A or provisional C of A.

(6) Where the operator of a waste disposal site is not the owner of the land on which the site is located, subsections (1) and (2) do not prevent the ownership of waste that is accepted or deposited at the site from being transferred to the owner of the land.

This transferring of responsibility away from waste generators is a major difference between the approach to waste management in Ontario and that used in some other jurisdictions, notably the United States where generators essentially are responsible for their wastes forever (Shaw, 1989).

4.4.2 Approvals

Section 27 of Part V specifies that no person shall use, operate, establish, alter, enlarge, or expand a waste management system or waste disposal site unless a C of A or a provisional C of A has been issued by the MOEE director and except in accordance with any conditions set out in such certificate. **Operating a waste system without a certificate is an offence.**

Section 39 allows an MOEE director to impose conditions on a disposal site or management system that are "in the public interest" (but does not expand upon that phrase).

Section 40 prohibits any person from depositing waste without a C of A "upon, in, into, or through any land or land covered by water or in any building that is not a waste disposal site" for which a C of A has been issued, except if in accordance with the terms and conditions of such a certificate.

Section 41 limits the equipment and facilities that may be used in conjunction with a waste management system in that "no person shall use any facilities or equipment for the storage, handling, treatment, collection, transportation, processing, or disposal of waste that is not part of a waste management system" for which a C of A has been issued and except in accordance with the terms and conditions of such a certificate.

4.4.3 Hearings

An MOEE director must order public hearings prior to deciding whether a C of A should be issued for any sites that will receive liquid industrial waste, hazardous waste, or any other waste equivalent to the domestic waste of more than 1,500 people. In other cases, the director can decide whether or not a public hearing should be held.

Public hearings convened under the EPA are limited in scope to the technical applicability of the proposal. Hearings also can be convened under the Environmental Assessment Act (EAA) in which case the scope must be expanded to consider alternatives to the proposed undertaking and alternative methods of carrying out the undertaking. The evaluation of options is a cornerstone of the EAA and also applies to the selection of technologies and sites.

There also are cases in which waste disposal proposals are subject to hearings under both the EPA and EAA. The Consolidated Hearings Act (CHA) permits the two hearings to be held together.

Whether convened under the EPA, the EAA, or the CHA, the types of information that are likely to be reviewed include:

- the purpose for the undertaking
- the reasons behind the proposed project
- a description of how the project will affect the environment
- a description of the actions proposed to prevent, change, mitigate, or remedy environmental effects
- an evaluation of advantage/disadvantage to the environment of the project

Sections 30 through 36 of Part V describe various aspects of the hearing process. For example, Section 31 authorizes an MOEE director to dispense with public hearings where an emergency situation exists. Section 36 authorizes a director to require a hearing to determine whether an existing or proposed disposal site or management system can be exempt from municipal by-laws.

4.4.4 Restoring or Re-using Disposal Sites

Section 43 of Part V provides MOEE directors with the statutory authority to order an occupant or the person having charge and control of land or a building to remove wastes and restore the site to a condition satisfactory to the director if the location has not been approved as a waste disposal site. Section 44 authorizes the director to require a waste management system or operator to comply with the requirements of the EPA.

Once a site has been classified as a waste management site, certain restrictions are imposed upon it. Section 46 of the EPA states that if a land site or land covered by water was used for disposal of waste, a period of 25 years from the year in which the waste disposal ceased is required before the land can be used for another purpose unless approval has been obtained from the Minister.

4.5 MANIFEST SYSTEM FOR SUBJECT WASTES

4.5.1 Overview

Regulation 347 describes a manifest system that must be used during the transportation, transfer, and disposal of all subject wastes. The system is compatible with the one required under TDGA regulation, so that only one piece of governmental paperwork needs to be filled out (see Figure 4.3) for transportation within Canada. Additional paperwork is required for international shipments.

Manifests are used to track each shipment of the waste as it passes from generator, to carrier, and eventually to the receiver. The MOEE oversees the whole system to make sure every aspect is being followed properly.

The six-copy manifest is divided into three parts:

Part A Completed by the Consignor (generator)
Part B Completed by the Carrier
Part C Completed by the Consignee (receiver)

4.5.2 Responsibilities of the Generator

A generator must fill out Part A of the manifest, including the name of the intended receiver. In addition, the generator must ensure that Part B of the manifest is completed by the carrier. The generator must then remove the **first copy** and forward it to the director of the Waste Management Branch within three working days of the transfer. The **second copy** is to be removed and retained on file by the generator for a period of two years. The four remaining copies of the manifest are to be given back to the carrier.

Within two weeks of the transfer of waste, the generator should receive the **sixth copy** of the manifest from the receiver of the wastes. If this doesn't happen, the generator should contact the receiver to ensure that the waste did in fact reach its intended destination. If unable to trace the waste within four weeks of the waste transfer, the director of the Waste Management Branch must be notified. These time periods may differ if sending waste outside Ontario (Tricil, not dated).

4.5.3 Responsibilities of the Licensed Carriers

A licensed carrier must obtain a C of A and comply with all of the transportation requirements imposed by Regulation 347 and any applicable requirements of the TDGA (see Section 4.7). The carrier must carry the C of A in the vehicle at all times and only transfer those wastes specified in the certificate.

The carrier must complete Section B of the manifest and retain the third through sixth copies of the manifest during the transfer of the waste. The carrier must only transport the wastes to a transfer station or disposal site that is operating under a C of A and transport only those waste specified in Section C of the manifest. Prior to leaving the site of a waste transfer, the carrier must obtain the **fourth copy** of the completed manifest from the receiver of the waste and retain the document for a period of two years.

Carriers may enter into contracts that offer various forms of assistance to waste generators. For example, a carrier can arrange for samples of the waste stream to be collected and analyzed, fill out necessary forms at the disposal site, arrange for the disposal codes to be put in place, and arrange the scheduling at the receiving site, be it a transfer site or a final disposal site (Shaw, 1989).

If the disposal site refuses to receive a load, the carrier is responsible for either finding an alternative approved receiver or taking the waste back to the generator. The generator is legally required to accept the material if returned (see Section 4.3).

4.5.4 Responsibilities of the Receiver

A receiver can only accept those waste classes for which the receiver has a C of A. The operation of the site must be in accordance with the conditions which are specified in the certificate.

The receiver must complete Section C of the four remaining copies of the manifest. The **third copy** of the manifest must be sent to the MOEE; the **fourth copy** is returned to the carrier; the **fifth copy** is retained by the receiver for two years; and the **sixth copy** is sent to the generator within three working days after the waste transfer.

If the waste is refused by the receiver, a load refusal report must be prepared outlining the manifest number, generator registration number and the reason for the refusal. The report must be sent to the director of the Waste Management Branch within three working days after the refusal (Tricil, not dated).

4.6 TRANSPORTING WASTES INSIDE ONTARIO

4.6.1 Carriers

To transport wastes regulated by Regulation 347, a carrier must have a Provisional C of A for a Waste Management System. The carrier must make an application to the MOEE and satisfy certain requirements with respect to driver training and insurance prior to obtaining a C of A. Regulation 347 requires that carriers must have automotive insurance coverage in the amount of $1,000,000. For certain wastes (PCBs and pathological waste), carriers must post additional security with the MOEE (Shaw, 1989).

A C of A will identify the vehicles that the carrier can use, the waste classes that the carrier can transport, and the disposal sites or transfer stations that the carrier can use. In addition to the conditions of the certificate, Regulation 347 imposes certain standards upon the carrier:

- waste collection vehicles and waste carriers must be of a design that ensures safe transfer of waste without leakage, emission of offensive odours or falling or blowing of waste material from the vehicle
- a vehicle used for transporting liquid industrial waste or hazardous waste must be clearly marked or placarded in accordance with the TDGA and display the name and number from the C of A
- driver training must be provided for the operation of the vehicle and waste management equipment, relevant legislation, environmental and safety concerns and emergency management procedures
- a copy of the C of A that authorizes the transport must be kept in the vehicle when liquid industrial waste or hazardous waste is being transported, and
- the driver, generator, or receiver must be present whenever liquid industrial waste or hazardous waste is being transferred

Under Section 2 of the DGTA, a permit may be issued by a Minister or a person designated by the Minister exempting from the application of the act, the transportation of dangerous goods in a vehicle.

4.6.2 Transfer Stations

The transfer station is an intermediate point between the original generator and the ultimate disposal site of the waste. For a transfer station to receive waste, it must have one of two types of certificates: a C of A for a waste disposal site (bulking), or a C of A for a waste disposal site (processing). A public hearing may be required to obtain the certificates (Shaw, 1989).

4.6.3 Transferring Responsibility or Ownership of Wastes

As noted in Section 4.3, Section 42 of Part V allows responsibility for the disposal of a waste to be transferred from the generator to a third party (a disposal site operator, the owner of a disposal site, or the owner of a transfer station). While a waste is being transported, both the generator of the waste and the carrier are liable should there be an incident involving the material. Contractual conditions can be used to transfer all liabilities to the carrier. Such a transfer of ownership may not be recognized in court if it is seen as trying to circumvent liability specified under Part X of the EPA (Shaw, 1989).

4.7 TRANSPORTING WASTES UNDER THE TDGA

4.7.1 Basic Responsibilities

The Transport of Dangerous Goods Act (TDGA) pertains to marine, air, rail, and interprovincial and international road transportation. The TDGA is administered by Transport Canada. Environment Canada provides technical advice and recommendations for regulatory initiatives or matters related to dangerous goods.

The basic responsibilities of the consignor (generator), carrier, and consignee (receiver) are presented in Figure 4.5. These include documentation, packaging, and notification requirements. Part IV of the TDGA requires all shipments of dangerous goods to be accompanied by a shipping document or manifest. The manifest should be compatible with provincial manifests and provide:

- detailed information on the types and amounts of hazardous waste being shipped
- a record of various firms or individuals involved in the shipment, and
- information on the treatment, storage and/or disposal of the hazardous waste when they reach their final destination

If the waste is hazardous, the consignor (i.e. the shipper) must insert the word "waste" immediately preceding the shipping name.

The Regulation 347 manifest presented in Figure 4.3 is sufficient for TDGA requirements. For intraprovincial and interprovincial shipments of hazardous waste, manifests must be distributed as follows:

Copy 1   mailed by the consignor to the appropriate authority of the province/territory in which the consignee is located within two days, exclusive of holidays, after the goods have been received by the carrier

Copy 2   retained by the consignor for a period of two years after the goods have reached their destination

Copy 3   mailed by the consignee to the appropriate authority in his province/territory within two days, exclusive of holidays, after the goods are received from the carrier

Copy 4   retained by the carrier for a period of two years after the goods have reached their destination

Copy 5   retained by the consignee for a period of two years after the goods have reached their destination, and

Copy 6   mailed by the consignee to the consignor

The province/territory of the consignor may also require copies of the manifest for wastes that are shipped to other jurisdictions. The appropriate authorities should be contacted and, if required, the consignor should send a photocopy of copy 1 and the consignee should send a photocopy of copy 3.

If dangerous goods are being transferred by road vehicle, a copy of the document must be kept in the cab within the driver's reach. If the driver is not in the cab, the documentation must be kept either on the driver's seat or in a pocket mounted on the driver's door.

When radioactive materials are involved, conditions of the Transport Packaging of Radioactive Materials Regulation also must be met.

4.7.2 Notification Procedures

Proposed shipments of hazardous waste from the United States to Canada should be preceded by notification to the Waste Management Branch of Environment Canada. If destined for a facility in Ontario, the documents will be forwarded to the MOEE Waste Management Branch and then to the MOEE district office where the facility is located to verify that all certificates have been issued and other forms of registration have been filed. Objections can be raised and routed back to Environment Canada and/or the U.S. Environmental Protection Agency.

If a "dangerous occurrence" occurs, notification of certain government agencies by the person in charge at the time must occur immediately. In Ontario, the MOEE Spills Action Centre (SAC) can be called (see Section 12.6.2). The analogous federal agency is the National Environmental Emergencies Centre in Hull, Quebec.

4.7.3 Container Markings and Packaging

All dangerous goods (which includes hazardous waste) must be properly packaged and marked with proper safety marks, labels, signs and placards. Part V and Schedule V of the TDGA describe the proper **markings** required for hazardous goods. Marking involves the use of dangerous good labels and safety marks on small containers, and the use of placards on large transport units. It is the generator's responsibility to ensure that the appropriate placards are in place prior to shipment. The carrier, however, is responsible during the transportation of the dangerous good. Examples of the placards are presented in Figure 4.4.

Before a container which has contained dangerous goods can be marked as EMPTY, the container must be emptied and cleaned or purged of all residue so that a hazard does not exist. The general rule is that containers should be rinsed three times with high-quality water. If a residue remains, the container must be marked EMPTY – LAST CONTAINED XXXX and all of the rules pertaining to placards and shipping documents still apply. There are exemptions for containers with residues if the containers are being returned to the original supplier.

Under the TDGA, designated officials have the power to stop a vehicle for **inspection** at any time, take samples of the goods, and examine and make copies of the shipping documents. Designated officials can be representatives of Transport Canada, the MOEE, provincial police forces, the Royal Canadian Mounted Police, and weigh-scale operators.

4.7.4 TDGA Classifications

Classification involves assigning dangerous goods to classes and divisions based on hazard criteria that are described in Part III of the TDGA regulation. Dangerous goods are classified by either picking the substance from a comprehensive list given in the regulation, or by comparing the properties of the substance to criteria given in the regulation. A comprehensive list of specific and generic dangerous goods is presented in Schedule II, List II of the TDGA.

There are nine different classes of dangerous goods:

1 Explosives
2 Gases
3 Flammable and Combustible Liquids
4 Flammable Solids
5 Oxidizing Substances and Organic Peroxides
6 Poisonous (toxic) and Infectious Substances
7 Radioactive Material
8 Corrosives
9 Miscellaneous Dangerous Goods

Each type of dangerous good is assigned one of the nine classes as its primary classification. In addition, one or more subsidiary classifications may be assigned. The primary classification describes the main hazardous properties of a particular dangerous good. A subsidiary classification describes other hazardous properties. These properties are considered to be of a secondary concern in transportation when compared with the main hazardous properties of the good. For example, Class 2 – Gases includes several divisions such as Division 2.1 – Flammable Gas; Division 2.2 - Non-flammable Gas; and Division 2.3 – Poisonous Gas.

Table 4.3 presents preliminary descriptions of each class of dangerous good. Note that in Class 9.2, the term "environmentally hazardous substance" refers to chemicals which bioaccumulate in the food chain and/or are persistent.

The following definitions of waste and hazardous waste are not part of the TDGA regulations but are widely used as working definitions (Environment Canada, 1986):

Waste: Any substance for which a consignor/generator has no further use and is discarded.

Hazardous Waste: Wastes which are potentially hazardous to human health and/or the environment due to their nature and quantity, and which require special disposal techniques.

4.7.5 Exempt Materials

The following materials are exempted from the requirements of the TDGA:

- gasoline
- retail purchases
- movement of less than one kilometre between plants or properties of the same owner
- service truck exemption for material being used in repair
- limited quantity exemptions

At one time, recyclable material was exempted if it was waste transferred by a generator and destined for a site where it was to be wholly utilized (but not by combustion or land application), promptly packaged for retail sale, or offered for retail sale; however, materials going for recycling must now be manifested as per Schedule 8 and 12 of the TDGA.

4.7.6 Other TDGA Requirements

The TDGA also specifies **safety standards** in Schedule III and in Part II. For example, temperatures must be kept within defined ranges for goods listed in Column IV of List II of Schedule II.

For some dangerous substances specified in Schedule XII of the TDGA regulation, the generator or consignor of the waste must file an **emergency response plan** with the director-general of the TDGA regulation. The documents for each shipment must show the emergency response plan number and the telephone number for activating the plan. These dangerous goods include infectious wastes, explosives, certain gases, and radioactive materials and wastes. The plan must outline the assistance that can be provided in the event of an emergency (Tricil, not dated).

Some industrial associations have been established at regional response centres to respond to emergencies. One example is the Canadian Chemical Producers Association of the Transportation

Emergency Assistance Program (TEAP). Chapter 12 provides a more detailed discussion of emergency response.

Any person who handles, offers for transport, or transports dangerous goods must be trained or be directly supervised by a trained person. The **training** must be relevant for the types of duties performed. Following the completion of training, employees must be given a certificate of TDGA training. The certificate is valid for three years and must be issued to each employee. After three years, the employee must be retrained. A trained person may be required to produce the certificate upon request by an inspector. Training sessions can be conducted in-house or by an external third party. The training of employees should also include the requirements under Regulation 347.

4.8 IMPORT/EXPORT OF HAZARDOUS WASTES

As noted in section 4.1, CEPA authorizes Environment Canada to regulate the export and import of hazardous wastes. As a signatory to the *Basel Convention on Control of Transboundary Movements of Hazardous Wastes and Their Disposal*, which came into force in 1992, Canada has developed the *Export and Import of Hazardous Wastes Regulations*. The requirements outlined in the regulations help to ensure that all shipments of hazardous wastes entering into, leaving, or passing through Canada are tracked and controlled. The regulations are administered by the Hazardous Waste Management Division, Office of Waste Management of Environment Canada.

4.9 REDUCING, RE-USING, AND RECYCLING WASTES

4.9.1 General

The ever-increasing costs of waste management, transportation, and disposal are constant incentives for all waste generators to seek ways to minimize the amounts of waste they create. Increasing numbers of organizations and agencies are emphasizing the three Rs: reduction, re-use, recycling. Recovery is sometimes included as the fourth R.

Reduction can be achieved several ways. The amount of materials needed at a facility often can be reduced by implementing changes to processes or better process control. Ongoing inventory tracking of wastes should be used to identify ways to achieve reductions and monitor their effectiveness. Examples of waste reduction approaches and potential waste exchanges are presented in Tables 4.4 and 4.5.

The Ontario Waste Exchange (OWE) is a technical assistance program that provides free assistance to industrial waste generators in Ontario.

The co-sponsors of the program are the Ontario Waste Management Corporation (OWMC) and the MOEE. The OWE is also seen as the active component of the Canadian Waste Materials Exchange Program (CWME) in Ontario. The CWME is a passive waste exchange which issues bulletins every two months on lists of wastes available and wastes wanted by different industry sectors (Varangu and Laughlin, 1988).

In 1988, approximately 3,500 companies participated in the OWE system and approximately 290 million kg of wastes were transferred. The economic incentive to reduce waste production became increasingly attractive in the late 1980s as disposal costs for both non-hazardous and hazardous wastes increased across Ontario.

The OWE provides assistance to the companies in the following form (Varangu and Laughlin, 1988):

- finds industrial users for wastes generated in different industrial sectors
- assists in finding sources of wastes as alternative raw materials
- provides recycling industry contacts
- conducts literature reviews for selected waste reduction topics
- conducts research on selected hazardous waste streams
- provides technical assistance in waste reduction
- conducts plant visits to assist in improving waste management practices

Both the OWE and the Ontario section of the CWME are operated by the Ontario Research Foundation. Both can be contacted by calling (416) 822-4111.

4.9.2 Waste Reduction Regulations

In March 1994, five waste reduction regulations under the EPA were promulgated. Also referred to as the **3Rs Regulations**, they set out various requirements for waste reduction, re-use, and recycling schemes. Four of the regulations impose new requirements on municipalities such as making composting and blue box recycling program mandatory. The fifth regulation will require that designated waste generators from the industrial, commercial, and institutional sectors conduct waste audits and formulate waste reduction plans.

"Waste audits" (really the preparation of waste inventories) will be used to determine the amount, nature, and composition of wastes being generated as well as to study the process or activities that generate the wastes. The audits also should critically examine the influence on waste generation of decisions or policies such as the processes used to procure supplies and equipment. The regulation recommends that the audits be performed annually.

Waste reduction plans will respond to the findings of the waste audits.

A plan should identify ways to reduce, re-use, and recycle waste and should be modified and updated annually. The plan must be communicated to employees. Work plans and waste audits should be kept on file for at least five years.

The designated waste generators and the types of materials that are to be source separated at each include:

- owners of retail shopping establishments or complexes with total floor area of 10,000 m^2 or greater will separate corrugated cardboard, fine paper, newsprint, and food and beverage containers made of glass, aluminum, or steel
- manufacturing establishments with more than 100 full-time employees (or equivalent part-time employees) will separate corrugated cardboard, fine paper, newsprint, wood, steel, aluminum, glass, and plastic
- construction or demolition projects involving 2,000 m^2 or more of floor area will separate corrugated cardboard (construction projects only), drywall (construction projects only), wood, steel, concrete, and brick
- owners of office buildings with total floor area of 10,000 m^2 or greater will separate corrugated cardboard, fine paper, newsprint, and food and beverage containers made of glass, aluminum, or steel
- restaurants that employ more than 100 full-time employees (or equivalent part-time employees) will separate corrugated cardboard, fine paper, newsprint, and food and beverage containers made of glass, aluminum, polyethylene terephthalate (PET), or steel
- hotels, motels, inns, resorts, or hostels with more than 75 units will separate corrugated cardboard, fine paper, newsprint, and food and beverage containers made of glass, aluminum, PET, or steel
- hospitals will separate corrugated cardboard, fine paper, newsprint, and food and beverage containers made of glass, aluminum, or steel
- educational institutions enrolling more than 350 students annually will separate corrugated cardboard, fine paper, newsprint, and food and beverage containers made of glass, aluminum, or steel

Additional requirements are laid out for major packaging users in four manufacturing sectors: food; beverages; paper and allied products; chemical and chemical products. Packaging audits and workplans must be undertaken.

4.10 SUMMARY

In Ontario, waste management is addressed primarily in Part V of the EPA and its associated Regulation 347. The identification and proper disposal of waste is clearly the responsibility of waste generators. Identification should be done in accordance with the classification system set out in Regulation 347. Every generator of subject and registerable wastes must file a Generator Registration Report and be issued a Generator Registration Number.

The transportation of hazardous waste via Ontario roads is governed by the DGTA. Transportation of wastes by other modes and between provinces must comply with the requirements of the federal TDGA. Transportation of hazardous wastes into, out of, or through Canada must comply with TDGA and CEPA.

Regulation 347 requires a six-copy manifest system to track the movement of waste materials. Carriers must be licensed in accordance with provincial and federal requirements. Similarly, owners/operators of waste management systems, disposal sites, and transfer stations must comply with provincial requirements.

The costs of waste management, transportation, and disposal are constant incentives for waste generators to seek ways to minimize the amounts of waste they create. The Ontario Waste Exchange (OWE) provides assistance to industrial waste generators in Ontario.

The 3 Rs Regulations define mandatory rules and requirements for waste reduction, re-use, and recycling activities in Ontario. They will require municipalities to implement recycling and composting programs and require that major waste generators undertake waste audits and implement waste reduction programs.

REFERENCES

Environment Canada. April 1986. *Users' Guide to Hazardous Waste Classification (Transportation of Dangerous Goods Regulation).* First edition.

Ontario Ministry of the Environment (MOE). August 1992. *Proposed Policy for Management of Excess Soil, Rock, and Like Materials.* Technical Consultation Document. Materials Management Policy Committee.

Ontario Ministry of the Environment (MOE). June 1989. *Interim Position on the Classification and Disposal of Coal Tar and Contaminated Soils, Sediment, and Water at Abandoned Sites.*

Ontario Ministry of the Environment (MOE). July 1985. *Registration Guidance Manual for Generators of Liquid Industrial and Hazardous Waste.*

Shaw, J. 1989. "An Insider's Perspective of Ontario's Waste Management Industry." *Environmental Science and Engineering* (October): 12-15.

Tricil. Not dated. *The Tricil Guide: Your Guide on What to Know, What to Do, and Where to Find Out about Hazardous Waste Legislation in Ontario.*

Varangu, L., and B. Laughlin. 1988. "The Ontario Waste Exchange Program: Helping Industries Reduce Waste." Presented at the 35th Ontario Waste Management Conference, 12 to 15 June, Toronto.

Table 4.1
MOEE WASTE CLASSES

INORGANIC WASTES

Acid Solutions	Examples
111 Spent pickle liquor	Acid solutions of sulphuric and hydrochloric acids containing ferrous salts from steel pickling.
112 Acid solutions, sludges and residues containing heavy metals	Solutions of sulphuric, hydrochloric and nitric acids containing copper, nickel, chromium, zinc, cadmium, tin, lead, or other heavy metals; chromic acid waste; acidic emission control sludges from secondary lead smelting.
113 Acid solutions, sludges and residues containing other metals and non-metals	Solutions of sulphuric, hydrochloric, hydrofluoric and nitric acids containing sodium, potassium, calcium, magnesium or aluminum; equipment cleaning acids; cation regenerant; reactor acid washes; catalyst acid and acid washes.
114 Other inorganic acid wastes	Off-specification acids; by-product hydrochloric acid; dilute acid solutions; acid test residues.

Alkaline Solutions

121 Alkaline solutions, sludges and residues containing heavy metals	Metal finishing wastes; plating baths; spent solutions containing metals such as copper, zinc, tin, cadmium; case hardening sludges; spent cyanide destruction residues; dewatered solids from metal and cyanide finishing wastes and cyanide destruction.
122 Alkaline solutions, sludges and residues containing other metals and non-metals, not containing cyanides	Alkaline solutions from aluminum surface coating and etching; alkali cleaner wastes; waste lime sludges and slurries; anion regenerants.
123 Alkaline phosphates	Bonderizing wastes; zinc phosphates; ferrous phosphates; phosphate cleaners.

Aqueous Salts

131 Neutralized solutions, sludges and residues containing heavy metals

Metal finishing waste treatment sludges containing copper, nickel, chromium, zinc or cadmium; neutral salt bath sludges and washes; lime sludge from metal finishing waste treatment; dewatered solids from these processes.

132 Neutralized solutions, sludges and residues containing other metals

Aluminum surface coating treatment sludges; alum and gypsum sludges.

133 Brines, chlor-alkali sludges and residues

Waste brines from chlor-alkali plants; neutralized hydrochloric acid; brine treatment sludges; dewatered solids from brine treatment.

134 Wastes containing sulphides

Petroleum aqueous refinery condensates.

135 Wastes containing other reactive anions

Wastes containing chlorates; hypochlorite; bromate or thiosulphate.

Miscellaneous Inorganic Wastes and Mixed Wastes

141 Inorganic wastes from pigment manufacturing

Wastewaters and sludges from the production of chrome yellow, molybdate orange, zinc yellow, chrome green and iron pigments; dewatered solids from these sources.

142 Primary lead, zinc and copper smelting wastes

Slurries, sludges and surface impoundment solids; treatment plant sludges; anode slimes and leachate residues; dewatered solids from these sources.

143 Residues from steel making

Emission control sludges and dusts; precipitator residues from steel plants; dewatered solids from these sources.

144 Liquid tannery waste sludges

Lime waste mixtures; chrome tan liquors; dehairing solutions and sludges.

145 Wastes from the use of paints, pigments and coatings

Paint spray booth sludges and wastes; paper coating wastes; ink sludges; paint sludges.

146 Other specified inorganic sludges, slurries or solids

Flue gas scrubber wastes; wet fly ash; dust collector wastes; metal dust and abrasives wastes; foundry sands; mud sediment and water; tank bottoms from waste storage tanks that contained mixed inorganic wastes; heavy sludges from waste screening/filtration at transfer/processing sites not otherwise specified in this table.

147 Chemical fertilizer wastes

Solutions, sludges and residues containing ammonia, urea, nitrates and phosphates from nitrogen fertilizer plants.

148 Miscellaneous waste inorganic chemicals

Waste inorganic chemicals including laboratory, surplus or off-specification chemicals, that are not otherwise specified in this table.

149 Landfill leachate

Surface run-off and leachate collected from landfill sites.

150 Inert inorganic wastes

Sand and water from catch basins at car washes; slurries from the polishing and cutting of marble.

ORGANIC WASTES

Non-halogenated Spent Solvents

211 Aromatic solvents and residues

Benzene, toluene, xylene solvents and residues.

212 Aliphatic solvents and residues

Acetone, methylethylketone and residues, alcohols, cyclohexane and residues.

213 Petroleum distillates

Varsol, white spirits and petroleum distillates, thinners.

Fuels

221 Light fuels

Gasoline, kerosene, diesel, tank drainings/washings/bottoms, spill clean-up residues.

222 Heavy fuels

Bunker, asphalts, tank drainings/washings/bottoms, spill clean-up residues.

Resins and Plastics

231 Latex wastes

Waste latexes, latex crumb and residues.

232 Polymeric resins   Polyester, epoxy, urethane, phenolic resins, intermediates and solvent mixtures.

233 Other polymeric wastes   Off-specification materials, discarded materials from reactors.

Halogenated Organic Wastes

241 Halogenated solvents and residues   Spent halogenated solvents and residues such as perchloroethylene, trichloroethylene and carbon tetrachloride (dry cleaning solvents); halogenated still bottoms; residues and catalysts from halogenated hydrocarbon manufacturing or recycling processes.

242 Halogenated pesticides and herbicides   2,4-D, 2,4,5-T wastes, chlordane, mirex, silvex, pesticide solutions and residues.

243 Polychlorinated biphenyls (PCB)   Askarel liquids such as Aroclor, Pydraul, Pyranol, Therminols, Inerteen, and other PCB contaminated materials.

Oily Wastes

251 Waste oils/sludges (petroleum based)   Oil/water separator sludge; dissolved air flotation skimming; heavy oil tank drainage; slop oil and emulsions.

252 Waste crankcase oils and lubricants   Collected service station waste oils; industrial lubricants; bulk waste oils.

253 Emulsified oils   Soluble oils; waste cutting oils; machine oils.

254 Oily water/waste oil from waste transfer/processing sites   Waste oil and oily water limited to classes 251, 252 and 253 that have been bulked/blended/processed at a waste transfer/processing site.

Miscellaneous Organic Wastes and Mixed Wastes

261 Pharmaceuticals   Pharmaceutical and veterinary pharmaceutical wastes other than biologicals and vaccines; solid residues and liquids from veterinary arsenical compounds.

262 Detergents and   Laundry wastes.
     soaps

263 Miscellaneous   Waste organic chemicals including laboratory
     waste organic   surplus or off-specification chemicals that are
     chemicals   not otherwise specified in this table.

264 Photoprocessing   Photochemical solutions, washes and sludges.
     wastes

265 Graphic arts wastes   Adhesives; glues; miscellaneous washes; etch
                           solutions.

266 Phenolic waste   Cresylic acid; caustic phenolates; phenolic oils;
     streams   creosote.

267 Organic acids   Carboxylic or fatty acids; formic, acetic, propi-
                           onic acid wastes; sulphamic and other organic
                           acids that may be amenable to incineration.

268 Amines   Waste ethanolamines; urea; tolidene; Flexzone
                           waste; Monex waste.

269 Organic non-halo-   Organophosphorus chemical wastes; arsenicals;
     genated pesticide   wastes from MSMA and cacodylic acid.
     and herbicide
     wastes

270 Other specified   Tank bottoms from mixed organic waste bulking
     organic sludges,   tanks at waste transfer sites; mixed sludges from
     slurries and solids   waste screening/filtration at waste transfer/pro-
                           cessing sites not otherwise specified in this
                           table.

**Processed Organic
Wastes from Transfer
Stations**

281 Non-halogenated   Blended/bulked non-halogenated solvents, oils
     rich organics   and other rich organics prepared at transfer/pro-
                           cessing sites for incineration.

282 Non-halogenated   Blended/bulked aqueous wastes prepared at
     lean organics   transfer/processing sites for incineration and
                           contaminated with non-halogenated solvents,
                           non-halogenated oils and other non-halogenat-
                           ed organics.

Plant and Animal Wastes

311 Organic tannery   Fleshings; trimmings; vegetable tan liquors; Bate
     wastes   solutions.

312 Pathological wastes   Human anatomical waste; infected animal car-
                            casses; other non-anatomical waste infected
                            with communicable diseases; biologicals and
                            vaccines.

OTHER WASTES

Explosive Manufacturing Wastes

321 Wastes from the   Wastewater treatment sludges; spent carbon;
     manufacture of   red/pink waters from TNT manufacturing;
     explosives and det-   residues from lead base initiating compounds.
     onation products

Compressed Gases

331 Waste compressed   Methane (natural gas); nitrous or nitric oxide;
     gases, including   propane; butane.
     cylinders

Table 4.2
SCHEDULE 4 — LEACHATE QUALITY CRITERIA

Hazardous Waste Number	Contaminant	Concentration (mg/L)
ON4001	2,4,5-TP/Silvex/ 2-(2,4,5,-Trichlorophenoxy) propionic acid	0.01
ON4002	2,4-D	0.1
ON4003	Aldrin + Dieldrin	0.0007
ON4004	Arsenic	0.05
ON4005	Barium	1.0
ON4006	Boron	5.0
ON4007	Cadmium	0.005
ON4008	Carbaryl/1-Naphthyl- N-methyl carbamate/ Sevin	0.07
ON4009	Chlordane	0.007
ON4010	Chromium	0.05
ON4011	Cyanide (free)	0.2
ON4012	DDT	0.03
ON4013	Diazinon/Phospordithioic acid, 0,0-diethyl 0-(2-iso- propyl-6-methyl- 4-pyrimidinyl) ester	0.0002
ON4014	Endrin	0.0002
ON4015	Fluoride	2.4
ON4016	Heptachlor + Heptachlor epoxide	0.003
ON4017	Lead	0.05
ON4018	Lindane	0.004
ON4019	Mercury	0.001
ON4020	Methoxychlor/ 1,1,1-Trichloro-2, 2-bis (p-methoxyphenyl) ethane	0.1
ON4021	Methyl Parathion	0.007
ON4022	Nitrate + Nitrite	10.0
ON4023	Nitrilotriacetic acid	0.05

ON4024	Nitrite	1.0
ON4025	PCBs	0.003
ON4026	Parathion	0.035
ON4027	Selenium	0.01
ON4028	Silver	0.05
ON4029	Toxaphene	0.005
ON4030	Trihalomethanes	0.35
ON4031	Uranium	0.02

Table 4.3
TDGA CLASSIFICATIONS OF DANGEROUS GOODS

Canada
Transportation of Dangerous Goods Regulation (TDGR)SOR/85-77
as amended under the Transportation of Dangerous Goods Act.
Discarded dangerous goods and listed industrial process waster types in quantities 5 kg (solid) or 5 L (liquid), listed in TDGR Schedule II, List II, PLUS:

Class I—Explosives (Never a waste by definition)
TDGR 3.9
Use TDGR, Schedule II, List I for listed explosives. Refer to Energy, Mines and Resources Canada for classification of unlisted explosives.
Definition of explosives:
- Capable, by self-sustaining chemical reaction, of producing gas at such temperature, pressure and speed as to damage the environment.
- Manufactured for the purpose of making a practical explosive or pyrotechnic effect.

Class 2—Compressed Gases
TDGR 3.10-3.11
Use TDGR, Schedule II, List II for specified gases. If not specified, use the following criteria and return to Schedule II, List II for best general name:
a) Critical temperature <50°C or absolute vapour pressure >294 kPa at 50°C.
b) Absolute pressure >275 kPa ± 1 kPa at 21.1°C.
c) Absolute vapour pressure >275 kPa at 37.8°C using Reid Vapour Test (ASTM-D323-82).
d) Refrigerated liquid gases boiling point <-84°C at 101.325 kPa.
e) Liquid carbon dioxide.
Class 2.1—Ignitable in mixture of 13% or less of air at normal pressure. Flammability range of at least 12.
Class 2.2—When not in any other division of Class 2.
Class 2.3—LC50 <5000 mL/m^3 by reason of toxicity.
Class 2.4—LC50 <5000 mL/m^3 by reason of corrosion on respiratory tract.

Class 3—Flammable Liquids
TDGR 3.12-3.14
Use TDGR, Schedule II, List II for specified flammable liquids. If not specified, use the following criteria and return to Schedule II, List II for best general name:
- Flash point <61°C, using one of the following tests: Tag Closed Tester (ASTM-D323-82); Pensky-Martens Closed Tester (ASTM-D93-80);

Setaflash Closed Tester (ASTM-D3828-81 or ASTM D3278-82) depending on the viscosity of the flammable liquid.

Division/Packing Group	Flash Point	Boiling Point
Class 3.1	<-18°C	
Class 3.2	>-18°C & <23°C	
Class 3.3	>23°C & <61°C	
Pack, Group I		<35°C at 101.325 kPa
Pack, Group II	<23°C	>35°C at 101.325 kPa
Pack, Group III	>23°C & <37.8°C	>35°C at 101.325 kPa

Class 4—Flammable Solids, Spontaneously Combustible, Flammable Gas When Wet
TDGR 3.15-3.16

Class 4.1—Solids which are ignitable and burn vigorously and persistently. They cause fire through friction or from related heat from manufacturing.

Class 4.2—Spontaneously combustible substances.

Class 4.3—Substances that on contact with water emit flammable gases or become spontaneously combustible.

Class 5—Oxidizing Substances & Organic Peroxides
TDGR 3.17-3.18

Use TDGR, Schedule II, List II for specified oxidizers and organic peroxides. If not specified, use the following criteria and return to Schedule II, List II for the best general name:

Class 5.1—Oxidizing substances which cause the combustion of other material by yielding oxygen, whether or not the substance is combustible.

Class 5.2—Organic compounds which contain the "-0-0-" bivalent structure.

Class 6—Poisonous (Toxic) & Infectious Substances
TDGR 3.19-3.23

Use TDGR, Schedule II, List II for specified poisonous or toxic substances. If not specified, use the following criteria and return to Schedule II, List II for best general name:

Class 6.1—

Substance Form	LD50	LC50
• Solid (oral toxicity)	<50 mg/kg	
• Liquid (oral toxicity)	<50 mg/kg	
• Substance (dermal toxicity)	<200 mg/kg	
• Dusts/mists (inhalation toxicity)		<2000 mg/m^3
• Substances with saturated vapour concentration LC50 (mL/m^3)		<3000 mL/m^3

Use the LD50 and LC50 formulae in TDGR 3.23, for various mixtures.

Class 6.2—Organisms and their toxins which are reasonably believed to be infectious to humans or animals. Use the list in TDG Regulations, Schedule

VII for infectious organisms and their toxins.

Class 7—Radioactive Materials (Never a waste by definition)
TDGR 3.24
Use TDGR, Schedule II, List II for listed radioactive materials. If unlisted, refer to Atomic Energy Control Board for classification.
Radioactive materials are defined as products or substances with activity >74 kBq/kg.

Class 8—Corrosives
TDGR 3.25
Use TDGR, Schedule II, List II for specified corrosives. If not specified, use the following criteria and return to Schedule II, List II for best general name:
a)   Corrodes SAE 1020 steel or 7075-T6 non-clad aluminum at a rate >6.25 mm/year at 55°C using Metal Corrosion Test (NACE TM-01-76).
b)   Has a pH factor <2.0 or >12.5

Class 9—Miscellaneous Dangerous Goods
TDGR 3.27
Use TDGR, Schedule II, List II for listed miscellaneous dangerous goods. If unlisted, they are not regulated. Class 9 substances are classified and listed by Transport Canada and Environment agencies only.
Class 9.1—Possess a hazard not already described in a previous class.
Class 9.2—Substance which is hazardous to the environment.
Class 9.3—Dangerous wastes that possess a hazard not described in a previous class.

Class 9—Basis for Listing
Class 9.2 and 9.3 are classified by Environment Canada and Provincial Environment Ministries. These agencies use a list of criteria not stated in the Regulations, and in addition to those used for Classes 1 to 8. The additional criteria enable them to determine all the characteristics of a substance or waste which may be hazardous to human health or the environment. The additional criteria include:
 • chronic toxicity (carcinogenic, teratogenic, genotoxic);
 • aquatic toxicity;
 • bioaccumulation;
 • persistence in the environment.
Substances or wastes that satisfy these additional criteria are assigned to Class 9.2 & 9.3.

Table 4.4
APPROACHES TO WASTE REDUCTION

Waste Abatement

Substitution of a new low-waste industrial process for an old process to eliminate or drastically reduce the quantity of waste produced.

– Replacement of sulphuric acid in steel pickling with hydrochloric acid
– Replacement of liquid of paints by powder coatings
– Replacement of solvent-based adhesives with water-based adhesives

Waste Minimization

The reduction of the quantity of waste through good house-keeping practices or by the application of concentration technologies. Also, the reduction in the degree of hazard of waste through simple in-plant treatment.

– Separation of waste streams to permit recovery
– Application of countercurrent rinsing to minimize volume discharge
– Neutralization of wastes and precipitation of smaller-volume sludges
– Fixing leaky taps and nozzles

Waste Re-use

The direct re-use of a waste stream, as is, or with a very minor modification.

– Re-use of surplus or salvage chemicals
– Use of blast furnace slag as aggregate
– Use of solvents from electronics industry in paints manufacture
– Use of refinery spent caustic in pulping wood
– Use of oil sludges in asphalt manufacturing
– Use of electronic circuit manufacturing plating baths in regular plating shops

Waste Recycle

The reclamation of value from waste streams through the application of reprocessing such as distillation, etc.

– Oil re-refining
– Solvent distillation
– Recovery of iron salts technologies from pickle liquor
– Recovery of heavy metals from sludges
– Recovery and re-use of spent foundry sands

- Recovery of scrap metal
- Landfarming of organic wastes
- Regeneration and re-use of activated carbon
- Recycling of grease and fats to renderers

Reference: Varangu and Laughlin, 1988

Table 4.5
WASTE EXCHANGES

Materials	Receivers
Acids	
Nitric Acid	Metal Reclaimer
Sulphuric Acid	Metal Reclaimer
Alkalis	
Calcium Hydroxide	Broker to New Business
Potassium Hydroxide	Chemical Company
Other Inorganic Chemicals	
Alumina	Abrasives Manufacturer
Asbestos (unused)	Manufacturer for Re-blend
Foundry Sands	Asphalt Manufacturer
Solvents	
Degreasing Solvents	Replace with Biodegradable Solvent Substitute
Ink Wastes	Recycling and Recovery
Other Organic Chemicals	
Paints	Salvation Army
Latex Materials	Manufacturer for Re-blend
Oils, Fats & Waxes	
Gasoline (Experimental)	Charity Organization
Oils (PCB Free)	Oil Recycler
Plastics and Rubber	
Polystyrene (Water-damaged Pack)	Plastic Recycler
Plastic Drums	Municipal Composting Programs

Reference: Varangu and Laughlin, 1988

Figure 4.1
WASTE IDENTIFICATION FLOWCHART

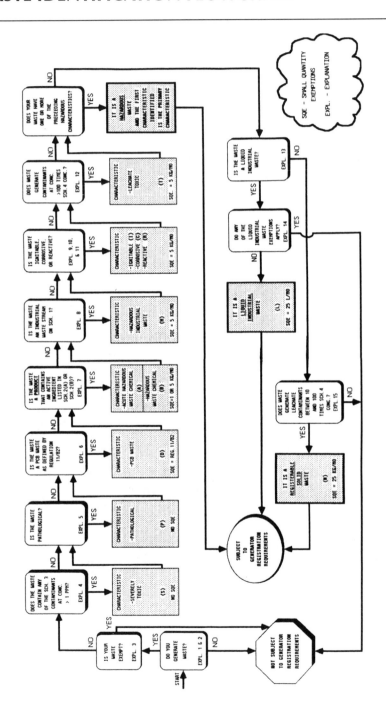

Figure 4.2
REGULATION 347 GENERATOR REGISTRATION REPORT

Ministry   Ministère
of the   de
Environment   l'Environnement

Ontario

Generator Registration Report
"Regulation 309, R.R.O. 1980, Form 2"

Rapport d'inscription du producteur
"Règlement 309, R.R.O. de 1980, formule 2"

NOTE: Regulation 309 requires generators of hazardous or liquid industrial wastes to submit a Generator Registration Report respecting each waste generation facility and each hazardous or liquid industrial waste.

REMARQUE: Le règlement 309 exige que les producteurs de déchets industriels liquides ou dangereux présentent un Rapport d'inscription du producteur en se servant de la présente formule pour chaque lieu de production de déchets et chaque déchet industriel liquide ou dangereux.

Part I – Generator Identification / *Partie I – Identification du producteur*

This report is / *Le présent rapport constitue:*

Generator Registration Number
Nº d'inscription du producteur

1. ☐   an initial generator registration report /
        un premier rapport d'inscription du producteur

or / ou

2. ☐   a revision – enter Ontario Generator Registration No
        une révision – veuillez inscrire le numéro d'inscription du producteur de l'Ontario

3. For generators located outside of Ontario, enter Registration/Notification number assigned by your local environmental authority. / Si vous êtes un producteur de l'extérieur de l'Ontario, veuillez inscrire le numéro d'inscription/d'identification attribué par les autorités locales en matière d'environnement.

Name of Generator (Enter the corporate name or, if a partnership or proprietorship, the name of the principal(s). If the generator intends to carry on business under a separate name or style, this should also be entered.) / *Nom du producteur (Veuillez inscrire la dénomination sociale ou, s'il s'agit d'une société en nom collectif ou d'une société à propriétaire unique, le nom du (des) principal (principaux) propriétaire(s). Si le producteur envisage d'exploiter une entreprise sous une dénomination ou un nom distinct, veuillez également le noter.)*

4. Name /Nom

5. Address / Adresse

6. Municipality / Municipalité   Province/State Province/État   Postal Code / Code postal

7. Site location / Lieu des installations

8. Municipality / Municipalité   Province/State Province/État   Postal Code / Code postal

9. Name of contact / Nom de la personne à contacter   Tel No. / Nº de tél

10. Standard Industrial Classification Codes (SIC) for Site noted in Section 7. / Codes de la classification des activités économiques pour les installations décrites au nº 7

11. Total number of wastes to be registered with this report / Nombre total de déchets à inscrire au moyen de ce rapport

12. Name of Company Official / Nom du représentant autorisé de la compagnie   13. Position / Poste

14. Signature / Signature   15. Date / Date

················· **PENALTY** ·················   ················· **PÉNALITÉ** ·················
Contraventions may be punished by fines of up to $2,000 (higher if environmental damage may result).   Toute infraction peut être sanctionnée par une amende maximale de 2 000 $
(Environmental Protection Act, sections 47 and 147)   (ou plus s'il peut en résulter une détérioration de l'environnement).
(Articles 47 et 147 de la Loi sur la protection de l'environnement)

16 **Ministry Use Only /**
    Réserve au ministère   County Code / Code de comté

                                      Regional/District Code / Code de région/district

                                      Municipal Code / Code de municipalité

                                      Inter City Tie Line / Ligne privée interurbaine

1487 (5/85) Page 1 of 2

Part 2 – Waste Identification / *Partie 2 – Identification des déchets*

1.   Description of Waste / *Description des déchets*

2.   Description of generating process / *Description du procédé de production*

3.   Waste quantity generated or accumulated / *Quantité des déchets produite ou accumulée*

     Continuous process / *Procédé continu*   **Batch process** / *par lots*

     or / ou

     kg/mo. / *kg/mois*   batches/mo..   kg/batch / *kg/lot*
     lots/mois

4.   Primary characteristic / *Caractéristique principale*

     Analytical data (if applicable). If the data has been estimated, attach separate sheet outlining the basis for the estimate. / *Données analytiques (le cas échéant). Si les données sont estimatives, veuillez annexer une feuille à part pour décrire sur quoi reposent les estimations.*

     Name of Laboratory (if applicable). / *Laboratoire (le cas échéant)*

Waste Class / *Catégorie des déchets*   Hazardous Waste Number / *Numéro des déchets dangereux*   Specific Gravity / *Gravité spécifique*   Physical State (Solid - S, Liquid - L, Gas - G) / *État physique (solide - S, liquide - L, gaz - G)*

For Ministry Use Only / *Réservé au ministère*

5.   Secondary Characteristic / *Caractéristique secondaire*

     Analytical data (if applicable) / *Données analytiques (le cas échéant)*

Part 3 – Waste Management / *Partie 3 – Gestion des déchets*

1.   Principal Intended Receiver / *Réceptionnaire principal prévu*

     Company name and address / *Nom et adresse de la compagnie*   Receiver No. / *N° du réceptionnaire*

     Municipality / *Municipalité*   Province/State / *Province/État*   Postal Code / *Code postal*

2.   Principal Intended Carrier / *Transporteur principal prévu*

     Company name and address / *Nom et adresse de la compagnie*   MOE Carrier No. / *N° du M. de l'E. du transporteur*

     A

     Municipality / *Municipalité*   Province/State / *Province/État*   Postal Code / *Code postal*

1487 (5/85) Page 2 of 2

Figure 4.3
REGULATION 347 MANIFEST

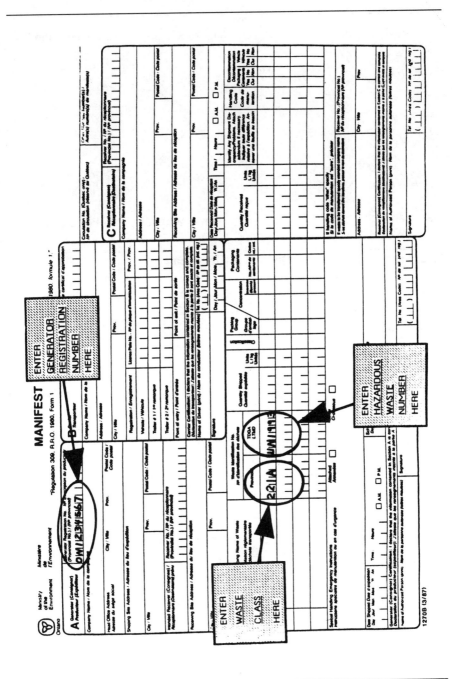

Figure 4.4
TDGA MARKING FOR CLASS 2—GASES

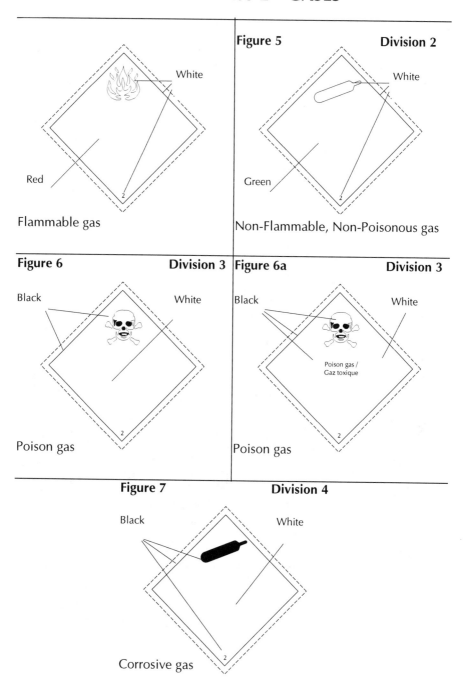

Figure 5   **Division 2**

White

White

Red

Green

Flammable gas

Non-Flammable, Non-Poisonous gas

Figure 6   **Division 3**

Black   White

Poison gas

Figure 6a   **Division 3**

Black   White

Poison gas / Gaz toxique

Poison gas

Figure 7   **Division 4**

Black   White

Corrosive gas

Figure 4.5
RESPONSIBILITIES DURING TRANSPORTATION UNDER TDGA

Consignor	Carrier	Consignee
Obtain a provincial number in the province of registration	Obtain registration program number for the province in which the vehicle is based	Obtain a provincial number for the province in which the facility is located
Complete Section A of the Manifest and pass on all necessary documents to carrier	Complete Section B of the Manifest and pass on all necessary documents to consignee	Complete Section C of the Manifest and forward appropriate copies to prescribed persons
Identify the physical state of the waste, shipping name, waste identification number, classification, packing group, quantity shipped, number of packages and special handling and emergency instructions	Display appropriate safety marks in proper manner and location Replace any safety marks that are damaged or lost while the consignment is in the carrier's charge Refuse consignments of dangerous goods that are offered for transport which do not meet the requirements of the regulation	Identify the quantity of waste, any discrepancy, (e.g. leaking containers), whether the waste has been refused for any reason, and whether or not decontamination of the vehicle was required Meet the requirements of a consignor when returning empty packages, containers or vehicles that are not purged or cleaned

5.0

Assessing and Remediating Contaminated Property

5.1 OVERVIEW

Few environmental issues have grown in importance as rapidly as those concerning the identification, assessment, and remediation of contaminated property. There are likely thousands of properties in Ontario where current soil or ground water quality could be considered to be "contaminated." Many of these properties are in areas where there are strong demands for redevelopment. When and how these properties are remediated will be influenced strongly by how the goals of remediation are defined and the responsibilities for remediating are distributed.

Numerous factors have contributed to the growing importance of contamination issues. Some originate in regulatory requirements. For example, the Environmental Protection Act contains the "no-excuse accountability" present in much of the new environmental legislation. It clearly places responsibility for making a site "acceptable" upon the current owner. (Previous owners also can be held responsible.) If a contaminated site is owned by a corporation or a site becomes contaminated as a result of the actions of a corporation, the individual officers of the corporation can be liable. As described later in this chapter, recent court decisions indicate that the liabilities associated with contaminated property can extend beyond owners to lenders, tenants, site managers, future owners, and others.

At the same time, some aspects of the regulatory framework for contaminated property are missing or incomplete. For example, the numerical guidelines or criteria used in Ontario to determine environmental "acceptability" address relatively few contaminants.

Other factors stem from changes in social expectations. These reflect the general heightened awareness of the public to environmental concerns. Increasingly, members of the public want to be informed about situations such as soil or ground water contamination, and be given opportunities to comment on remediation or redevelopment plans. Finally, there are factors that are technological in nature. For example, many methods for remediating contaminated sites are in the developmental or demonstration stage, but few have been approved for use in Ontario. This need for approved technologies is compounded by the rapidly declining availability of options frequently used in the past such as excavation and off-site disposal.

Collectively, these conditions pose several obstacles to the buying, selling, leasing, remediating, and redeveloping of contaminated property. They also clearly illustrate the need for current property owners to protect the environmental quality of their sites. While there are several initiatives in progress which will eventually clarify various facets of this issue, it is anticipated that the remediation, redevelopment, and transfer of contaminated property will continue to be hampered by uncertainty and lack of precedent for several years.

5.2 THE REGULATORY FRAMEWORK

5.2.1 Provincial Legislation

While all three levels of government are involved in contaminated sites issues, this is largely a matter of provincial jurisdiction. Given the relatively recent growth in importance of site contamination issues, it is not surprising that many aspects of site assessment and remediation are sparsely addressed in provincial statutes and regulations.

When Part X (Spills) of the Ontario Environmental Protection Act (EPA) came into effect in 1985, it had the effect of creating two categories of contaminated sites (when viewed from the perspectives of assigning responsibilities to remediate and providing the MOEE with the means to encourage prompt remediation). One category includes all sites where the contamination has been caused by spills that began after 29 November 1985. For those cases, Section 93 of the EPA clearly imposes a duty to restore the environment upon the owner or the person having charge of the pollutant that is spilled. Other sections in Part X of the EPA authorize the Minister to order clean-ups, take whatever remedial actions are necessary, and to sue the person(s) responsible for the costs.

The second category includes all sites contaminated by events other than spills and all sites contaminated before 29 November 1985. Section 17 of the EPA authorizes MOEE directors to issue remedial orders for contaminated sites regardless of when the contamination occurred. Such an order can be issued to "the person who causes or permits the discharge of a contaminant into the natural environment". Recent court decisions indicate that responsible persons can include past and present owners, tenants, site managers, and operators of properties.

There is no automatic obligation to remediate contaminated sites that fall into this second category. It is possible for a site to be contaminated for many years before an owner or the MOEE is aware of the contamination. (This is most likely to be true where the contamination is relatively immobile, present at only "mild" levels of contamination, limited in physical extent, or otherwise kept distant from neighbouring properties or receptors.) The resources of the MOEE do not allow it to seek out or investigate potentially contaminated properties except when prompted by circumstances such as looking for the cause of a contaminated water supply (i.e. when an adverse effect has been noted).

Despite these limitations, the number of properties in Ontario being investigated has increased rapidly in recent years, and large sums have been paid to clean up some properties. These actions largely have been in response to the growing desire of owners, purchaser, lenders, and insurers to avoid the potential liabilities that contaminated property can pose. In addition to these market forces, the MOEE can become aware of contaminated property via several regulatory processes:

- When a change in land use or municipal plan amendment is proposed, the MOEE may be asked by the municipality or the Ministry of Municipal Affairs to comment on the suitability of the site for the proposed use. The MOEE can recommend to the approving authority to withhold approval of a land use change unless certain site conditions are met.
- Like municipalities, some conservation authorities and federal agencies will ask the MOEE for opinions of environmental suitability of proposed projects and applications.
- If a project is the subject of the environmental assessment process, the MOEE may recommend that site assessment and/or remediation be required as conditions to the approval or exemption of the project.

While the general intent of the EPA is to have persons responsible for contamination to restore the environment, the ability to do so has been hampered by uncertainty about clean-up objectives and goals. Missing from the EPA are quantifiable definitions of contamination, ways to determine when clean up is necessary, and ways to determine when clean-up activities should be terminated. These deficiencies, which are described in greater detail in Sections 5.3 through 5.7, have led to considerable confusion and in some cases unwillingness to proceed with remediation.

Two other pieces of provincial legislation require remediation where petroleum products have been released from storage tanks. Both are administered by the Ministry of Consumer and Commercial Relations (MCCR). The Fuel Oil Code, which is Regulation 329 under the Energy

Act, applies to storage tanks for standby generators and heating systems. Section 4 of the Code requires that the owner of a supply tank shall ensure that escaped fuel oil is recovered and contaminated soil is removed forthwith. Section 5 of the Code states that where the soil around an underground tank is contaminated with oil from the tank, the contaminated soil should be removed. The Code does not define "contamination."

General Regulation 521/93 under the Gasoline Handling Act applies to the storage of petroleum products (except storage tanks regulated under the Energy Act). Section 17 of the Regulation adopts the Gas Handling Code as part of the Regulation. The Code imposes numerous requirements upon owners and operators of tanks used to store petroleum products. Sections 5, 7, and 8 require the removal of all contamination during removal or replacement of storage tanks. Section 12 authorizes MCCR directors to request that remediation reports be prepared and corrective actions taken. The level of remediation to be achieved on the property where the tank is located is outlined in the document entitled *Interim Guidelines for the Assessment and Management of Petroleum Contaminated Sites* (MCCR, 1993). (This document is described further in Section 5.3.) The level of remediation beyond the site should result in conditions similar to those found adjacent to the property in areas not contaminated by the spill or leak. Upon completion of remediation, the director can request that a confirmatory report be submitted.

5.2.2 Municipal Legislation

Most municipal government agencies defer to the MOEE on site assessment and remediation issues; however, this pattern is changing in some urban areas. For example, during the past few years the Environmental Protection Office of the Toronto Health Department has reviewed numerous site assessment studies and remediation plans. Municipal agencies in other cities and regions also are becoming more involved in remediation, particularly when it is part of a redevelopment proposal or when the lands are owned by a municipality.

5.2.3 Federal Legislation

Federal agencies participate in soil resource issues in several ways. Various federal agencies are responsible for facilities such as international airports, harbours, federal research facilities, and defence facilities including any environmental assessment or remediation that may be required. Federal agencies are responsible for establishing clean-up requirements for radioactive materials if associated with nuclear fuel cycles and specifically regulated substances such as polychlorinated biphenyls (PCBs). Environmental quality criteria developed by federal programs or bodies such as the Canadian Council of Ministers of the Environment are described in Section 5.3.4.

5.3 ENVIRONMENTAL QUALITY CRITERIA AND GUIDELINES

5.3.1 The Role of Ambient (Background) Concentrations

In principle, remedial action is required wherever contaminants are present at concentrations above ambient (background) levels. The MOEE defines ambient or background concentrations as the level of a substance in the local area. Often it is necessary to undertake a sampling program to determine these concentrations. There are situations in which background concentrations of parameters in soil or ground water are elevated throughout an area. Examples can include areas of mineralization and areas which have been used for industrial purposes for many years. Where this is the case, it may be necessary to collect samples from locations outside the immediate area of interest.

The MOEE has established Upper Limit of Normal (ULN) concentrations for some parameters in soil (see Table 5.1). ULN values represent the expected maximum concentrations of substances in surface soil from areas not subject to the influence of point sources of emissions. "Urban" ULN values are based on samples collected from centres with a minimum population of 10,000. "Rural" values are based on samples collected from areas that have not been developed. The MOEE has stressed that ULN values are not clean-up guidelines but serve as levels which if exceeded should prompt further investigation on a case-by-case basis to determine their significance (MOE, 1989b).

In 1990, an initiative was established at the MOEE to re-evaluate the ways that ULN values were determined and used. The decision was made to replace the ULNs with new guidelines referred to as Ontario Typical Range (OTR) values. The MOEE is working to establish OTRs for several types of samples (soil, vegetation, snow, etc.) in different types of environments (rural, urban), and for different types of land uses (residential, parkland, agricultural, commercial/industrial). As the OTR values are established, it is expected that they will be used in place of the ULNs in assessments of contamination. A draft report of OTR values was issued in 1992 and a final report is expected early in 1994. OTR values are incorporated into the proposed set of "soil placement guidelines" described in Section 5.3.3.

The MOEE suggests that background levels in water should be defined according to the objectives outlined in the MOEE document entitled *Water Management: Goals, Policies, Objectives and Implementation Procedures* (MOE, 1992a). This document does not provide much guidance for evaluating ground water quality, except perhaps where ground water enters surface water.

5.3.2 Options for Setting Clean-up Guidelines

Wherever soil or ground water has become contaminated and the contamination poses a threat to people or the environment, a series of questions inevitably emerges: Does the property need to be cleaned? What level of residual contamination is acceptable? These and other concerns often are expressed by the simple phrase "how clean is clean?". Unfortunately, the answer is not so simply stated. At present, few jurisdictions have established guidelines, and those that have address relatively few types of substances.

As noted in Section 5.3.1, remedial action may be required wherever contaminants are present at concentrations above ambient (background) levels; however, the MOEE identifies three basic options for developing clean-up guidelines above background levels provided that they are protective of human health and the environment (MOE, 1989a):

1 application of relevant MOEE policies and guidelines;

2 application of clean-up criteria developed in other jurisdictions, where appropriate;

3 development and application of site-specific guidelines.

If clean-up guidelines above background levels are proposed, specific reference must be made to the future use of the site. The MOEE typically considers five broad categories of land use: agricultural, residential, parkland, commercial, and industrial. Generally, more stringent clean-up requirements are need for agricultural, residential, and parkland redevelopment.

5.3.3 Using Relevant MOEE Policies and Guidelines

The most straightforward approach to selecting clean-up objectives is to use the guidelines and provisional guidelines presented in the MOEE publication entitled *Guidelines for the Decommissioning and Clean-up of Sites in Ontario* (MOE, 1989a). The MOEE has developed soil guidelines for the 22 parameters listed in Table 5.2. Initially recommended by the Phytotoxicity Section of the Air Resources Branch, many of the values are based primarily on phytotoxicological considerations. Some are based on human health or the health of grazing animals. The guidelines do not address specific organic compounds. Table 5.3 presents the interim soil quality guidelines that the MOEE has adopted for dioxins and furans (MOE, 1990) and for PCBs (MOE, 1988).

In 1992, the MOEE issued guidelines for remediating petroleum contamination at commercial sites in Ontario. The document subsequently was reissued in 1993 to address all types of fuel outlets and bulk transfer stations (MOEE, 1993). The same document also was issued by the MCCR (1993). Both documents provide guidelines for benzene, toluene, ethylbenzene, and xylenes (four common, volatile components of petroleum fuels) and for total petroleum hydrocarbon. As shown in Table 5.4, three guidelines are specified for each contaminant. Determining which of the three guidelines to used is based upon the sensitivity of the site. Sensitivity is a function of the distance to the nearest user of ground water and the hydraulic conductivity of subsurface materials. The guidelines and the method of determining site sensitivity are patterned after guidelines drafted by Alberta Environment (Alberta MUST, 1990).

Other MOEE policies that can be used to establish clean-up guidelines include:

- provincial objectives for surface water quality if contaminants are reaching surface waters such as a river or lake via ground water (see Section 3.2)
- provincial drinking water quality objectives if contaminants are present in local ground water which is used as a drinking water source (see Section 3.2)
- the appropriate sewer-use by-law if contaminants are reaching the local sewer system (for example, the MOEE Model Sewer-Use By-law or the Toronto Sewer-Use By-law as described in Section 3.5)
- policies and guidelines related to resolving ground water quality problems (see MOEE, 1994; MOE, 1992a; MOE, 1986); and
- Regulation 346 concerning emissions to the atmosphere (see Section 2.2)

In addition to the numerical guidelines shown in Table 5.3 and 5.4, the MOEE has aesthetic guidelines which are based upon qualities such as appearance and odours. The aesthetic guidelines used to assess soil quality during the decommissioning of two former petroleum refinery sites near Toronto included (Reades, 1989):

- absolutely no remaining refinery-related odours in the soil
- no discolouration or staining of soil
- no hydrocarbons or sheen if a soil sample is placed in water

In 1992, the MOEE proposed a policy for managing "excess materials" which would include excavated soil (MOE, 1992b). The policy provides new guidance for determining where excess materials can be placed. It also recommends that more chemical parameters be considered when characterizing soils than the 22 noted in the decommissioning guideline document. One of the principal reasons given by the MOEE for recommending the new soil placement guidelines (SPGs) is to avoid sending relatively uncontaminated soils to municipal landfills. As of March 1994, the Minister had not announced whether the proposed policy would be adopted.

Late in 1993, the MOEE announced a series of possible changes to the existing soil quality guidelines and the ways in which the guidelines are to be used. The proposed changes included:

- a greatly expanded list of parameters
- the use of a more rigorous and effects-based rationale to derive the guidelines
- consistency with other guidelines such as those presented in MOEE, 1993
- guidelines that vary according to whether or not local ground water is used as a source of potable water, and
- soil guidelines that are less stringent for some parameters at depths beyond 1.5 m (provided that the extent of remediation is registered on title)

Other implications of the proposed changes are described in Sections 5.5 and 5.6. The MOEE anticipates that the new guideline for managing contaminated sites will be ready for implementation by mid-1994. Supporting documents that describe the underlying rationale in detail and that present sampling and analytical protocols are planned to be issued in 1994.

5.3.4 Using Soil Guidelines Developed in Other Jurisdictions

This option is most likely to be used when provincial guidelines have not been established for the contaminants being encountered at a site. Proponents of guidelines from other jurisdictions must be sure that the methodology(s) used to derive those values are consistent with the over-all MOEE objective of establishing criteria that are fully protective of human health and the environment.

Table 5.5 lists several documents that contain guidelines from other jurisdictions. Some of these guidelines have been developed for use at specific sites, others are for certain types of sites, and yet others are intended for broad application. Proponents need to review any statements from the developers of the guidelines concerning their application or interpretation before values are proposed for a specific site.

The Canadian Council of Ministers of the Environment (CCME) started a process in 1990 to develop site assessment and remediation criteria suitable for use at "orphan" sites (those for which a responsible party cannot be identified) across Canada. One of the first products of this effort is a set of interim environmental criteria for soil and ground water (CCME, 1991). The "assessment" criteria of the CCME can be used to assess the degree of contamination at a site and to determine the need for further action. The "remediation" criteria can be used to determine if further investigation or remediation is needed. The development of scientifically defensible guidelines is an ongoing process. As specific parameters are reviewed, criteria may be revised and/or the "interim" modifier removed. The CCME also is investigating ways to advise potential users how to modify the criteria to specific sites and the ways that site-specific criteria might be established.

Regulatory agencies from other provinces have established guidelines for parameters not addressed by the MOEE. Three examples include the guidelines from the British Columbia Ministry of Environment, Lands, and Parks; the Ministère de l'Environnement du Québec (MENVIQ); and Alberta Environment.

Examples of agencies from other countries that can be sources of guidelines include several specific U.S. states. (The U.S. EPA prefers that soil quality criteria be set by individual states). One of the most frequently cited efforts concerning soil quality guidelines are the "ABC" values developed by a federal ministry in The Netherlands (Moen, 1988).

5.3.5 Developing Site-Specific Guidelines

For situations where the MOEE has not established clean-up guidelines, the party(s) responsible for the assessment or remediation of a property can choose to develop site-specific guidelines. Obviously, the onus is on the proponent to undertake whatever effort is required and to demonstrate that the proposed values are sufficiently protective of the environment and human health. Efforts in that regard should consider the following issues:

- environmental mobility of the contaminants of concern
- the pathways by which the contaminants of concern may impact on human health or the environment
- the risks posed to human health
- the risks posed to non-human site users such as terrestrial or aquatic species of plants and animals
- anticipated future uses of the site
- surrounding land uses
- possible synergistic or antagonistic effects of the contaminants of concern
- possible exposures to off-site receptors by pathways such as diet or water supplies
- physical features and environmental conditions of the site such as soil type, ground water regime, local meteorology
- background concentrations of contaminants
- possible phytotoxicological effects
- possible aesthetic considerations
- compatibility with other relevant environmental guidelines or criteria

Risk assessment and management are likely to be major components of efforts to develop site-specific guidelines. Such techniques appear to

offer a more defensible alternative than some of the methods that historically have been used such as basing guidelines on analytical detection
limits, background conditions, or technological capabilities. Failure to
consider risks can result in limited resources being used to reduce
already low levels of risk at one situation while higher risks go unattend-
ed at other situations.

While the phrase "how clean is clean" often has been used in the past
to discuss clean-up requirements, a more appropriate phrase might be
"how clean is fair" when risk assessment and management techniques are
to be used. In this context, the concept of fairness must address several
aspects including the costs that will be incurred by those who will pay
for the clean-up, the risks that will be experienced by site users and
neighbours as a result of residual contaminants that may remain after
clean-up, and the benefits that will be realized by the owners of the site
and possibly future site users or neighbours. (Chapter 11 describes the
way(s) in which risk assessment and management can be used to resolve
environmental issues.) While it would be misleading to present risk management as a panacea for resolving complex issues, it is equally true that
risk management is critical to identifying cost-effective actions and ensuring that resources are used efficiently.

To date, site-specific guidelines have only been developed for a few
sites in Ontario. One of the better-known of these efforts culminated in
the development of values for two former petroleum refinery sites west
of Toronto (ICCC, 1988).

Among the possible changes in contaminated site management guidelines announced by the MOEE late in 1993 is the possibility that this
option will need to be used for some conditions (i.e. when there are no
guidelines for the contaminants of concern and at sites where existing
guidelines may not be sufficiently protective of sensitive environments or
receptors) but not be available for other types of conditions. Whether this
change is adopted by the MOEE should be known by mid-1994.

5.4   ASSESSING SITE CONDITIONS

5.4.1 Recent Trends towards Standardizing Terminology

Over the past few years, the potential problems, responsibilities, and
costs associated with owning contaminated land has resulted in many
financial institutions avoiding any situations where there is even a suspicion of contamination. To minimize the chance of unknowingly taking on
the responsibilities of owning or financing contaminated land, advisors to
potential owners (including lawyers, lenders, and property managers) are
requiring that certain types of environmental information be reviewed as
a prerequisite to closing property transfers.

Many terms have been used to describe this gathering of environmental information including site inspection, site assessment, site evaluation, site characterization, site audit, property audit, real estate audit, historical audit, and transaction audit. Efforts are underway in Canada and elsewhere (notably the United States) to standardize the terminology and tasks for various types of site assessment studies. From these efforts, the terms "transaction screen" and "environmental site assessment" (ESA) are gaining wide acceptance; however, buyers and sellers of site assessment services need to ensure that there is a clear understanding of the work to be done prior to undertaking such activities. (Environmental audits are discussed in Chapter 10.)

5.4.2 Transaction Screen

A transaction screen (sometimes referred to as a Phase 0 ESA) usually takes the form of a questionnaire about current and past activities at a site. The questions are phrased so that simple "yes", "no", or "don't know" answers will suffice. The screens often are developed by financial institutions for use by in-house staff. The results indicate whether a transaction should proceed, stop, or requires further assessment by environmental professionals.

Examples of questions that might be addressed in a transaction screen are presented in Table 5.6. A positive response to any of the questions should raise a red flag and hence require a more detailed assessment (i.e. a Phase I or Phase II ESA). The more red flags, the greater is the need to consult with environmental specialists.

5.4.3 Phase I Environmental Site Assessment

A Phase I ESA typically consists of four tasks:

- gathering information about past and present activities and uses of the site
- an inspection of the site by an environmental professional, usually accompanied by someone familiar with the property (i.e. a site manager, plant manager, or long-time employee)
- a review of environmental files maintained by the site owner and regulatory agencies
- the preparation of a report that identifies existing and potential sources of contamination on the property

A Phase I ESA report may also identify the types of studies needed to confirm or deny suspected conditions. It is important to note that Phase I ESAs do not include the collection of any samples for analysis or the taking of any measurements.

The **review of historical information** can offer clues as to the types of contaminants that might be at a site and locations where contamination is most likely be found. Some types of industrial activities are recognized as being probable sources of contamination. These include coal gasification works, salvage yards, rail spurs and maintenance yards, petroleum refineries, fuel storage and distribution facilities, metal foundries, metal-plating operations, wood-preserving facilities, leather tanneries, chemical producers, pesticide manufacturers, and paint and ink manufacturers.

Transfers of ownership can complicate the review of historical information. With each new owner, the clues by which contamination can be identified may become more difficult to uncover. The title search that often is a legal prerequisite for a transfer of ownership can identify previous owners of a property and the types of activities which may have occurred on the site. Legal title searches often extend back 40 years. This may not be sufficient for a Phase I ESA where historical information sources (such as aerial photographs, military maps, fire-insurance plans, and municipal directories) should be traced back to the point that there is a long period of agricultural use or non-use.

Ground water is a special concern wherever it is used as a drinking water supply. Attention should always be paid when reviewing historical information to possible off-site migration of contaminated ground water. The legal and financial consequences of off-site contamination are much greater and more complicated than on-site contamination.

The overall objectives of a **site inspection** are to develop a general appreciation for site layout and activities. At properties where chemicals are used or stored, a general understanding should be developed of all chemicals used, the ways in which chemicals may be released to the environment (i.e. emission release points), and all chemical handling and waste-management procedures.

Even at properties where activities do not involve the use, storage, or production of chemicals, there are numerous conditions that need to be noted during a Phase I ESA. The topography or physical layout of the property should be checked for obvious signs of waste-disposal practices such as lagoons, pits, ponds, or standing water. Note should be made of areas with sparse vegetation since the presence of contaminants can impede plant growth.

Facilities should be checked for the presence of any hazardous materials (as defined by Regulation 347) or designated substances (as defined by the Ministry of Labour). All PCB-containing equipment such as transformers and capacitors should be identified. Any equipment no longer in service must be stored in properly designed facilities (see Section 7.1). Asbestos (a generic term that applies to naturally occurring hydrated mineral silicates) was used extensively for ceiling and floor tiles, pipe insulation, cement and insulating materials. The presence of asbestos-containing materials (ACM) will complicate and increase the costs of demolition or clean-up efforts.

Storage tanks and piping can be the source of leaks and contaminated soil and/or ground water. Underground storage tanks often are indicated by the presence of vent or filler pipes. Leaking tanks can go undetected for several years. It has been estimated that approximately 20% of all underground storage tanks have leaked (Rush and Metzger, 1991).

Finally, any activities on nearby properties that have the potential to adversely affect the surrounding environment should be noted.

A **review of company files and records** can provide information on site conditions and the environmental performance of a facility. Files to review include previously prepared ESA reports or environmental audits, reports of incidents such as spills or unscheduled releases, and waste manifests and chemical-use records.

Environmental audit files can provide an account of how well a company has complied with environmental requirements. Conversely, audit reports may ignore significant environmental risks at a facility (e.g. inadequate spill containment or prevention at a discharge adjacent to a sensitive fish habitat). Reviews of past documents must consider the terms of references of those who prepared the previous reports.

Records of waste manifests and chemical inventories/purchases should allow a list to be prepared of the chemicals used, stored, or produced at the facility.

Under the Freedom of Information Act, any citizen has the ability to request and **review MOEE files**. Information regarding processes/chemicals, the names of individuals registered on complaints, and information used in a current court proceeding may be confidential.

An MOEE "approval" file may contain Certificates of Approval for air emissions, water discharges and waste treatment, and/or disposal systems. The certificates for solid waste stored on-site should be critically reviewed for the types of chemicals stored, volumes, and the abatement technology employed to stop ground water contamination, if any. An approval file should also contain violation notices, control orders, or tickets issued under the EPA (see Section 8.5). The file may contain information concerning unscheduled releases of contaminants onto the property.

The MOEE also maintains "complaint" files. For contaminated property, these files will provide little information as they often are focused on issues such as odour or noise. Some complaints, however, can help in the assessment (e.g. the detection of odour and/or colour in well water or runoff to an adjacent property).

The MOEE Spills Action Centre should be contacted for information about spills on the subject property and adjacent properties (see Chapter 12).

Another potential source of information is the MOEE Public Information Dataset which contains summarized information about the generators, carriers, and receivers of hazardous and liquid industrial waste. The Dataset is updated annually.

Interviews with knowledgeable personnel can provide information regarding on-site contaminants which may not have been recorded. Informal discussions with long-time plant personnel can identify past practices or unusual events, such as spills that should be investigated further. Interviews with neighbours may be useful, especially if on-site activities cause odours, dust, noise, or other conditions that tend to be noticed by neighbours. Some judgments, however, may be required to separate the facts from fiction.

Phase I ESA reports should identify existing and potential sources of contamination on the property, document all findings, indicate the relative degree of uncertainty associated with evidence of potential contamination, describe steps that could be taken to confirm, refute, or delineate contamination (i.e. Phase II ESA activities), and provide preliminary estimates of the costs associated with those steps. Facts should be clearly distinguished from opinion (CSA, 1993).

5.4.4 Phase II Environmental Site Assessment

While Phase I ESAs rely on existing information, the focus of Phase II ESAs is to gather new information about a property. Phase II ESA tasks can include:

• collecting and analyzing environmental samples
• directly measuring environmental conditions such as noise levels or radiation
• comparing the analytical data and measurements to environmental quality criteria to determine the types of contaminants present, the physical extent of contaminants present, and the potential volumes of material that may need to be treated, removed, or otherwise managed, and
• using environmental fate or transportation models to evaluate the potential implications of the contamination

Initial **sampling** efforts should be based on information (typically gathered during a Phase I ESA) about historical and current operations at the site, observations made during a site inspection, the results of previous sampling, and the future use of the site. Numerous sample-gathering techniques are available. Factors such as the type(s) of material to be samples (such as soil, ground water, etc.), the accessibility of the materials to be sampled (i.e. whether they are located at or near the surface, at substantial depths, beneath buildings, etc.), and the type(s) of analyses to be performed will influence the selection of sample-gathering techniques.

Monitoring wells can be used to study the hydrogeology of a site and the potential extent of ground water contamination. Monitoring wells are required for determining water levels, ground water flow directions, and ground water quality.

Boreholes are one of the most commonly used ways to investigate the physical and chemical quality of soil strata. Test pits can often give a more complete picture of local stratigraphy, but are best-suited when depths of interest are shallow (less than 3 m), and the surface disruption associated with test pits is not a concern. Test pits may not reveal contamination that occurs in thin layers or is of a low level (Reades, 1989).

Geotechnical investigations conducted primarily for construction purposes may provide data regarding the extent of any contamination at a site. In addition, observations made during excavation for building additions, the installation of utilities or for the removal of pipelines or underground structures are not only relevant, but provide an indication of the potential extent of contamination (Reades, 1989).

Non-disruptive investigations using geophysical techniques such as near-surface conductivity surveys and total field (proton) magnetometer surveys can be used to delineate buried metallic objects such as tanks, drums, pipelines, and debris. All of the anomalies should be thoroughly examined prior to excavating since anomalies can be induced by nearby objects such as buildings, fences, and surface debris.

While most sampling programs generate samples that are taken off-site for analysis, there are a growing number of options for on-site monitoring. For example, it has become commonplace to use an organic vapour analyzer to measure organic compounds during field programs. Vapours can be analyzed quickly in soil or ground water samples by analyzing the headspace that develops in sample containers or by analyzing the vapours from soil samples as they are obtained from boreholes or test pits. Other on-site monitoring techniques include test kits which are being developed to address an increasing number of parameters and the use of portable gas chromatographs.

For the initial phase of sampling programs, it may be cost-effective to analyze samples for indicator parameters such as pH, total organic carbon, total organic halogens, total oil and grease, or Analytical Test Group 9 (metal scan). The results of these analysis should indicate if further sampling is required. There may need to be more than one campaign of sample gathering and analysis with subsequent campaigns used to improve the delineation of contamination.

Off-site sampling of adjacent surface water into which a facility's direct discharge or storm water flows may be appropriate in some cases. In addition, surface water should also be sampled at locations where ground water emerges.

Phase II ESA reports should document all findings and criteria used to define contamination, indicate the methods used to estimate the volume(s) of contaminated materials present, present preliminary options for managing the contamination, describe steps that could be taken to develop a remediation plan. Although remediation planning sometimes is referred to as a Phase III ESA (with implementation of the plan being called Phase IV ESA), that terminology is somewhat misleading and not as helpful as the preferred terms "remediation planning and implementation" (which are described below).

5.5 REMEDIATION

5.5.1 When Is Remediation Necessary?

Remediation can be broadly defined as the actions taken to manage contamination. These actions can include physical actions (such as the destruction, removal, isolation, or immobilization of contaminants) or administrative actions (such as restricted site access, signs, attachments to title, the "holding" designation in municipal plans).

The need for remediation usually is prefaced upon the findings of an ESA, environmental audit, or an accidental release of a substance. The evidence most often cited as demonstrating the need for remediation is concentrations of substances (usually in site soil or ground water) that exceed whatever guidelines or criteria are appropriate to use.

The reasons for remediation can include the need to improve conditions as a prerequisite for changing land use (see Section 5.7 - Decommissioning); as a means of preventing contamination from migrating off-property (and avoiding the various types of liability that such a condition can pose); the desire to improve property value and/or the ability to show that a property is "clean"; or the desire to avoid possible future liability (if the site was suspected to be a source of adverse effects).

The possible changes in contaminated site management guidelines announced by the MOEE late in 1993 include the dividing of the remediation process into four phases:

- Phase I would be "Property Assessment" and would consist of the activities described above for a Phase I ESA
- Phase II would be "Site Investigation and Sampling" and would consist of the activities described above for a Phase II ESA
- Phase III would be "Site Clean-up Plan" and would consist of the activities described in the next two subsections, and
- Phase IV would be "Formal Reporting and MOEE Acknowledgement" and would consist of the activities described in Section 5.5.4

5.5.2 Remediation Planning

Many kinds of information may be needed to plan remediation activities. The kinds of information required concern the types of contaminants present and their locations; site conditions such as soil type(s) present and depth to ground water table; the clean-up objectives to be achieved; capabilities of the option(s) to be used; etc. Even with that information, it still will be necessary to strike a balance in terms of costs, schedules, the degree to which options have been proven, etc.

At all but relatively simple sites, more than one remediation option may be needed to address contamination. It may also be necessary to clean certain portions of a site or specific contaminants before other problems can be addressed. The considerations of timing, sequencing, logistics, and combining (either in series or in parallel) various technologies all need to be taken into account in planning remediation. As noted in Section 5.5.1, remediation plans can include options other than those that remove contaminants. Other types of options can include isolating contaminants (so that they are immobile in the environment), on-site or off-site storage, or pairing future use to clean-up efforts (for example, in areas where a clean-up to meet residential requirements is difficult, it may be designated for commercial/industrial use).

Remediation planning often will begin by reviewing numerous options and identifying those that appear to be best suited for application to a specific site. Several dozen options are available for soil and a similar number of options are available for ground water (see Section 5.6.2). Factors that may need to be considered when selecting options include the ability of technologies to meet clean-up guidelines; the time required to implement and carry out the clean-up; the risks to workers and neighbours during clean-up; and costs.

Procedures such as environmental fate modelling, pathways analysis, risk assessment, and financial analysis may be used to evaluate various aspects of a site remediation plan. The results produced by these procedures may need to be reviewed by regulatory agencies such as the MOEE. For many remediation technologies, bench-scale and/or pilot-scale investigations will be needed to demonstrate their effectiveness, to develop detailed plans for full-scale implementation, and/or gather data necessary to receive certificates of approval.

5.5.3 Implementation

While implementation is the phase of remediation in which much of the physical work gets done, it also is a relatively straightforward phase if site assessment and remediation planning have been done carefully. There are numerous companies (also referred to as contractors or vendors) that provide treatment, disposal, and storage services. Independent inspectors may be used while remediation efforts are underway.

Before a plan can be implemented, environmental approvals may be required. The approvals will not be for the plan *per se* but for any releases of contaminants to the environment caused by activities of the plan. Approvals may be needed that address the atmospheric emissions of activities, the treatment or disposal of waste waters or residues produced, and noise levels along the site boundary. Before the MOEE issues approvals, sufficient information characterizing the releases must be submitted and reviewed. Obtaining approvals for various types of options is a major area of uncertainty currently surrounding the remediation of contaminated sites.

Toward the completion of the site remediation plan, soil and/or ground water monitoring can be used to verify that clean-up objectives have been met. The MOEE should be provided with the results of the verification testing. In some instances, the MOEE may want to conduct its own verification testing.

5.5.4 Documentation/Registration

At the conclusion of implementing the site remediation plan, a final comprehensive report should be submitted to MOEE. Reports prepared during site assessment or remediation planning can be used to facilitate producing the final report.

Once clean-up is complete, the MOEE will provide a written statement that outlines the level of clean-up achieved at a site if requested to do so. Such a **statement of completion** in no way amounts to the MOEE accepting liability for any problems that may arise at the site. A copy of the statement may be forwarded to other agencies or attached to the title of the property.

Among the possible changes in contaminated site management guidelines announced by the MOEE late in 1993 is the possibility that this task may represent the only formal reporting requirement for remediation activities (aside from obtaining Cs of A, if necessary). Where full clean-up has been achieved, the MOEE may issue an "acknowledgement letter." Where the less stringent guidelines being considered by the MOEE for some contaminants at depths beyond 1.5 m are used, the MOEE may issue a Director's Order to be registered on title. Whether these changes are adopted by the MOEE should be known by mid-1994.

5.6 REMEDIATION OPTIONS

5.6.1 Options for Remediating Soil

Many ways to manage contaminated soil have been developed in response to the multitude of contaminants and site conditions that are possible. Continuing research and development efforts are expected to expand the number of available options. Discussions of these options can be simplified by grouping the options according to common, basic characteristics. Six categories are used in the following discussion which only briefly touches upon clean-up technologies that are available or are in the process of being developed. There is extensive documentation for virtually each of the technologies and the amount of literature is growing rapidly as demonstrations and actual applications are published.

Off-site Disposal – This category involves removing material from a property without prior treatment. Excavation and off-site disposal of contaminated soils long has been the most commonly used option in Ontario. The type of facility to which the excavated soil should be taken is determined by the types of contaminants present, their concentrations, and their leachability (ability to solubilize and be transported by ground water). For example, material classified as "hazardous waste" using the Regulation 347 leachate test must be disposed at a hazardous waste management facility. The only such facility currently in Ontario is located near Sarnia. Less contaminated materials can be suitable for disposal at municipal landfills.

Destruction – The options in this category destroy organic contaminants. The options usually involve converting the contaminants to other, usually simpler, forms such as water, carbon dioxide, and acid gases. Most destruction methods generate intermediate products (vapours, ash, or wastewater) that need to be managed. Many of the methods can be implemented in place (*in situ*), in reactor vessels (typically large tanks), or off-site. Some are limited to taking place off-site at treatment facilities.

Bioremediation refers to the destruction of organic contaminants in soil and ground water through microbial degradation. Indigenous microorganisms can be used to degrade or detoxify most organic materials, as can non-indigenous bacteria specifically designed to metabolize particular compounds or classes of compounds. Bioremediation options can be applied to soil *in situ*, in a prepared soil bed (e.g. land farming), or in a reactor tank.

All bioremediation options require the careful monitoring and adjusting of nutrients (phosphorus, nitrogen, sulphates, trace minerals, etc.) and oxygen, as well the control of water content, pH, and soil temperature. These factors are more easily controlled in reactor tanks than *in situ*. Bioremediation options have the potential to create noxious or hazardous gases and/or leachable biodegradation products.

Chemical destruction options employ the chemical reactivity of the contaminant to alter the form of the material or destroy it completely and render it inert or less reactive. Thermal destruction options use extreme temperature to destroy organic soil contaminants via combustion. The emissions are chiefly gases (such as carbon dioxide), water, and acid gases such as sulphur dioxide and nitrous oxides.

Separation – This category of options involves separating the contaminants from the soil by transferring the contaminants to another media such as air, liquid, or solid. Most separation options take advantage of the physical properties of contaminants such as their volatility, solubility, or density. The media that receive the contaminants usually need to be managed.

Volatilization transfers the contaminant from the soil or the ground water to air spaces present in the soil, which subsequently is collected for release or treatment. Solubilization transfers the contaminant from the soil to a liquid (often ground water) which subsequently is collected for release or treatment. Adsorption separates contaminants from soil by physically binding the contaminants to an inert material that can be subsequently removed. The contaminants can be stripped from the inert material so as to regenerate and recycle the inert material.

Electrokinetics applies an electrical field to soil, causing a complex set of phenomena to occur. The two principal effects are electroosmosis (fluids and dissolved species are forced through stationary media) and electrophoresis (solid particles are induced to move through a stationary fluid). Electroosmosis potentially is more important to site remediation.

Immobilization – The options in this category use physical or chemical processes that permanently solidify or immobilize the contaminants present in soil. These processes prevent the contaminants from migrating into the ground water or air.

Solidification usually involves the production of solid blocks of material in which the contaminants are permanently, physically locked. Stabilization involves adding materials that ensure the contaminants are converted and maintained in their least mobile form. Encapsulation methods coat or enclose contaminants with a non-permeable substance.

Isolation – In this category, contaminated soil is neither treated or removed from the site. The soil can be excavated and placed in surface storage facilities or left in place and isolated from the environment by the use of physical barriers such as impermeable liners, caps, and walls.

Re-use – This category involves either the conversion of contaminated soil into a useful product (such as asphalt) or to use the soil as fill material where it is acceptable to do so.

5.6.2 Options for Remediating Ground Water

Many of the technologies used to remediate soils have analogous versions for treating ground water. Several of these options involve bringing the water to the surface and having it flow through a container or tank where a treatment process occurs. Collectively, these are referred to as **pump and treat** approaches. Types of treatment processes can include bioremediation, adding chemicals that destroy contaminants, air stripping (a form of enhanced volatilization), adsorption, and the use of ultraviolet light (to break down organic contaminants by photolysis). Treated water may be discharged to the sewer system or surface water if its quality is acceptable. Alternatively, treated water may be re-injected into the ground to assist with the movement of ground water. Atmospheric emissions from the treatment component may need to be monitored, and/or require treatment of the off-gases before release.

All pump and treat approaches work best in permeable soils. Non-homogeneous conditions in the subsurface can prevent clean-up of pockets of contamination. Even in homogeneous soils, "residual" contamination held in place by interstitial forces can act as a long-term source of contamination. As a result, there are many cases of pump and treat efforts continuing for several years without reaching clean-up targets.

There also are techniques for treating ground water in place. Such techniques typically involve injecting chemicals to destroy contaminants or to encourage indigenous bacteria to degrade contaminants. *In situ* techniques are subject to many of the same limitations as pump and treat options.

Finally, there are techniques that can be used to limit the physical migration of contaminated ground water. These include the use of interceptor wells and the use of subsurface barriers (usually in combination with extraction wells).

5.6.3 The Current Status of Soil Remediation

Table 5.7 lists more than 20 remediation options that are used in Canada, the United States, and Europe. The options that are described as being "commonly used" in Ontario involve off-site disposal (at two types of facilities) and surface storage (which is used for PCB wastes across Canada).

It could be argued that biostimulation and subsurface containment also are commonly used options. Biostimulation has been used at landfarms for decades as a means of managing organic wastes, particularly at petroleum facilities, but that practice is now discouraged by the MOEE. Subsurface containment has been described as "not used" because most applications to date have been for geotechnical purposes, not to resolve concerns about contaminated soil.

Seven of the options in Table 5.7 are described as being "rarely used" in Ontario or being in the demonstration stage. They include two forms of bioremediation, dechlorination, soil vapour extraction, low temperature thermal desorption, and metal chelation. Some of the options in this group likely will assume increasingly important roles as they become better known to site clean-up managers and regulatory agencies.

The remaining options either have not been used in Ontario or their use is not well documented. Some of these options will need to overcome opposition from regulatory agencies and/or the public before they can be widely used. Examples include options that use thermal destruction (due to concerns about atmospheric emissions), immobilization (due to concerns about the long-term integrity of immobilized materials), and subsurface containment (due to concerns about the long-term integrity of the containment features).

The costs of the options listed in Table 5.7 range from $20/m^3 to more than $1000/m^3. Most of the options that destroy, remove, or immobilize contaminants in soil have costs in the range of $150 to $300/m^3. Such generalized costs are highly susceptible to misinterpretation and misuse; however, they are similar to those reported for U.S. Department of Energy sites (which often have relatively high degrees of contamination) where average costs in 1989 were reported to be $170/yd^3 (*Pollution Engineering*, 1992) or approximately $300/m^3 in current Canadian dollars.

All of the options shown in Table 5.7, except those classified as being commonly used, also face the challenge that the MOEE is reluctant to comment on the appropriateness of technologies when there is a lack of local experience and/or proven effectiveness. Several initiatives are underway that should help to address the lack of experience. At the federal level, the Development and Demonstration of Site Remediation Technology (DESRT) Program is designed to investigate, demonstrate, and test remediation technologies. Agreements have been reached between the federal government and several provinces, including Ontario, to use funds from this program to demonstrate clean-up technologies. The sites in Ontario where this funding is being applied include oily wastes and other by-products from burning rubber at a former tire storage compound in Hagersville that was the scene of an immense fire in 1990; a former waste oil transfer station in Smithville where the soil and ground water have been contaminated with PCBs; a site in Rednersville that was illegally used for the disposal of solvents and other hazardous wastes; and arsenic contamination at a gold mining and mineral processing operation at Deloro.

There is also the national Groundwater and Soil Remediation Program (GASReP), which is jointly sponsored by government and the petroleum industry. GASReP focuses on the development and assessment of technology for cleaning ground water and soil contaminated by petroleum hydrocarbons.

The MOEE has indicated a willingness to assist remediation technology vendors to obtain approvals for pilot projects that demonstrate new or innovative technologies. One example is metal chelation which was being demonstrated in 1992/1993 at two projects supported by the Environmental Technologies Program of the MOEE. Section 4 of the EPA provides the Minister with the option of establishing or operating experimental systems and may not require certain approvals for work that clearly is research or is experimental in nature.

5.7 DECOMMISSIONING

As noted in Section 5.5.1, remediation can be undertaken for several reasons, but it is most often discussed in the context of decommissioning, a broad term that most often refers to the permanent closing of an industrial facility (or part of a such facility) and whatever activities are required to make the site suitable for redevelopment or re-use. Those activities can include partial or total dismantling, demolition, and remediation. While some form of remediation is often necessary, it is not a mandatory component of decommissioning. Conversely, there are many examples of commercial and industrial facilities, where remediation is the critical and most expensive component of decommissioning.

The MOEE publication entitled *Guidelines for the Decommissioning and Clean-up of Sites in Ontario* (MOEE, 1989a) often is cited as the basic MOEE reference when proponents start to discuss site decommissioning in Ontario. The guidelines apply to the closing of any provincially, municipally, and privately owned site or facility at which environmental contamination has occurred. The document can also be used, as appropriate, where remedial action may be necessary to clean-up a site regardless of whether the facility is to be decommissioned. The MOEE has also indicated that the guidelines can be used when sites are offered for sale, even if a decommissioning is not anticipated or planned.

The guidelines do not apply to the closure of waste disposal sites or to other facilities if closure conditions have been stipulated in a Certificate of Approval issued for the site, or if terms and conditions have been attached to an exemption order issued under the Environmental Assessment Act, unless the approval or order identifies the guidelines as being applicable.

The MOEE suggests that decommissioning typically consists of four phases:

Phase I – Planning the Decommissioning
- prepare initial documentation that describes the site, preliminary inventory of potential contaminants, current zoning, and the proposed decommissioning/clean-up schedule
- initiate public communications and consultation
- identify clean-up guidelines to be used or develop site-specific values

Phase II – Designing and Implementing the Decommissioning/Site Clean-up

- design the remedial work program
- implement the remedial work program

Phase III – Verifying Completion of a Satisfactory Decommissioning/ Clean-up

- verify that objectives have been met
- inform regulatory agencies that decommissioning has been completed
- Phase IV – Signing Off (Statement of Completion)
- submit final comprehensive report to MOEE and local municipal office
- register on title documents created in previous phases
- MOEE can provide written statement of completion
- affidavit may be deposited on title setting out remaining matters of concern

The terminology used in MOEE decommissioning document may need to be amended to reflect the new definitions being assigned to other terms such as ESA and/or to become compatible with the terminology described in Section 5.5.1 that is being considered by the MOEE. A possible new structure could be:

- Phase I may be reworded to include the undertaking of Phase I and II ESAs as well as dismantling and demolition.
- Phase II might be divided into two phases: Remediation Planning and Implementation.
- Phase IV might be renamed Formal Reporting and/or Registration to better reflect the actual tasks at hand and be expanded to include the possibility of long-term monitoring (for sites where that may be required).

Regardless of the terminology used, each of the decommissioning phases can be subdivided into tasks similar to those discussed in Sections 5.4, 5.5, and 5.6. The proper sequence of tasks is highly site-specific, as is the timing of the overall process. A more detailed description of each phase is provided in the decommissioning document.

There is no requirement to notify the MOEE about decommissioning plans; however, there are several ways which the MOEE may become aware of such plans. The Employment Standards Act requires that the Ministry of Labour be informed of all employment terminations involving 50 or more employees. The Ministry of Labour will share this information with the MOEE. Regional MOEE staff usually will be aware of local decommissioning activities and plans. Concerned individuals or public organizations may inform the MOEE. If a change in land use is proposed, it will be necessary to describe to the MOEE and/or municipal agencies how the environmental conditions at a site will be made compatible and suitable for a proposed use. Given all of the above, it is usually in a proponent's best interest to initiate an open exchange of information with the MOEE (and possibly other interested parties) at an early stage of decommissioning.

Communication with interested public groups and the news media is another essential component of the overall decommissioning process. Depending on the size and profile of the decommissioning, proper communication can include providing opportunities for public input at several occasions, making a file of information available to the public at locations such as local libraries, distributing written material to local residents that describes the project, or establishing a public liaison committee.

If a decommissioning project eventually will include a rezoning application or planning amendment, the Planning Act contains statutory requirements for public meetings. Some Ontario municipalities are requiring that area residents be consulted during the preparation and implementation of decommissioning programs.

The size and location of a facility to be decommissioned will greatly influence the amount of attention that the public or news media pay to specific projects; however, it is increasingly unlikely that any decommissioning project in urban areas of Ontario will not draw the attention of one or more groups. In the context of the overall process, it is always in a proponent's interest to consider the concerns and opinions of such groups.

5.8 LEGAL ASPECTS OF BUYING OR SELLING CONTAMINATED PROPERTY

5.8.1 The Role of Common Law

Notwithstanding the recent use of the transaction screens and ESAs described in Section 5.4, there remains the basic tenet of common law that the onus is on buyers to protect themselves by an express warranty that premises are fit for their purpose and free from specified defects. The *caveat emptor* principle applies when a buyer purchases a property that has a defect which could have been discovered during a careful inspection. If the defect could not be discovered, the onus may be on the vendor; however, the purchaser must prove that the vendor knew of the latent defect. At many sites, it is difficult to prove that the owner knew of contamination. Examples can include ground water contamination resulting from a leaking tank or historical disposal activities that occurred before the owner took possession.

The *caveat emptor* principle may not apply if misrepresentation has occurred during the purchase of the contaminated property; however, the misrepresentation must be actual fraud to rescind the contract and recover out-of-pocket losses. If an innocent misrepresentation occurs (i.e. the owners believed they were acting in good faith), the contract may be rescinded but recovery of out-of-pocket losses may not be allowed. Several other torts (civil wrongs excluding breach of contract), may be applicable during a property transfer. These include negligence, nuisance, and trespass. (Section 8.7 discusses common law as it pertains to torts.)

Where responsibility for contamination is complicated by changes in ownership, the MOEE can elect to issue an order to all parties that can be legally associated to the cause of the contamination. Because of the broad definitions in the EPA of "owner" and "operator", liability for past contamination can extend through unsuspecting parties (Hall, 1990).

5.8.2 The Role of Contract Law

To maximize protection from assuming a property that poses environmental liabilities, a **purchaser's offer** should contain the following provisions (Ruderman, 1989):

* The purchaser has the right to access files, documents, etc. pertinent to the property, inspect the property, and conduct environmental tests during a conditional period.
* The purchaser has the right to use agents, consultants, etc. to perform the above inspection, testing and/or review of records.
* If not satisfied with the inspection, the purchaser must be given the right to terminate the agreement or proceed with the agreement such that it is not deemed to be a waiver of non-compliance with any of the vendor's warranties.
* The vendor must provide an absolute warrant that there are no noxious, dangerous, toxic substances or conditions on the property (including urea formaldehyde, asbestos, PCB or any radioactive substance).
* The vendor must provide an absolute warrant that the vendor has not received notice or has knowledge of any judicial or administrative action or action by adjacent or affected land owners related to the use of the property or the presence or discharge of noxious, dangerous, or toxic substances.
* The vendor must provide an absolute warrant that all necessary licenses to operate the business have been obtained and the business is in compliance with all government laws and regulations.
* A requirement to inform the vendor promptly in writing if any of the aforementioned warranties are untrue or if the vendor has knowledge of any event or likely event which may result in the warranty no longer being true.
* A statement that the warranties will survive closing.
* The purchaser has the right to terminate if warranties are found to be untrue and potential recovery of inspection costs.

- The requirement that vendor rectify the breach of warranty prior to closing and that a portion of the purchase price is held back as security on the completion of the work.
- The purchaser has the right to obtain information on all government files related to the property, a right to cause various government departments to inspect the property, and a requirement that the vendor sign consents permitting such release and inspection.

The decision to include any or all of the above points will depend upon many factors including the extent of potential contamination and the value of the property.

In recent years, the rights of a purchaser to claim damages arising from non-disclosure of facts relating to the condition of the property appears to have expanded. Therefore, if a vendor has any knowledge of potentially hazardous conditions, the vendor may not be protected by an offer which contains no warranties. The knowledge portion of this liability can extend to a corporation's officers, directors, and agents.

The **vendor's counter-offer** may contain the following (Ruderman, 1988):

- A requirement that the purchaser acknowledge the previous uses of the property which may have resulted in the existence of hazardous, noxious, or toxic conditions or substances in the soil and structures.
- The purchaser will conduct a thorough inspection, including soil test, at its own expense and that the purchaser is buying on an "as is" basis. The vendor makes no representation or warranties regarding the presence or absence of toxic or hazardous substances or conditions, especially urea formaldehyde, asbestos, PCB or radioactive materials.
- If the purchaser does not terminate the agreement during the inspection period, the purchaser is deemed to have accepted the conditions of the property and the existence of any toxic or hazardous substances or conditions. As such, the purchaser is solely responsible for any remedial action.
- The purchaser is to indemnify the vendor during and after closing from all claims, liabilities, and obligations respecting such substances or conditions.
- If the purchaser terminates the agreement following the inspection he will be responsible for all costs and will not be entitled to make any claim for damages arising out of breach of warranty.

Such clauses will not fully protect the vendor from liability if there is an actual concealment of conditions relating to the property, a direct false statement about the condition of the property, or an intentional withholding of facts (Ruderman, 1988).

The above counter-offer terms may conflict with those described in the offer to purchase and may scare off a purchaser. It is best to have a lawyer knowledgeable in the field of environmental law involved in the transaction to ensure that the appropriate steps are being taken, especially if there is the possibility that the property is contaminated.

Note that the various types of **professional advisors** (such as engineers, lawyers, real estate agents, etc.) that may participate during the transfer of ownership have a duty to act with a reasonable degree of care. A person under contractual duty to make an inspection may be liable for breach of contract and/or negligence by his or her failure to perform the task properly (Sefton, 1988).

5.9 SUMMARY

Owners, prospective buyers, and sellers of property need to be aware of environmental legislation in Ontario that influences site assessment, remediation, redevelopment, and the assignment of liabilities. At greatest risk are individuals who deal with properties that have a history of industrial or commercial use. Past practices have resulted in conditions at many sites that are not environmentally acceptable today.

The Environmental Protection Act clearly places responsibility for making a site acceptable upon the current owner, but previous owners or site operators can also be held responsible. Where responsibility for contamination is complicated by changes in ownership, the MOEE can elect to issue an order to all parties that can be legally associated to the cause of the contamination. Where the transfer of property is concerned, the adage "let the buyer beware" is more applicable today than ever before.

The MOEE publication entitled *Guidelines for the Decommissioning and Clean-up of Sites in Ontario* is often cited as the basic reference when proponents consider site remediation and decommissioning in Ontario; however, that document is does not have force of law (unless cited in an order) and many issues concerning decommissioning and clean-up are not addressed. Numerous changes were proposed late in 1993 which would modify the numerical criteria and the ways in which they are used during site remediation and decommissioning. Whether these changes are adopted by the MOEE should be known by mid-1994.

There is a growing body of information and cases which are setting precedents, procedures, and/or criteria for determining the environmental "acceptability" of site conditions or of clean-up efforts; however, "approved" technologies and methods to achieve acceptable levels of clean-up are generally lacking. Many methods for remediating sites or addressing various types of site contamination are in the developmental and demonstration stages, but very few of the methods have been approved for use in Ontario.

Given the gaps in regulatory guidance and the need to demonstrate to the MOEE and/or municipal agencies that the environmental conditions at a site are compatible and suitable for a proposed use, it is usually in a proponent's best interest to inform all of the agencies directly and to initiate an open exchange of information and concerns at an early stage of decommissioning.

Collectively, theses conditions pose serious obstacles to the buying, selling, remediation, and redevelopment of contaminated property. They also clearly illustrate the need for current property owners to protect the environmental quality of their sites.

REFERENCES

Alberta MUST Project. 1991. *Subsurface Remediation Guidelines for Underground Storage Tanks.* DRAFT. A Joint Project of the Departments of Environmental and Labour.

Canadian Council of Ministers of the Environment (CCME). September 1991. "Interim Canadian Environmental Quality Criteria for Contaminated Sites." Report CCME EPC-CS34.

Canadian Standards Association (CSA). September 1993. *Phase I Environmental Site Assessment.* CSA Publication Z768. DRAFT.

Hall, A. 1990. "Decommissioning and Cleanup – Regulatory Framework." Presented at Cleaning Up Contaminated Sites, Toronto, Ontario, 23 January.

Inter-Ministry Committee on Clean-Up Criteria (ICCC). 1988. *Report on Clean-Up Criteria for Shell, Oakville and Texaco, Port Credit Refinery Properties.*

Moen, J.E.T. 1988. "Soil Protection in The Netherlands." *Contaminated Soil '88:* 1495-1503.

Ontario Ministry of Consumer and Commercial Relations (MCCR). August 1993. *Interim Guidelines for the Assessment and Management of Petroleum Contaminated Sites in Ontario.* Report GH 13.

Ontario Ministry of Environment and Energy (MOEE). January 1994. "Revised Tables of Objectives for MOEE's Publication *Water Management*."

Ontario Ministry of Environment and Energy (MOEE). August 1993. *Interim Guidelines for the Assessment and Management of Petroleum Contaminated Sites in Ontario.* Report of the Petroleum Contaminated Soils Working Group.

Ontario Ministry of the Environment (MOE). 1992a. *Water Management: Goals, Policies, Objectives and Implementation Procedures of the Ministry of the Environment.*

Ontario Ministry of the Environment (MOE). August 1992b. *Proposed Policy for Management of Excess Soil, Rock and Like Materials.* Technical Consultation Document. Materials Management Policy Committee.

Ontario Ministry of the Environment (MOE). 1990. *Dioxins and Furans Background – An Environment Information Bulletin.*

Ontario Ministry of the Environment (MOE). February 1989a. *Guidelines for the Decommissioning and Clean-up of Sites in Ontario.*

Ontario Ministry of the Environment (MOE). 1989b. *Upper Limit of Normal Contaminant Guidelines for Phytotoxicology Samples.* Phytotoxicology Section, Air Resources Branch. ARB-138-88-Phyto.

Ontario Ministry of the Environment (MOE). 1988. *Interim Guidelines for PCBs in Soil.*

Ontario Ministry of the Environment (MOE). 1986. *Guidelines for the Resolution of Ground Water Quality Interference Problems.* Policy 15-10-01.

Pollution Engineering. January 1992. *Pollution Engineering News.* 1:9.

Reades, D.W. 1989. "Hydrogeological Investigation during Environmental Audits." Presented at the Regulatory Compliance Workshop, Toronto, 11 October.

Ruderman, J.C. 1988. "Negotiating the Agreement of Purchase and Sale to Reduce Risk of Environmental Hazards." Presented at the Environmental Real Estate Transaction Conference, Toronto, 19 September.

Rush, R., and K. Metzger. 1991. "Leaking Storage Tank Costs Could Rival Our Federal Deficit." In *Environmental Science & Engineering* (July): 38-41.

Sefton, C.R.C. 1988. "Remedies: Litigation the Toxic Real Estate Case." Presented at the Environmental Real Estate Transaction Conference, Toronto, 19 September.

Table 5.1
UPPER LIMIT OF NORMAL (ULN) VALUES FOR SOILS

Parameter	Urban Soil	Rural Soil
antimony	8	1**
arsenic	20	10
boron	15	10**
cadmium	4	3, 4*
calcium	hv	hv
chromium	50	50
cobalt	25***	25
copper	100	60
iron	3.5%***	3.5%
lead	500	150
magnesium	ne	1%
manganese	700	700, 1000*
mercury	0.5	0.15
molybdenum	3	2**
nickel	60***	60
selenium	2	2
sulfur	ne	0.1%
vanadium	70	70
zinc	500	500

Notes

All values in μg/g (unless indicated otherwise) on dry weight basis and apply to soil in the top 5 cm.

* - The first value is based mainly on data from southern Ontario. The second is based on Northeast Region data.

** - Provisional value estimated from range of results, pending additional data.

*** - Rural results higher than urban results; urban guideline based on rural results.

ne - not established
hv - highly variable, not established

Table 5.2
MOEE SOIL CLEAN-UP GUIDELINES

Parameter	Agricultural/Residential/Parkland		Commercial/Industrial	
	Type of Soil		Type of Soil	
	Medium & Fine	Coarse[2]	Medium & Fine	Coarse
pH	6 to 8	6 to 8	6 to 8	6 to 8
EC (mS/cm)	2	2	4	4
SAR	5	5	12	12
nitrogen (%)[3]	0.5	0.5	0.6	0.6
oil & grease (%)[4]	1	1	1	1
arsenic	25	20	50	40
cadmium	4	3	8	6
chromium (VI)	10	8	10	8
chromium (total)	1000	750	1000	750
cobalt	50	40	100	80
copper	200	150	300	225
lead	500	375	1000	750
mercury	1	0.8	2	1.5
molybdenum	5	5	40	40
nickel	200	150	200	150
selenium	2	2	10	10
silver	25	20	50	40
zinc	800	600	800	600
Provisional Guidelines:				
antimony	25	20	50	40
barium	1000	750	2000	1500
beryllium	5	4	10	8
vanadium	250	200	250	200

Notes

- All values in µg/g unless indicated.
1 For comparison with these guidelines, analyses for metal and metalloids must be conducted using an approved strong, mixed-acid digestion procedure.
2 Defined as greater than 70% sand and less than 17% organic matter.
3 If nitrogen levels exceed the guidelines, the mineralization of the soils should be evaluated. Additions of nitrogen-based fertilizer may be counter productive.
4 Guideline is for fresh oil; for weathered oil (minimum of 2 years exposed on site), the guideline is 2%.

Table 5.3
MOEE INTERIM SOIL QUALITY GUIDELINES

Polychlorinated Dibenzo-p-dioxins and Polychlorinated Dibenzofurans:

1 µg TEQ/kg (1 part per billion)

- where the TEQ (toxicity equivalent quantity) of dioxins and furans in soil is the sum of the concentrations of each isomer group times the toxicity equivalent factors (TEF) for each group. TEF values range from 1 for 2,3,7,8-tetrachlorodibenzo-p-dioxin to 0.001 to octachlorodibenzo-p-dioxin and octachlorodibenzofuran.

- assumed to apply to all types of soil and land use

Reference: MOEE, 1990

Polychlorinated Biphenyls (PCBs):

0.5 µg/g for agricultural land
5 µg/g for residential and park land
25 µg/g for commercial and industrial land

Reference: MOEE, 1988

Table 5.4
INTERIM SOIL REMEDIATION CRITERIA FOR PETROLEUM CONTAMINATION

Contaminant	Level I	Site Sensitivity Level II	Level III
benzene	0.05	0.5	2.0
toluene	1.0	10.0	100
ethylbenzene	0.5	5.0	100
xylenes (total)	1.0	5.0	50
TPH1 (gas/diesel)	100	1000	5000
TPH2 (heavy oil)	1000	5000	5000

Notes

All values in µg/g on dry weight basis.
1 -Total of purgeables and cold extractables.
2 -Hot extractables.
Level I corresponds to "high" sensitivity. Level II to "moderate" sensitivity, and Level III to "low" sensitivity. See MOEE, 1993 for further discussions of determining site sensitivity.

Table 5.5
OTHER SOURCES OF CLEAN-UP GUIDELINES

Alberta Environment. 1990. *Alberta Tier I Criteria for Contaminated Soil Assessment and Remediation.* DRAFT. Wastes and Chemical Division, Soil Protection Branch.

Bell, C.E., P. T. Kostecki, and E.J. Calabrese. 1990. "An Update on a National Survey of State Regulatory Policy: Cleanup Standards." In *Petroleum Contaminated Soils* (Vol. 3). P.T. Kostecki and E.J. Calabrese, (eds.).

British Columbia Ministry of the Environment. 1989. *Criteria for Managing Contaminated Sites in British Columbia.* DRAFT. Prepared by the Waste Management Program, 21 November.

Canadian Council of Ministers of the Environment. March 1991. *National Guidelines for Decommissioning Industrial Sites.* CCME TS/WM-TRE013E.

Canadian Council of Resource and Environment Ministers. 1988. *Proposed Interim Guidelines for PAH Contamination at Abandoned Coal Tar Sites.* Prepared for the Waste Management Committee, Toxic Substances Advisory Committee, by the Ad Hoc Federal-Provincial Working Group on Interim PAH Guidelines.

Canadian Council of Resource and Environment Ministers. 1987. *Interim Guidelines for PCBs in Soil.* Prepared by J.D. Clarke, M. Richardson, B. Hanna Thorpe, and M. Bealieu.

Department of the Environment. 1990. *Contaminated Land.* Select Committee on the Environment Report on Contaminated Land: Government Response. United Kingdom.

Fitchko, J. 1989. *Criteria for Contaminated Soil/Sediment Cleanup.* Pudvan Publishing Co., Inc.

Interdepartmental Committee on the Redevelopment of Contaminated Land. 1987. *Guidance on the Assessment and Redevelopment of Contaminated Land.* ICRCL 59/83 (second edition). Department of the Environment, United Kingdom.

Ministère de l'Environnement du Québec. 1988. *Contaminated Sites Rehabilitation Policy.*

Siegrist, R.L. 1989. *International Review of Approaches for Establishing Clean-up Goals for Hazardous Waste Contaminated Land.* Institute for Georesources and Pollution Research, Norway.

Table 5.6
EXAMPLES OF TRANSACTION SCREEN QUESTIONS

Q1. Were significant volumes of hazardous chemicals used, produced, or stored at the site?

Q2. Have waste materials been disposed on-site or nearby?

Q3. Are there any tanks or pipelines (above or below ground) on the site? Are there records or indications that any of the tanks or pipelines have leaked?

Q4. Are there unexplained earthworks or vegetation damage on the site?

Q5. Are there signs of stained or discoloured soils or building surfaces? Are oily sheens present on surface waters (including puddles)?

Q6. Are there facilities in the vicinity which may pose a health or environmental risk or nuisance problem because of there current or past operation?

Q7. Are PCBs, asbestos, or other designated substances present in on-site equipment or structures?

Q8. Is ground water used by nearby residents and/or does ground water discharge to a nearby water course?

Table 5.7
SUMMARY OF EXTENT TO WHICH OPTIONS HAVE BEEN USED AND THE CONTAMINANTS THEY ADDRESS

Category/Option	Extent of Use*	Contaminants Addressed
OFF-SITE DISPOSAL		
Hazardous Waste Facility	common	all**
Municipal Landfill	common	all
DESTRUCTION, BIOREMEDIATION		
Biostimulation	rare (except landfarms)	best on BTEX, some PAHs
Biological Seeding	rare	best on BTEX, some PAHs
DESTRUCTION, CHEMICAL		
Oxidation	not used	chlorinated organics
Dechlorination	rare	PCBs
DESTRUCTION, THERMAL		
Fluidized Bed Incineration	used in U.S.	BTEX, PAHs, cyanides
Rotary Kiln Incineration	rare, common in U.S.	BTEX, PAHs, phenols
Pyrolysis	used in U.S.	organics and volatile metals
SEPARATION, VOLATILIZATION		
Soil Vapour Extraction	rare	BTEX, solvents, some PAHs
Low Temperature Thermal	rare	BTEX, some PAHs
SEPARATION, SOLUBILIZATION		
Soil Washing	not used	most organics, most metals
High Pressure Soil Washing	used in Europe	all

Table 5.7 (continued)

Category/Option	Extent of Use*	Contaminants Addressed
SEPARATION, ADSORPTION		
Metal Chelation	demonstrated only	most metals, cyanides
SEPARATION, ELECTROKINETICS		
Electrokinetics	demonstrated in U.S.	most metals
IMMOBILIZATION, SOLIDIFICATION		
Cement Solidification	used in U.S.	metals, PCBs
Lime-Silicate Solidification	used in Australia, Europe metals, oils, solvents	
Glassification	demonstrated in the U.S.	all
IMMOBILIZATION, ENCAPSULATION		
Thermoplastic	not used	metals, some organics
ISOLATION		
Surface Storage	common	PCBs
Subsurface Containment	not for soil issues	all
REUSE		
Asphalt Batching	used in U.S.	BTEX, PAHs

Notes

  * - extent of use in Ontario unless noted otherwise

** - except PCBs and radionuclides (this note applies to each entry shown as "all")

BTEX - benzene, toluene, ethylbenzene, and xylenes

PAHS - polycyclic aromatic hydrocarbons

6.0

Noise and Vibration

6.1 OVERVIEW

Noise is defined as unwanted or disturbing sound. The types of situations where noise is an issue most often involve commercial operations, industrial facilities, or transportation corridors in proximity to residential areas. The effect that a sound has on the surrounding environment (i.e. the extent to which it can be considered to be noise) depends on many variables including the acoustic characteristics of the sound source, the path the sound must travel, characteristics of the areas around the source and the receiver, the nature of the receiver, and the effects of other ambient sound levels.

Vibrations involve the flow of energy through the ground. As energy travels further from its source, it decreases in strength at a rate which is dependent upon distance, soil conditions, and mode of transmission. Depending on the amount of energy involved and its duration, vibration can be merely perceived, be annoying, or, in the extreme, cause structural damage.

Both sound and vibration are defined as environmental contaminants in the Environmental Protection Act (EPA) and should be treated no less seriously than an atmospheric emission or liquid effluent. In Ontario, residents can file complaints with various agencies including the MOEE, local municipality, city, or township. There are many examples where noise abatement actions have been initiated as a result of the complaints of neighbours. There are also instances in which noise has been the source of initial aggravation and prompted those being disturbed to investigate and complain about other environmental issues concerning the source of the noise.

Some of the factors that influence community tolerance to noise include (Thumann and Miller, 1986):

- the presence of clearly visible noise sources, such as outdoor cooling towers, vents, stacks, etc.

- an obvious change or fluctuation in sound level
- pure tones or discrete-frequency sounds
- noises which interfere with sleep or communications
- unusually low background noise levels
- low frequency noise which induces vibrations (e.g. rattling windows) in residences
- impulses or startling noises
- noise which conveys displeasing information (e.g. glass breaking)

The units of measurement for sound and vibration span several orders of magnitude when used to describe conditions typically found in the environment. For example, the frequencies of sound in the environment can range over one million hertz (cycles per second). Even larger ranges can be encountered for sound intensity and sound pressures. To preserve constant-percent accuracies in measuring or describing noise, and to avoid large exponents in the numbers involved, logarithmic scales are used for several noise and vibration parameters (Beranek, 1971). The logarithmic parameter most commonly associated with acoustics is the decibel. The logarithmic nature of sound is illustrated in Table 6.1 which provides examples of sound pressures (decibels) and sound power levels of several common sources.

6.2 LEGISLATION

6.2.1 Environmental Protection Act

Sound and vibration are defined as contaminants under the Environmental Protection Act (Section 1(1)). As noted in Section 2.2, the EPA contains a general prohibition against the discharge of a contaminant into the natural environment that causes or is likely to cause an adverse effect. The EPA definition of "adverse effect" includes:

- impairment of the natural environment for any use that can be made of it
- harm or material discomfort to any person
- loss of enjoyment of normal use of property, and
- interference with the normal conduct of business

In the context of sound and vibration, key parts of the definition, especially with respect to complaints from neighbours, include the loss of enjoyment of normal use of property and material discomfort.

In Ontario, the courts have stated that when a person with average sensibilities is bothered by noise impinging on his property, the person is entitled to complain and the courts will assist in having the bothersome noise checked. In addition, the courts have also stated that one cannot acquire a right to inflict noise on another's property unless the other property owner is actually there, suffering the noise, and taking no action to prevent it (Working Group on Noise Control, 1989).

Section 178(1) of the EPA provides local municipalities with the power to pass sound and vibration by-laws, subject to the approval of the Minister.

6.2.2 Municipal Noise By-Laws and Guidelines

Municipalities can establish by-laws for several aspects of sound and vibration:

- to regulate or prohibit the emission of sounds or vibrations
- to provide for the licensing of persons, equipment, and premises with respect to the emission of sounds or vibrations
- to prescribe maximum permissible levels of sounds or vibrations that may be emitted
- to prescribe procedures for determining the levels of sounds or vibrations that are emitted

By-laws may make different provisions for different areas of a local municipality and may make provisions for exempting any person, equipment, or premises from any provision of the by-law for such period of time and subject to such terms and conditions as may be set out or provided for in the by-laws.

To assist municipalities to develop noise by-laws and provide a consistent basis for noise control across Ontario, the MOEE issued the *Model Municipal Noise Control By-Law* in 1978. Table 6.2 lists various MOE Noise Pollution Control (NPC) publications that support the Model Municipal Noise Control By-Law. Table 6.3 lists noise guideline documents issued in recent years by the Ontario Ministry of Housing and the MOEE.

Several of the MOEE publications listed in Table 6.2 address sound level limits from specific types of sources or in specific situations. The following is a brief description of key NPC publications.

NPC-105 (Stationary Sources) and NPC-132 (Guidelines for Noise Control in Urban Areas) address sound level limits from Stationary Sources. In NPC-105 the applicable sound level limit, excluding specific impulsive sounds, is the one-hour equivalent sound level (L_{eq}) specified by NPC-106 and is the higher of the measured or estimated road traffic levels, or published values for minimum hourly L_{eq}.

The published minimum hourly levels are dependent upon the time of day: ranges from a L_{eq} of 40 dBA (A-weighted decibels) from 0300-0400 to an L_{eq} of 50 dBA from 0700-1900. Refer to Table 106-2 in NPC-106 for additional information on minimum hourly L_{eq} values.

For specific impulsive sounds from stationary sources which are industrial metal working operations (including but not limited to forging, hammering, punching, stamping, cutting, forming and moulding), the applicable sound level is 50 dBAI (A-weighted decibels impulsive sound). If the source was in operation before 1 January 1980, the sound limit is 60 dBAI. If the impulsive sound from the stationary source is so infrequent that it cannot be normally measured using procedures mentioned in NPC-103, the sound applicable sound level is 100 dBAI. These limits do not apply to the discharge of firearms at a licensed gun club.

If more than one type of sound is occuring, the most restrictive applicable sound level limit shall prevail. No restrictions apply to a stationary source resulting in an equivalent sound level (L_{eq}) of 40 dBA or less at a point of reception.

Penalties may have to be applied to the following types of sound (as per NPC-104) prior to comparing to the limits specified in NPC-105 and NPC-106: intermittence, tonality, cyclic variations, and quasi-steady impulsive sound.

Publication NPC-115 sets out sound emission standards for various items of **construction equipment** according to the date of manufacture. It includes limitations for excavation equipment, dozers, loaders, backhoes, pneumatic pavement breakers, portable air compressors, and tract drills.

Publication NPC-131 specifies the sound level limits for the assessment of **proposed residential land developments** and alterations to or conversion of any existing developments or construction. Quantitative sound level limits for use in land use planning decisions include:

	Limit	*Hours*	
Outdoor	L_{eq} = 55 dBA	0700-2300	
	L_{eq} = 50 dBA	2300-0700	
Indoor	L_{eq} = 45 dBA	0700-2300	living rooms, hotels, motels reading rooms, classrooms, and individual or semi-private offices
	L_{eq} = 50 dBA	0700-2300	general offices, reception areas retail shops and stores
	L_{eq} = 40 dBA	2300-0700	bedrooms, sleeping quarters, hospitals

Outdoor recreational areas refers to those outdoor amenity areas where the enjoyment of the outdoor environment is important. These amenity areas include, but are not limited to, yards (front and back) and terraces of dwellings, common outdoor areas for recreational purposes such as areas outside apartment buildings, schools, etc., and parks and open spaces allocated for recreational purposes within a plan of a subdivision.

Control measures to ensure compliance with limits may include site planning (e.g. orientation of buildings and other outdoor recreational areas), acoustical barriers (e.g. berms, walls), architectural design (e.g.

placement of windows, balconies), and construction (e.g. acoustical treatment of windows and doors).

If the predominant sound has a pronounced tonal quality such as a whine, screech, buzz, or hum or contains pronounced narrow bands of energy, then 5 dBA should be deducted from the sound level listed above for indoor sound level limit.

Two problems have arisen in recent years with regards to the interpretation of NPC-131. The first is that the allowable levels in some circumstances are higher than those specified in NPC-105, thereby potentially putting adjacent industry at risk of non-compliance. The second issue is the applicability of the 40 dBA level for bedroom windows. The measurement location stipulated in NPC-103 for an open exterior window is the "plane" of the window. This location was put forth when the Ontario Building Code (1990) explicitly stated that bedroom windows could not be sealed. The revised Building Code (1990) allows sealed windows for bedrooms. Hence, several groups have argued that the sound level should be measured or estimated inside the bedroom thereby allowing for greater sound mitigation. Both issues are currently being addressed by the MOEE in a publication entitled LU-131 which will replace NPC-131 in 1994.

Publication NPC-133 provides information for the assessment of **planned stationary sources**. The guidelines provided apply to new sources of sound as well as expansion, alteration, or conversion of existing sources. The information required in the document can be used to obtain a Certificate of Approval for the source from the MOEE. The document includes measurement standards and procedures as well as sound level limits for urban and rural areas.

Publication NPC-134 provides information for the assessment of **planned new land uses**. Guidelines are provided for changes to official plans, rezoning, applications for subdivision approval, and all new land uses adjacent to major transportation and energy corridors, industries, and airports. The document also provides measurement standards and procedures.

6.2.3 Vibration Guidelines

Acceptable levels of vibration are based upon perceptibility. One method of evaluating the perceptibility of vibration has been developed by the Canadian National Railroad (CNR). The CNR approach is based on the premise that vibrations with frequencies between 4 and 200 hertz have the potential to cause annoyance at a sensitive residential receptor location if the velocity exceeds 0.14 mm/s during an averaging time of one second. Below this speed, vibration is not a concern; above it, consideration should be given to mitigation measures. The MOEE has adopted the same values in draft form but has not yet included them in official guidelines.

Stronger vibration levels are usually needed to produce annoyance or inconvenience in commercial or industrial areas than those at a sensitive residential location; however, there are no guidelines for acceptable vibration levels in commercial or industrial spaces. If complaints arise, each situation is assessed individually according to the activities occurring in the space and the perceptibility of the vibration intrusion.

6.2.4 Land Use Compatibility

MOEE Policy 07-03, Land Use Compatibility, identifies the direct interest of the MOEE in recommending separation distances and other control measures on land-use planning proposals to prevent future incompatibilities between land uses. The intent is to achieve a reasonable degree of protection that supplements practicable emission controls, without unduly restricting land use. The following is the Policy Statement:

> It is the policy of the MOEE to recommend the separation of incompatible land uses, where necessary, in the review of land use plans as a preventative means of achieving environmental objectives of the Ministry. There is an influence area around certain facilities or land uses, subject to emissions, usually of a nuisance nature, where exposures of residents and other sensitive uses should be minimized. These areas should be identified at an early stage in land-use planning. Necessary environmental control measures, such as placing Buffer Areas between emission sources and residential or sensitive land uses, should be applied to supplement practicable emission controls but not to take the place of such controls.

In the MOEE Central Region publication, *Buffers: Use and Design Guidelines,* a buffer is defined as a space or feature interposed between two conflicting land uses for the purpose of reducing or eliminating the adverse effects of one land use upon the other. The guideline indicates that buffers should not be used as a substitute for adequate control of the source. They are an added safeguard against process upsets, control equipment breakdown, or malfunction and spills. They are also necessary controls for fugitive sources for which there is no other practical means of control.

The following are proposed buffer distances for various land uses:

Residential–Commercial: A separation distance of 30 metres between residential buildings and commercial buildings is considered an acceptable minimum. A visible separator designed to disrupt "sight lines" should be developed on the intervening lands. The siting of commercial units should be cognizant of noise, dust, and odours generated by loading and unloading of trucks, and the location of any restaurants which should be provided with a greater separation distance.

Residential–Light Industrial: Separation distance of 60 metres between residential building and industrial buildings is considered minimum. A visible separator as discussed above should be developed. Examples of light industry include light warehousing, electronics, light assembly, auto service garage, car wash, and small industrial malls (does not include fibreglass operations).

Residential–Medium Industrial: Separation distances of 90 to 300 metres between residential buildings and medium industrial-use buildings are considered acceptable minimums. A visible separator as discussed for Residential–Light Industrial should also be developed. Examples of land use requiring the smaller separation distance (90 to 150m) include heavy assembly, heavy outside storage, and general manufacturing. Examples of land uses requiring larger separation distances (150 to 300m) include meat and poultry processing, small foundries, metal fabricating, and fibreglass fabrication plants.

Residential–Heavy Industrial Uses and Other Potentially Non-Compatible Uses: A separation distance greater than 300 metres is required. The specific distance will vary depending on the nature of the industrial activity, etc. The intervening lands should be separate and used for light industrial and/or commercial use subject to the aforementioned guidelines, or some other insensitive use. Examples of land uses include steel mills, rendering plants, metal recovery plants, large foundries, pesticide manufacturing, and refineries.

6.3 OBTAINING APPROVALS

As outlined in Section 9 of the EPA, a C of A must be issued by the MOEE director to any person who intends to:

- construct, alter, extend, or replace any plant, structure, equipment, apparatus, mechanism, or thing that may emit or discharge or from which may be emitted or discharged a contaminant into any part of the natural environment other than water; or
- alter a process or rate of production with the result that contaminant may be emitted or discharged into any part of the natural environment other than water or the rate or manner of emission or discharge of a contaminant into any part of the natural environment other than water may be altered.

Failure to obtain a C of A, especially for an industrial operation, may result in prosecution.

Exemptions to the C of A requirements with respect to noise and vibration include:

- routine maintenance carried out on any plant, structure, equipment, apparatus, mechanism, or thing
- any equipment, apparatus, mechanism, or thing in or used in connection with a building or structure designed for the housing of not more than three families where the only contaminant produced by such equipment, apparatus, mechanism, or thing is sound or vibration
- any plant, structure, equipment, apparatus, mechanism, or thing used in normal agricultural practice
- any motor or motor vehicle that is subject to the provisions of Part III of the EPA

It is current MOEE policy to approve development applications even if the sound levels described in Section 6.2 for outdoor recreation and at bedroom windows are exceeded, provided that appropriate mitigative measures can be taken.

6.4 MONITORING

6.4.1 Estimating Noise Levels

Sound pressure levels are measured in A-weighted decibels (dBA). The term "A-weighted" indicates that factors are assigned to specific frequencies to approximate the relative sensitivity of the normal human ear to different frequencies (pitches of sound). Sound pressure level is defined according to the equation (Thumann and Miller, 1986):

$$L_p = 20 \log P/P_o \qquad (6.1)$$

where L_p = sound pressure level (dBA)
            P = sound pressure (micropascals)
            P_o = reference pressure = 20 micropascals

The reference pressure is the pressure equivalent to 10 to 12 watts/m^2, the threshold of human hearing.

To estimate sound pressure levels outdoors, the basic power formula can be used (Thumann and Miller, 1986):

$$L_p = L_w + 10 \log [Q/(4 \pi R^2] + 0.02 \qquad (6.2)$$

where L_w = sound power level (dBA)
                   = $10 \log (W/10^{-12})$
            R   = distance from the source (m)
            Q   = directivity factor of the source
            W   = acoustic power (watts)
            10^{-12} = standard reference power (watts)

The parameter Q takes into account the directivity of the source and the reflecting surfaces:

Q = 1 for point sources radiating uniformly in all directions with no reflecting surfaces

Q = 2 for sources radiating from flat surfaces

Q = 3 for noise source radiating from corners

A simple formula can be used to predict noise levels at a plant boundary based on measurements taken adjacent to the source (Thumann and Miller, 1986):

$$L_{p,X} = L_{p,Y} - 20 \log (X/Y) \qquad (6.3)$$

where   X = distance at which noise is being estimated for (m)

Y = distance at which noise monitoring data are available (m)

Equation 6.3 will result in a level decrease of 6 dBA when the distance is doubled (i.e. the inverse square law) in free space. The above relationship does not apply directly adjacent to the noise source (also referred to as the "near field"). Sound measurement should be made at a minimum distance of two machine dimensions and at least one wavelength. If information on the wavelength is unavailable, a good rule of thumb is to monitor at a distance of several times the equipment dimensions (Thumann and Miller, 1986).

When more than one source exists, the overall noise level is not the additive of each acoustic power level (W). Two equal sound sources result in the overall noise level being 3 dBA higher than either source alone.

Noise within a community fluctuates with time; thus a single measurement of sound level is insufficient for an assessment. The statistical method which is most commonly used to describe environmental noise is the equivalent sound level (L_{eq}). The L_{eq} is a time-weighted, mean square, A-weighted sound pressure.

To present the random fluctuation of community noise, especially where traffic is present, values for L_{90}, L_{50}, L_{10}, and L_1 may be used. These are the noise levels that are exceeded 90% of the time (also referred to as background or ambient), 50% (median), 10% (intrusive), and 1% (the "peak" noise levels), respectively.

6.4.2 Noise Measurement

Sound measuring devices typically consist of a microphone, electronic amplifier, filters and a readout meter. When measuring noise, the microphone should be located at least 1.2 m above the ground and 3 m away from significant sound-reflecting surfaces. Average wind speeds of greater than 15 km/h may invalidate the data. Short-term (less than 5 minutes) wind gusts up to

20km/h are acceptable. Steady precipitation can also invalidate monitoring.

It is essential that the device be calibrated in the laboratory and in the field. Field calibration should be conducted prior to and after each set of sound level readings. Table 6.4 lists several helpful publications concerning the measurement of sound.

To be qualified to assess noise as it relates to land use planning, a certificate of competency in environmental acoustic technology should be obtained from the MOEE. The MOEE conducts certification courses and provides manuals based on the guidelines available from the Model Municipal Noise Control By-Law and other documents. MOEE publication NPC-135 lists the requirements of certification.

6.4.3 Vibration Measurement

Sources of vibration include road traffic, rail traffic (including streetcars), and large-scale industrial equipment. Vibration may be measured using instruments similar to those used for monitoring noise, or by specialized vibration-measuring instruments.

The results of vibration surveys can be used to identify locations where remedial actions are warranted or to identify appropriate setback distances to avoid excessive vibration levels.

6.5 SUMMARY

Sound and vibration should be treated as any other pollutant which may cause the loss of enjoyment of normal use of property. As such, it is important that a company be aware of its contribution to the surrounding noise and vibration levels, and reduce levels if they are having a detrimental impact on local residents.

Noise control for the most part is regulated by municipal by-laws. The MOE has published a Model Noise Control By-Law as a means of providing a uniform base for noise control across Ontario. The Model By-Law includes Noise Pollution Control documents which describe guidelines for noise levels, assessments, monitoring, and abatement.

REFERENCES

Beranek, L.L. (ed.). 1971. *Noise and Vibration.* New York: McGraw-Hill Book Company.

Ontario Ministry of the Environment (MOE). August 1978. "Model Municipal Noise Control By-Law." Final Report.

Ontario Ministry of the Environment (MOE). 1979. *ORNAMENT: Ontario Road Noise Analysis Method for Environment and Transportation.* ISBN 0-7729-6376.

Thumann, A., and R. Miller. 1986. *Fundamentals of Noise Control Engineering.* The Fairmont Press.

Working Group on Environmental Noise. March 1989. "National Guidelines for Environmental Noise Control." Federal-Provincial Advisory Committee on Environmental and Occupational Health.

Table 6.1
REPRESENTATIVE SOUND SOURCES AND LEVELS AT CLOSE RANGE

Source	Decibels (dB)	Power (in Watts)
human breath	10	0.00000000001
rustling leaves	20	0.0000000001
soft whisper	30	0.000000001
small electric clock	40	0.00000001
ventilation fan	60	0.000001
conversation	70	0.00001
shouting	90	0.001
blaring radio	110	0.1
small aircraft engine	120	1
large pipe organ	130	10
turboprop aircraft at takeoff	150	1000

Table 6.2
PUBLICATIONS WITHIN THE MOE MODEL MUNICIPAL NOISE CONTROL BY-LAW (1978)

NPC-101	Technical Definitions
NPC-102	Instrumentation
NPC-103	Procedures
NPC-104	Sound Level Adjustments
NPC-105	Stationary Sources
NPC-106	Sound Levels of Road Traffic
NPC-115	Construction Equipment
NPC-116	Residential Air Conditioners
NPC-117	Domestic Outdoor Power Tools
NPC-118	Motorized Conveyances
NPC-119	Blasting
NPC-131	Guidelines for Noise Control in Land Use Planning
NPC-132	Guidelines for Noise Control in Rural Areas
NPC-133	Guidelines on Information Required for the Assessment of Planned Stationary Sources of Sound
NPC-134	Guidelines on Information Required for the Assessment of Planned New Uses with Respect to Sound and Vibration Impacts
NPC-135	Certificates

Table 6.3
INDEX OF NOISE GUIDELINES

Ministry of Housing:

- Land Use Policy Near Airports (1978)

- Guidelines on Noise and New Residential Development Adjacent to Freeways (1979)

Ministry of the Environment:

- Ontario Hydro Protocol for Community Noise Control (1981)

- Noise Level Guidelines (1984)

- Guidelines for Landfill Sites (1979)

- Ontario Road Traffic Noise Prediction Methodology—"ORNAMENT" (1989)

- Guidelines for Noise Impact Assessment for Off-Site Vehicular Traffic (1988)

- Low Frequency Noise Criteria

- Guidelines for Quarries (1986)

- Manual for Certificate Course—Environmental Noise (1989)

- Environmental Noise Assessment in Land Use Planning (1989)

Table 6.4
SELECTED REFERENCES CONCERNING SOUND
MEASUREMENT

American Society for Testing and Materials (ASTM). 1984. *Standard Method for Measurement of Outdoor A-Weighted Sound Levels.* ASTM Standard E1014-84.

Canadian Acoustical Association (CAA). 1985. *Industrial Noise Control Manual.*

Canadian Standards Association (CSA). 1983. *Recommended Practice for the Prediction of Sound Levels Received at a Distance from an Industrial Plant.* CSA Standard Z107.55.

International Organization for Standardization (ISO). Not dated. *Assessment of Noise with Respect to Community Response.* Publication No. 1996.

Ontario Ministry of the Environment (MOE). 1983. *Procedures for the Measurement of Sound.* Publication NPC-203.

7.0

Special Materials

7.1 POLYCHLORINATED BIPHENYLS (PCBs)

7.1.1 Overview

Polychlorinated biphenyls (PCBs) is a class of 209 compounds. Each PCB consists of two, fused benzene rings on which are located one or more chlorine atoms. The physical, chemical, and toxicological properties vary widely among PCB compounds, but all are stable at elevated temperatures and sparingly soluble in water. These characteristics made PCBs suitable for various uses including dielectric fluid in electrical equipment and in hydraulic fluids, paints, and inks. PCBs came into commercial use in the late 1920s. The major Canadian use was in dielectric fluid for industrial electrical equipment.

In 1973, the Organization for Economic Cooperation and Development (OECD) urged all member countries to limit PCBs to enclosed uses and to develop control mechanisms to eliminate the release of PCBs into the environment. In 1977, PCBs became the first class of substances to be regulated under the Canadian Environmental Contaminants Act, and subsequently most non-electrical uses of PCBs were prohibited in Canada. Since that time, regulations have been issued by the MOEE as well as federal agencies that address virtually every aspect of the use, management, and disposal of PCBs. These are summarized in Table 7.1.

The same properties that made PCBs well-suited for use as dielectric fluid also have resulted in PCBs becoming widely dispersed in the environment. Airborne transport probably is an important contributor to their environmental distribution.

PCBs can accumulate in living organisms and have been found in animals in remote areas of Canada and at low levels in the fatty tissue and blood of Canadians (CCREM, 1986). Table 7.2 presents physical characteristics for a few PCB compounds. The octanol-water partition coefficient (K_{OW}) is a good indicator of the potential for bioaccumulation.

Birds, aquatic invertebrates, and most species of fish are particularly sensitive to PCBs. Effects which have been observed include the reduction in litter sizes of otters and minks, as well as birth defects such as crossed beaks in birds (CCREM, 1986). It is these effects on wildlife, the persistence of PCBs, and their ability to bioaccumulate, which prompted the federal government to regulate PCBs.

PCBs were identified as a suspected human health hazard approximately 20 years ago. Recent research indicates that, except for causing skin rashes (chloracne), many PCBs do not pose substantial human health risks. PCBs with relatively high numbers of chlorine atoms are considered capable of causing some cancers in laboratory animals if exposed to high concentrations for prolonged periods. PCBs with high numbers of chlorine atoms are found in small amounts in the PCBs supplied to the electrical industry.

Long-term occupational exposure to PCBs has not been shown to result in any statistical increase in cancer. No direct evidence has linked PCBs to birth defects or chromosomal changes in humans (Environment Canada, not dated). According to the American Council on Science and Health, there have been no reported cases of deaths attributed to PCBs (Miller, 1989).

Despite the recent scientific evidence concerning human health effects, PCBs must be handled, stored, and transported as if they were highly toxic because of the requirements that legislation has imposed. Although PCBs may be less hazardous to humans than previously suspected, PCBs can be converted to dioxins and furans if heated sufficiently. The oily soot produced at fires involving PCBs can be hazardous.

7.1.2 Definitions and Classifications

Provincial and federal regulations define several key terms such as PCB material, PCB liquid, PCB waste, and PCB equipment. The prime provincial regulation, issued under the Environmental Protection Act, is Waste Management — PCBs Regulation (Regulation 362). The prime federal regulations are the Chlorobiphenyls Regulations (SOR/91-152) and the Storage of PCB Material Regulations (SOR/92-507). Both of these regulations are issued under the Canadian Environmental Protection Act.

The provincial and federal definitions generally are consistent with one another. There are subtle differences as would be expected given that the regulations have different purposes. The provincial regulation outlines the need to manage PCB waste materials while the federal regulation goes into considerable detail as to how PCB materials should be stored. The following definitions are those from Ontario Regulation 362 with differences in federal definitions noted as appropriate. As with other components of environmental legislation, provincial requirements take precedent when they exist. In provinces without PCB regulations, the federal regulations are used in their entirety.

All PCBs have the molecular formula $C_{12}H_{10-n}Cl_n$ where "n" represents the number of chlorine atoms. Ontario Regulation 362 defines PCBs as having $n \geq 1$ while the Canadian Environmental Protection Act (in the List of Toxic Substances of Schedule I) defines PCBs as having $n \geq 2$.

The definition of PCB waste in Ontario Regulation 362 is built upon the definitions of PCB material, PCB liquid, and PCB equipment. **PCB material** is any material that contains more than 50 ppm by weight of PCB regardless of whether the material is liquid or not. A **PCB liquid** is defined as:

(i) liquids, other than liquids used or proposed for use for road oiling, containing PCBs at a concentration of more than 50 ppm by weight

(ii) liquids used or proposed for use for road oiling, containing PCBs at a concentration of more than 5 ppm by weight, and

(iii) liquids made by diluting liquids referred to in subclause (i) or (ii)

PCB equipment means equipment designed or manufactured to operate with PCB liquid or to which PCB liquid has been added. It also includes drums or other containers used to store PCB liquid. The federal definition of PCB equipment is similar but does not extend to include drums or containers.

Regulation 362 does not define PCB solid or PCB substance (both of which are defined in federal Regulation 92-507 as materials that contain more than 50 ppm of PCBs).

Collectively, these definitions are used in Regulation 362 to define **PCB waste** to include PCB material, PCB liquid, and PCB equipment. Exceptions include:

(a) PCB material or PCB equipment that has been decontaminated pursuant to guidelines issued by the MOEE or instructions issued by the director.

(b) PCB equipment that is,

(i) an electrical capacitor that has never contained over 1 kg of PCBs

(ii) electrical, heat transfer, or hydraulic equipment or a vapour diffusion pump that is being put to the use for which it was originally designed or is being stored for such use by a person who uses such equipment for the purpose for which it was originally designed, or

(iii) machinery or equipment referred to in sub-subclause (c)(i).

(c) PCB liquid that,

(i) is at the site of fixed machinery or equipment, the operation of which is intended to destroy the chemical structure of PCBs by using the PCBs as a source of fuel or chlorine for purposes other than the destruction of PCBs or other wastes and with respect to which a certificate of approval has been issued under the EPA

(ii) is in PCB equipment referred to in sub-subclause (b)(ii).

The exemption in sub-subclause (b)(i) also is found in Ontario Regulation 347. Although capacitors that have never contained more than 1 kg of PCBs need not be registered as PCB waste, the MOEE asks large-scale owners of such capacitors to collect them voluntarily so that they ultimately can be disposed in an environmentally acceptable manner.

Regulation 362 does not address the length of time that equipment can go unused before it needs to be stored or is considered to be PCB waste. Federal Regulation 92-507 indicates that storage is required for equipment shut down for greater than six months. Similarly, Regulation 362 does not define any minimum quantities of material that might be exempt. Federal Regulation 92-507 applies to materials not being used daily in quantities of more than 100 L of PCB liquid, more than 100 kg of PCB solids or sub-stance, or anything containing greater than 1 kg of PCBs.

Regulation 362 defines **PCB related waste** as waste containing low levels of PCBs or waste arising from a spill or clean up of PCB liquid or PCB waste. No further guidance is provided as to what constitutes "low levels" of PCBs.

Section 3 of Regulation 362 classifies every site containing PCB waste and PCB related waste, but not containing other wastes, as a **PCB waste disposal site**. Sections 4 and 8 of the regulation impose various duties upon the operators of such sites (see Section 7.1.7).

Since there are relatively limited opportunities to destroy PCB wastes in Ontario, storage is the predominant method of currently managing these materials. Regulation 362 provides few details as to how PCB mate-rials should be stored; however, federal Regulation 92-507 describes proper storage requirements in detail.

Askarel is a generic name for PCB liquids used as electrical insulating materials. Askarels range from crystal clear to pale yellow in colour and are denser than water. Environment Canada defines askarel as any fluid mixture that contains PCBs in excess of 30% by weight (Environment Canada, not dated).

7.1.3 Environmental Guidelines and Allowable Release Rates

The MOEE has issued guidelines for allowable concentrations of PCBs in water, air, and soil, as well as used concentrations as a basis for defin-ing PCB wastes. These guidelines are summarized in Table 7.3.

Federal agencies have recommended guidelines for concentrations of PCBs in ambient water, air, and soil. The Chlorobiphenyls Regulations (SOR/91-152) prohibit the release of more than 1 g per day of PCBs from any one piece or package of equipment in the course of operation, servicing, maintenance, decommissioning, transportation, or storage of this equipment. It also prohibits the use of oils that contain more than 5 ppm by weight for the application to road surfaces, and the release of PCBs from all sources, except those discussed above, in excess of 50 ppm by weight.

The Fisheries Act prohibits the deposition of deleterious substances into water frequented by fish or waters leading to fish-frequented waters except as may be permitted by regulations.

Although the Ocean Dumping Control Act was repealed in June 1988, the regulations issued under that act still govern the disposal of PCBs at sea, including incineration, through permits and regulations which specify environmental operating requirements. These regulations will eventually come under the jurisdiction of CEPA (CCME, 1989). The first of the amendments proposed under Part IV of CEPA were published in *Canada Gazette* in September 1993.

7.1.4 Manufacture, Importation, and Use

PCBs were first synthesized in 1881, but not manufactured on a commercial scale until 1929. Most PCBs used in Canada were imported from the United States either in pure form or as askarel. In 1977, production in the United States was terminated voluntarily, while in Canada, most non-electrical uses of PCBs were prohibited under the former Canadian Environmental Contaminants Act and a national inventory of PCB-filled equipment was undertaken by Environment Canada.

While the major Canadian use of PCBs was in dielectric fluid for industrial electrical equipment, they also were used in waxes, adhesives, heat exchange fluids, vacuum pump oil, paints, de-dusting agents, hydraulic fluids, specialized lubricants, painting inks, pesticides, cutting oils, sealants, plasticizer, and carbonless copying paper. Some of the trade names under which PCB fluids were sold include Aroclor, Askarel, Chlorinol, Diachlor, Hyvol, Inchlor, Inerteen, Pyranol, and Sovol.

The Chlorobiphenyls Regulations (SOR/91-152) prohibit the manufacture, use, sale, or import of PCBs in excess of 50 ppm for any of the following commercial, manufacturing, or processing uses:

- the operation of any product or equipment other than
  - electrical capacitors and transformers and capacitors
  - heat transfer equipment, hydraulic equipment, electromagnets and vapour diffusion pumps that were designed to use PCBs other than those that were in use in Canada before 1 September 1977
- the operation of electromagnets that are used to handle food, animal feed, or any additive to food or animal feed
- as a constituent of any product, machinery, or equipment manufactured in or imported into Canada on or after 1 September 1977

other than electrical capacitors and transformers

- as a constituent of electrical capacitors and transformers manufactured in or imported into Canada on or after 1 July 1980
- in the servicing or maintenance of any product, machinery, or equipment other than electromagnets and electrical transformers and associated electrical equipment from which PCBs are removed to allow servicing and maintenance
- as new filling or as make-up fluid in the servicing or maintenance of electromagnets or electrical transformers and associated electrical equipment

Exemptions to these prohibitions include the sale of PCB-filled equipment which is a necessary and integral part of a building, plant, or structure that is offered for sale; the sale of PCB-filled equipment for destruction or for storage awaiting destruction of the PCBs contained therein; and the importation of PCB-filled equipment for destruction of the PCBs contained therein. The latter exemption was required to develop a reciprocal agreement between Canada and the U.S. for the use of PCB-destruction facilities (CCME, 1989).

Equipment in service that contains PCBs does not need to be registered with the MOEE or Environment Canada. Labelling of in-service equipment will assist in inventory control as well as during handling, storage, and disposal. Figure 7.1 presents a label that should be used on large pieces of equipment such as transformers. Once the label is affixed, it should only be removed if the equipment has been decontaminated and the MOEE and/or Environment Canada are satisfied that the PCB concentration is less than 50 ppm.

For smaller items, the label presented in Figure 7.2 can be used. If several smaller pieces of PCB equipment are found together, one label may be sufficient. The label should have an Environment Canada registration number at the bottom. The registration numbers allow Environment Canada to keep track of the amounts and locations of askarel equipment and liquids.

Figure 7.3 presents a general warning label that should be placed in a clearly visible position at the entrances to locations where PCB equipment is found.

Both the MOEE and Environment Canada maintain inventories of all askarel and PCB-contaminated equipment that has been labelled. Both agencies should be informed as to the status of a piece of PCB equipment (e.g. if it is taken out of service, relocated, stored, decontaminated, or disposed). Environment Canada recommends that owners of PCB equipment retain inventory records for five years after equipment is removed from service.

7.1.5 Decommissioning PCB Equipment

When PCB equipment is to be taken out of service, whether through failure, retrofit, or redundancy, it must be carefully decommissioned. The following suggested procedures are taken from guidelines issued by the CCME (1989).

Notification and Record-Keeping – Prior to decommissioning equipment, the MOEE must be notified and both the site and material must be registered. Before the equipment is decommissioned, the following information should be recorded: nameplate data, serial numbers, dates of decommissioning and shipment, destination of equipment, and names of decommissioning personnel, as well as the Environment Canada label identification number, if applicable.

Planning – All persons assigned to handle the PCB equipment should be thoroughly instructed in the proposed procedures, particularly with respect to safety precautions, the use of safety equipment and the applicability of federal and provincial regulations. Prior to decommissioning, aspects such as containment, ventilation, and working space available should be examined. The type, condition, and level of PCBs in the equipment dictates the extent of precautions to be taken. The maximum allowable emission rate from a piece of equipment during decommissioning is 1 g per day.

If the equipment is located in an open area, suitable curbs, barriers and/or metal pans should be provided to prevent the release of PCBs in the case of a spill during handling operations. All floor drains should be plugged and air ducts leading to other parts of the building should be closed. If cracks or leaks are apparent, liquids should be removed from the equipment prior to movement. The area of work should be appropriately identified and unauthorized persons prohibited from entering the area.

Protective Clothing and Apparatus – The required protective clothing will depend upon the individual circumstances, such as concentration, quantity of PCBs, and whether the material is in solid or liquid form. If workers are to come into direct contact with askarel, protective clothing impervious to PCBs should be worn. Federal and provincial regulations pertaining to the wearing of protective clothing and equipment must be observed at all times.

Procedures – Sealed capacitors should be placed into 205-L drums made of 18-gauge steel (or heavier), fitted with removable steel lids and gaskets made of PCB-resistant material such as nitrile rubber, cork, or Teflon. Capacitors should be stored with the terminals up to prevent leakage from the capacitor bushings. As many capacitors as space allows may be placed in each drum. Drums or containers smaller than 205 L may be used when the size or quantity of capacitors does not justify the larger container.

Leaking capacitors should be drained and then placed in heavy-duty polyethylene bags before storing in a drum (one capacitor per bag). The drum should be packed with adsorbent material to adsorb PCBs which may escape from the bags.

Non-leaking capacitors that are too large to fit into a 205-L drum should be wrapped in heavy gauge polyethylene and crated for transfer to a storage area. If the capacitor is leaking, it should be drained and stored in a drip pan containing sufficient adsorbent to adsorb any remaining liquid.

Small transformers may be stored or transported in leakproof containers, without draining, in a manner similar to that for capacitors. Transformers stored on-site need not be drained as long as they are structurally sound, external parts are protected from the weather, and spill containment is provided. Where large askarel transformers are being stored pending transportation or disposal, the askarel should be removed or stored in double-bung drums made of 16-gauge steel (or heavier). PCB liquids may be stored in tanks rather than drums provided the tanks are above ground and are sound, properly labelled, regularly inspected, protected from the weather, and spill containment provided.

7.1.6 Decontamination of PCB Equipment

The removal of PCBs from equipment or mineral oil is called "decontamination." There are two general approaches to decontamination: solvent cleaning and retrofilling.

Solvent cleaning is used for metal equipment that contains PCBs. Once the PCB fluid is removed, the metal hulk or carcass is rinsed with an organic solvent (such as hexachlorobenzene) to remove residual PCBs. Double- or even triple-rinsing may be necessary. Cleaned equipment may be suitable for disposal or re-use, or be sold for its scrap metal content.

Retrofilling involves the removal of PCBs from a piece of equipment and replacement with a non-PCB fluid. Several weeks after retrofilling, the new fluid should be analyzed to determine whether residual PCBs in the equipment have migrated into the new fluid. Two or more refills may be needed to reach acceptably low concentrations of PCBs in the fluid.

Proposed changes to federal legislation include lowering the maximum PCB concentration in non-PCB-contaminated materials and equipment from 50 ppm to 3 ppm. This proposed change could challenge the usefulness of retrofilling.

There is also an *in situ* method for refilling in which a decontamination unit is connected directly to the transformer. The oil is continuously recycled through the unit until the PCB concentration is reduced to an acceptable limit.

Depending upon the level of contamination, size of equipment, transportation regulations, and draining, decontamination can take place at the point of removal from service, or at some other location prior to transportation. Decontamination can also take place at a disposal site.

Like decommissioning, decontamination must be undertaken carefully. A valid C of A specifically applicable to PCB wastes is required to decontaminate liquid PCBs. The following suggested procedures are taken from guidelines issued by the CCME (1989).

Non-electrical, Askarel-filled Equipment – Non-electrical equipment which contains askarel can be decontaminated by triple-rinsing. Metal components may then be suitable for recovery.

Electrical, Askarel-filled Equipment – For electrical equipment that contains askarel, the procedure is complex and the success of the retrofilling is dependent on the type of transformer.

Contaminated Mineral Oil Equipment – Equipment which contained mineral oil contaminated with PCBs at concentrations <500 ppm may be drained and refilled with clean oil for re-use. Scrapping for metal recovery is considered acceptable once all free liquid is removed from the hulk by an approved method. The drained oil is a PCB waste.

Containers – Askarel-contaminated containers, such as drums or tanks, should be decontaminated by triple-rinsing with an appropriate solvent. Containers that held PCB-contaminated mineral oil or solvent should be rinsed in a manner appropriate to the degree of contamination and the intended use of the empty container or to the disposal method.

Solvent Disposal – Solvents used for PCB decontamination are classified as PCB waste if they contain more than 50 ppm of PCB by weight. It is acceptable, however, to use rinse solvent contaminated with greater than 50 ppm PCB as the first rinse when more than one PCB article is being decontaminated and the article being rinsed is more highly contaminated than the rinse solvent.

7.1.7 Storage of PCB Waste

As noted in Section 7.1.2, PCB waste can include PCB materials, PCB liquids, and PCB equipment. Regulation 362 defines all sites used to store PCB wastes as PCB disposal sites. This is somewhat misleading since there are few true disposal opportunities in Ontario at present. It has become commonplace to refer to storage facilities as being "interim".

Regardless of the terminology used, Regulation 362 describes various administrative requirements for operating a PCB waste disposal or storage site. For example, Section 4 outlines the responsibilities that a site operator has with respect to record-keeping and reporting to the MOEE. Section 5 requires that certain activities such as removing and transferring PCB waste can only take place in accordance with written instructions from an MOEE director. Section 7 requires that every person storing PCB waste shall ensure that the waste is in a safe and secure location so as to prevent waste coming into contact with any person and so that any liquid containing PCBs that may escape can be readily recovered and will not discharge directly or indirectly into a watercourse or ground water.

Regulations proposed in 1993 under the Ontario Environmental Bill of Rights will require that Director's Instructions for establishing new PCB storage sites must be placed in the provincial environmental registry for at least 30 days. The electronic registry is intended to provide the public with information about environmental proposals before decisions are made.

The MOEE directs owners of PCB waste to CEPA Regulation 92-507 for a description as to what constitutes proper storage. The aspects of storage addressed in that regulation include site security and access, the types of containers to be used, the precautions that should be taken to prevent releases to the environment, the stacking of containers, fire protection and emergency procedures, maintenance and inspection practices, labelling requirements, and record-keeping. Table 7.4 presents a list of features that facilities used to store PCB materials should have.

Figure 7.4 shows the label that should be used to identify drums, tanks, or packaging where contaminated mineral oils, rinsing fluids, or other low-level PCB wastes are stored. The label allows for the entering of the PCB concentration, date of analysis, company name, and the signature of an authorized company official.

Drums or other containers that contain PCB liquids in concentrations above 10,000 ppm require special identification to alert people to separate these liquids from low-level wastes in the storage area and that special disposal requirements may be necessary. The label presented in Figure 7.5 can be used.

Environment Canada recommends that the owner of PCB wastes retain an inventory record for five years after removal or disposal of the last of their PCBs.

Regulation 347 requires that the owner of a site where PCB wastes are stored must be registered as a hazardous waste generator and must meet various requirements for safety, storage of waste, and record-keeping.

The MOEE has considered developing a regulatory amendment which would define a "small PCB generator" on some measurable basis. For example, total square footage of a building might be used to determine whether the quantity of PCBs present in fluorescent light ballasts requires the owner to be registered as a generator, establish a storage facility, or determine the rate at which such ballasts can be disposed. At present, owners of more than one waste PCB-containing capacitor are required to store them, usually on their own property, until an approved method of disposal becomes available. While individual capacitors may not be PCB waste, once bundled together they may be classified as either PCB waste or PCB-related waste, and therefore be subject to the provisions of Regulation 362.

7.1.8 Transportation

The movement of PCB wastes in Ontario is governed by Regulation 347. The requirements specified in that regulation are described in Chapter 4.

Federally, the transportation of equipment and wastes that contains PCBs is governed by the Transportation of Dangerous Goods Act (TDGA) as described in Chapter 4. Under the TDGA regulations, PCBs or articles containing PCBs have a primary classification of 9.1, a subsidiary classification of 9.2 and a Product Identification Number (PIN) of 2315.

All equipment and wastes that contain PCBs at concentrations greater than 50 ppm should be labelled. **Safety marking and documentation** requirements are set out under TDGA regulations. When PCB wastes or equipment is offered for transport, it must be labelled as shown in Figures 7.5 and 7.6. All containers, articles, or equipment must clearly show the shipping name and the PIN number. When PCBs are transported in a large container or transport unit, a Class 9 placard (see Figure 7.7) must be displayed. An exception to this rule is for road vehicles travelling solely on land and when the gross quantity of PCB goods is less than 500 kg. No such exception applies for PCB wastes.

PCB equipment requires a TDGA shipping document. (The waste manifest system required by Regulation 347 satisfies this requirement when PCB waste is being transported.) People involved in shipping must be trained and certified in accordance with the TDGA or under direct supervision of a trained, certified person.

Recent amendments to the TDGA regulations provide certain **exemptions for small-quantity items** such as samples, articles of wastes, and some types of electrical equipment containing PCBs. Securely packaged (including adsorbent) samples, solids in quantities less than 10 kg gross weight, and liquids when their net quantity is the lesser of 2 L or 2 kg are exempt. When a waste is a PCB mixture containing less than 50 ppm of PCBs, or an article containing PCBs or electrical equipment containing a PCB mixture, it is also exempt if the quantity of PCB mixture is not greater than 500 g. PCB articles in leak-free condition and containing not greater than 500 g of PCB mixture are exempt from all TDGA regulations.

The **documentation requirements** of the TDGA include:

- 60-day advance notification for PCB shipments destined for or imported from any international location
- the Canadian party must forward a letter to Environment Canada and Transport Canada confirming that arrangements have been made by the Canadian party, when dealing with a party outside of Canada, to receive completed copies of the Waste Manifest

- 30-day prenotification of interprovincial shipments and a seven-day prenotification for inspection by the appropriate authority

The advance notification for international shipments can cover a series of consignments over a 12-month period if estimated shipping dates for each consignment are provided. However, seven days before the intended shipping date of the second and each subsequent consignment, the shipper must again notify both Transport Canada and Environment Canada.

The TDGA regulation requires that articles containing PCB mixtures be securely enclosed in leak-proof **containers and packaging** suitable for PCBs. Serviceable electrical equipment used as emergency replacement for stationary equipment must be permanently mounted on a railway or road vehicle. This type of equipment, if it is drained, must have any remaining PCB mixture contained in the base below the drain opening. When transportation occurs by road vehicles, the equipment must be inspected by the carrier every two hours or every 200 km, whichever occurs first.

The Dangerous Goods Transportation Act in Ontario adopts the TDGA requirements for provincially regulated modes of transportation.

The U.S. banned the importing of PCB waste in 1980, and most European sites will no longer accept international shipments. Federal PCB Waste Export Regulations under CEPA ban overseas export of PCB wastes. The regulations will help Canada meet its international obligations under the United Nations Basel Convention to minimize hazardous wastes imports and exports, or place strict environmental controls if they cannot be avoided.

7.1.9 Destruction

The most widely used technology in Europe and the United States for the destruction of PCB liquids and PCB wastes is that of high-temperature incineration. In Canada, high-temperature incinerators approved for the destruction of PCB wastes are located at Swan Hills, Alberta (which only accepts PCBs from Alberta and the Northwest Territories) and Smithville, Ontario.

The Mobile PCB Treatment and Destruction Regulations (SOR/90-5) govern the operation of mobile PCB destruction units at federal facilities. The regulations require that destruction systems must have a minimum PCB destruction limit of 99.9999%. A mobile PCB incinerator was used at the Canadian Forces Base in Goose Bay, Labrador.

Ontario has given approval-in-principal to mobile destruction units and has passed a regulation specific to their establishment and control. The Mobile PCB Destruction Facilities Regulation (Regulation 352) describes siting, operation, environmental control, monitoring, and bonding requirements for two types of mobile PCB destruction technologies: mobile incineration and mobile chemical destruction facilities. The regulation outlines the requirements for record-keeping and record-retention at disposal facilities.

7.1.10 Disposal

As noted in Section 7.1.2, the disposal of PCB wastes in Ontario and the operation of disposal sites are addressed in Regulation 362. To receive PCB wastes at a disposal site, written instructions are required from an MOEE director, or the site must be operated under a certificate of approval that specifies the circumstances under which PCB waste may be accepted.

Once accepted at a site, the PCB waste can not be disposed, decontaminated, or otherwise managed or diluted if in the form of a liquid unless the conditions are specified in the certificate of approval or in accordance with written instructions of an MOEE director.

Section 7 of Regulation 362 requires that the PCB waste be placed in a safe and secure location so as to prevent waste coming into contact with any person and so that any liquid containing PCBs that may escape can be readily recovered and will not discharge directly or indirectly into a watercourse or ground water.

A PCB waste disposal site is exempt from Sections 27, 39, and 40 of the EPA which deal with the requirement for a Certificate of Approval or provisional C of A for a waste management system or waste disposal site. However, the exemption is subject to the following conditions:

- record-keeping (as discussed below) must be provided
- either written instructions from the director prior to the removal of PCB waste are required or the waste management system or waste disposal site must have a certificate of approval which states that PCB wastes may be stored, handled, treated, collected, transported, processed, or disposed of
- if the waste being removed contains over 50 L of PCB liquid, the removal must be in accordance with written instructions of the director, regardless of its destiny, and
- PCB liquid must not be removed from equipment or a container except to transfer the liquid from a leaking container (after notifying the director of the transfer) or pursuant to instructions of the director

If a C of A or provisional certificate has been issued which specifies the manner in which the PCB waste may be stored, handled, treated, collected, transported, processed, or disposed of, the conditions of EPA Sections 27, 39, and 40 apply.

Certain conditions apply if a PCB waste disposal site is offered for sale or lease. The prospective purchaser, tenant, or person taking possession of the site must be made aware of the existing legal requirements of the site in addition to notifying an MOEE director of the change. The director must be notified 10 days after the sale, lease, or change in possession of the location of the site and the nature and quantity of PCB waste.

The record-keeping requirements of Regulation 362 for waste disposal sites include:

- method and time of PCB delivery to and from the site
- the source of the PCB waste and/or destination and the contact person
- description of the nature and quantity of PCB waste at the site
- the location of the waste disposal site
- the method of storage of the PCB waste at the site
- notification to the director immediately by telephone, and in writing within three days, after PCB waste first comes on the site, and
- notification to the director within 30 days after any other PCB waste is taken to or from the site

The operator must maintain the records until two years following written notice to the director that he has ceased to be a holder of PCB wastes.

7.1.11 Summary

Polychlorinated biphenyls (PCBs) are a family of compounds which bioaccumulate in the food chain. Birds, aquatic invertebrates, and most species of fish are particularly sensitive to PCBs. Recent research indicates that, except for causing skin rashes, many PCBs are virtually harmless to human beings.

PCBs came into commercial use in the late 1920s. The major Canadian use was in dielectric fluid for industrial electrical equipment. All non-electrical uses of PCBs were prohibited in Canada in 1977. There remain many pieces of electrical equipment in service that contain PCBs.

The use of PCBs and equipment that contains PCBs is governed by several acts including the EPA (and its Regulations 347, 352, and 362), CEPA (and its Regulations SOR/91-152 and 92-507), and the TDGA. These pieces of legislation define various types of PCB materials, place several prohibitions on their use and importation, and impose requirements on their storage, transportation, destruction, and disposal. There also are guidelines and criteria that identify maximum acceptable concentrations in air, water supplies, soils, and sediments. Ontario Regulation 362 defines material that contains more than 50 ppm of PCBs as PCB waste.

7.2 ASBESTOS

7.2.1 Overview

Asbestos is a generic term that applies to naturally occurring hydrated mineral silicates that are separable into flexible, incombustible fibres. The family of asbestos minerals can be subdivided into serpentine and amphibole fibres. Chrysotile is the most common fibrous serpentine and accounts for more than 90% of the world's production of asbestos.

Canada, specifically the Thetford area of Quebec, has been a major producer of asbestos for more than 100 years. Canada was the world's largest producer of chrysotile (white) asbestos, accounting for over 40% of world production.

Asbestos has been used for ceiling and floor tiles, pipe insulation, cement, and insulating materials. In addition, asbestos is incorporated into cement construction materials (roofing, shingles, and cement pipes), friction materials (brake linings and clutch pads), venting and gaskets, asphalt coats, and sealants (Mossman *et al.*, 1990).

Around the turn of the century, asbestos was shown to cause asbestosis (a fibrotic lung disease). The association with the causation of lung and pleural tumours in asbestos miners and workers was demonstrated in the 1950s and 1960s, respectively (Mossman *et al.*, 1990). The inhalation of asbestos fibres has also been shown to produce lung cancer and mesothelioma (a cancer of the lining of the lung and chest cavities). Epidemiological research in the 1960s revealed that insulation workers who had dealt with asbestos for 20 years or more were dying of lung cancer and the complications of asbestosis at alarming rates, particularly those who had smoked (Zurer, 1990).

7.2.2 Regulatory Framework

Much of the regulatory framework for asbestos in Ontario has been passed under the Occupational Health and Safety Act (OHSA). Asbestos was one of the first **designated substances** to be regulated. The original regulation (Regulation 570/82) addressed uses of asbestos-containing materials (ACMs) except in construction projects (which was to be addressed in a second regulation). Subsequent to the findings of a Royal Commission into the use of asbestos, a regulation for the use of asbestos on construction projects and in buildings and repair operations (Regulation 645/85) was filed. Both Regulation 570/82 and Regulation 645/85 were amended between 1985 and 1992. In the latest revisions to provincial regulations, Regulation 570/82 has become Regulation 837 and addresses the mining of asbestos and the manufacture of asbestos parts. Regulation 645/85 has become Regulation 838 and addresses the use of asbestos on construction projects and in buildings and repair operations.

The only "environmental" regulation that pertains to asbestos is Regulation 347 which defines asbestos waste and the requirements for the management of that waste (see Section 7.2.4).

7.2.3 Removal versus Management

ACMs were used widely in large buildings including offices, schools, and hospitals. While ACMs in buildings do not spontaneously shed fibres, physical damage by decay, renovation, or demolition can lead to the release of airborne fibres.

Public pressure, fuelled by concepts such as the theory that inhaling one fibre of asbestos will cause cancer, has resulted in the removal of asbestos from many schools and public buildings even though ACMs are used most commonly in boiler rooms and other areas which are relatively inaccessible to building occupants.

ACMs removal in large buildings can cost millions of dollars. Removal must be done carefully and thoroughly. The improper removal of previously undamaged or encapsulated asbestos can lead to increases in airborne concentrations of fibres in buildings, sometimes for months afterwards. (Mossman *et al.*, 1990).

In the United States, the 1986 Asbestos Hazard Response Act (AHERA) provides the Environmental Protection Agency (U.S. EPA) with the mandate to require schools to develop plans to manage (not necessarily remove) asbestos. It also requires asbestos-removal consultants and workers to have some minimal training and requires that asbestos be taken out of buildings before they are demolished or renovated (Zurer, 1990).

The U.S. EPA has published several documents to help school owners identify and control asbestos hazards in buildings:

- Guidance for Controlling Friable Asbestos-Containing Materials in Buildings, 1983 (EPA-560/5-83-002)
- Guidance for Controlling Asbestos-Containing Materials in Buildings, 1985 (EPA-560/5-85-024)
- Measuring Airborne Asbestos Following an Abatement Action, 1985 (EPA-600/4-85-049)

In 1984, a U.S. National Research Council (NRC) Committee concluded that breathing the asbestos present in ambient air may be hazardous and that some cancers will result. The NRC panel reached that conclusion by extrapolating from high occupational doses to low doses of asbestos (Zurer, 1990). Since that time, two points have become clear that contradict the NRC conclusions (Mossman *et al.*, 1990). The first is that chrysotile asbestos, the asbestos which predominates in buildings, is not nearly so dangerous as other forms of asbestos. By lumping all kinds of asbestos together, the risk assessments undertaken by NRC, U.S. EPA, and the Occupational Safety and Health Association (OSHA) exaggerated the risk from chrysotile. The second point is that the estimates of the amount of asbestos that a building's occupants inhale were too high. Fibre concentrations from recent studies in buildings are comparable to levels in outdoor air.

If asbestos is suspected of being present the following action should be taken:
- A sample should be taken as visual inspection of fireproofing materials is unreliable.
- The type of asbestos should be identified. Chrysotile asbestos forms curly fibres while amphibole types of asbestos including crocidolite and amosite crystallize as sharp needles.
- Indoor air monitoring should be conducted.
- If air quality levels are unacceptable, a detailed assessment should be made of physical damage to ACM.
- Damaged areas should be repaired and/or encapsulated.
- If conditions warrant removing the ACM, it should be removed by trained individuals (as per Regulation 838) and the material disposed as per Section 17 of Regulation 347.
- The ACM should be wet prior to stripping to suppress dust.
- Individuals involved in the removal must wear appropriate protective clothing including respirator, coveralls, and gloves.

7.2.4 Management of Asbestos Waste

Ontario Regulation 347 defines **asbestos waste** as solid or liquid waste that results from the removal of asbestos-containing construction or insulation materials or the manufacture of asbestos-containing products and contains asbestos in more than a trivial amount or proportion. No definition is provided for what constitutes "a trivial amount or proportion".

Section 17 of Regulation 347 specifies various aspects of managing asbestos waste. The management of asbestos waste must be carried out in accordance with the provisions outlined in Table 7.5. One of the requirements of Section 17 is that every precaution must be taken to avoid the asbestos waste from becoming airborne.

Asbestos waste does not require registration in accordance with Regulation 347 as it is specifically identified in Section 1 of the regulation as non-hazardous solid industrial waste. It therefore does not require manifesting and can be disposed at a non-hazardous landfill site; however, TDGA does require that the asbestos waste be manifested.

Regulation 347 requires that the word "CAUTION" in letters at least 10 cm high be present on both sides of all rigid containers and vehicles used to transport asbestos waste. The words "CONTAINS ASBESTOS FIBRES", "Asbestos May Be Harmful To Your Health", and "Wear Approved Protective Equipment" also need to be present. The TDGA also requires that labels and placards be present during shipment.

7.2.5 Acceptable Concentrations in Air

The MOEE has established an interim half-hour point-of-impingement limit for total asbestos of 5 fibres per cm^3, and an ambient air quality criterion of 0.04 fibres per cm^3 for fibres greater than 5 µm in length (MOE, 1991).

7.2.6 Summary

As early as the turn of the century, asbestos was shown to cause asbestosis. The link to lung and pleural tumours in asbestos miners and workers was not demonstrated until the 1950s and 1960s. Research has demonstrated that the inhalation of asbestos fibres may produce asbestosis, lung cancer, and mesothelioma.

Asbestos-containing materials have been used widely in public buildings, including schools and hospitals, as well as commercial and industrial establishments. Asbestos in buildings does not spontaneously shed fibres, but physical damage to ACM by decay, renovation, or demolition can lead to the release of airborne fibres. It is therefore important that an assessment be made by experienced personnel of the condition of ACM in a building. If the material is damaged, it should be repaired and/or encapsulated, or if conditions warrant be removed. The removal must be done by trained individuals.

In Ontario, the management of asbestos is covered by Regulation 838 (construction projects and buildings) and Regulation 837 (mining and manufacturing of asbestos parts). The management of asbestos waste is specified under Regulation 347. The regulation covers the storage, removal, transportation, and disposal of asbestos waste. The transportation of asbestos waste must comply with the requirements of Regulation 347, DGTA, and TGDA.

REFERENCES

Canadian Council of Ministers of the Environment (CCME). August 1986. "The PCB Story."

Canadian Council of Ministers of the Environment (CCME). September 1989. *Guidelines for the Management of Wastes Containing Polychlorinated Biphenyls (PCBs).* CCME-TS/WM-TRE008, Manual EPS 9/HA/1 (revised).

Environment Canada. Not dated. *Handbook on PCBs in Electrical Equipment.* Third edition. Commercial Chemicals Branch, Conservation and Protection.

Environment Canada. 1989. *Environment Canada Release Regulations on the Operation of Mobile PCB Incinerators.* PR-HQ-089-37.

Miller, J. 1989. "Myth or Menace?" *Toronto Star.* D.1, 2 September.

Miller, M.M., P.W. Stanley, G.L. Huang, W.Y. Shiu, and D. Mackay. 1985. "Relationships between Octanol-Water Partition Coefficient and Aqueous Solubility." *Environ. Sci. and Technol.* 19 (No. 6): 522-528.

Ontario Ministry of the Environment (MOE). October 1992a. *Water Management — Goals, Policies, Objectives and Implementation Procedures of the Ministry of the Environment.*

Ontario Ministry of the Environment (MOE). June 1992b. *Fill Quality Guidelines for Lakefilling in Ontario.* Prepared by A. Hayton, D. Persaud, and R. Jaagumagi, Water Resources Branch.

Ontario Ministry of the Environment (MOE). August 1991. *Summary of Point of Impingement Standards, Ambient Air Quality Criteria (AAQCs), and Approvals Screening Levels (ASLs).* Air Resources Branch.

Mossman, B.T., J. Bignon, M. Corn, A. Seaton, and J.B.L. Gee. 1990. "Asbestos: Scientific Developments and Implications for Public Policy." *Science* 24 (January).

Zurer, P.S. 1990. "Many Asbestos Removal Projects Cited as Needless, Costly, and Risky." *C & EN.* February 5.

Table 7.1
SUMMARY OF PCB REGULATIONS

Environmental Criteria	MOEE Provincial Water Quality Objectives MOEE Drinking Water Objectives MOEE Air Quality Criteria and Standards MOEE Soil Quality Guidelines MOEE Fill Quality Guidelines CCME Ambient Water Quality Guidelines CCME Interim Environmental Quality Criteria Ocean Dumping Control Act
Environmental Releases	CEPA Chlorobiphenyls Regulations SOR/91-152 CEPA Mobile PCB Treatment and Destruction Regulations SOR/90-5 Fisheries Act
Importation, Manufacture, and Use	CEPA Chlorobiphenyls Regulation SOR/91-152
Decommissioning Equipment	MOEE Notification CCME Guidelines
Decontaminating Equipment	CCME Guidelines
Equipment Storage	MOEE and Environment Canada Notification
Waste Storage	Ontario Regulation 362 CEPA Chlorobiphenyls Regulations SOR/91-152
Movement/Transportation	Ontario Regulation 347 Ontario Dangerous Goods Transportation Act Transportation of Dangerous Goods Act
Labelling	Dangerous Goods Transportation Act Transportation of Dangerous Goods Act
Mobile Destruction	Ontario Regulation 352 CEPA Mobile Treatment and Destruction Regulations SOR/90-5
Disposal	Ontario Regulation 362
Record-Keeping	Ontario Regulation 362
Import/Export	CEPA Waste Export Regulations SOR/90-453

Table 7.2
PHYSICAL PARAMETER VALUES FOR SELECTED PCBS

Compound	Molecular Wt. g/mol	Solubility mol/m3	Log Kow
biphenyl	154.2	4.35×10^{-2}	3.76
2-	188.7	2.68×10^{-2}	4.50
2,6-	223.1	6.23×10^{-3}	4.93
2,4,6-	257.5	8.76×10^{-4}	5.51
2,3,4,5-	292	7.17×10^{-5}	5.72
2,3,4,5,6-	326.4	1.68×10^{-5}	6.3
2,2',4,4',6,6'-	360.9	1.13×10^{-6}	7.55
2,2',3,3',4,4',6-	395.3	5.49×10^{-6}	6.68
2,2',3,3',5,5',6,6'	429.8	9.15×10^{-7}	7.11
2,2',3,3',4,5,5',6,6'-	464.2	3.88×10^{-8}	8.16

Reference: Miller et al., 1985

Table 7.3
ALLOWABLE CONCENTRATIONS OF PCB

WATER

1 µg/L in drinking water — interim maximum acceptable concentration (MOE, 1992a)

1 ng/L in ambient water — provincial water quality objective (MOE, 1992a)

1 ng/L in ambient water — Canadian Water Quality Guideline (CCME, 1989)

5 µg/L — maximum in liquid effluents (CEPA Mobile PCB Treatment and Destruction Regulations SOR/90-5)

AIR

35 ng/m^3 (annual average) — ambient air quality criterion (CCME, 1989; MOE, 1991)

150 ng/m^3 (24-h average) — ambient air quality criterion (CCME, 1989; MOE, 1991)

450 ng/m^3 (0.5-h average) — point-of-impingement limit (MOE, 1991)

1 mg/kg — maximum in gaseous releases (CEPA Mobile PCB Treatment and Destruction Regulations SOR/90-5)

SOIL

0.5 ppm for agricultural sites — MOEE and CCME Interim Guideline (CCME, 1989)

5 ppm for residential and public access sites — MOEE and CCME Interim Guideline (CCME, 1989)

25 ppm for industrial and commercial sites — MOEE and CCME Interim Guideline (CCME, 1989)

SEDIMENT

0.01 µg/g (dry weight) — no effect level: provincial sediment quality guideline (MOE, 1992b)

0.07 µg/g (dry weight) — lowest effect level: provincial sediment quality guideline (MOE, 1992b)

WASTE

50 ppm by weight — Ontario Regulation 362

RELEASE RATE

1 g/d — CEPA Chlorobiphenyls Regulations SOR/91-152

Table 7.4
PCB STORAGE REQUIREMENTS

1 Spill containment (have a collection system for rain water if storage is outdoors; can place PCB-adsorbent material in drain lines).
2 There should be a fire alarm system and suitable portable or flood-type fire extinguishers.
3 Emergency response training for personnel.
4 The storage facility should be separate from processing and manufacturing operations.
5 Access to the site should be restricted.
6 An isolated room (alternatively a 2 m high woven mesh fence with lockable gate).
7 Placement of personnel protection equipment and clean-up kits within easy access.
8 Adequate ventilation (air intake and exhaust outlets should be on the exterior walls of buildings).
9 If the storage site is equipped with a mechanical exhaust system that exhausts into a building, the system must be provided with a smoke sensory control to stop the fan and close the damper(s) in the event of a fire.
10 Ventilation switch placed outside of storage room if mechanical ventilation (the system should allow for several minutes of ventilation prior to entry).
11 Floors should be made of steel, concrete, or similar durable material.
12 The storage area should have continuous curbing (designed to accommodate the larger of two times the largest piece of equipment or 25% of the total volume of PCB liquid at the location; or for a single unit 125% of the containers volume).
13 Concrete should be sealed with a PCB-resistant sealant.
14 All floor drains, pumping systems, and sumps leading from the storage location should be sealed.
15 The storage facility should be located and engineered so that no PCBs will be released in the event of flood, storm, or runoff from fire fighting.
16 Use storage containers as described in Section 9 of CEPA Regulation SOR/92-507.
17 Drums or other portable containers should be placed on skids or pallets.
18 Stacking should be limited to two containers high, unless special shelving, bracing, strapping, etc. is provided.
19 If equipment containing liquid PCBs is stored outside, equipment and containment should be covered by a weatherproof roof or barrier that protects the equipment or liquids and the curbing or drip pans under them.

20 Solids, including drained PCB equipment, may be stored outside without being covered by a roof or other secondary covering providing the drained equipment and containers are structurally sound.

21 Bulk containers (e.g. large international shipping containers or approved commercially manufactured metal storage containers or structures) may be used for either primary or secondary containment for outdoor storage.

22 There should be an emergency fire plan which has been approved by the local fire department.

Table 7.5
REQUIREMENTS FOR MANAGING ASBESTOS WASTES

1 Asbestos waste that leaves a site must be sent to a waste disposal site where the operator has previously agreed to accept the material and has been advised of its arrival time.

2 Unless transported in bulk, asbestos waste must be stored in a rigid, impermeable, sealed container capable of accommodating the weight of the material.

3 Only a waste management system operating under a certificate of approval that specifically authorizes the transportation of asbestos in bulk can be employed to transport bulk asbestos.

4 If a cardboard box is used for storage, the asbestos must be sealed in a polyethylene bag 6 mm thick placed within the box and must be transported within a closed vehicle.

5 The external surfaces of the container and the vehicle or vessel used for transportation must be free of asbestos waste.

6 Asbestos waste shall not be transported in a compaction type waste haulage vehicle.

7 Both sides of the vehicle transporting the asbestos wastes and every container (see item 2) must display in large, easily read letters that contrast in colour with the background the word "CAUTION" in letters not less than 10 cm high. The words "CONTAINS ASBESTOS FIBRES", "Asbestos May Be Harmful To Your Health", and "Wear Approved Protective Equipment" also need to be present.

8 The driver must be trained in the management of asbestos waste.

9 Asbestos waste shall not be transported with any other cargo in the same vehicle.

10 The vehicle must be equipped with emergency spill equipment.

11 Asbestos waste may be deposited at a landfilling site only while the depositing is being supervised by the operator of the site or a person designated by him for the purpose and the person supervising is not also operating machinery or the truck involved.

12 If deposited in a landfill, the location within the site must have been adapted for this purpose and at least 125 cm of garbage or cover material must be place forthwith over the deposited asbestos waste.

13 Protective clothing and respiratory equipment must be worn.

Figure 7.1
PCB LABEL FOR LARGE EQUIPMENT

ATTENTION
PCB   BPC

CONTAINS	CONTIENT DES
POLYCHLORINATED BIPHENYLS	BIPHÉNYLES POLYCHLORÉS

| A TOXIC SUBSTANCE SCHEDULED UNDER THE CANADIAN ENVIRONMENTAL PROTECTION ACT. IN CASE OF ACCIDENT, SPILL OR FOR DISPOSAL INFORMATION, CONTACT THE NEAREST OFFICE OF ENVIRONMENTAL PROTECTION, ENVIRONMENT CANADA. | SUBSTANCE TOXIQUE MENTIONNÉE DANS L'ANNEXE DE LA LOI CANADIENNE SUR LA PROTECTION DE L'ENVIRONNEMENT. EN CAS D'ACCIDENT, OU DE DÉVERSEMENT, OU POUR SAVOIR COMMENT L'ÉLIMINER, CONTACTER LE BUREAU DE LA PROTECTION DE L'ENVIRONNEMENT, MINISTÈRE DE L'ENVIRONNEMENT LE PLUS PRÈS. |

OR 26900

Figure 7.2
PCB LABEL FOR SMALL EQUIPMENT

CAUTION   ATTENTION

CONTAINS   CONTIENT DU

PCB BPC

A   UNE

TOXIC   SUBSTANCE

SUBSTANCE   TOXIQUE

OR 12882

Figure 7.3
PCB GENERAL WARNING LABEL

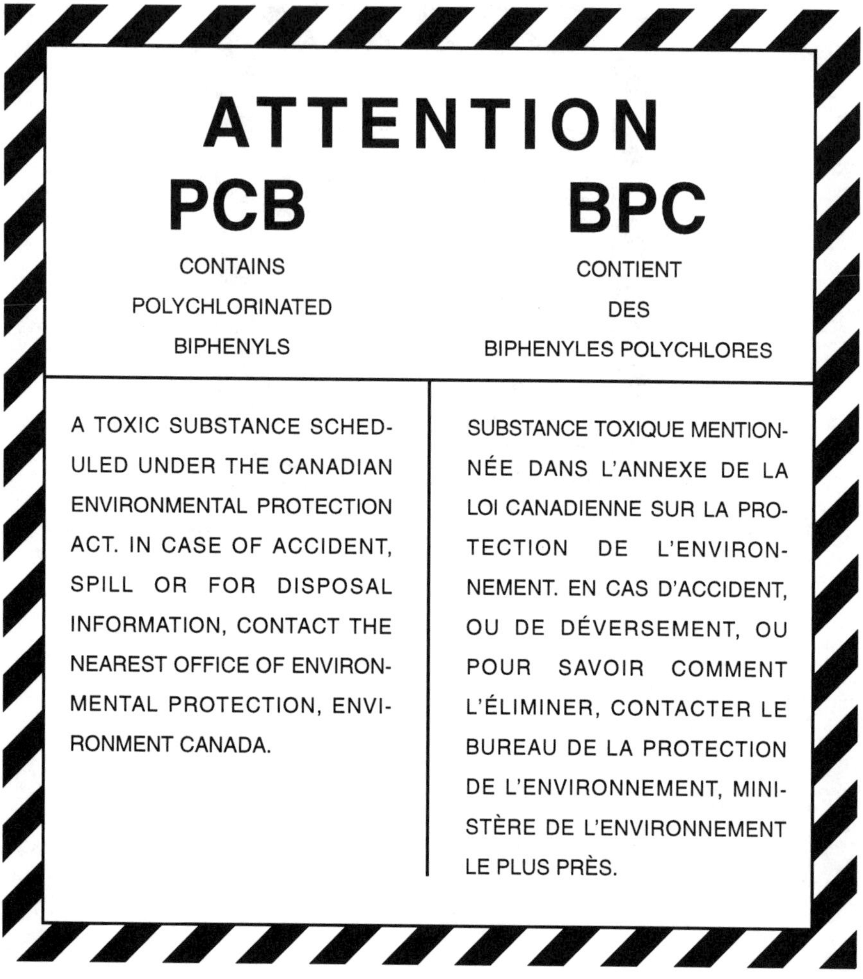

ATTENTION
PCB   BPC

CONTAINS	CONTIENT
POLYCHLORINATED	DES
BIPHENYLS	BIPHENYLES POLYCHLORES

| A TOXIC SUBSTANCE SCHEDULED UNDER THE CANADIAN ENVIRONMENTAL PROTECTION ACT. IN CASE OF ACCIDENT, SPILL OR FOR DISPOSAL INFORMATION, CONTACT THE NEAREST OFFICE OF ENVIRONMENTAL PROTECTION, ENVIRONMENT CANADA. | SUBSTANCE TOXIQUE MENTIONNÉE DANS L'ANNEXE DE LA LOI CANADIENNE SUR LA PROTECTION DE L'ENVIRONNEMENT. EN CAS D'ACCIDENT, OU DE DÉVERSEMENT, OU POUR SAVOIR COMMENT L'ÉLIMINER, CONTACTER LE BUREAU DE LA PROTECTION DE L'ENVIRONNEMENT, MINISTÈRE DE L'ENVIRONNEMENT LE PLUS PRÈS. |

Figure 7.4
PCB WARNING LABEL FOR CONTAMINATED EQUIPMENT

ATTENTION

CONTAMINATED WITH PCBs (POLYCHLORINATED BIPHENYLS)	CONTAMINÉ PAR BPCs (BIPHÉNYLES POLYCHLORÉS)
THE CONTENTS OF THIS EQUIPMENT ARE CONTAMINATED WITH PCBs, A TOXIC SUBSTANCE SCHEDULED AND REGULATED UNDER THE CANADIAN ENVIRONMENTAL PROTECTION ACT. IN CASE OF ACCIDENT, SPILL OR FOR DISPOSAL INFORMATION, CONTACT THE NEAREST OFFICE OF ENVIRONMENTAL PROTECTION, ENVIRONMENT CANADA.	LE CONTENU DE CET APPAREIL EST CONTAMINÉ PAR DES BPCs, UNE SUBSTANCE TOXIQUE ANNEXÉE ET RÉGLEMENTÉE EN VERTU DE LA LOI CANADIENNE SUR LA PROTECTION DE L'ENVIRONNEMENT. EN CAS D'ACCIDENT, OU DE DÉVERSEMENT, OU POUR SAVOIR COMMENT L'ÉLIMINER, CONTACTER LE BUREAU LE PLUS PROCHE DE LA PROTECTION DE L'ENVIRONNEMENT, MINISTÈRE DE L'ENVIRONNEMENT.

PCB CONCENTRATION (parts per million)
CONCENTRATION DE BPC (parties par million) _____

DATE ANALYZED
DATE D'ANALYSE _____

COMPANY NAME
NOM DE LA COMPAGNIE _____

AUTHORIZED COMPANY OFFICIAL
AGENT OFFICIEL AUTORISÉ_____

Figure 7.5
TDGA PCB LABEL

Black —— **ATTENTION**   White

PCB-BPD

CONTAINS   CONTIENT DES
POLYCHLORINATED BIPHENYLS   DIPHÉNYLES POLYCHLORÉS

A TOXIC SUBSTANCE SCHED-
ULED UNDER THE CANADIAN
ENVIRONMENTAL PROTECTION
ACT. IN CASE OF ACCIDENT,
SPILL OR FOR DISPOSAL
INFORMATION, CONTACT THE
NEAREST OFFICE OF ENVIRON-
MENTAL PROTECTION, ENVI-
RONMENT CANADA.

SUBSTANCE TOXIQUE MENTION-
NÉE DANS L'ANNEXE DE LA
LOI CANADIENNE SUR LA PRO-
TECTION DE L'ENVIRON-
NEMENT. EN CAS D'ACCIDENT,
OU DE DÉVERSEMENT, OU
POUR SAVOIR COMMENT
L'ÉLIMINER, CONTACTER LE
BUREAU DE LA PROTECTION
DE L'ENVIRONNEMENT, MINI-
STÈRE DE L'ENVIRONNEMENT
LE PLUS PRÈS.

Figure 7.6
TDGA CLASS 9 LABEL

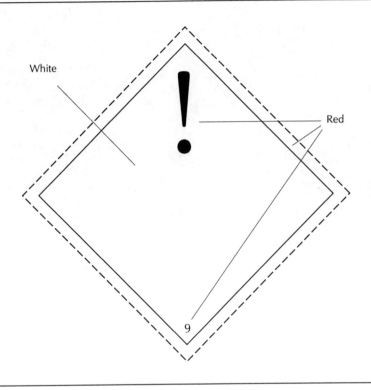

Figure 7.7
TDGA CLASS 9 PLACARD

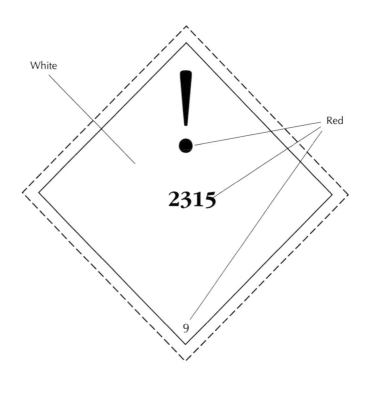

8.0

Enforcement

8.1 BACKGROUND

Prior to 1985, the enforcement activities of the MOE were seen by some as being somewhat lethargic and ineffective. The majority of non-compliance issues were resolved through discussions between the MOE regional personnel and industry. Approximately 50 cases per year went to court, convictions were few, and penalties did not seem to be adequate deterrents. Since 1985, several events have occurred in Ontario that are causing those perceptions to change:

- Since the formation of the Investigations and Enforcement Branch (IEB) in 1985, the number of cases going to court has increased. In 1992, there were 399 convictions (221 individuals and 178 companies) from 2,163 charges laid.
- The Environmental Enforcement Statute Law Amendment Act of 1986 extended liability to directors and officers of companies who do not comply with statutes and regulations and greatly increased the penalties possible for violations.
- Individuals can be fined $2,000 to $100,000 and given jail terms and made responsible for other costs. The fines for corporations range from $2,000 to $2,000,000. Total fines for provincial convictions for 1992 were $3,633,095 as compared to $605,668 for 1985/86.
- The annual publication entitled *Offences against the Environment* presents a comprehensive listing of environmental convictions and highlights interesting and significant cases from the realm of environmental law.

As a result of these changes and the importance that regulatory agencies (including the MOEE) are placing on enforcement, companies and their employees face the increasing likelihood of being inspected or interviewed. If violations are observed or suspected, regulatory agencies can be expected to pursue corrective actions actively and, if necessary, seek convictions.

The **IEB** was created to clearly separate the roles of abatement work from environmental enforcement. The branch has approximately 54 investigators, 11 enforcement officers, and 10 technical support specialists.

It has two primary objectives (MOEE, 1993):

1 to conduct investigations of illegal environmental activities
2 to provide sufficient evidence to Crown prosecutors to bring cases before the courts

The IEB visits facilities primarily to determine whether or not a law has been broken. Staff members come from a broad background. Many have extensive experience in environmental science while others are former members of police forces.

The **Legal Services Branch (LSB)** of the MOEE is largely composed of lawyers specializing in environmental law. LSB lawyers are accountable to the Ministry of the Attorney General, not the MOEE. The branch's primary role is to determine which cases go forward for prosecution and conduct prosecutions under provincial environmental legislation.

8.2 INSPECTIONS

8.2.1 Authority and Responsibilities of Provincial Officers

Provincial Acts that provide designated representatives (referred to in this discussion as provincial officers) with the right to inspect sites or premises as part of investigations include the Environmental Protection Act (EPA) and the Ontario Water Resources Act (OWRA). Analogous powers of inspection are provided in federal legislation including the Canadian Environmental Protection Act (CEPA) and the Transportation of Dangerous Goods Act (TDGA).

In broad terms, a provincial officer administers the Acts by attempting to identify, contain, clean up, and prevent emissions or spills being repeated. In addition to administering the Acts, the provincial officer is also responsible for obtaining evidence for prosecution. Table 8.1 lists the powers of a provincial officer under the EPA.

A provincial officer must have **reasonable cause** before exercising the prescribed powers. It may be difficult to determine if the provincial officer is restricting his activities to those reasonably related to the administration of the EPA and its regulations, or whether, in fact, an investigation is taking place to obtain evidence for a prosecution (Cotton, 1989).

In addition to the authority granted by legislation, provincial officers may in certain circumstances be required to obtain an Order of the Justice of the Peace or a search warrant. The latter is obtained by making a sworn declaration to the Justice of the Peace concerning the offence that has been committed and the items being sought (McKenney, 1989).

Recent case law on the Canadian Charter of Rights and Freedoms strongly suggests that provincial officers should not search premises to seize or obtain evidence of an offence without a search warrant or order of a court (Jetten and Smith, 1989).

8.2.2 Timing of Inspections

A provincial officer may enter a business premise at any **reasonable time** to check for compliance with the EPA. What constitutes a reasonable time may vary with the circumstances. It is generally accepted that routine inspection should be conducted during normal business hours. In contrast, a search based on the suspicion of an offence may be reasonable even if carried out at other times of the day.

The MOEE may give a company notice of any incident or situation into which it is investigating. The company and government representatives should attempt to establish procedures for conducting any investigation such as when and where interviews are to be conducted.

If the time suggested by a provincial officer is not convenient, an alternative time may be requested by the company. It is not unreasonable to request that an inspection be delayed to allow the company to consult a lawyer.

If prearrangements have not been made and an inspector or officer arrives to investigate a situation, he should be treated courteously and the concerns addressed without delay. Some companies, fearing that incriminating evidence or practices may be uncovered, may refuse entry or assume an uncooperative attitude. This type of conduct may give rise to a charge of obstructing a provincial officer in the execution of his duty.

If an inspector or officer arrives unannounced, he should be asked to show his credentials or badges, etc., to indicate the department he represents and then asked questions concerning:

- the purpose of the investigation and/or the nature of the problem
- whether there is a specific date or series of dates that are of concern
- whether a specific location or source is under investigation
- the section of which Act or regulation may have been violated

If the responses indicate that the inspection is with regard to an investigation into a possible violation, copies of the responses should be sent to a lawyer.

8.2.3 Obligations of Those Being Inspected

Some legislation contains sections that, in effect, impose obligations on individuals to cooperate when an investigation by an inspector is launched. Sections 156, 160, 161, and 167 of the EPA prohibit an individual from hindering, obstructing, or providing false information to a provincial officer in the lawful performance of his or her duties. In addition, an individual may not refuse any **reasonable request** for information for the purposes of the Act or regulation.

Under Section 14(4 and 5) of the federal Transport of Dangerous Goods Act (TDGA), specified individuals are required to give an inspector all reasonable assistance so that he can carry out his duties and functions. The Act also specifies that no person shall provide false or misleading information to the inspector or remove, alter or interfere in any way with anything seized or removed by the inspector.

If the search is requested because of a suspicion that an offence has been committed, the company should object to any search before legal counsel is consulted.

8.2.4 Information Gathering

An inspector may take photographs, conduct tests, or inspect equipment as long as the requests are reasonable. Nonrelated pictures should not be taken. To protect confidential business information, and prevent the inclusion of extraneous information, the company should have the right to approve pictures used in reports.

All testing and sampling procedures should be reviewed to ensure that they were done properly and allow for a fair conclusion. It may be appropriate to take a duplicate sample and have the sample analyzed by an independent laboratory.

A list should be kept of all documents or photocopies provided to the MOEE. Documents which have been passed to the MOEE should be numbered to avoid confusion.

It is preferable to designate one company representative to show the inspector the facility and coordinate responses to questions. The individual should be familiar with the legal implications of the inspection and should have a working knowledge of the facility. In addition, the employee should take careful notes of what is seen and photographed, who is interviewed, what is said, and sampling procedures and locations.

8.2.5 Confidentiality

One approach to the unwanted disclosure of documents is to use the concept of solicitor-client privilege. In most cases, information passing between a lawyer and client is privileged if it is secured for the purpose of obtaining legal advice.

To claim this privilege, the following conditions must be met:

- the information/study must be requested by the corporation and/or officers and directors
- the request must be in anticipation of litigation
- the information must be delivered by the lawyer to the corporation and/or officers and directors
- the information must be kept confidential

A more detailed discussion of the confidentiality as it can pertain to environmental audits is presented in Section 10.6. If the question of confidentiality does arise during an investigation, especially over a potentially sensitive document, legal counsel should be sought.

8.3 INTERVIEWS

A company should try to prearrange the procedures used for interviews. Individuals should be briefed by the company in advance of an interview on their individual rights and what is required of them. In cases where this is not possible, or for some other reason the prearrangement has not been made, individuals should be made aware of their individual rights at the beginning of the interview.

Individuals should approach interviews with the attitude that **statements made may be used in a court of law** whether or not the individual being interviewed is charged or not. Some guidelines to remember during an interview include (Rovet, 1988):

1 Stick to the facts; do not speculate.
2 Make sure you understand the question, or ask for clarification or a repeat of the question.
3 Take your time answering the questions.
4 Do not wander off the topic.
5 Do not volunteer information.
6 If you do not know an answer, say so.
7 Take notes during the interview.

If the sole purpose of the questioning is to obtain evidence of an offence for the purpose of prosecution, a person may refuse to answer. An inspector cannot force a person into self-incrimination. If the provincial officer has reasonable or probable grounds to believe that the individual being interviewed has committed an offence, the officer must recognize the rights against self-incrimination and give a warning (McKenney, 1989). During the interview, an individual is required to give only the information that is pertinent to the investigation. Most MOEE officers have been trained as interviewers and may try to get an individual to be open. This may reveal information which in some cases is not pertinent to the investigation.

A company can be incriminated and convicted through statements made by an employee during the course of an inspection. Damaging statements given by employees must be made voluntarily without threat, promise, or inducement. Any threat to prosecute the individual employee if he or she doesn't give a statement would remove the voluntary nature of the statement (Rovet, 1988).

A provincial officer may write a narrative of the answers while interviewing a person and ask the person to sign it as his or her own statement. The statement will be paraphrased in words selected by the inspector to highlight issues which the officer feels are important. The statement may omit salient facts (Rovet, 1988). None of the statutes or regulations requires individuals to sign or initial anything. The choice of whether to sign or not sign the document is up to the individual being interviewed.

An inspector may suggest the use of a tape recorder for interviewing purposes. There is no statutory authority or obligation which would require an individual to participate in tape-recorded interviews, and therefore it is entirely up to the individual to object to the use of tape recorders. A person should not feel embarrassed or be afraid to refuse to participate in recorded interviews.

Whenever possible, a company representative not related to the incident but familiar with the particular Act under which the investigation is being conducted should be present at all meetings and interviews during the investigations. If this has not been prearranged, the person being interviewed can request the right to have someone present. The inspector has the legal right to disallow a third party to be present during the interviews (Section 156(4) of the EPA) unless the third party is the person's legal counsel.

8.4 RESPONSES TO VIOLATIONS

8.4.1 MOEE Responses

Enforcement officials, whether, municipal, provincial, or federal, are expected to respond to violations according to the sufficiency of the evidence and predetermined response criteria. In April 1994, the MOEE released its *Compliance Guideline F-2* (formerly Policy 05-02). The guideline covers the following areas:

- identification and evaluation of non-compliance
- voluntary abatement
- mandatory abatement
- public notification and consultation
- review and enforcement
- prosecution

It is important to note that all non-compliance situations which may require abatement or enforcement action shall be fully documented in an "Occurrence Report." Where the investigating officer is of the opinion that a violation has occurred, the original report shall be given to the Regional Supervisor of the Investigations and Enforcement Branch.

The MOEE views the laying of charges as only one of many remedies to reduce or eliminate pollution. Other remedies include voluntary compliance, warnings, and control documents. A control document is any written instrument which covers statutory authority. These include the Minister's reports, orders, licences, permits, Certificates of Approval, requirements and directions, and program approvals.

In general, a control document will require that intermediate steps in a control order be completed in a timely and regular fashion, that pollution control equipment be installed by the specified date, and that pollution control equipment be properly maintained and operated. The control document will also specify the allowable emissions or discharges, and the monitoring requirements that must be met.

The EPA provides for various types of orders that can be issued. When a discharge or emission is found to be in non-compliance, the Minister can issue a control order under Section 7 of the EPA. A **control order** may specify directions or the manner of discharge, additional studies of the discharge, and implementation of procedures.

Section 8 of the EPA allows an MOEE director to issue a **stop order** to immediately cease polluting activities. There must be an immediate danger to human life or health or property for a stop order to be issued.

Under Sections 17 and 97 of the EPA, the Minister may issue a **clean-up order** to any individual or company who caused or permitted a discharge or spill of a contaminant compelling the individual or company to take necessary steps to repair the injury or damage. This can include the restoration of the environment.

Section 18 of the EPA empowers the Minister to issue a **prevention order** for the discharge of a contaminant if it is believed that the discharge likely will cause an adverse environmental effect. This type of order may require specific facilities, equipment, or procedures to be followed. A prevention order may also require monitoring or the study of the effects of the contaminant (Shier, 1989).

During Phase I of the Municipal, Industrial Strategy for Abatement (MISA) program (refer to Section 3.3.3), the MOEE outlined the following steps which are to be taken if a company is found to be in non-compliance:

1 An Occurrence Report outlining the nature of the non-compliance will be completed.

2 This would be followed up by abatement action which would involve communication with the company as the first step. The Ministry may contact the company by telephone or in person, then follow up with a letter to confirm that the violation has occurred and to request that the company respond. It is essential that response to the Ministry is made promptly and that every reasonable effort is made to return to compliance. If there is no response or a poor response, the occurrence would then be referred to the IEB.

3 If the violation is deliberate, involves an attempt to conceal, or is a repeated occurrence of an earlier violation, then the Occurrence Report would be referred directly to the IEB. The IEB investigation could result in a recommendation for prosecution.

8.4.2 Federal Responses

When a violation of the Canadian Environmental Protection Act (CEPA) is discovered, enforcement officials consider the nature of the violation, the desired response by the violator, and consistency in enforcement when deciding what action to take (Environment Canada, 1988).

The **nature of the violation** covers the seriousness of the harm or potential harm, the intent of the alleged violation, whether the occurrence has been repeated, and if there were attempts to conceal information or otherwise subvert the objectives and requirements of the Act.

The desired result of any response is compliance with the Act within the shortest possible time and with no further occurrence of violation. The violator's history of compliance, willingness to cooperate with enforcement officials, evidence of corrective action already taken, and the existence of enforcement actions by other federal or provincial authorities as a result of the same activity may be considered.

To achieve **consistency in enforcement**, officials will consider how similar situations were handled when deciding what enforcement action is taken.

Like the MOEE, Environment Canada has various types of responses available to deal with violations of CEPA and its regulations (Environment Canada, 1988).

A **warning** may be issued if it is believed that a violation is continuing or has occurred, and the degree of harm or potential harm to the environment, human life, or health appears to be minimal. A warning may be issued if the violator has a record of compliance and/or made reasonable efforts to remedy or mitigate the consequence of the offence.

In response to a release of a substance in contravention of the CEPA, an inspector may give **directions** to remedy a dangerous condition or reduce any danger to the environment, human life, or health that results from the release of a substance.

When there is a minimal threat to the environment or human life or health, a **ticket** may be issued. Ticketable offences include failure to provide information on a new substance, or failure to provide, within the allowable time, a pre-shipment notice. For any offence that is designated as ticketable, inspectors will always issue a ticket except when a warning is considered appropriate.

The Minister may issue four types of **orders**: an order that prohibits activities involving new substances to Canada; a recall of substances and products; requirements for additional information on, or testing of, substances suspected of being toxic, and to prohibit their manufacture or importation, or to limit these two activities until the expiration of the assessment period to determine the risk that they present to the environment; or interim orders for immediate action to prevent a significant danger to the environment, human life, or health.

Under the CEPA, the Minister has the authority to seek **injunctions** to stop or prevent violations. If an individual or company is not complying with the injunction, the Minister can return to the court to seek a contempt of court ruling.

Inspectors can lay a charge and seek a **prosecution** for every violation under CEPA, except where warnings, tickets, and/or orders are considered to be more appropriate. If a violation involved death or bodily harm, serious harm or risk to the environment or human health, false information/concealment of information, or less than all reasonable measures being taken to comply with Environment Canada responses, prosecution can be expected.

If there is no prosecution, or prosecution has resulted but an order to recover cost was not obtained, or the prosecution did not result in a conviction, the Crown may seek a **civil suit** to recover the cost of a clean-up (including the hiring of third parties) or action taken to prevent an unauthorized release of a regulated substance.

8.4.3 Municipal Responses

Like their provincial and federal counterparts, municipalities can respond to environmental violations with various informal and formal actions. Informal actions include informal notice (e.g. a telephone conversation), meeting, warning letter, and/or meeting to show cause. At the latter, the municipality would present the facts concerning the non-compliance and request the violator to show cause as to why the municipality should not proceed with one or more formal enforcement actions. Formal actions include the issuance of a compliance program, civil action, an order of prohibition, and/or contempt of court.

Where a by-law of a municipality or local board, passed under the authority of the Municipal Act or any other general or special act, is contravened and a conviction entered, the court in which the conviction has been entered (or any court of competent jurisdiction), may make an order prohibiting the continuation or repetition of the offence by the person convicted (Section 326 of the Municipal Act).

Table 8.2 presents a typical example of enforcement strategy that a municipality may follow when ensuring compliance with the local Sewer-Use By-law.

8.5 PENALTIES AND LIABILITIES

8.5.1 Ontario Environmental Protection Act

Subsection 192 of the EPA deems the actions and omissions of an officer, official, employee, or agent of a corporation in the course of his or her employment, or in the exercise of his or her powers or the performance of his or her duties, as the actions or omissions of the corporation.

It is up to the discretion of the Crown prosecuting a case whether the individual employee will be charged along with the corporation. Often the Crown is not interested in convicting individuals except those with considerable corporate authority.

Prior to 1986, the liability of officers and directors was limited to persons who could be said to be the directing minds and wills of the corporation. This artificial distinction between those who make policy and those who implement it no longer exists. Officers and directors must now communicate adequate information and specific instructions through the management structure and arrange for the training, supervision, and monitoring so that adverse effects to the environment are prevented (Petrie, 1989).

Subsection 194(1) of the EPA clearly states that every director or officer of a corporation that engages in an activity that may result in the discharge of a contaminant into the natural environment contrary to the Act has a **duty to take all reasonable care** to prevent the corporation from causing or permitting such unlawful discharge. Furthermore, it is an offence for anyone who fails to carry out that duty and permits a prosecution and conviction of an officer or director despite the fact that the corporation has not been prosecuted or convicted for the offence (Petrie, 1989).

The EPA creates a positive duty to educate and instruct employees to prevent environmental damage, and that duty is a personal one assumed by directors and officers of a company. The officers must implement environmental policy, ensure that an adequate system for environmental protection is set up, and act upon the findings of environmental compliance reports.

In a leading decision (*Queen v. the City of Sault Ste. Marie*), the minimum duty of officers and directors was expressed to be (Glenn *et al.*, 1988):

1 Officers report back periodically to the board on the operation of the company's environmental system.
2 Officers report substantial non-compliance to the board in a timely manner.

In a more recent ruling *(Queen v. Bata Industries Limited),* the minimum duty on the officers and directors was expanded to include the following (Mansell, 1993):

- The Board of Directors is ultimately responsible for environmental compliance.
- If the Board chooses to delegate its responsibilities, it must ensure that a system of adequate and effective supervision is in place, that the Board is kept regularly informed on environmental matters, and that the persons to whom the responsibility has been delegated are properly educated in environmental matters and have the resources to deal with environmental problems.
- The Board is entitled to place reasonable reliance on delegates, and on the reports such delegates prepare.
- An environmental policy, approved by the Board, dealing with the prevention of pollution (including waste management and disposal), and an assurance to the Board that the policy is being complied with are

essential. One way to establish compliance is through comprehensive environmental review or audit.

- The Board should be aware of the standards in its own industry as well as other industries that may deal with similar environmental concerns.
- Directors should ensure that minutes of the Board's meetings accurately reflect the consideration of environmental matters.
- The Board should be informed of and react to environmental concerns that affect the company as quickly as possible.

Table 8.3 presents a summary of EPA penalties. There are penalties for individuals and corporations. The financial penalties can be levied for each day a violation occurs. In addition to the fines, violators can be required to pay an amount equal to the monetary benefit obtained due to the violation. There are provisions for imprisonment (terms of up to one year) for violations of specific sections or subsections of the Act.

When there is minimal or no threat to the environment or human life or health, a provincial officer may issue a **ticket**. Table 8.4 presents examples of ticketable offenses and the corresponding fines. The fines themselves may not be large but the conviction will affect a company's compliance record—a record that may be used against the company should they be charged and/or convicted of a more serious offence.

8.5.2 Ontario Water Resources Act

Like the EPA, Section 116 of the OWRA addresses the concept of personal duty of care in that every director or officer of a corporation that engages in an activity that may result in the discharge of any material into or in any waters or on any shore or bank or that may impair the quality of the water has a duty to take all reasonable care to prevent the corporation from causing or permitting such unlawful discharge.

The penalties for the contravention of any part of the OWRA are presented in Table 8.5. In addition to fines, a conviction under Section 109 (the protection of public water supplies) may result in imprisonment for not more than one year.

8.5.3 Canadian Environmental Protection Act

The offence sections of CEPA refer to "every person". Therefore, individual employees of the company may be prosecuted where they had care and control of the deleterious substance which escaped into the natural environment and caused damage.

Section 122 states that where a corporation commits an offence, any officer, director, or agent of the corporation who directed, authorized, assented to, acquiesced in or participated in the commission of the offence is a party to and guilty of the offence, and is liable, whether or not the corporation has been prosecuted or convicted.

Subsection 124(1) goes one step further in that an employee may not necessarily be prosecuted but his actions may implicate an officer, director and/or company.

Table 8.6 presents a summary of penalties under CEPA. The Act provides for maximum fines of $1 million, five years in jail and taxing of profits perceived to have been gained by polluting. The CEPA also provides a civil cause of action to any person who has suffered loss or damage as a result of conduct contrary to the Act or the regulations, including the right to seek injunctive relief.

8.5.4 Transport of Dangerous Goods Act

Under the Transport of Dangerous Goods Act (TDGA), any officer, director, or agent of a corporation who directed, authorized, or consented to the commission of an offence is guilty of the offence and liable to conviction whether or not the corporation is prosecuted. Penalties for violations under the TDGA are presented in Table 8.7. The Act provides for maximum fines of $100,000 a day for a summary conviction and imprisonment for up to two years if the conviction is on indictment.

8.5.5 Fisheries Act

To be prosecuted under the Fisheries Act, the Ministry does not have to prove that fish were actually harmed, but only that a "deleterious" substance was deposited into waters frequented by fish, or that the fish habitat was harmed. Special regulations made under the Act allow for specific material to be discharged under certain circumstances. Such regulations have been developed for chloro-alkali effluents, liquid mercury effluents, petroleum refinery effluents, and pulp and paper effluents.

The penalties prescribed under the Fisheries Act are presented in Table 8.8. The penalties cover the addition of a deleterious substance, the harmful alteration of a fish habitat and throwing material overboard. The first carries a maximum fine of $100,000 a day, plus the cost of mitigative action and income lost by commercial fishermen.

8.5.6 Municipal Act

Table 8.9 presents the maximum penalties under the Model Sewer-Use By-Law. The penalties range from a maximum of $5,000 a day for a first offence to $50,000 a day for a second offence.

The Municipal Act allows a municipality or a local board to obtain an order prohibiting the continuation or repetition of a contaminant discharge to a sewer by a person convicted of an offence. If the offender knowingly acts in contravention of the order of prohibition, an application can further be brought for an order citing the offender in contempt of court and committing the offender to jail (MOE, 1988).

In a court case involving a metal plating company and the Municipality of Metropolitan Toronto, the court granted a prohibition order under Section 326 of the Municipal Act against the company after 40 convictions for violating Metropolitan Toronto sewer-use by-laws. Following the making of the order there were four further convictions. Metropolitan Toronto commenced contempt proceedings against the company and its president. Both were found in contempt. The company was fined $100,000, its president was sentenced to six months in jail, and a fine of $25,000 was levied. The fine was levied to cover in part the legal fees of Metropolitan Toronto (Vialanic, 1989).

8.5.7 Significant Fines and Other Convictions

In the following section, significant fines and other convictions are briefly summarized. Additional information on these cases can be obtained from the MOEE document entitled *Offenses against the Environment* (MOEE, 1993):

- Robert Len Brown and Robert Len Brown Construction Ltd. were fined a total of $364,000 for numerous offences resulting from the illegal storage of tires. In addition, Mr. Brown was also ordered to pay $250,000 worth of related costs for a total of $614,000 in monetary penalties.
- Two officers of a multinational company (president and vice-president/plant general manager) were found guilty under the director's liability section of the Ontario Water Resources Act. Each individual was fined $12,000. The judge noted that he would have preferred to blend the fine with probation and community service orders; however, the two company officials had been transferred to Malaysia. The company was also ordered to pay $60,000 to the Central and South Hastings Waste Management Board to assist in funding the Reduce/Return Strategy for Household Hazardous Waste, and an additional $60,000 to the Consolidated Revenue Fund of the province. In addition to the monetary aspects of the sentence, the corporation was ordered to publish the facts leading up to the conviction in their international newsletter, publish a Technical Advisory Circular on toxic waste disposal for all of their facilities, place a caution on their land warning future purchasers of environmental damage, not pay the company's officers fines for them, and make environmental issues a mandatory agenda item in all Board of Director meetings for the two-year probationary program. The case is currently being appealed.
- $125,000 for the discharge of ethylbenzene from a chemical company into the St. Clair River and failing to report the spill to the MOEE.

8.5.8 Creative Sentencing

Creative sentences are different from, or in addition to, jail terms or fines. These sentences are gaining favour in environmental law as the courts look for additional ways to make convicted offenders pay their debt to society by directly helping the environment they harmed through restoration, repayment, education, and training.

Examples of recent cases involving creative sentencing include:

• A large chemical company repaid the MOEE $26,000 for outside laboratory costs it incurred as a result of a spill. These monies were in addition to the $125,000 fine for the incident.

• A waste disposal company was ordered to forfeit $70,000 in profits made from an offending operation; the operation was in repeated violation of conditions in the company's Certificate of Approval. This type of creative sentencing is known as profit-stripping. This payment was in addition to a fine of $70,000 by the company and fines of $10,000 and $7,500 levied against two company directors.

• A large forest products company was ordered to make a $25,000 contribution to a graduate scholarship in environmental and forestry management at Lakehead University following a conviction for failing to report a spill. The company was also fined $5,000.

• A development company was orderd to put $25,000 in fines into a fund to be used by the Ministry of Natural Resources to restore fish habitats damaged by the actions of the company.

8.6   DEFENSES AND MITIGATING FACTORS

8.6.1 Criminal Offences

For offences under the Criminal Code or other statutes with significant penal sanctions, the burden of proof to be overcome by the prosecution is: proof beyond a reasonable doubt; strict proof as to the identification of accused; and proof of causal connection to the offence (Petrie, 1989).

The prosecution must show that the source of the pollution was a specific company or individual, or at least demonstrate that there is no reasonable likelihood of another source of the pollution. This can be demonstrated by the use of photographs showing the plume of smoke dispersing from the stack on the roof of the plant, by testimony of witnesses who saw effluent pouring from the drain pipe into a stream, by scientific methods of "fingerprinting" the chemical and matching that fingerprint to a product known to be used by the accused, or by eliminating other likely sources (Petrie, 1989).

Once the accused has been positively identified, a causal connection to the environmental damage must be made. Neighbours may testify that they could smell, taste, or feel the pollutant settling on their properties. Experts may testify as to the probable health effects of the pollution. Alternatively, it may be sufficient to prove that the regulatory standards or performance standards in a Certificate of Approval were exceeded. Types of technical defenses, although rare, may include (Petrie, 1989):

- improper service of court documents
- lapse of the limitation period (usually two years)
- unreasonable delay in reaching trial
- failure of investigating officer to inform you of your rights to retain and instruct counsel upon detention or arrest

8.6.2 Quasi-Criminal Offences

Absolute liability offences must be specified as such in the statute. Absolute liability means that, once the Crown proves that the accused has committed the offence, the accused cannot raise a defense such as mistake of fact, due diligence, or Act of God. The defendant, subject to the Canadian Charter of Rights and Freedoms, may be free of fault and yet liable under an absolute liability offence (Petrie, 1989). An example is failure to obtain a C of A.

The CEPA and EPA offences create **strict liability** offences. An example is in Section 125(1) of the CEPA which states that "no person shall be guilty of an offence under this act, if the person established that he exercised all **due diligence** to prevent its commission."

To establish a defense based on due diligence, the onus of proof is on the defendant to establish that **reasonable care** was taken. The defendant must show that the care taken was

- consistent with general standards of care common to the business activity in question
- if special circumstances of the case indicated a different level of care than that of the standard practice was required, that indeed it was achieved

In a recent court case (*Queen v. Courtaulds Fibres Canada*), the judge ruled that:

> "Reasonable care and due diligence do not mean superhuman efforts. They mean a high standard of awareness and decisive, prompt and continuing action . . . The decision of how long a company must prove that it was duly diligent before it can become a valid defence, cannot be clearly answered by considering only how long the company was so engaged. The state of the facility, the age of the facility, the problems to be addressed, and the scope of the actions taken to deal with them, as well as the time the company was engaged in remedial action, must all be weighed and balanced.

In cases where reasonable care does not afford a full defense of due diligence, the efforts may still be used as a mitigating factor in determining sentence. Best efforts to remedy the situation after a pollution event may be another mitigating factor (Petrie, 1989).

Part X of the Environmental Protection Act lists several possible defenses:

- due diligence

- an act of war, terrorism, insurrection, or hostile act of a foreign government
- a natural phenomenon of an exceptional, inevitable, and irresistible character
- an act or omission of a person for whom the owner or contractor of the pollutant is not responsible under the law

8.7 THE ROLE OF COMMON LAW

Sections 8.4 (Responses to Violations) and 8.5 (Penalties and Liabilities) cover environmental statutory law. In recent years, especially in the United States, there has been a significant increase in private lawsuits for pollution-related activities such as clean-up activity, contaminated property transfers, and elevated exposures to nearby residents from various types of activities. However, the statutory context in the United States (e.g. Comprehensive Environmental Response Compensation and Liability Act—CERCLA) is substantially different from that in Canada. In essence, fault does not have to be proven in the United States and all related parties must bear a share of the responsibility and financial burden.

Common law has its origins in the morals, traditions, and business practices of England. The law has evolved over the centuries through the decisions of judges interpreting these norms and legislation which codified society's standards. Torts are part of common law. They are civil wrongs other than breach of contract. Courts may remedy a wrong by awarding damages or injunctive relief (prohibitive or mandatory orders) to compensate the injured property and prevent further wrongs. Tort causes of action may include negligence, nuisance (*Rylands v. Fletcher*), trespassing, and riparian rights (Petrie, 1989).

Negligence occurs when a person's conduct falls below the standard regarded as reasonable among his peers. To prove negligence, one must show that the standard of reasonable care was breached and that the defendant should have foreseen the damage that resulted.

Nuisance is the unreasonable interference with the comfort or enjoyment of property, or causing damage to another's property. Noise, odours, vibrations, and actual physical intrusions of deleterious substances can create a cause of action in nuisance.

The law recognizes both private and public nuisances. Private nuisance involves the interference with an interest in land, such as the occupier's interest in the use and enjoyment of the land. Public nuisance is the interference with the public in its exercise of public rights. A nuisance against the public is normally pursued by the Attorney General. An individual does not have to be negligent to be found liable in nuisance.

Nuisances can be continued or adopted by the subsequent owner of property who, with the knowledge or presumed knowledge of the nuisance, allows it to continue after a reasonable period of time available to stop the nuisance.

A long-standing example of the role of common law in environmental matters is the 1868 decision of the British House of Lords in the case of *Rylands v. Fletcher.* The decision supported the proposition that a party who brings onto his land a non-natural use is answerable for the damages which the thing causes if it escapes or is discharged from that party's land. A water reservoir constructed on land which contained an abandoned mine shaft ruptured through the shaft flooding the neighbouring coal mine. The degree of care exercised by the defendant was not an issue. Liability was a direct consequence of proof of the physical damage resulting from the non-natural use of the land. Liability can be imposed even if there is no negligence.

Trespass is a direct, unauthorized interference with private property. Liability for trespass can occur where there is no actual damage suffered by the person in actual possession of the property. The discharge of pollution onto another's property is a form of trespass.

The owner of land which borders on a watercourse has a **riparian right** to the continued flow of the water in its natural quantity and quality subject to the ordinary, reasonable use of owners upstream along the watercourse. The right to sue for damages and injunctive relief is created not only with diminished quantity or quality of water; one can also sue if surface water flow is altered so that another's property is flooded.

8.8 ONTARIO ENVIRONMENTAL BILL OF RIGHTS

The Ontario Environmental Bill of Rights (EBR) was passed in the Spring of 1994. The EBR will provide increased government accountability for the environment. Ministries within the government will be required to:

- develop "Statements of Environmental Values" that will outline how it will include environmental issues in its decision-making process
- determine which of their laws, regulations, and policies have an impact on the environment

The EBR has provisions to increase protection to employees who "blow the whistle" on polluting employers. The EBR also introduces increased public participation in environmental issues, including:

- an electronic registry where any member of the public will have access to information
- increased public participation in environmental decision making by government (public notice will be will be given in the Registry of proposed Acts, policies and regulations which are environmentally significant to allow for public comment)
- increased access to the courts for Ontario residents to protect the environment

The newly introduced Environmental Commissioner's Office will be the conduit through which the public will lobby the government for change or introduce an investigation regarding an environmental matter. The Environmental Commissioner will assist Ministries in screening public complaints to determine if a full investigation is warranted. The public may also issue, through the Environmental Commissioner, a request for a review of a Ministry's Acts, policies, or regulations.

8.9 SUMMARY

The enforcement activities of the MOEE have changed in recent years from that of cooperation between MOEE regional personnel and industry to prosecution. Under various environmental statutes, provincial officers have a wide variety of powers which allow them to inspect sites or premises as part of investigations. Provincial officers must have reasonable cause, however, before exercising their statutory powers.

Some environmental legislation imposes obligations on individuals to cooperate with an investigation. As part of the information-gathering, the inspector may take photographs, conduct tests, or inspect equipment as long as the requests are reasonable. It is important that employees be made aware of their individual rights prior to being interviewed and the legal obligation to cooperate. If the sole purpose of the question is to obtain evidence of an offence for the purpose of prosecuting an individual, that person may refuse to answer. An inspector cannot force a person into self-incrimination.

Enforcement officials may respond to violations by issuing an order (e.g. control order, clean-up order) or lay charges. The laying of charges may result in anything from a small fine for a ticketable offense to a substantial fine ($1,000,000) and/or imprisonment if environmental impairment occurs.

REFERENCES

Cotton, R. 1989. "101 New Liabilities under MISA: Your Rights and Responsibilities." Presented at Effluent Management for the 1990s. 5 and 6 June, Toronto.

Environment Canada. May 1988. *Canadian Environmental Protection Act (CEPA): Enforcement and Compliance Policy.*

Glenn, W., D. Shier, K. Sisson, and J. Whilms. June 1988. *Toxic Real Estate Manual.* Corpus Information Services.

Jetten, B., and B. Smith. November 1989. "When the Environmental Police Call, It Could Become a Corporate Nightmare." *Environmental Science and Engineering.*

Mansell, R. June 1993. "Personal Communications."

McKenney, M. 1989. "Environmental Enforcement in Ontario." Presented at the Environmental Auditing Workshop, 10 and 11 October, University of Toronto.

Ontario Government. 1989. "Penalties Adjustment Act." S.O. 90, 6.72. Statutes of Ontario.

Ontario Ministry of the Environment (MOE). August 1987. *Short Form Wordings and Set Fines: Pursuant to Part 1, Provincial Offences Act, Schedule 55.*

Ontario Ministry of the Environment (MOE). August 1988. *Model Sewer-Use By-Law.* ISBN 0-7729-4419-9.

Ontario Ministry of Environment and Energy (MOEE). 1993. *Offenses Against the Environment.*

Ontario Government. 1990. *Environmental Protection Statute Law Amendment Act.*

Petrie, P. 1989. "What Management and Staff Should Know about Environmental Laws to Minimize Personal and Corporate Liability." Presented at the Environmental Auditing Workshop, 10 and 11 October, University of Toronto.

Rovet, E. 1988. *Canadian Business Guide to Environmental Law.* Vancouver: International Self-Counsel Press Limited.

Shier, D.S. 1989. "Negotiating Environmental Provisions in Real Estate Transactions to Avoid Costly and Unnecessary Disputes." Presented at the Environmental Auditing Workshop, 10 and 11 October, University of Toronto.

Vialanic, M. (ed.) March 1989. "Municipality of Metropolitan Toronto v. Siapas." *Canadian Environmental Law Reports* 1 (Part 3). Toronto: Carswell Legal Publications, Vol. 1, Part 3.

Table 8.1
POWERS OF PROVINCIAL OFFICERS UNDER EPA

A provincial officer can:

- enter any place where it is believed that a contaminant has been discharged or may be discharged into the natural environment;

- enter any place where it is believed that relevant documents are likely to be found;

- take samples and record or copy any information by any method;

- make inquiries of any person, orally or in writing;

- detain or remove anything, including a vehicle or vessel, that is discharging or is likely to discharge a contaminant into the natural environment which causes or is likely to cause an adverse effect; and

- seize anything that is produced, or that is in plain view, during an inspection if the officer reasonably believes that there has been a contravention of the Act or the regulations and the thing being seized will afford evidence of the contravention.

Reference: Jetten and Smith, 1989

Table 8.2
EXAMPLES OF MUNICIPAL ENFORCEMENT
STRATEGY USING THE MODEL SEWER-USE BY-LAW

Sample Violations	Responses
Informal Actions	
Minor exceedance of discharge limit—one-time violation	Informal meeting
Minor exceedance of discharge limit on an infrequent basis	Warning letter
Failure to notify about a one-time minor spill into sewage works	Show cause meeting
Major exceedance of discharge limit—one-time violation	Show cause meeting
Formal Actions	
Exceeding of discharge limits on a regular basis	Civil action
Failure to notify municipality of a major spill into the sewage works	Civil action
Exceeding discharge limit with known damage to sewage treatment plant or failure to comply with compliance program	Order of prohibition
Exceeding discharge limits with known damage to sewage treatment plant on a regular basis	Order of prohibition
Failure to comply with order of prohibition to stop discharging sewage exceeding by-law limits and causing sewage treatment plant damage	Contempt of court

Reference: MOE, 1988

Table 8.3
PENALTIES UNDER THE ONTARIO EPA

Offence	Occurrence	Maximum Daily Penalty	
		Individual	Corporation

Section 186
Contravention of any part of
the Act or regulations
OR
Failure to comply with an order
or a C of A under Sections 8 or 14

	Occurrence	Individual	Corporation
	First*	$10,000	$50,000
	Second*	$25,000	$100,000

Subsection 187
Discharge of contaminant to the
environment (Section 14(1))
OR
Disobey a stop order (Section 130)

	Occurrence	Individual	Corporation
	First**	$10,000	$2,000-$200,000
	Second**	$25,000	$4,000-$400,000

Notes:

* Additional penalties can include:
- amount equal to the monetary benefit accrued due to the violation
- court can order action to prevent or eliminate effects on the environment
- any other conditions the court thinks appropriate
- changes to conditions can be made as court sees fit
- must comply even if in jail
- suspension of one or more existing or pending licences if fines are not paid

** Additional penalties can include those above plus:
- imprisonment for one year
- prevent repetition of offence

Section 193
Contravention of the Act or
regulations with respect to
hauled liquid industrial waste
or hazardous waste

a) which may result in environmental impairment:

First	$2,000-$10,000	$2,000-$100,000
Second	$4,000-$25,000	$4,000-$200,000
	Plus imprisonment for one year	

b) which results in environmental impairment:

First	$2,000-$50,000	$2,000-$1,000,000
Second	$4,000-$100,000	$4,000-$2,000,000
	Plus imprisonment for one year	

References: Ontario, 1989 and Ontario, 1990

Table 8.4
EXAMPLES OF TICKETABLE OFFENCES UNDER EPA

Regulation	Activity	Penalty

I)   Regulation 347

Operate a Landfilling Site:

	• allow use by unauthorized persons	$103.75
	• allow access while attendant not on duty	$103.75

Operate Waste Management System:

	• vehicle valves not locked with driver absent	$78.75
	• fail to clearly mark vehicle	$103.75
	• fail to keep Certificate of Approval in vehicle	$103.75

Asbestos Handling:

	• permit asbestos waste to leave location in inadequate containers	$153.75
	• asbestos waste not covered with suitable tarpaulin or net in unenclosed vehicle	$153.75

Transporting Waste:

	• carrier - fail to promptly transport subject waste to proper receiving facility	$103.75
	• carrier - fail to complete Section B of manifest	$78.75

Regulation	Activity	Penalty
	• carrier - fail to give manifest to generator at time of transfer	$78.75
	• generator - fail to complete Section A of manifest	$78.75
	• generator - fail to retain copy 2 of manifest for two years	$78.75
II) Regulation 346		
	• cause or permit visible emission - obstruct passage of light more than 20%	$153.75
	• burn or permit burning in combustion unit of type of fuel or waste for which unit not designed	$153.75
	• emit contaminants beyond property limits from prescribed activities	$153.75
III) Reg. 362 PCB		
	• operation - fail to keep records of all PCB waste held	$103.75
	• fail to report required information to MOEE director in writing within 3 days	$103.75

Table 8.5
PENALTIES UNDER THE OWRA

Offence	Occurrence	Maximum Daily Penalty Individual	Corporation
Section 108: Contravention of any part of the Act or regulations			
	First	$10,000	$50,000
	Second	$25,000	$100,000
Section 109: Discharge of contaminant into any waters, including a public water supply (Sec. 30(1) or 33(2)(b))			
	First	$10,000	$2,000-$100,000
	Second	$25,000	$4,000-$200,000
	Plus imprisonment for not more one year		

Reference: Ontario, 1992

Table 8.6
PENALTIES UNDER THE CEPA

Type of Offence	Conviction	Maximum Penalty
Sections 111 and 112 Failure to notify or provide information to an inspector OR Providing misleading information OR Hindering an investigation (Sections 16, 26, 27, 50, 102, and 103)		Maximum fine of $200,000 Up to six months in prison
Section 113 Failure to properly store, handle, register, and/or dispose of a hazardous chemical	Summary Conviction	Maximum fine of $300,000 and/or Up to six months in prison
Failure to properly import a hazardous chemical (Sections 17, 18(1)(c), 29(1)(a), 29(1)(b), 26(1)(b), 27, 29(2), 34(1), 35, 36, 40, 42, 43, 46, 54, 56, 57, 64, 65, 68(4), 69 and 70)	Indictment	Maximum fine of $1 million and/or Up to 3 years in prison
Section 114 Providing Minister with false information (Sections 16, 17, 18(1)(a), 18(1)(b), 26, 27, and 29(1)(b))	Summary Conviction	Maximum fine of $300,000 and/or Up to six months in prison

Type of Offence	Conviction	Maximum Penalty
	Indictment	Maximum fine of $1 million and/or Up to 5 years in prison
Section 115 Every person in contravention of the Act who intentionally or recklessly causes loss of environment or risk of death or harm to others		
	Indictment	Liable to a fine and/or Up to 5 years in prison
	If death or bodily harm	Subject to prosecution and punishment under the Criminal Code (Section 203 and 204)
Section 133 The contravention or failure to comply with an order or direction once convicted of an offence (Sections 127, 128, 130 and 132)		
	Summary Conviction	Maximum fine of $200,000 and/or Up to six months in prison
	Indictment	Maximum fine of $1 million and/or Up to 3 years in prison
Section 116 Contravention of any regulation not already covered		
		Maximum fine of $200,000 and/or Up to six months in prison

Table 8.7
PENALTIES UNDER THE TDGA

Type of Offence	Conviction	Maximum Penalty	
Subsection 6(1) Failure to provide proper safety requirements (Sections 4 and 5) OR Failure to obey a directive to cease or alter the activity (Section 28)			
	Summary Conviction	First Second	$50,000 $100,000
	Indictment	Imprisonment for a term not exceeding two years	
Subsection 6(2) Failure to comply with any provision of the Act or regulations			
	Summary Conviction		$10,000
	Indictment	Imprisonment for a term not exceeding one year	

Table 8.8
PENALTIES UNDER THE FISHERIES ACT

Type of Offence	Conviction	Maximum Daily Penalty
Subsection 33(5)(b) The deposit of a deleterious substance (Section 33(2))		
	First	$50,000
	Second	$100,000
	Plus cost for mitigative measures, and liable for loss of income by any licensed commercial fisherman	
Subsection 31(1) Harmful alteration, etc. of fish habitat		
	First	$5,000
	Second	$10,000
Subsection 33(3) Throwing overboard certain substances		
	First	$5,000
	Second	$10,000

Table 8.9
PENALTIES UNDER THE MODEL SEWER-USE BY-LAW
(SECTION 321 OF THE MUNICIPAL ACT)

	Individual	Corporation
First Offence	$5,000/day	$25,000/day
Second Offence	$10,000/day	$50,000/day

Reference: MOE, 1988

9.0

Environmental Fate

9.1 WHY BE CONCERNED ABOUT ENVIRONMENTAL FATE?

Anyone who deals with environmental issues can benefit from having a basic understanding of the factors that influence the fate of chemicals in the environment. An understanding of environmental fate can be applied to tasks as diverse as responding to recently introduced or proposed legislation, assessing treatment options, developing monitoring programs, and assessing the potential risks from a chemical during its production, use, and disposal.

Recently introduced and proposed legislation, including the Municipal, Industrial Strategy for Abatement (MISA) and Canadian Environmental Protection Act (CEPA), consider the impact of chemical releases on the environment. MISA requires water-quality assessments for sensitive receiving water bodies; CEPA requires a "cradle-to-grave" approach for managing chemicals.

A basic understanding of the environmental fate of a chemical can be used to assess the effectiveness of treatment options. For example, consider two water treatment options — an activated carbon column and air stripping — and two compounds of concern — benzo(a)pyrene and trichloroethylene (TCE). Because benzo(a)pyrene has a relatively high octanol-water partition coefficient and strongly adsorbs to carbon, the carbon column should be effective. Conversely, air stripping would not be expected to be as cost-effective because of the compound's low vapour pressure. For TCE, which has a high vapour pressure and low affinity for carbon, air stripping is the preferred option.

To develop cost-effective monitoring systems, companies and environmental agencies must be able to predict the compartment of the environment where a chemical is most likely to be found. The compartments that usually are considered include air, water, soil, sediment, and biota.

For example, a decision must be made whether to sample sediment or water for PCBs near an old dump site. Because of its high affinity for sediment, the majority of the PCB likely will be found in the sediment. Water column samples would be expected to show nondetectable or very low concentrations.

Understanding the environmental behaviour and fate of a chemical is an essential component of a risk assessment. The behaviour of a chemical will strongly influence which exposure routes or pathways are likely to occur. For example, if a sudden release occurs of a highly volatile compound, it may be necessary to evacuate the area downwind. If the chemical is soluble and could reach a nearby river or water supply, then appropriate interceptors (such as dykes or trenches) may be needed.

The Pesticides Act requires that exhaustive tests be conducted, both in the laboratory and field, prior to the introduction of a new pesticide to the marketplace. These tests are used to assess the environmental fate of a pesticide and determine if it can adversely affect the environment. CEPA will require a similar approach for all new chemicals being produced or imported into Canada. One of the main objectives of CEPA is to avoid the introduction of chemicals that may cause an adverse effect on the environment in the short and long term.

9.2 KEY CHEMICAL PROPERTIES

Every substance possesses a unique set of physico-chemical properties. While many such properties exist, the following five are important determinants of overall environmental behaviour and fate.

Vapour pressure is a measure of the volatility of a chemical in its pure state. Vapour pressure indicates the maximum concentration that a chemical may achieve in the air compartment.

Water-solubility is the maximum concentration of a chemical that dissolves in pure water. Highly soluble chemicals are easily and quickly distributed by the hydrologic cycle. These chemicals tend not to adsorb to soil or sediments and to bioconcentrate only slightly in organisms. Most tend to be biodegradable by microorganisms in soil, surface water, and sewage treatment plants.

Density can indicate how a chemical will move in the environment. For example, dense non-aqueous phase liquids (DNAPL) sink in aquatic environments or, if released into the ground water regime, will migrate to the confining layer of the saturated zone. Similarly, a release of dense vapours will follow the contours of the land and may gather in low-lying areas.

Melting point and boiling point determine whether a chemical is a gas, liquid, or solid according to the temperature of the environment of concern.

Molecular weight is important when stoichiometric relationships can be used to estimate various processes such as dissolution, precipitation, and hydrolysis.

9.3 KEY ENVIRONMENTAL PARAMETERS

Several key environmental parameters are presented in Table 9.1. These can influence the behaviour of a chemical in a particular compartment. There are many more parameters that can be used when a finer level of detail is required.

The majority of the parameters associated with the **air compartment** describes the transport, diffusion, and/or convection of a chemical in that compartment. The atmospheric stability class indicates whether a gaseous emission may readily rise and disperse or be trapped by an inversion condition.

In the **water compartment,** the behaviour of a chemical will be influenced by the flow velocity, flow rate, and residence time (or turnover rate) of a water body. Fast-moving streams may promote uniform mixing within a short distance, whereas large lakes can stratify into several layers. The pH and cation/anion balance are useful in determining the precipitation and dissolution of ionic species.

The accumulation of a chemical in the **sediment compartment** is influenced by the rates of sediment deposition and resuspension. It is also influenced by the adsorptive capability and porosity of the sediment.

In the **soil compartment**, the movement of a chemical which has been applied to soil or deposited on the surface can be influenced strongly by hydrological factors (runoff and rainfall), soil type (porosity and adsorption capability), and chemical properties of the soil such as pH and organic carbon content.

The movement of chemicals in the **ground water compartment** is influenced by soil type and flow conditions (hydraulic conductivity and gradient). It is also influenced by the recharge rate to the aquifer (the amount of water flowing into the aquifer).

9.4 PARTITION COEFFICIENTS

Partition coefficients are parameters that describe the transfer of a substance between environmental compartments such as from water to air or soil to air. Table 9.1 presents a list of equilibrium partition coefficients.

For non-equilibrium conditions, the partition coefficients described in Table 9.1 may be used in combination with other parameters such as kinetic rate constants, although the relationships can become mathematically complex. Usually the assumption of equilibrium conditions is valid for a first approximation of the fate of a chemical, especially if several months or years have passed since the chemical was introduced to the environment.

Henry's Law Constant or the air-water partition coefficient relates the concentration of a chemical in the air phase to its concentration in the water phase:

$$H = C_a \div C_w \qquad (9.1)$$

where H   = Henry's Law Constant
       C_a = concentration in air (g/m^3)
       C_w = concentration in water (g/m^3)

Values of Henry's Law Constant of range from greater than 10 for a highly volatile chemical to less than 10^{-6} for a low-volatility chemical.

The **Octanol/Water Partition Coefficient** is defined as:

$$K_{ow} = C_{oc} \div C_w \qquad (9.2)$$

where K_{ow} = octanol/water partition coefficient
       C_{oc} = concentration in octanol (i.e. an alcohol with eight carbons)
       C_w = concentration in water

Scientists have found that octanol is a good surrogate for the lipid materials present in the fat portion of fish. Hence, K_{ow} is used to estimate the amount of an organic chemical which can be bioaccumulated by biota. The coefficient is also used in correlations to predict adsorption partition coefficients for organic chemicals in soils and sediments.

K_{ow} values range from 10^{-3} to 10^7 and are usually expressed as logarithms. A chemical with a log K_{ow} greater than 3 is considered to have a high affinity for lipids in biological media and the organic carbon portion of soil and sediment, while a chemical with a log K_{ow} value less than 1 is considered to have a higher affinity for air or water.

The **Organic Adsorption Coefficient,** or K_{oc} value, is a measure of the relative sorption potential of organic chemicals:

$$K_{oc} = S_{org} \div C_w \qquad (9.3)$$

where K_{oc} = organic carbon partition coefficient
       S_{org} = ratio of chemical adsorbed per unit weight of organic carbon
       C_w = concentration in water compartment

The K_{oc} value indicates the tendency of an organic chemical to be adsorbed, and it can be largely dependent on soil properties. The K_{oc}

parameter may not be as straightforward for ionic organic compounds such as pentachlorophenol.

Several empirical relationships have been developed for estimating K_{oc} using other properties, including octanol/water partition coefficient, solubility, and bioconcentration factors. For example:

$$\log K_{oc} = a \log (S, K_{ow}, \text{ or } BCF) + b \qquad (9.4)$$

where   S   = solubility
  K_{ow} = octanol/water partition coefficient
  BCF = bioconcentration factor
  a,b = constants

Two widely used correlations are:

$$\log K_{oc} = 1.00 \log K_{ow} - 0.21 \qquad (9.5)$$

$$\log K_{oc} = 0.544 \log K_{ow} + 1.377 \qquad (9.6)$$

The former is intended for aromatic hydrocarbons, polyaromatic hydrocarbons and some chlorinated aromatic hydrocarbons (Karickhoff *et al.*, 1979). The latter is intended for pesticides (Kenaga and Goring, 1978). Other correlations are available in the literature for other compounds.

Sorption distribution coefficients are used for both organic and inorganic chemicals:

$$C_s = C_w K_d \qquad (9.7)$$

where C_s = soil concentration
  C_w = aqueous phase concentration
  K_d = sorption distribution coefficient

For organic chemicals, the K_d value can be determined from:

$$K_d = K_{oc} F_{oc} \qquad (9.8)$$

where K_d = adsorption distribution coefficient for an organic compound
  K_{oc} = organic sorption partition coefficient
  F_{oc} = fraction of organic carbon in the soil

For inorganic parameters, no simple correlation exists for sorption, and hence literature K_d values must be sought. The K_d value selected should reflect the inorganic chemical as well as the type of soil and the pH of the soil.

In addition to sorption, solubility-controlled dissolution should be considered when assessing inorganic substances. To estimate the dissolution rate, additional information may be required, such as soil-water pH, ionic balance, concentrations of other ionic species in ground water, and solid phases present.

The **bioconcentration factor,** or BCF, is used to estimate the concentration of the chemical in biotic phases (such as fish). For some chemicals, especially organic compounds, this concentration may be orders of magnitude higher than the water phase. Several correlations have been developed for BCF. The following simple correlation is one of the more widely used ones or organic chemicals (Mackay, 1982a):

$$BCF = L_F K_{OW} \tag{9.9}$$

where BCF = Bioconcentration factor
L_F = lipid content of fish (typically about 0.05)

Some compounds partition into fish very slowly. Hydrophobic chemicals have low solubilities and therefore a large volume of water must passed through the fish to accomplish the necessary transfer. For relatively large molecules, there may be additional resistance to bioconcentration due to the molecule–cell membrane interaction (Mackay and Hughes, 1984).

Equation 9.9 does not take into account biomagnification effects that may be caused by fish feeding on other aquatic organisms, or the ability of fish to metabolically convert a substance. Rates of metabolism for fish are poorly documented. If fish are the organism of interest, consideration also must be given to the migratory nature of the fish.

Plant uptake factors are used to estimate the transfer of substances from soil, water, and air to plants. There are three ways for plants to take up a chemical in the environment: foliar deposition, root uptake, and uptake of vapours via leaves. The first two mechanisms are considered to dominate most scenarios and various equations have been formulated to estimate uptake. For certain compounds (those which are not soluble, persistent, and sparingly volatile), recent studies suggest that the uptake of vapours may be the major long-term uptake route; however, appropriate equations have not yet been published.

One equation developed to estimate the uptake of compounds due to foliar deposition is (Hetrick and McDowell-Boyer, 1984):

$$K_{pf} = R/(Y\ W)\ [1 - e^{(-W\ t)}\ /(W\ t)\ D_p] \tag{9.10}$$

where K_{pf} = uptake factor due to foliar deposition (on a dry weight basis)
R   = initial fraction of material intercepted

Y   = vegetative productivity or yield
W   = weathering constant
t   = crop growth period
D_p = deposition rate of particulate matter

A relatively simple equation for estimating root uptake of organic compounds in soil is (DSC, 1989):

$$\log K_{pr} = 0.97 - 0.5 \, (\log K_{ow}) \qquad (9.11)$$

where K_{pr} = root uptake factor for an organic (on a dry weight basis)

Other equations as well as variations of Equations 9.10 and 9.11 have been developed; however, in general, plant uptake is not well understood.

9.5 REACTION RATES AND HALF-LIVES

9.5.1 Reaction Rates

An organic compound in the environment can be subjected to many types of reactions, most of which involve the degradation of the compound and therefore influence its concentration in the environment. The overall effect of the reaction rates often is referred to as a compound's persistence or environmental stability. Various reaction rates are identified in Table 9.1.

Hydrolysis is a chemical transformation process in which an organic molecule reacts with water, forming a new carbon-oxygen bond and cleaving a carbon bond in the original molecule. Typically, the net reaction is the direct displacement of a component of the organic molecule by a hydroxyl ion (Harris, 1982). For example, acetic acid and ethanol are formed by the hydrolysis of ethyl acetate.

Photolysis is the degradation of a chemical due to exposure to light. Degradation typically results via the rupture of covalent bonds. The process is most relevant to chemicals in the atmosphere but also occurs in surface water and on the surface of soils.

Biodegradation involves the breakdown of organic or inorganic materials by organisms, most often microorganisms. Bacterial metabolism alone accounts for 65% of the total metabolism of a soil community because of high bacterial biomass and metabolic rates (Scow, 1982). Biodegradation may occur in the presence of oxygen (aerobic conditions) or absence of oxygen (anaerobic conditions).

Chemical oxidation can involve the addition of oxygen, removal of hydrogen, or the removal of electrons. A chemical that is responsible for oxidizing another is called an oxidizing agent or an oxidant. Examples of oxidizing agents include ozone (O_3) and potassium permanganate ($KMnO_4$).

9.5.2 Overall Rate Constants

In addition to specific reaction rate constants, total compartment rate constants are sometimes used to express the overall rate of loss of a chemical from a compartment. For example, published accounts indicate that the total soil loss rate constant for acetone is about of 1×10^{-7} per second. This value was derived from laboratory studies in which the loss of acetone through soil volatilization, soil leaching, and runoff were measured. A similar value for arsenic would be 2×10^{-10} per second (Environ, 1988).

9.5.3 Half-Lives

An alternative to the use of reaction rates or soil loss rate constants is the half-life which can be calculated, once reaction rate constants (k values) are known, according to the equation:

$$T_{1/2} = \ln 2/k = 0.693/k \qquad (9.12)$$

For each environmental compartment, a persistence half-life can be estimated and used to assess the chemical's fate. The use of half-lives when expressing persistence is sometimes easier to interpret. For example, a half-life of 10 days for toluene in soils following a spill may be easier to understand than a rate constant of 0.069 days^{-1}.

9.6 USING ENVIRONMENTAL FATE TO EVALUATE RELEASES

9.6.1 Overview

The release of a chemical into the environment, even in a small quantity, may be disruptive or lead to adverse effects. A chemical may be transported by several pathways, reaching unsuspecting or non-target organisms (including humans) that may experience subtle and delayed effects (Mackay, 1982b). Such long-range transportation is demonstrated by the presence of trace organic compounds at measurable concentrations in Canadian snow (Gregor and Gummer, 1989).

Wherever chemicals have been released to the environment or a release is being considered, an understanding of environmental fate can be used to ensure that the relevant transport and transformation processes are assessed. The underlying objective of assessing environmental fate is to assist in estimating the exposures that humans and biota may experience and to determine how environmental concentrations of the chemical likely will change with time. This is particularly relevant in light of the environmental policy being advocated by growing numbers of regulatory agencies towards the virtual elimination of persistent toxic chemicals.

9.6.2 Stack and Fugitive Emissions to the Atmosphere

The emission rate and behaviour of a chemical from a stack may be strongly influenced by the type of pollution control equipment used and its operating parameters, production rates, and stack exit gas velocity. In recent years, there has been a shift towards longer residence times (more than two seconds) and higher temperatures (greater than 1000 °C) during the combustion of organic chemicals to ensure complete destruction.

In addition to stack emissions, fugitive emissions can be major sources of releases to the air. Fugitive emissions may result from leaks, storage tanks, vents, open windows near process areas, and waste disposal and treatment site emissions.

Once a chemical is emitted to the atmosphere, it can be transported by turbulent mixing and convection to the surrounding area or even to distant locations. The distance a chemical can travel is a function of several parameters, including the release height, location of adjacent buildings, atmospheric stability, wind speed, and prevailing long-range transport phenomena. For example, the Atlantic Ocean appears to be the major sink for PCBs, accounting for 80% to 90% of the PCB burden in the environment (Doskey and Andren, 1981).

The processes that may act upon a chemical in the air compartment are illustrated in Figure 9.1. From the air compartment a chemical may be deposited on water, land, or plants.

Transformation in the form of photochemical degradation or reaction with other compounds is also important for compounds in the atmosphere. An example of the latter is the formation of acidic precipitation from the interaction of water vapour with emissions of sulfur and nitrogen compounds.

9.6.3 Spills onto Water

Whenever a chemical is stored, used, or transported near an aquatic environment, there exists the risk that a spill may occur and the chemical may reach a river, stream, lake, etc. Releases also can result from inadequate effluent treatment at a manufacturing plant, spillage during manufacturing and distribution, losses during transportation, or leakage from disposal sites.

The Exxon *Valdez* released approximately 42 million litres of oil into the marine environment. When oil is spilled at sea, various processes act on it, most of which are influenced by the oil's properties. Early behaviour is dominated by the spreading tendency of the oil. The spreading process is very complex, involving unsteady-state transient behaviour of an oil of changing composition as material evaporates on a mobile water surface. The usual behaviour is for the oil to form slicks less than a millimetre thick surrounded by sheens only a few micrometres thick (Mackay *et al.*, 1983).

The oil will also drift and potentially form a heavy water-in-oil emulsion (mousse) which is almost impossible to pump. Eventually, wind and waves may shear the mousse into pieces referred to as "pancakes," which in turn break into tar balls and may wash ashore.

Evaporation is often an important source of loss for chemicals spilled in aquatic environments. The evaporation rate is a function of the chemical's vapour pressure, temperature, and characteristics of the air above the chemical (primarily wind speed). In the case of an oil spill, the most soluble components are also the most volatile and hence will evaporate readily (Mackay *et al.*, 1983).

Other processes that will act upon the chemical are illustrated in Figure 9.2. The chemical may dissolve into the water column resulting in the potential uptake by biota, sorption onto suspended solids or interaction with sediment. The material may undergo oxidation, hydrolysis, and biodegradation in the water column and in the sediment. Oil drops will form by either breaking waves or a local surface convergence which may occur on steep waves. The smaller drops may be conveyed by eddy diffusion currents to depths in the water and become essentially permanently incorporated in the water column (Mackay *et al.*, 1983).

Spilled chemicals that have densities greater than water will sink to the bottom and may interact with sediment. These "sinkers" may become a source of contamination over an extended period of time as components gradually dissolve from the material and enter the water column.

9.6.4 Leaks from Underground Storage Tanks

If a small volume of non-aqueous phase liquid (NAPL) is lost from an underground storage tank into a relatively homogeneous, permeable soil, the liquid will move downward towards the water table. It will pass through the more permeable corridors in the soil. The liquid will continue to move towards the water table as long as the volume is sufficient to offset the absorption of the chemical into the soil void space. Unless the leak is large or ongoing, the leading edge of the liquid plume eventually will become static (Farmer, 1983).

Five potentially damaging conditions may develop (Farmer, 1983):
- light NAPL may migrate along the top of the water table
- residual, but immobile, pockets of chemical, are left as NAPL moves downward
- evaporation of the liquid phase results in vapour dispersing through the unsaturated zone to surface
- NAPL can dissolve into the aquifer and subsequently be transported by the ground water

- as "lighter" constituents leave the NAPL, "sinkers" may form and move to the bottom of the aquifer; these are difficult to detect and will act as a contaminant source

When contaminants come into contact with a water well or a basement or reach a surface water course, an environmental problem may be created. If the NAPL readily volatilizes, the volatile components will migrate into the air-filled pores potentially resulting in exposure through inhalation for individuals at the site.

If the density of the NAPL is less than that of water (such as oil) the material will eventually spread out horizontally above the water table. If the material has a density greater than water (often referred to as a dense, non-aqueous phase liquid or DNAPL), it will pass through the aquifer and sink until it reaches a confining or relatively impermeable layer of soil or rock. The direction of the DNAPL movement at that point will be similar to the slope of the confining layer.

9.7 ENVIRONMENTAL FATE MODELS

In recent years, many models have been developed to assess the environmental fate of contaminants. These types of models can be used to assess potential environmental hazards (Cohen, 1986).

Many of the models focus on a specific environmental compartment or fate process. For example, Table 9.2 presents a sampling of models that address vapour transport from soils, chemical movement in both the unsaturated and saturated zones of soil, and chemical fate in surface water environments.

Three of the models that can be used to estimate the loss of chemicals from soil due to volatilization were developed to evaluate the releases of chemicals from landfills. The other two models were developed to assess pesticide movement in soil.

The majority of the unsaturated zone models address the influences of runoff, infiltration and volatilization on chemicals applied to soil. The MINTEQ model (Battelle, 1984) predicts the aqueous speciation, adsorption, and precipitation dissolution of inorganic substances.

The saturated zone models presented on Table 9.2 simulate the movement of a chemical in the saturated zone under the influence of convection, dispersion, adsorption, and reaction processes.

The surface water quality models address the tendency of a substance to distribute itself among the various compartments of aquatic environments. These can include the water column, suspended material, biota, sediment, and overlying air.

There are also models that can be used to assess environmental fate in a broader or more general context. Those often are assemblies or combinations of models such as those identified in Table 9.2.

REFERENCES

Baker, L.W., and K.P. Mackay. 1985. "Screening Models for Estimating Toxic Air Pollution Near Hazardous Waste Landfill." *J. Air. Poll. Control Ass.* 35: 1190-1195.

Battelle Pacific Northwest Labs. February 1984. *MINTEQ — A Computer Program for Calculating Aqueous Geochemical Equilibrium.* Prepared for the U.S. Environmental Protection Agency, PB84-157148.

Burns, L.A., D. M. Cline, and R.R. Lassiter. 1982. *Exposure Analysis Modeling System (EXAMS): User Manual and System Documentation.* EPA-600/3-82-023, U.S. EPA, Athens, GA.

Carsel, R.F., C.N. Smith, L.A. Mulkey, J.D. Dean, and P.P. Jowise. 1984. *User's Manual for the Pesticide Root Zone Model (PRZM) — Release 1.* U.S. Environmental Protection Agency, Office of Research and Development, EPA-600/3-84-109.

Cohen, Y. 1986. "Organic Pollutant Transport." *Environ. Sci. Technol.* 20 (No. 6): 538-544.

Dean, J.D., P.P. Jowise, and A.S. Donigan, Jr. 1984. *Leaching Evaluation of Agricultural Chemicals (LEACH) Handbook.* U.S. Environmental Protection Agency, Office of Research and Development, EPA-600/1-84-068.

Decommissioning Steering Committee (DSC). 1989. "The Development of Soil Clean-Up Criteria in Canada." *Report on the "Demonstration" Version of the AERIS Model (An Aid for Evaluating the Redevelopment of Industrial Sites).* Vol. 2. Prepared for Environment Canada, Conservation and Protection.

Electronic Power Research Institute (EPRI). August 1981. *Unsaturated Groundwater Flow Model (UNSATD) Computer Code Model.* Palo Alto, CA. CS-2434-CCM.

Environ Corporation. January 1988. "Site Assessment Phase 4B: Risk Assessment — Vol. 2, Appendices A through D." Prepared for the Ontario Waste Management Corporation.

Farmer, V.E. 1983. "Behaviour of Petroleum Contaminants in an Underground Environment." Presented at the Seminar on Ground Water and Petroleum Hydrocarbons: Protection Detection, Restoration. Toronto, 26 to 28 June.

Gregor, D.J., and W.D. Gummer. 1989. "Evidence of Atmospheric Transport and Deposition of Organochlorine Pesticides and Polychlorinated Biphenyls in Canadian Arctic Snow." *Envir. Sci. and Tech.* 23 (No. 5): 561-565.

Harris, J.C. 1982a. "Rate of Hydrolysis." In *Handbook of Chemical Property Estimation Methods.* W.J. Lyman, W.F. Reehl, and D.H. Rosenblatt, eds. New York: McGraw-Hill Book Company.

Hetrick, D.M., and L.M. McDowell-Boyer. 1984. *User's Manual for TOX-SCREEN: A Multimedia Screening-Level Program for Assessing the Potential Fate of Chemicals Released to the Environment.* Prepared by the Oak Ridge National Laboratory for the U.S. EPA Office of Toxic Substances, EPA Report 560/5-83-024.

Javandel, I.C., C. Doughty, and C.F. Tsang. 1984. *Groundwater Transport: Handbook of Mathematical Models.* Water Resources Monograph Series 10, American Geophysical Union, Washington D.C.

Jury, W.A., R. Grover, W.F. Spencer, and W.J. Farmer. 1980. "Modeling Vapor Losses of Soil-Incorporated Triallate." *Soil Soc. Am. J.* 4: 445-450.

Karickhoff, S.W., D.S. Brown, and T.A. Scott. 1979. "Sorption of Hydrophobic Pollutants on Natural Sediments." *Water Res.* 13: 241-248.

Kenaga, E.E., and C.A.I. Goring. 1978. "Relationship between Water Solubility, Soil-Sorption, Octanol-Water Partitioning, and Bioconcentration of Chemicals in Biota." Pre-publication copy of paper dated 13 October 1978 given at the American Society for Testing Materials, Third Aquatic Toxicology Symposioum, 17-18 October 1978, New Orleans, LA.

Kincaid, G.T., and P.J. Mitchell. 1986. "Review of Multiphase Flow and Pollutant Transport Models for the Hanford Site." Pacific Northwest Laboratory, PNL-6048.

Mackay, D. 1982a. "Correlation of Bioconcentration Factors." *Environ. Sci. Technol.* 16: 274-278.

Mackay, D. 1982b. "Nature and Origin of Micropollutants." *Wat. Sci. Tech.* 14: 5-14.

Mackay, D., and A.I. Hughes. 1984. "Three-Parameter Equation Describing the Uptake of Organic Compounds by Fish." *Environ. Sci. and Technol.* 18 (No. 6): 439-444.

Mackay D., W. Stiver, and P.A. Tebeau. 1983. "Testing of Crude Oils and Petroleum Products for Environmental Purposes." Proceedings 1983 Oil Spill Conference, San Antonio, TX. American Petroleum Institute, Washington, D.C.: 331-337.

Mackay, D., S. Patterson, B. Cheung, and W.B. Neely. 1985. "Evaluating the Environmental Behavior of Chemicals with a Level III Fugacity Model." *Chemosphere* 14 (No. 3/4): 335-374.

Mayer, R., J. Letey, and W.J. Farmer. 1974. "Models for Predicting Volatilization of Soil-Incorporated Pesticides." *Soil Sci. Soc. Am. Proc.* 38: 563-568.

Scow, K.M. 1982. "Rate of Biodegradation." In *Handbook of Chemical of Property Estimation Methods.* Previously cited.

Shen, T. August 1981. "Estimating Hazardous Air Emissions from Disposal Sites." *Pollution Engineering.*

Short, T.E. "Mathematical Modeling of Land Treatment Processes." Invited presentation to the National Specialty Conference on Land Treatment, University of Texas, Austin TX, 16 to 18 April.

Thibodeaux, L.J. 1981. "Estimating the Air Emissions of Chemicals from Hazardous Waste Landfills." *J. Haz. Mat.* 4: 235-244.

Table 9.1
KEY ENVIRONMENTAL PARAMETERS

CHEMICAL PARAMETERS
- vapour pressure
- density
- molecular weight
- solubility
- melting point and boiling point

PHYSICAL PARAMETERS

Air
- wind velocity and direction
- physical topography
- temperature and rainfall
- atmospheric stability class

Water
- pH and temperature
- concentration of suspended sediment
- water velocity and flow
- residence time of water
- cation/anion balance

Sediment
- oxygen concentration
- resuspension rate
- porosity
- organic carbon content
- deposition rate

Soil
- pH and temperature
- runoff
- soil type (density and porosity)
- surface vegetation
- rainfall
- organic carbon content
- soil water content
- solid phases present (e.g. carbonate)

Ground Water
- organic carbon content
- hydraulic conductivity/gradient
- dispersion
- aquifer soil type (density and porosity)
- pH and cation/anion balance
- infiltration rate

PARTITION COEFFICIENTS
- Henry's Law constant (H)
- bioconcentration factor (BCF)
- adsorption coefficient (K_d)
- octanol/water partition coefficient (K_{ow})
- organic partition coefficient (K_{oc})
- plant uptake factor (K_p)

REACTION RATES
- hydrolysis
- biodegradation
- reaction with other chemicals
- photolysis
- chemical oxidation

Table 9.2
SELECTED ENVIRONMENTAL FATE MODELS

Volatilization from Soil
Jury, Grover, Spencer and Farmer, 1980
- vapour/non-vapour movement in soil

Shen, 1981
- estimates emissions from landfill

Thibodeaux, 1981
- estimates exposure from landfill emission

Baker and Mackay, 1985
- four models for estimated exposure from landfill emissions

Unsaturated Zone
Electric Power Research Institute, 1981
- Unsaturated Flow Model (UNSAT1D) estimates infiltration, vertical seepage and uptake by water roots

Battelle, 1984
- Metal Speciation Equilibrium Model (MINTEQ) is a thermodynamic equilibrium model for aqueous speciation, adsorption and precipitation dissolution of solid phases

Carsel et al., 1984
- Pesticide Root Zone Model (PRZM) estimates runoff, erosion, plant uptake, leaching, decay, foliar wash-off and volatilization

Dean et al., 1984
- Leaching Evaluation of Agricultural Chemicals (LEACH) is used to assess the leaching potential of pesticides

Short, 1985
- Regulatory and Investigative Treatment Zone Model (RITZ) estimates movement of chemicals following land treatment of oily wastes

Saturated Zone
Yeh and Ward, 1981*
- Finite Element Model of Waste Transport (FEMWASTE) simulates the transport of dissolved constituents in two-dimensional ground water (unsaturated/saturated zones)

Prickett, Naymik and Lonnquist, 1981*
- "RANDOM WALK +" can be used to evaluate one- or two-dimensional flow and solute transport

Garabedian and Konikow, 1983
- "Front-Tracking Model" is a finite difference model for convective transport of a conservative tracer dissolved in ground water under steady or transient flow

Voss, 1984**
- "SUTRA +" simulates two-dimensional, transient, or unsteady state, saturated or unsaturated, transport of energy or chemically reactive single species

UCLA Davis, 1985**
- "GS2" is a two-dimensional horizontal or vertical finite element model to simulate flow and solute movement in ground water (unsaturated/saturated zones)

Surface Water
Mackay *et al.*, 1985
- Fugacity Level III is a steady-state, non-equilibrium chemical fate model; fugacity is a thermodynamic concept that represents the tendency of a chemical to escape from one environmental compartment to another

Burns *et al.*, 1982
- EXAMS (Exposure Analysis Modeling System) estimates chemical fate in various types of aquatic environments including lakes, rivers, and estuaries; has steady-state and non-steady-state options

Notes
*   **Reference:** Javendel *et al.*, 1984
**   **Reference:** Kincaid and Mitchell, 1986

Figure 9.1
ATMOSPHERIC TRANSPORT AND
TRANSFORMATION PROCESSES

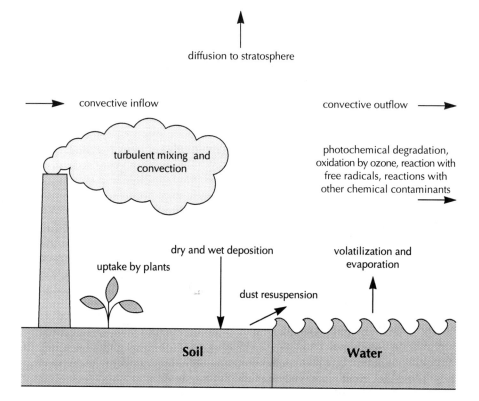

Figure 9.2
TRANSPORT AND TRANSFORMATION OF
CHEMICALS IN WATER

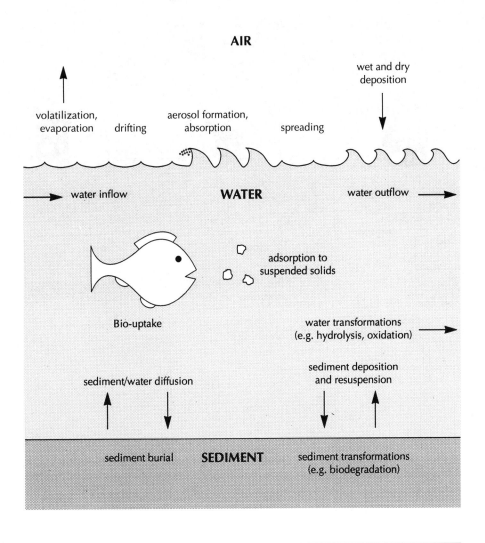

Figure 9.3
LEAKAGE FROM AN UNDERGROUND
STORAGE TANK

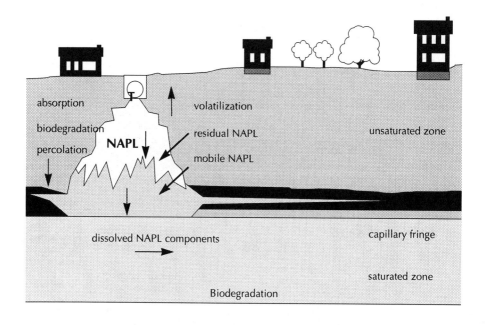

10.0

Environmental Audits

10.1 WHAT IS AN ENVIRONMENTAL AUDIT?

10.1.1 Canadian Activities

During the past several years, the term "environmental audit" (EA) has been used to describe various types of environmental studies. Most often, these studies have focused on the degree to which a company, facility, or property complies with appropriate environmental legislation. Examples of the range of objectives met by performing an EA rapidly swelled to include:

- assessment of compliance with environmental legislation, published guidelines for environmental management systems (EMS), industrial codes of practice, or corporate policies, procedures, and objectives
- identification of potential environmental impacts and liabilities imposed on company and employees
- identification and prioritization of resources needed to comply with areas of potential non-compliance, and
- improving or protecting the environmental reputation of a company

Changes to the Ontario Environmental Protection Act and the Canadian Environmental Protection Act in the late 1980s delineated the responsibility of officers and directors for communicating adequate information and specific instructions through the management structure, and for arranging training, supervision, and monitoring so that adverse effects to the environment are prevented. In order to reduce potential liability and ensure ongoing compliance, senior management of numerous companies have initiated environmental auditing programs. Recent court decisions (e.g. *Queen v. Bata Industries Ltd.*), and publication of standards by various organizations on EMS (e.g. Canadian Standard Association – CAN/CSA Z750) have reinforced the need to perform environmental audits.

Most large industries perform periodic audits of their operations. The frequency of auditing and procedures employed in the audit may differ, but there is a growing consensus that it is an integral part of an environmental management system. There is general agreement that an environmental audit is a systematic and objective evaluation of a facility, process, or site from an environmental perspective.

As the numbers of EAs being performed grew rapidly, confusion began to set in over terminology, tasks, and the qualifications needed to be an environmental auditor.

To help clarify this situation, the Canadian Standards Association (CSA) and the Canadian Environmental Auditing Association (CEAA) drafted a document entitled *Guidelines for Environmental Auditing: Principles and Practices* (CAN/CSA Z751). This document provides an overview of the principles and practices that are applicable to all types of environmental audits. The definition for EAs employed in the document is as follows:

A systematic process of objectively obtaining and evaluating evidence regarding a verifiable assertion about an environmental matter, to ascertain the degree of correspondence between the assertion and established standards and criteria, and then communicating the results to the client.

The aforementioned definition does *not* include environmental site assessments (ESA), internal plant inspections performed by facility personnel, or on-site monitoring programs. According to the proposed principles, only verification sampling should be performed during the audit. It is recommended that these principles and practices be followed to ensure auditor objectivity, professional competence and due care, and that well-defined and systematic procedures and relevant standards and measures are being used.

The CSA is currently working on developing practices and procedures for EAs. It is anticipated that the practices and procedures for conducting an EA will become "generally accepted." The voluntary guidelines on EAs are part of a series of documents under development by the CSA dealing with various aspects of EMS.

The CEAA is an independent association of individuals dedicated to the development of environmental auditing as a profession. The association encourages the development of the profession of environmental auditing and the improvement of environmental management of Canadian private and public organizations through the creation and application of generally accepted environmental auditing principles and standards. The CEAA is currently assessing certification of environmental auditors. It is anticipated that certification may be available in 1994.

The following discussion of EA activities tries to be consistent with the latest CSA and CEAA initiatives. Readers also should note the differences between an EA and an ESA (see Chapter 5). One characteristic they share is that both are now seen as key components of environmental management systems.

10.1.2 International Auditing Activities

Several international organizations have prepared or are in the process of preparing guidelines/specifications for EAs. These include:

- International Organization for Standardization (ISO), 14000 series
- European Community Eco-Audit Scheme
- National Environmental Auditors Registration Board (United Kingdom)
- Environmental Auditing Roundtable (United States)
- Environmental Auditing Institute (United States)
- Environmental Auditing Foundation (United States)

The following are brief discussions of three key programs.

The International Organization for Standardization (ISO)/ Strategic Advisory Group on Environment (SAGE) has prepared draft guidelines on environmental auditing. It is anticipated that these guidelines will become part of ISO 14000 series. Based upon the draft guidelines, the document will consist of sections on general principles; protocols (or detailed principles) for different types of environmental audits; qualifications for environmental auditors; and the management of the environmental auditing programs for different types of audits. The *ISO Guidelines for Auditing Quality Systems* (ISO 10011) may be a useful reference until the EA guidelines are available.

The European Community (EC) recently adopted a proposal for a Council Regulation allowing voluntary participation by companies in a Community Eco-Audit scheme. The objective of the Council Regulation is to encourage companies to introduce EMS and to provide the public with details of their environmental performance in relation to its policies and objectives.

Participating companies are required to implement an environmental protection system (EPS) and undertake environmental audits. The EPS must include an effective management control of practices relevant to the environment. The EAs are to involve a comprehensive analysis of the environmental issues and impacts and performance relating to a site. Following the audit, an environmental statement regarding the performance of a company's environmental activities must be made public. The audit methodology and procedures must be undertaken in accordance with the guidelines set out in ISO 10011 and the principles and requirements of the Council Regulation.

The National Environmental Auditors Registration Board (NEARB) is a United Kingdom-based working group which certifies and publishes a registry of environmental auditors. NEARB classifies auditors into three categories: provisional environmental auditors, environmental auditors, and principal environmental auditors. A person's categorization is based upon his or her technical and academic background, professional membership, and relevant training and experience.

10.2 PRE-AUDIT DECISIONS

10.2.1 Prerequisites

Since there are many reasons for undertaking an EA, there is broad variability in the scope, objectives, and procedures associated with EAs. However, there also are some common, prerequisite elements that need to be in place to demonstrate the benefits that an audit can provide. Whenever a company decides that an EA is to be performed — regardless of whether the audit is to be performed by outside auditors or by in-house staff — it is necessary that:

- the audit is supported by the company's senior management
- the audit team is given the authority, resources, and training to conduct a thorough and proper job
- the audit receives good cooperation from staff at the facility to be audited, and
- the company's management is prepared to respond to any deficiencies identified during the audit

10.2.2 Objectives, Scope and Boundary Conditions

The objectives, scope, and boundary conditions of an audit will depend upon who is requesting the audit and reasons why the audit is to be undertaken. These aspects need to be conveyed to the auditor before the audit begins. Uncertainties in the scope of the audit may result in large variances in quotations to perform the work, or the writing of an audit report which does not respond to the objectives of the client.

Objectives will normally make reference to the types of audit criteria to be employed (e.g. compliance to environmental legislation, published EMS, industrial codes of practices and corporate policies and procedures). The objectives should be clearly documented prior to initiating the audit.

The **scope** of the audit should define the activities required to meet the audit's objectives and summarize the boundary conditions discussed below. The current approach to auditing as indicated by CSA is that an environmental audit includes a report on findings. Conclusions, recommendations, and/or the development of an action plan are all "extras" which should be discussed with the client and defined by the internal scope of the work or in the request for proposal.

Boundary conditions which must be included in the scope of the audit include the following:

- geographical area to be assessed
- industrial processes
- time period (i.e. current and/or past operations)
- verification sampling
- assessment of off-site impacts (e.g. air dispersion modelling)
- on-site subcontractors/lessees
- interaction with government agencies
- involvement of third parties, and
- inclusion/exclusion of occupational issues

It is important that the role of the relevant boundary conditions be clearly documented.

10.2.3 Types of Audits

The following are examples of three broad categories of environmental audits: compliance audits, risk (liability) audits, and environmental management system audits. As indicated in Section 10.1.1, Environmental Site Assessments (ESA) are not considered environmental audits according to the CSA guidelines and hence are not discussed under types of audits.

A **compliance audit** is directed toward determining whether or not a facility meets all of its current environmental requirements. The requirements can include laws, regulations, standards, criteria, guidelines, by-laws, and permits. Failure to comply may result in fines or other penalties such as the revocation of permits and control orders, adversarial relations with regulatory agencies, court injunctions, and even criminal prosecution of corporate officials (Palmisano and Margolis, 1987).

The definition of failure to comply has recently been broadened to include failure to notify regulatory agencies of events or conditions. Regulatory reporting requirements have increased dramatically in recent years. The Environmental Protection Act (EPA) and the Ontario Water Resources Act (OWRA) contain extensive reporting requirements. Failure to notify agencies forthwith of an environmental incident (such as a spill or unscheduled release) has become one of the most frequently cited violations of non-compliance.

A compliance audit also may consider self-imposed requirements. For example, a company may want to establish its own environmental objectives or may strive to comply with a code of practice established by an industrial association.

A **risk audit** is used to assess the probability of potential adverse effects that a facility or operation may pose to staff members, neighbours, or the natural environment. All of the routes or pathways by which released substances can move around in the environment or which affect public health need to be considered. Typically these include air, surface water, ground water, and soil pathways.

The release of gases from the Union Carbide facility in Bhopal, India or the warehouse fire at Sandoz Ltd. in Basel, Switzerland and subsequent discharges into the Rhine River illustrate that companies and facilities do not exist in isolation. Most often they are located where they may affect the air quality, water supplies, and recreational or agricultural activities of nearby communities, as well as adjacent businesses, wildlife, aesthetics, and other features of the local setting. The sorts of risks considered in a risk audit can include direct or indirect health effects, environmental damage, negative publicity, erosion of public confidence, and being named in legal proceedings.

One important way in which risk audits differ from compliance audits is that risk audits are not usually required by law or are not part of a facility's items of compliance. One advantage of risk audits is that they can allow a company to be proactive in dealing with existing or potential concerns rather than being reactive.

An **environmental management system audit** comprises a critical review of a facility's environmental management systems. The components of an EMS audit may include the company's environmental policies and procedures, organizational structure, assignment of responsibilities, reporting protocols, environmental training, and inspection programs. An EMS audit should include a review of environmental departments and personnel, job responsibilities and accountability (Palmisano and Margolis, 1989). Special attention should be paid to internal training because many companies are finding it increasingly difficult to keep employees informed about new or revised legislation.

This type of audit can draw attention to communication deficiencies, gaps or overlap in responsibilities, schedule delays (especially with regard to obtaining Certificates of Approval), and unnecessary costs. The identification of problems or situations that appear to pose excessive liability signal the need for improved management systems.

A comprehensive environmental audit program at a facility likely would include all three types of audits described above. In practice, many companies modify, merge, or otherwise make facility-specific audit programs which also tend to evolve and become more sophisticated over time.

10.2.4 Audit Confidentiality

Two issues related to confidentiality can arise during an environmental audit. The first is related to **confidentiality between an auditor and the company**. Sensitive information collected during an audit may significantly impact a company's competitiveness and reputation if passed on to competitors, members of the financial community, or the press. Contract conditions can be used to restrict the release of information collected during the audit.

The second issue concerns the **accessibility of audit reports** by government agencies or through court-directed disclosure. Both industry and regulators continue to struggle with this issue. Environment Canada recognizes that environmental audits are an effective management tool for assessing environmental compliance. Under the Canadian Environmental Protection Act (CEPA), audit reports may be required when inspectors/investigation specialists have reasonable grounds to believe that:

- an offence has been committed
- the audit findings will be relevant to a particular violation, necessary to its inspector/investigation specialist, and required as evidence, or
- the information being sought cannot be obtained from other sources through the exercise of the inspector's/investigation specialist's powers (Environment Canada, 1988)

Environment Canada has stated that an environmental audit must not be used to shelter monitoring/compliance or other information that would otherwise be accessible to inspection under CEPA. In addition, the demand for access to an environmental audit during an investigation can be made under the authority of a search warrant. An exception can be made when the delay necessary in obtaining a warrant would likely result in danger to the environment or human health, or the loss or destruction of evidence (Environment Canada, 1988).

The MOEE has proposed a policy in *Access and Use of Self-Initiated Environmental Evaluations*. In the policy, the MOEE recognizes the power and effectiveness of environmental evaluations as a method of protecting and conserving the natural environment, and as a management tool for business, public institutions and individuals, and intends to promote their widespread use.

This policy is meant to promote proactive self-initiated environmental evaluations which identify compliance problems — those weaknesses that are intended to apply to initiatives which exceed the current dictates of law. The policy currently does not apply to monitoring/compliance and other information municipalities or provincial or federal authorities presently require to ensure compliance with environmental law. Nor does the policy deal with information such as incident reports or reports prepared in response to the Ministry's spill reduction program which are produced in reaction to specific discharges, spills, or contaminant concentrations in effluent or air emissions which exceed the allowable levels.

The exact details of the draft policy are beyond the scope of this book as they are currently being negotiated with industrial representatives. We do recommend that auditors and environmental managers obtain a copy of the policy when it is finalized.

Prior to initiating an audit, a client should discuss the issue of confidentiality with legal counsel. Two schools of thought on the confidentiality of environmental audit revolve around the concept of attorney-client privilege and due diligence.

Option 1: Solicitor-Client Privilege

Several companies use "solicitor-client" privilege when conducting an environmental audit and restricting access to the audit report. To be in force, the lawyer must take the lead role and ensure that the following conditions are met:

- the information/study must be requested by the corporation and/or officers and directors
- the request must be in anticipation of litigation
- considered legal advice
- the information/study must be delivered by the lawyer to the corporation and/or officers and directors
- the information/study must be kept confidential

The above conditions do allow for an outside consultant and/or corporate staff to assist the lawyer in the preparation of report.

Counsel responsible for an audit should develop procedures for maintaining confidentiality and ensure that those procedures are followed by everyone who participates in the audit.

One disadvantage of this approach is that it may deny report access to individuals who will implement the corrective action.

Option 2: Due Diligence

Several companies are choosing the due diligence option (as opposed to solicitor-client privilege) on the premise that the benefits flowing from an auditing program may far outweigh any negative concerns associated with disclosure (Villeneuve, 1989). Advocates of this approach can argue that a defense of due diligence based on an active audit program which critically and impartially identifies and corrects environmental deficiencies may be the best defense.

10.3 PRE-VISIT ACTIVITIES

10.3.1 Selecting the Audit Team

An essential element of all audits is that the auditors must be objective and impartial. The auditor may be completely external to the facility to be audited and the client. Conversely, the auditor (or team of auditors) may include in-house personnel provided that their objectivity is not compromised. The use of in-house personnel will not jeopardize audit independence if certain criteria such as auditor proficiency and non-accountability to the facility are met. If audits are to be performed on a regular basis, it may be appropriate to select and train several individuals (i.e. a pool of auditors) from different facilities to audit their counterparts. The use of external auditors, especially for a first audit, can be beneficial. External auditors can assist in training internal audit staff. It may also be appropriate to have external consultants perform periodic audits to assess the adequacy of the internal audit program depending upon the degree of potential non-compliance and regulatory changes.

Audit team members should be selected based upon the scope and type of audit to be undertaken. Audit team members should include professionals with appropriate specialist skills. These skills may include:

- environmental affairs and policy
- regulatory affairs expertise
- management systems expertise
- specific environmental and engineering expertise
- scientific expertise such as biologists, chemists, toxicologists, or hydrogeologists
- familiarity with operations

Collectively, the team must understand the operations of the facility or company from a technical perspective and also be familiar with the applicable environmental laws and regulations. The responsibilities of each member of the team must be clearly established. One of the members of the audit team should be appointed as leader. The leader should have a general level of familiarity with the facility and auditing principles and practices, and leadership qualities to ensure that audit objectives are met.

When organizing the audit team, the availability of team members for the required time period must be unequivocal. The amount of time required to audit a facility will depend on the objective of the audit, the size of the facility and its complexity, as well as the number of people on the audit team. A two-person team may need two to four days to audit a small or medium-size chemical plant, while a four-member team may require two to five days for a larger facility.

Audits initiated by regulatory agencies tend to be performed by government staff or hired consultants. In Ontario, the MOEE on occasion has designated consultants as provincial officers during the course of the audit thereby providing the auditors greater access to records. Section 10.6 discusses steps that can be taken when a facility is the subject of an external audit.

10.3.2 Identification of Criteria

Criteria must be employed to assess the degree of compliance, performance, or liability. Depending upon the type of audit to be undertaken, the criteria may include, but may not be limited to, federal and provincial environmental Acts, regulations, standards, policies, guidelines, objectives, municipal by-laws; industrial codes of practice; published guidelines and standards on EMS; and the organization's policy requirements and internal codes of practice.

Table 10.1 lists relevant pieces of legislation for Ontario industries. Individuals who conduct environmental audits must have a good working knowledge of the environmental legislation that pertains to the situation being evaluated. The relative importance of the legislation listed in Table 10.1 largely will be influenced by the type of industrial operations to be audited and the location of its emissions/discharges. An example of the latter is the selection of appropriate legislation to assess a water discharge. Discharges to municipal storm sewers and sanitary/combined sewers (i.e. indirect discharges) are usually regulated by municipal by-laws, whereas direct discharges are regulated by the MOEE under the Ontario Water Resources Act using Certificates of Approval (C of A), Provincial Ambient Water Quality Objectives, and industrial discharge guidelines.

It also is necessary to use most recent versions of legislation and regulations. During the past ten years, many regulatory requirements have changed, and further widespread changes to legislation are expected. An audit performed without an appreciation of the relevant legislation may fail to identify non-compliance situations.

The Municipal, Industrial Strategy for Abatement (MISA) monitoring program in Ontario is an example of legislation which contains extensive monitoring and reporting requirements. Such requirements increase the likelihood of procedural violations and hence must be considered during an environmental compliance audit of a facility under the MISA program.

10.3.3 Develop an Audit Plan

A plan should be developed for the collection of evidence using substantiative procedures relevant to the objectives of the audit. The plan should contain the proposed schedule for the audit, names of audit team members, the evaluation criteria to be used, and the auditing procedures. The criteria should be referenced and documented.

Clearly understood protocols should be implemented to ensure consistency in information gathering and interpretation. The protocols must ensure that only "verifiable assertions" are recorded — a declaration or statement about a specific subject matter which is supported by documented factual data (CSA, 1993). Much of the information gathered during an audit initially may be recorded on checklists or other types of working papers.

Questions in a compliance audit checklist should be worded in ways such that they can be answered "yes" or "no." This allows the audit team to quickly assess and summarize non-compliance issues. In the case of a management system audit, the question may be worded to "How do you ensure . . . ?"

The checklist should also require all responses to be referenced. The protocols should document how references are to be recorded (e.g. numerically numbered and presented at the back of the checklists) and whether copies of all pertinent parts of documents (letters, reports, and pictures) indicating non-compliance are to be copied and attached to the audit report.

The audit procedures should also include **tests** to assess specific items on the checklists. For example, the number of manifests to be randomly selected and reviewed for compliance with Ontario Regulation 347 should be identified. The use of specific statistically-sound test methods can allow the audit to be conducted in a reasonable amount of time while minimizing the audit risk.

It may also be appropriate to assess the **audit risk** (i.e. the probability of reaching an incorrect conclusions before an audit is undertaken). The level of risk is determined by the type of audit, the objectives of the audit, and the materiality, extent, and nature of the collected data and evidence. An example of an audit risk is the aforementioned practice of randomly selecting manifests to assess compliance with Ontario Regulation 347. Once the potential risks are identified, the audit plan and level of investigation can then be formulated so that the risk is reduced to an agreed-upon level.

10.3.4 Data Request and Review

Ideally, the audit team should have been provided with and reviewed various types of information before actually visiting a facility. The request for information will be strongly influenced by the type, scope, and boundary conditions of the audit.

Foremost among the data that should be provided in advance is a **comprehensive site plan**. The plan should show the locations of all buildings, storage and on-site transportation facilities, waste storage/treatment/disposal facilities, waste discharge or release points, environmental monitoring equipment, sewer connections, site drainage, neighbouring properties, environmentally sensitive areas, and similar pertinent information (Jolliffe and Gorelle, 1989). Environmentally sensitive areas can include drinking water supplies, streams, wetlands, parks, areas frequented by birds or animals, and any areas used by endangered species.

A **process and emissions block diagram** showing the physical or chemical processes conducted on the site, the handling of raw materials brought onto the site, and all points where waste products (solids, liquids, or vapours) leave the facility also should be provided to the team, or the team should produce one. A typical block diagram is presented on

Figure 10.1. A block diagram is critical since it is impossible to assess compliance if all the emissions or waste streams leaving the facility have not been identified.

All documentation relating to **previous environmental inspection reports** must be collected. Notices of complaints, violations, and prosecutions should also form part of the pre-audit materials. The audit team should be provided with **hazardous materials reports** that identify the locations of materials such as asbestos insulation, equipment that contains PCBs, radioactive materials, or solvents.

Depending upon the agreed-upon scope of the audit and boundary conditions, it may be appropriate to contact the MOEE to obtain copies of available Certificates of Approval, Waste Registration information, complaints and orders, and to discuss any concerns they may have with the facility. A similar request can be made of the municipal representatives to identify potential problems with discharges to sewer system and noise levels.

Travel arrangements may need to be made along with arranging for **permission to inspect** the facility. In most instances, an initial meeting with plant personnel to discuss the audit and a tour of the facility should be arranged in advance. The availability of plant personnel must also be established prior to the audit. At many types of facilities, various forms of safety equipment or special security passes are needed. Safety equipment may range from hard hats and safety glasses to respirators and hazard suits. Passes may be required to ensure security and also safety in the event of an accident. Once again, arrangements must be made prior to the site visit.

10.4 ON-SITE VISIT ACTIVITIES

10.4.1 Opening Meeting and Orientation Tour

A meeting between the audit team and appropriate representatives of the facility being audited should be the first on-site activity. The meeting should allow the groups to review and discuss the scope and objectives of the audit, coordinate the audit activities, and identify those personnel who have a responsibility for environmental activities.

Following this meeting, it may be appropriate to perform an orientation tour to provide an overview of the facility and its operations. The tour is relatively brief and auditors should note areas of concern where further follow-up is required. A plot plan should be taken with the audit team as part of the orientation.

The following activities described in Section 10.4.2, Record Review, 10.4.3. Site Investigation, and 10.4.4, Interviews with Facility Personnel should all be seen as methods by which to collect **evidence** to complete the checklists or working papers described in the Audit Plan. Information collected during any one of these activities should be tested to an appropriate extent by acquiring corroborating information during another activity.

10.4.2 Record Review

A major component of almost any audit the is the review of environmental records. The review may include waste manifests and inventories, observations of all discharges or releases to the environment, the performance logs of environmental control equipment, calibration reports for measuring devices, written environmental procedures and policies, the results of environmental monitoring efforts, Certificates of Approval or control orders issued by regulatory agencies, and reports of unusual or unscheduled events.

The review of environmental records can be very time- consuming. The practices and theory from financial accounting can be used to advantage in some instances. For example, the review of shipping documentation for dangerous goods can be time-consuming if every document must be reviewed. Instead, a representative sample of the documentation can be retrieved from the files and reviewed for compliance. As discussed in Section 10.3.3, the number of manifests to be randomly selected should be identified in the audit plan.

When reviewing certificates or permits care must be taken to check for any major additions, alterations, or modifications that have occurred since the C of A was originally issued. These may require either an amendment to the current approval or the obtaining of a new approval. Note that emissions sources older than 29, June 1988 which have not been modified, altered, or added to after that date, are exempted from C of A (Bill 148). They must still be operated, however, in compliance with appropriate legislation covering the quality of discharges/emissions.

10.4.3 Site Investigation

The audit team should conduct a thorough site investigation of all operations, equipment and storage facilities, and all waste discharge, removal, and environmental release routes. All existing and potential hazards must be noted. The actual information to be collected will be dictated by the questions listed on the audit checklists.

All pollution-control equipment, flow measurement devices, and monitoring equipment (on-line and continuous samplers) should be inspected. Examples of items to include on a checklist when assessing a facility involved in the MISA monitoring program may include:

- all samples must be stored in an environment maintained between the freezing point of the sample and 10°C

- the maximum time interval between sub-samples when using an automatic sampling device (combines equal volume sub-samples) is 15 minutes, and
- an automatic flow proportional composite sampling device must collect sub-samples at intervals not exceeding 30 minutes

All team members should make sure that they have the appropriate safety equipment to enter all parts of a facility (i.e. hard hat, safety glasses, ear protection, etc.)

10.4.4 Interviews with Plant Personnel

During the site visit, plant staff who are aware of current and historical site conditions should be interviewed. Plant personnel may possess significant knowledge of past chemical and waste storage sites, above/below ground tanks, and spills. It is important to talk to plant personnel who have been at the facility or operation for several years. Current and former or retired operators in an area may also be interviewed.

The degree of training received by staff to operate pollution-control equipment and their knowledge of environmental regulations should be investigated. In addition to evaluating routine or regular events, emergency or accident-response training also should be evaluated.

It is important to use the checklist when asking questions to ensure that all areas are covered and to confirm or identify discrepancies with information collected during the walk around and record review.

10.4.5 Exit Meeting

An exit meeting should be held upon the completion of site-related activities. At this meeting the key observations and findings should be reported. It also provides the opportunity for site management to point out errors or misconceptions in the audit team's work at a time and place where further verification can be undertaken at a minimal cost.

10.5 POST-SITE VISIT ACTIVITIES

10.5.1 Preparing the Audit Report

The report should be based on the review of the pre-audit materials, the site tour, the review of environmental records, and interviews with plant personnel. The report should describe the scope of the audit and the criteria and standards employed, and present the audit findings.

Conclusions and/or recommendations may be provided if stipulated in the scope of work. All findings should be fully supported by back-up documentation. Any major obstacles encountered in performing the audit should also be documented.

If the audit was performed under lawyer-client privilege, the draft and final report must be submitted to the lawyer directly. The lawyer can then assess potential non-compliance issues and provide legal advice to the client.

If the report has not be prepared under lawyer-client privilege, it should be marked "preliminary" or "draft" until plant management and legal counsel have had a opportunity to review it and make written comments. The distribution of the report usually will be determined by plant, divisional, or corporate management, and/or corporate environmental staff with some input from legal counsel.

10.5.2 Post-Audit Activities

Senior management should be made aware of all findings from the audit. Ideally, a summary table presenting the findings from the audit should be provided to senior management along with comments from legal counsel if areas of non-compliance have been encountered. If stipulated in the scope of work, cost estimates and a proposed schedule to implement corrective action for areas of non-compliance may be prepared.

The preparation and implementation of an action plan is essential for an effective audit program. In essence, it closes the loop and ensures that all deficiencies are corrected in a timely and cost-effective manner. It represents the due diligence element of the program.

Little good is accomplished if the paper trail of positive responses does not result in specific action. In some cases, inaction on the findings can be damaging. Procedural controls cost little to implement, and large capital projects can be implemented in phases.

10.6 REACTING TO AN EXTERNAL AUDIT

If an environmental audit is being performed as a result of external actions (i.e. it has originated with a government agency or a potential purchaser), the corporate environmental staff and the legal department should be made aware of the upcoming audit, and the scope of the audit should be determined as soon as possible.

Pertinent regulations, Certificates of Approval, control orders, permits, compliance history, previous audits, and environmental reports should be assembled and reviewed prior to the visit of the external auditors with a critical eye to identifying potential areas of vulnerability.

It is important that the auditors not be given misleading or false information. If a point is raised that has not been considered or the answer is not known, seek clarification of the question and the type of answer being sought. It may be appropriate to respond to the auditor at a later time when more information becomes available. **Do not speculate** for the sake of providing an answer.

A qualified individual should accompany the auditors throughout the audit, assisting where possible. It is a good idea to carry a notebook and write down important questions, as well as the responses provided.

Record all documents that are provided to the external auditors. All written information provided to the auditors should be formally transmitted (i.e. with a covering letter).

10.7 SUMMARY

Environmental audits are generally recognized as an essential component of an environmental management system. Environmental audits can assist a company in the identification of compliance or risk issues and thereby prevent incidents of pollution or, in the event of an incident, assist in establishing the defense of "due diligence."

Recent publications by the Canadian Standards Association, the Canadian Environmental Auditing Association, and similar organizations in Europe and the United States reinforce the need to perform environmental audits using recognized principles and practices. Generally, these principals and practices require the use of trained auditors – who are independent of the activities being audited — to develop audit protocols to provide verifiable assertions about the degree of compliance and the communication of the results to the client. It is anticipated that in time these principles and practices will be become "generally accepted" — analogous to those employed in financial audits.

REFERENCES

Canadian Standards Association. June 1993. *A Guideline for a Voluntary Environmental Management System.* CAN/CSA Z750, Draft Revision 6.0.

Canadian Standards Association in Association with the Canadian Environmental Auditing Association. 1993. *Guidelines for Environmental Auditing: Principles and General Practices.* CAN/CSA Z751.

Environment Canada. May 1988. *Canadian Environmental Protection Act: Enforcement and Compliance Policy.*

International Organization for Standardization (ISO) and Strategic Advisory Group on Environment (SAGE). October 1992. *Environmental Auditing.* Draft.

Jolliffe, R.S. and L. Gorelle, 1989. "The Environmental Audit: An Ounce of Prevention." *Engineering Dimensions* (July/August): 34-36.

Palmisano, J. and J. Margolis. 1987. "Environmental Audits as the Core of a Risk Management Program." In *Managing Environmental Risks,* Proceedings of an APCA International Specialty Conference, Washington D.C.

Villeneuve, E. 1989. "Overview of an Environmental Auditing Program." Presented at the Environmental Auditing Workshop, 10 and 11 October, University of Toronto.

Table 10.1
LEGISLATION THAT MAY BE RELEVANT TO AN
ENVIRONMENTAL AUDIT OF AN ONTARIO FACILITY

PROVINCIAL LEGISLATION

A - ENVIRONMENTAL PROTECTION ACT (EPA)

PART II	GENERAL PROVISIONS
PART V	WASTE MANAGEMENT
PART X	SPILLS
PART XI	ORDERS
PART XVII	MISCELLANEOUS (INCLUDES PENALTIES)

REGULATIONS WITHIN EPA

AIR REGULATIONS
REG. 346   - Air Pollution
REG. 356   - Ozone Depleting Substances
REG. 336   - Emissions, Ferrous Foundries
REG. 338   - Boilers

WASTE/SPILLS REGULATIONS
REG. 347   - Waste Management
REG. 362   - PCB Wastes
REG. 360   - Spills

MISA REGULATIONS

B - ONTARIO WATER RESOURCES ACT (OWRA)
C - GASOLINE HANDLING ACT
D - PESTICIDES ACT

FEDERAL LEGISLATION
A - CANADIAN ENVIRONMENTAL PROTECTION ACT (CEPA)
B - TRANSPORTATION OF DANGEROUS GOODS ACT (TDGA)
C - FISHERIES ACT

MUNICIPAL BY-LAWS
A - SEWER-USE BY-LAW
B - NOISE BY-LAW

Table 10.2
CHECKLIST FOR PREFORMING AN
ENVIRONMENTAL AUDIT

PRE-VISIT ACTIVITIES
- Determine the objective, scope, and boundary conditions of the audit
- Organize audit team and schedule
- Identify audit criteria
- Develop audit plan
- Ensure that client is in agreement with components of audit plan
- Request and review information from the facility (e.g. site plan, process flow sheets, etc.)
- Request and review information from the MOEE or municipality if acceptable to client
- Schedule site visit

ON-SITE ACTIVITIES
- Conduct opening meeting and orientation tour
- Review all records dealing with environmental compliance and performance
- Perform site investigation
- Conduct interviews with site personnel
- Conduct exit meeting

POST-AUDIT ACTIVITIES
- Prepare audit report
- Prepare action plan if stipulated by client

Table 10.3
WHAT GETS AUDITED

LIQUID EFFLUENTS OR DISCHARGES

Assemble and Review the Documentation Concerning:

1) Files concerning discharges to surface waters, storm sewers, and sanitary sewers
2) Maintenance records and operation logs for wastewater treatment systems, samplers, and flow measurement devices
3) Unscheduled releases/incident reports and sampling equipment malfunction reports
4) Certificates of approval for recent construction, alterations, extensions, or replacement
5) Integrity tests and maintenance record for above- and below-ground storage tanks
6) Control orders or violation notices
7) Previous environment reports dealing with effluents
8) Reporting and monitoring requirements
9) MISA monitoring reports, updates, and non-compliance reports
10) Calibration records for flow measuring devices (primary/secondary)
11) Sampling procedures, schedule, and list of chemicals

Inspect During the Site Visit:

1) The physical condition and operation of process equipment where liquids are used
2) The physical condition of all elements of wastewater treatment systems including any lagoons
3) All effluent samplers and flow measurement devices
4) All above- and below-ground storage tanks
5) Dykes and berms around aboveground storage tanks
6) Record-keeping including backing-up of computer disks

ATMOSPHERIC EMISSIONS

Assemble and Review the Documentation Concerning:

1) Files concerning emissions from stacks, vents, etc.
2) Maintenance records for air pollution control systems, monitors
3) Unscheduled releases/incident reports
4) Operation logs of control equipment systems
5) Certificates of approval for recent construction, alterations, extensions, or replacements

6) Previous environmental reports dealing with emissions or air quality
7) Notices of violations, complaints from neighbours on odours, dust, etc.
8) Reporting and monitoring requirements

Inspect During the Site Visit:
1) All stacks, vents, etc.
2) Dust from plant operation on building roofs, pavement, and surrounding property
3) All air quality monitors
4) The behaviour of emissions from stacks (i.e. initial opacity, plume rise, etc.)

NOISE

Assemble and Review the Documentation Concerning:
1) Review of data on noise emissions and levels
2) Noise complaint records

SOLID WASTES

Assemble and Review the Documentation Concerning:
1) Data on waste analysis as per Reg. 347 classification
2) Shipment manifests as per Reg. 347
3) Certificates of Approval for recently established waste disposal systems or site
4) Inventory of waste stored on-site and registration
5) PCB storage facility specifications

Inspect During the Site Visit:
1) Types and integrity of waste storage vessels
2) Housekeeping in storage areas
3) Labelling of containers and designation of waste storage areas
4) PCB storage facility

TRANSPORTATION OF DANGEROUS GOODS

Assemble and Review the Documentation Concerning:
1) TDG manifests
2) TDG emergency procedures
3) Proper registrations of carriers

Inspect During the Site Visit:
1) Labels on containers and trucks

MANAGEMENT SYSTEM

Assemble and Review the Documentation Concerning:
1) Defined responsibilities of environmental staff
2) Internal/external reporting system
3) Response to issues of non-compliance and environmental risk
4) Qualifications of environmental personnel

LABORATORY FACILITIES

Assemble and Review the Documentation Concernimg:
1) Laboratory QA/QC procedures
2) Analytical test methods, protocols, and method detection limits
3) Sample labels and chain-of-custody tracking system
4) MISA monitoring reports and updates

PROCEDURES/TRAINING PROGRAMS

Assemble and Review the Documentation Concerning:
1) Incident reporting procedures
2) Emergency response procedures
3) Wastewater treatment operator training
4) Training of shippers in TDG classification and registration
5) Environmental legislation and updating
6) Hazardous chemical handling and storage procedures

Figure 10.1
TYPICAL BLOCK DIAGRAM OF EMISSIONS, DISCHARGES, AND WASTE STREAMS

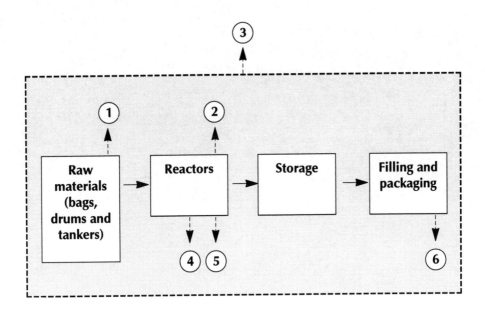

Process flow   ──────►
Emission/
discharge
waste streams   ------►

1. Duct from raw material storage
2. Stack for reactor discharge
3. Fugitive emission to atmosphere
4. Water discharge to sanitary sewer
5. Solid waste
6. Spoiled product for off-site disposal

11.0

Risk Assessment and Management

11.1 OVERVIEW

Risk often is defined as the probability or likelihood that an adverse outcome will be caused by an action or condition. In the context of environmental issues, the actions and conditions of concern usually are associated with the exposure to a chemical or physical agent such as noise, heat, or radiation.

Risk assessment is the process of determining the adverse outcomes that can occur. This can include evaluating the types of potential effects (also referred to as hazards), estimating the probability of an effect occurring, and estimating the numbers of people or other organisms that might be exposed and/or suffer the consequences of exposure. **Risk management** is the process of evaluating possible courses of action and selecting among them with the objective of minimizing risks. In this framework, risk assessment is the vital precursor to risk management. Figure 11.1 shows one interpretation of the steps that make up risk assessment and risk management and how these two processes are related.

During the last two decades, there has been a growing trend to incorporate risk assessment and management into various decision-making processes including the setting of environmental policies and regulations. These efforts have often proven to be cumbersome and onerous. Like most new technologies, there are differences of opinion as to how risk management should be used and what its role should be. There are also uncertainties as to its value and a lack of consensus on the terminology that should be used. As a result, a certain amount of scepticism and caution has been directed toward the risk assessment and management processes.

In part, these shortcomings may be the unavoidable outcome of expecting too much too soon from a relatively new aid for decision-making. Risk assessment and risk management often are expected to bring order to large pools of information and resolve conflicting interests and uncertainties en route to identifying appropriate options. Some of the factors with which a risk manager often must contend include situation-specific economic, social, political, and legal considerations. The complexity of such situations can be overwhelming.

Despite the difficulties that have been experienced (and no doubt will continue to be experienced), risk assessment and management are likely to play increasingly important roles in decision-making processes. Factors that will continue to support the need for risk assessment and management include:

- the realization that there are insufficient resources to address all concerns (and therefore priorities need to be set)
- the need to compare the relative importance of an ever-increasing number of environmental issues
- government agencies that are asked to use risk as a basis for regulatory decisions more than ever before
- the increasing number of issues, such as acidic precipitation, global warming, or exposure to carcinogens, which are complex and require careful assessment

11.2 RISK ASSESSMENT

11.2.1 Purpose and Elements

Risk assessment is directed toward determining the types and probabilities of adverse effects occurring as a result of some activity or condition. Consider the example of a proposed stack which will emit vapours that may be inhaled by downwind residents and cause adverse health effects. To assess the potential risks, it first is necessary to determine the characteristics of release (how much? when? at what exit velocity and temperature?). It then is necessary to determine how the release will behave in the atmosphere (how much dilution will occur? will the substance degrade while airborne?). Various characteristics of the person(s) who could inhale the vapours need to determined (how much air do they breathe? will they breathe the vapours all day? every day?). Of obvious importance is the toxicological nature of the substance (what kinds of adverse effect can it cause? how much does a person need to inhale to experience an adverse effect?). Finally, the estimated doses need to be described in terms of the risk or the probability of adverse effects occurring.

Many descriptions of these elements or steps have been prepared and there is considerable variability in the terminology used and the number of steps involved. The remainder of this section uses the steps and terminology suggested by the U.S. National Academy of Science, which considers risk assessment as consisting of four steps (NAS, 1983):

- hazard identification
- exposure assessment
- dose-response assessment
- risk characterization

11.2.2 Hazard Identification

The first step in a risk assessment is the identification of potential hazards, which in environmental management usually involves identifying where and how chemicals are being released (or have been released) into the environment. Examples of release points include:

- **air emissions** from stacks and vents, open storage tanks, pressure relief valves, waste ponds and lagoons, fugitive sources, land farms, open process tanks and vessels, tank and drum loading/unloading operations
- **liquid discharges** from point sources to surface water, discharges to municipal sewers, releases to ground water, leaky storage tanks and ponds
- **solid waste** shipments to off-site disposal, transfer to on-site disposal, on-site disposal/treatment facilities

At U.S. Superfund sites where soil or ground water is contaminated, the U.S. Environmental Protection Agency has described this step as data collection and evaluation since it typically involves the collection and analysis of environmental samples (soil, water, biota, air, etc.) and the identifying of potential chemicals of concern (U.S. EPA, 1989).

The types of activities that are likely to identify hazards include environmental inspections, assessments (see Chapter 5), audits (see Chapter 10), or gathering information to comply with regulatory requirements such as completing a Waste Inventory Survey as required by the Ontario Municipal Model Sewer-Use By-Law or the National Pollutant Release Inventory (NPRI).

11.2.3 Exposure Assessment

When a **receptor** (usually a person but the term can also be used to refer to an animal or plant) comes into contact with a chemical that has been released into the environment, **exposure** occurs. For example, a person may be exposed to a chemical in the air by inhaling it. Exposure assessment involves determining the environmental fate of the chemicals released from each release point (see Chapter 9) and the ways in which a individual can be exposed to those chemicals. Exposure **pathways** can include:

- ingestion of water
- ingestion of soil
- inhalation of vapours

- inhalation of particulate matter
- ingestion of fish
- ingestion of milk and dairy products
- ingestion of produce
- ingestion of dust
- dermal absorption

In many situations, one or two pathways are the major contributors to total exposures. For example, the ingestion of meat and milk accounts for 99% of human exposure to 2,3,7,8-TCDD, one of the more toxic forms of dioxin (Travis and Hattemer-Frey, 1987). The factors that determine which pathways predominate is a function of the physicochemical properties of the substance, characteristics of the receptor, the receptor's behaviour in the environment where contact occurs, and characteristics of the environment. Determining which substances and pathways are of greatest concern is a major step in determining the form that remedial measures may need to take.

For compounds with established provincial or federal guidelines such as ambient air and water quality guidelines or criteria, the estimated or measured concentration of a substance at the point where a receptor makes contact can be compared to the guidelines as a measure of relative hazard if the guidelines have been set to avoid a hazard. Some guidelines are not based on potential hazards but on other factors such as aesthetics or analytical detection limits.

The **dose** is the amount or mass of chemical taken up by the receptor via the pathways noted above. Dose and exposure often are used incorrectly as synonyms. For example, a receptor may be exposed to a substance present at a concentration of 3 mg/L in water. Upon drinking 2 L of the water, the receptor's intake is 6 mg of the substance. If the receptor weighs 30 kg, their dose is 0.2 mg/kg of body weight (bw). If they drink 2 L of the water every day, the dose is 0.2 mg/kg-bw/d. Dose is a function of several parameters:

- quantity of material taken into the receptor's body
- characteristics of the receptor, for example body weight
- concentration of chemical in the material taken in by the receptor
- frequency of occurrence of exposure
- bioavailability factor(s) specific to the chemical and exposure route

The bioavailability factor refers to the percentage of material taken into the body that actually enters the body tissue or blood. It is the dose at the target tissue that determines the response, not the level of external exposure. Some researchers have suggested that the term "dose" be replaced by "potential dose" if bioavailability is ignored or assumed to be 100% (as in the case described above), and that the term "internal dose" be used once bioavailability is taken into account (Lioy, 1990). It has also been suggested that the fraction of the internal dose which actually leads to a specific effect or physiologic change be called the "biologically effective dose."

It is important to state all of the assumptions employed to derive doses as the results can vary widely depending upon the assumptions made. There are at least two basic philosophies that have been used to estimate dose:

1 Calculate a maximum or upper extreme dose using conservative assumptions (those deliberately made to avoid underestimating risks) to arrive at a so-called upper bound estimate of the risk.

2 Make assumptions about receptors and pathways that are consistent with what the evidence and the best current scientific information suggest are probable or typical (as opposed to extreme). At the end of the process, apply a final safety factor to ensure public protection.

The first method puts the onus on the risk assessor to make decisions about conservative safety factors as opposed to leaving these assumptions to the judgement of the risk manager. Taken to extremes, the first "conservative" approach can lead to gross overestimations of exposures or portray receptors with unrealistic behaviours or characteristics. As a result, the second method is beginning to gain favour (Deisler, 1988).

In evaluations that use the first approach, it often is assumed that the receptor is a hypothetical individual who spends all of his time (24 hours a day, 365 days a year) for 70 years (the receptor's lifetime), outdoors at the location of highest contaminant concentration attributable to the source of the substance. In addition, it is often assumed that the source continuously emits the chemical for the receptor's lifetime. Information about the behaviour of people indicates that it would be more realistic to assume that the receptor spends one-third of his time indoors at the site, even less outdoors, and a substantial portion of his time off-site.

In the conservative approach, the maximum level of exposure is assumed to occur for the duration of the exposure. This requires a constant or infinite source of the substance, which seldom is the case. For example, soil containing organic compounds may be the source of vapours that a receptor can inhale. The vapour emissions of a compound, especially one that volatilizes rapidly, will deplete the amount of the compound in the soil, especially from the top soil layer. In turn, this will lead to a steady decrease in the exposures and doses with time.

In the conservative approach, it often is assumed that 100% of a substance is bioavailable for each pathway (i.e. all the chemical is absorbed or metabolized by body tissue or the bloodstream). In many cases, this assumption is made because there is insufficient evidence to support the use of a different value; however, there is a growing amount of data indicating that **bioavailability** often is substantially less than 100%. This likely is the case for the bioavailability of many organic substances that are ingested in the diet and the bioavailability of substances associated with inhaled particles.

To facilitate the calculation of exposures and doses, mathematical **models** can be used. Such models should take into account the emission or discharge rate of a chemical, its behaviour or fate in the environment, and the conditions under which receptors come into contact with the chemicals. Many such models exist. Some are highly specialized and may be limited to specific types of release points (for example, point sources such as factories), particular risk agents, or specific types of environmental settings such as watersheds or lakes (Cohrssen and Covello, 1989).

By their very nature, these models are only partial representations of real systems and contain a number of parameters which are either imperfectly known or inherently variable by nature. Uncertainties also arise when these models are used to predict effects over conditions and periods of time different from those for which the models and model parameters were developed. As a result, the outcomes generated by models, or for that matter any other exposure/risk assessment approach, contain a degree of **uncertainty.**

Until recently, uncertainty has been addressed in models indirectly. The traditional approach has been to run a model with conservative values of the parameters, typically near the upper or lower extreme of the expected range of the probability distributions for the parameters. The result of such an approach is generally a very conservative estimate of the effects.

An alternative approach is to use some form of **probabilistic analysis**. This approach attempts to take uncertainty into account explicitly by specifying probability distributions rather than single values for parameters that are model inputs. The model is run many times with new values selected for the input parameters on each run. The parameter values used in each run are randomly selected from the appropriate distributions. The model output is a probabilistic distribution of possible effects.

Output data from the uncertainty analysis can be used to assess the relative importance of the various model parameters by assessing their relative contribution to overall uncertainty in model predictions and determining how sensitive the predicted values are to small changes in model input parameters.

The benefits of this approach are that more realistic estimates of exposure and risk can be made, and the reliance on worst-case assumptions is reduced.

11.2.4 Dose-Response Assessment

The relationship between dose and response is based upon a thorough analysis of relevant data which may include epidemiological, clinical, environmental, animal toxicological, biochemical, structure-activity, and exposure data. Figure 11.2 presents a schematic plot of various levels of response (lethal, sublethal, and behavioral) versus exposure (environmental and laboratory).

The exposure levels of interest associated with most environmental issues are often orders of magnitude less than those which cause obvious adverse effects (such as lethality). As a result, it is often necessary to extrapolate the response data into regions which are experimentally impossible for statistical reasons (i.e. natural variation exceeds the effect), and in which the knowledge about the extent or existence of the toxic event may be simply inaccessible (Mackay, 1982).

In terms of response, chemicals can be broken into two groups: carcinogens and non-carcinogens. **Carcinogens** are defined as chemicals that produce self-propagating lesions. It is commonly and conservatively assumed that there is some risk associated with any exposure to carcinogens, no matter how small the dose. Similarly, it has become common practice to assume that the relationship between dose and response for carcinogens is linear; however, there is considerable scientific debate regarding the linearity of dose-response relationships, whether or not there may be thresholds below which adverse effects do not occur, and whether the linear models currently used are unduly or inadequately conservative.

Non-carcinogens are substances for which the information indicates that there is a dose below which measurable adverse effects should not occur even if there is a lifetime of exposure. The threshold below which no observable response occurs is defined as the no-observable-adverse-effect-level (NOAEL).

11.2.5 Risk Characterization

Risk characterization should include a description of the qualitative factors that help to establish the existence of a hazard and a risk; descriptions of the human population subject to risk and the possible responses; and estimates of the background or natural rates at which the responses occur and of their upper and lower statistical bounds (Deisler, 1988).

Once a dose has been calculated for a given situation and set of conditions, it may be compared to an **acceptable** level based solely on human health. Establishing acceptability of a dose is a complex process influenced by economic, social, political, and technical factors as well as scientific factors and therefore is not part of the risk characterization but is part of risk management.

For **carcinogens**, acceptability in terms of human health usually is expressed in terms of the lifetime risk levels that doses present. Until recently, one of the most commonly used approaches was to establish "virtually safe dose" (or VSD) values for carcinogens. A VSD often was set as the dose which presented a lifetime cancer risk probability of one in a million. Such a risk was thought to be acceptable and "virtually safe" because it represented a level of risk that most individuals willingly accept. To avoid the possible implications or misunderstanding of using the term "virtually safe," many agencies now use the term **"risk-specific dose" (RSD)** for carcinogens. This terminology clearly indicates that there is a risk level (i.e. a probability of developing cancer given a lifetime of exposure) associated with the dose. Whether that risk level should be one in a million or a higher or lower value is an issue that regulatory agencies must address.

An RSD value is usually calculated by extrapolating from health effects observed (at relatively high doses) in laboratory test to low doses using one of several mathematical models which have been developed for this purpose. The dose-response models employed are simplistic probabilistic representations of highly complex biological phenomena.

RSD values (or other couplets of dose and risk levels) can be converted into **slope factors** (often represented as q_{1*}) as follows:

$$\text{dose} = q_{1*} \times \text{risk level} \qquad (11.1)$$

Slope factors are expressed in units such as $(\text{mg/kg-bw/day})^{-1}$. When multiplied times a daily dose averaged over the lifetime of a receptor, a result is an estimate of the lifetime risk associated with the dose.

Non-carcinogens are substances for which measurable adverse effects should not occur below a specified dose. Until recently, such a dose was called an "acceptable daily intake" (ADI). Because of the possible implications of using the term "acceptable" to describe such doses, agencies now use the term **"reference dose" (RfD)**. An RfD value is calculated by dividing the lowest no-observable-adverse-effect-level by an extrapolation or safety factor (values of 10, 100, 1000 or more are used). The magnitude of the extrapolation factor depends on the confidence that can be placed in the allowable data, judging the relevance of the data to humans, the severity and the type of effects observed, and the types of test systems studied. Unlike RSD values, there is no risk level associated with RfD values.

Another approach that some agencies use to judge acceptability is to compare exposures or doses to **background conditions**. Nuclear scientists have led the way in using natural background exposures as a baseline from which to assess acceptability. The background approach is also one option for setting clean-up levels noted in the MOEE publication for decommissioning sites in Ontario (see Chapter 5). This approach cannot be used when the substance in question is man-made and therefore should not be present in "uncontaminated" environments or when there is uncertainty as to how background conditions are to be defined. For example, it is unclear as to whether clean-up levels for an urban site should be based on background concentrations measured at a rural site. Because RSD values have an associated risk level while RfD values do not, it is difficult to assess the risks posed when a receptor is being exposed to both types of substances. One potential way to assess the risks from both carcinogens and non-carcinogens is the use of **Relative Margin of Safety (RMOS)** values:

$$RMOS = observed\ dose \div acceptable\ dose \qquad (11.2)$$

The "acceptable" dose can be either an RSD or an RfD.

An RMOS value greater than 1 indicates that the estimated dose exceeds the acceptable dose and indicates potentially unacceptable health hazard. RMOS values between 0.1 and 1.0 indicate a situation of potential concern, although not necessarily unacceptable. Such values can be used to identify situations where additional assessment of releases, exposure parameters, and/or health evaluation criteria likely are warranted.

The RMOS approach is used in the California Air Pollution Control Districts reference manual for non-carcinogens. The manual provides a step-by-step approach to estimating and assessing the public health impacts of sources of air contaminants (CAPCD, 1987).

For carcinogens, the RMOS value is also termed the individual lifetime cancer risk. It represents the probability of an individual contracting cancer. The individual **cancer incidence rate** can be multiplied by the population residing within a predefined area to estimate the annual cancer incidence rate for that area. Estimates of annual cancer incidence rates have been used by regulators in the United States to assess control options for toxic chemicals.

Individuals seldom are exposed to a single chemical; most exposures are to complex mixtures of assorted compounds. Assessing human exposure to such mixtures is a formidable task. Firstly, it is generally impractical or impossible to measure the concentration of all constituents contained in a complex mixture. Secondly, even if all constituents were known, their respective toxicities are often unknown. Thirdly, even if the toxicities of individual components are known, the toxicity of a mixture can be substantially different from the composite of the toxicities of its constituents.

Chemicals can interact synergistically or antagonistically to form a mixture that is more or less toxic than expected. Many such interactions are reported in the toxicological literature. For example, cigarette smoke and asbestos are known to interact synergistically, thereby increasing the incidence of lung cancer in asbestos workers. Benzene and toluene interact antagonistically to decrease damage resulting from benzene exposure. While direct exposure of experimental animals to complex mixtures in the laboratory is one way to overcome these limitations of information, it is difficult to duplicate complex environmental conditions in a laboratory setting. The exact composition of environmental mixtures can be unknown and may change over time.

11.3 RISK MANAGEMENT

11.3.1 The Need for Risk Management

While there are uncertainties associated with virtually every aspect of assessing risks, there also are ways that the uncertainties can either be overcome or at least highlighted so that assessors are aware of them. Risk management, on the other hand, is not so restricted in scope and often must try to balance factors that are not easily compared or quantified.

Risk management is generally portrayed as an interactive process of identifying the options available for abating unacceptable risks, evaluating the cost-effectiveness of those options, and identifying the preferred course of action for achieving the desired risk reductions.

The management process may need to consider both actual and perceived risks. The preferable outcome of risk management is the abatement of an actual risk in a cost-effective manner. The reduction of risks for reduction sake alone has little long-term benefit and may be detrimental if it consumes resources that could be used more effectively to reduce other sources of risk.

As noted in Section 11.2.5, regulatory agencies must decide how to define acceptable risks and recognize that there is little merit or economic justification in striving for lower levels of risk. For example, adopting analytical detection limits is not considered a viable method of defining acceptable exposure, dose, or risk levels. The search for hazardous micropollutants has on occasion been compared to a "witch hunt" in which the hunters will never be fully satisfied because there is no clear proof of innocence (Mackay, 1982).

11.3.2 Factors that Often Need To Be Considered

Figure 11.1 illustrates some of the non-technical factors that often need to be incorporated into the risk management process. These factors add layers of complexity to risk management and, while they are essential, they also can make the process become rather "messy" (Fischhoff, 1985).

Benefit to Society–All other factors (e.g. size of exposed population, potency) being similar, a chemical that makes vegetables more colourful ought not to be subject to the same standard of "acceptable risk" as one that is released from the processing of raw materials for important industries. Society's willingness to forgo some of those benefits in the course of reducing the risks to the public are vastly different (Dwyer and Ricci, 1989).

Litigation–The possibility of litigation by one or more parties makes the task of risk management much more difficult. Litigation may introduce delays and the possibility of additional financial risks into the process (Deisler, 1988).

Economics–The expenditures required to clean up a site, decommission a facility, or comply with air and water emission criteria can be substantial to both the company and the economy as a whole. The Municipal, Industrial for Abatement program requires that for certain types of discharges, the best available technology that is "economically achievable" be used.

11.3.3 Possible Applications for Risk Management

Risk management can be used to address several types of issues:

* Is remedial action required?
* What level of risk is acceptable?
* What is the optimum remedial action?
* What priorities should be assigned to action items?

The first two issues can arise when evaluating situations such as the decommissioning of a property or during the assessment of air emissions or liquid discharges. Once a decision has been made that remediation is required, options must be assessed. A preliminary risk assessment of each option can assist in the identification of the optimal alternative.

Assigning priorities to action items is critical when resources such as funding, manpower, technical equipment, and technical expertise are scarce. No government agency or company can immediately implement activities for all actual or potential situations which require remediation. Some of the activities must wait until additional resources can be made available.

An example of a need for prioritization is the clean-up of hazardous waste sites in Canada and the United States which for various reasons have become the responsibility of federal and/or provincial agencies. The average cost of cleaning up such sites is likely several million dollars. In the United States, there now are more than 1,000 sites on the National Priority List (NPL) of the Superfund Program.

The highest priority of these programs should be to identify sites that pose a clear and immediate threat to human health and the environment and to remediate them using proven and effective technologies.

11.4 RISK COMMUNICATION

11.4.1 Overview

Risk communication must be an integral part of risk management. It cannot merely be passed along to the public relations staff or community affairs department, especially if most of the inquiries will be handled by the plant or environmental manager. These individuals also must be able to communicate effectively to avoid damaging the company's reputation (Sandman, 1986).

11.4.2 The Media

Most managers would probably prefer that the media and the public go away and leave them to do their jobs. Since it is highly likely that the media and public will persist, it is imperative that the managers understand how to communicate effectively with the media and the public and to anticipate the sorts of information that are likely to be of greatest interest. While communications often becomes a source of confusion, the risks of avoiding the media may be far greater than the risks of working with them (Sandman, 1986).

Preparation–It is important to remember that a reporter's job is news, not education: events, not issues or principles. The news is the "risky" thing that has happened, not the difficult determination of the numerical risk value. A reporter may seek answers to simple direct questions such as: What happened? How did it happen? Who's to blame? and What are the authorities/company doing? The media focuses on the politics of risk rather than the science of risk (Sandman, 1986).

Response–It is important that a company makes its position known and realizes that a story will be covered, whether or not it arranges to be included. Environmental risk stories often turn into political stories in part because political content is more readily available and understood than technical content.

In responding to questions from the media or members of the public, keep the following points in mind (Sandman, 1986):

- provide facts; never guess or lie
- if you do not know, say so but get back to the reporter
- remember that journalists, deadlines are measured in minutes not months
- decide on the main points of your story in advance
- stress points consistently and repetitively
- leave out technical qualifiers
- leave in important qualifiers
- do not use technical jargon
- explain technical terms if considered essential

The journalists will want the response to be on one side or another of a situation (i.e. safe versus unsafe, legal versus illegal.) They do not want to dwell on the complex nuances of intermediate positions because the length of their news story seldom allows for a lengthy response. Managers, scientists, and technical staff often resent the pressure from journalist to dichotomize and simplify an issue.

11.4.3 Members of the Public

Successful communication begins with the realization that risk perception is predictable, that the public overreacts to certain sorts of risks while ignoring others, and that you cannot know in advance whether the communication problem will be panic or apathy (Sandman, 1986). There is no way to present risk data which is neutral, but only ways that are alarming or reassuring in varying degrees.

It is important to remember when communicating to the public that society has reached a near-consensus that pollution is morally wrong. Some individuals and agencies are quick to realize this and present environmental risk in terms of "good and evil" instead of "costs and benefits."

The use of processes such as quantitative risk assessments, risk-benefit calculations, risk-cost ratios, and risk comparisons are difficult for individuals to accept when they are being asked to bear the risks while someone else makes the decision. The process of who decides can be a key factor, in most cases much more that the substantive issues. Consider the example of a town being selected as the future site of a hazardous waste treatment facility. The community, offended at this infringement of local autonomy, prepares to stop the facility by collecting information on the unacceptability of the site and initiates litigation. Both their anger and the legal process itself encourage community members to overestimate the risk of the proposed facility and to resist any argument that some package of mitigation, compensation, and incentives might actually yield a net gain in the community's health and safety, as well as its prosperity (Sandman, 1986).

People will participate more if they exercise some real control over an ultimate decision. In response to this need, regulatory agencies are trying to encourage public participation on various issues. Many previous public participation exercises have been perceived as being too little too late, and often involving only draft decisions. As a result, many members of the public believe that they will not be taken seriously.

Table 11.1 presents rules and guidelines published by the U.S. Environmental Protection Agencies for effective risk communication. Rules and guidelines like these can be used as a foundation for a risk communication program and lead to a constructive interaction with the community.

Ever-increasing numbers of occasions require risk-related information to be shared with the public. This poses a major challenge to risk assessors, managers, and scientists since their perceptions about risk acceptability and uncertainty are likely to be substantially different than those of members of the general public.

The Ontario Environmental Assessment Act (EAA) and Environmental Protection Act (EPA) both allow for input from the public. For example, there is a requirement to conduct a public hearing before issuing a certificate of approval for the use, operation, establishment, alteration, enlargement, or extension of a waste disposal site (see Section 4.4.3).

The MOEE has clearly indicated that it intends to increase the opportunities that members of the public have to participate in environmental decision making. Bill 26, the Environmental Bill of Rights, which became law in March 1994, increases public access by several means. One is to create an environmental registry which will record all significant environmental proposals and decisions by government including the issuing of approvals and permits. All decisions will be available on the registry for public comment for a period of at least 30 days. Longer periods will be used for decisions of regional or provincial significance.

In Ontario, the Canadian Chemical Producers' Association (CCPA) has taken the bold step of establishing a "Community Right to Know Policy" in its *Responsible Care: A Total Commitment* document. The policy recognizes the need and the right of the public to know the risks associated with the operations and products present in or transported through communities (CCPA, not dated).

11.5 SUMMARY

Risk assessment and risk management are likely to play an increasingly important role in environmental decision-making. The ever-increasing number of environmental issues and the realization that there are insufficient resources to address all concerns will continue to support the need for risk assessment and management.

The process of assessing risks often consists of four parts: hazard identification, exposure assessment, dose-response assessment, and risk characterization. The information obtained from a risk assessment is only one part of the overall package needed to conduct risk management. Risk management is an interactive process of identifying the options available for abating unacceptable risks, evaluating the cost-effectiveness of those options, and identifying the preferred course of action for achieving the desired risk reductions.

An integral part of risk management is risk communication. It is imperative that managers understand how to communicate effectively with the media and the public and to anticipate the sorts of information that are likely to be of greatest interest. Risk-related information may need to be presented to the public in response to regulatory requirements or voluntary programs It is important that the information be communicated effectively.

REFERENCES

California Air Pollution Control Districts. October 1987. *Toxic Air Pollutant Source Assessment Manual for California Air Pollution Applications for Air Pollutant Control District Permits.* Prepared by the Inter-Agency Working Group.

Canadian Chemical Producers' Association (CCPA). Not Dated. *Responsible Care: A Total Commitment.*

Cohrssen, J.J., and V.T. Covello. 1989. *Risk Analysis: A Guide to Principles and Methods for Analyzing Health and Environmental Risks.* United States Council on Environmental Quality, Executive Office of the President. ISBN 0-934213-20-8.

Deisler, P.F. 1988. "The Risk Management-Risk Assessment Interface." *Environ. Sci. and Technol.* 22 (No.1): 15-19.

Dwyer, J.P., and P.F. Ricci. 1989. "Coming to Terms with Acceptable Risks." *Environ. Sci. and Technol.* 23 (No. 2): 145-146.

Fischhoff, B. 1985. *Issues in Science and Technology* 2 (No. 1): 83-96.

Lioy, P.J. 1990. "Assessing Total Human Exposure to Contaminants — A Multidisciplinary Approach." *Envir. Sci. and Technol.* 24 (No. 7): 938-945.

Mackay, D. 1982. "Nature and Origin of Micropollutants." *Wat. Sci. Tech.* 14: 5-14.

National Academy of Science. 1983. *Risk Assessment in the Federal Government: Managing the Process.* National Academy Press.

Sandman, P.M. 1986. *Explaining Environmental Risk.* U.S. Environmental Protection Agency, Office of Toxic Substances, Washington, D.C.

Travis, C.C., and H.A. Hattemer-Frey. 1987. "Human Exposure to 2,3,7,8-TCDD." *Chemosphere* 16: 2331-2342.

United States Environmental Protection Agency (EPA). 1989. *Risk Assessment Guidance for Superfund Human Health Evaluation Manual (Part A).* Office of Emergency and Remedial Response, Office of Solid Waste and Emergency Response, U.S. EPA, EPA 540/1-89/002.

FURTHER READING

The Conservation Foundation. 1985. *Risk Assessment and Risk Control.* Washington, D.C.

Covello, V.T., and E. Allen. 1988. *Seven Cardinal Rules of Risk Communication.* U.S. Environmental Protection Agency, Office of Policy Analysis, Washington, D.C.

Covello, V.T., P.M. Sandman, and P. Slovic. 1988. *Risk Communication, Risk Statistics, and Risk Comparisons: A Manual for Plant Managers.* Chemical Manufacturers' Association, Washington, D.C.

Paustenbach, D.J. (ed.). 1989. *The Risk Assessment of Environmental and Human Health Hazards: A Textbook of Case Studies.* New York: John Wiley and Sons.

Table 11.1
EPA RULES AND GUIDELINES FOR EFFECTIVE RISK COMMUNICATION

Rule 1. ACCEPT AND INVOLVE THE PUBLIC AS A LEGITIMATE PARTNER
Guideline: Demonstrate your respect for the public and your sincerity by involving the community early, before important decisions are made. Make it clear that you understand the appropriateness of basing decisions about risks on factors other than the magnitude of the risk. Involve all parties that have an interest or a stake in the particular risk in question.

Rule 2. PLAN CAREFULLY AND EVALUATE PERFORMANCE
Guideline: Begin with clear, explicit objectives such as providing information to the public, motivating individuals to act, stimulating emergency response, or contributing to conflict resolution. Classify the different subgroups among your audience. Aim your communication at specific subgroups. Recruit spokespersons who are good at presentation and interaction. Train your staff, including technical staff, in communication skills, rewarding outstanding performance. Whenever possible, pretest your messages. Carefully evaluate your efforts and learn from your mistakes.

Rule 3. LISTEN TO YOUR AUDIENCE
Guideline: Do not make assumptions about what people know, think, or want done about risks. Take the time to find out what people are thinking: use techniques such as interviews, focus groups, and surveys. Let all parties that have an interest or a stake in the issue be heard. Recognize people's emotions. Let people know that you understand what they said. Recognize the "hidden agendas," symbolic meanings, and broader economic or political considerations that often underlie and complicate the task of risk communication.

Rule 4. BE HONEST, FRANK, AND OPEN
Guideline: State your credentials, but do not ask or expect to be trusted by the public. If you do not know an answer or are uncertain, say so. Get back to people with answers. Admit mistakes. Disclose risk information as soon as possible (emphasizing any appropriate reservations about reliability). If in doubt, lean toward sharing more information, not less – or people may think you are hiding something. Discuss data uncertainties, strengths and weaknesses – including the ones identified by other credible sources. Identify worst-case estimates as such, and cite ranges of risk estimates when appropriate.

Rule 5.   COORDINATE AND COLLABORATE WITH OTHER CREDIBLE SOURCES

Guideline: Closely coordinate all inter- and intraorganizational communications. Devote effort and resources to the slow, hard work of building bridges with other organizations. Use credible intermediates. Try to issue communications jointly with other trustworthy sources such as credible university scientists, physicians, trusted local officials, and opinion leaders.

Rule 6.   MEET THE NEEDS OF THE MEDIA

Guideline: Be open with and accessible to reporters. Respect their deadlines. Provide information tailored to the needs of each type of media, such as graphics and other visual aids for television. Provide background material for the media on complex risk issues. Follow up on stories with praise or criticism, as warranted. Try to establish long-term relationships of trust with editors and reporters.

Figure 11.1
RISK ASSESSMENT AND RISK
MANAGEMENT PROCESSES

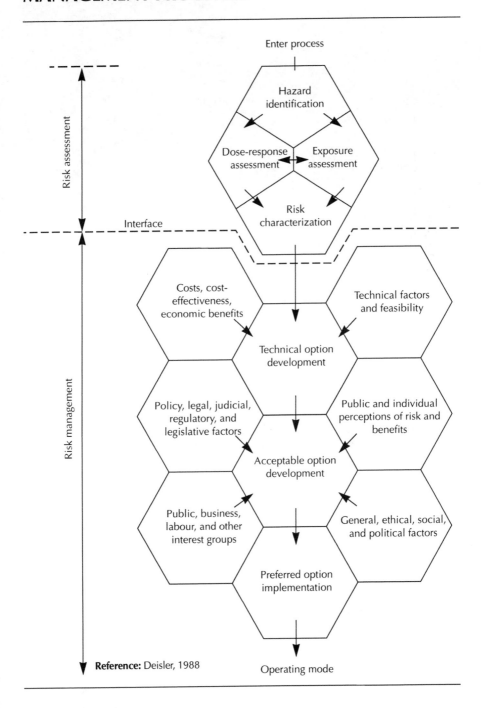

Reference: Deisler, 1988

Figure 11.2
SCHEMATIC PLOT OF RESPONSE AS A FUNCTION OF EXPOSURE

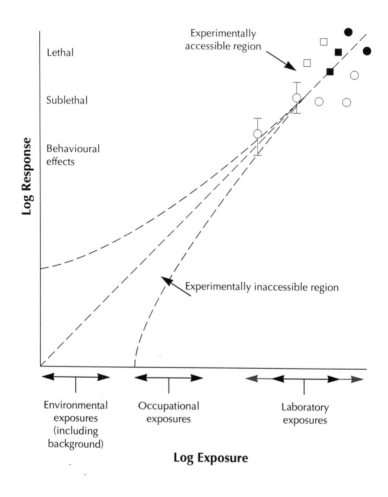

Reference: Mackay, 1982

12.0

Emergency Planning and Spills

12.1 BACKGROUND

Despite the training, procedures, and other precautions that may be taken, unscheduled releases or discharges of materials to the environment still occur as a result of equipment failure, mishandling, transportation accidents, and human error. More than 5,000 spills are reported each year to the Ontario Spills Action Centre (SAC).

Ontario legislation places far-reaching obligations on companies and individuals to report and clean up spills. It is a corporation's responsibility to show reasonable care by ensuring that records of inspection and maintenance of equipment are kept, employees receive adequate spill training, and that equipment and procedures are available to respond to spills.

12.2 PROVINCIAL LEGISLATION AND REGULATIONS

12.2.1 Environmental Protection Act

Part X of the EPA deals specifically with spills of pollutants. It establishes a prompt notification requirement and a duty to respond. It applies to spills that have occurred since 29 November 1985. Several key terms are described in Section 91 of the EPA:

spill – a discharge of a pollutant into the natural environment from a container, structure, or vehicle that is abnormal in quantity or quality

pollutant – a contaminant other than heat, sound, vibration, or radiation and including any substance from which a pollutant is derived

substance – any solid, liquid, or gas, or combination thereof

owner of a pollutant – the owner immediately before the first discharge

person having control of a pollutant – the person, employee, or agent having charge, management, or control immediately before the first discharge

Two other key terms to understanding Part X are "discharge" and "natural environment." Section 1 of the EPA indicates that **discharge** (when used as a verb) can mean to add, deposit, leak, or emit, while **natural environment** includes the air, land, and water, and any combination thereof in Ontario.

The Duty to Report

Section 92 of the EPA describes the **duty to report (or notify)**. This duty applies to every person having control of a spilled pollutant and every person who causes or permits the spill. The onus is on that person to determine if a spill is causing or is likely to cause an adverse effect. If any of the adverse effects described in Section 1 of the EPA is likely, a report must be made "forthwith" to the MOEE (see Section 12.6.2), the municipality, the owner of the pollutant, and the person having control of the pollutant. This duty comes into force as soon as a person learns of a spill or should know about a spill. The term "forthwith" is interpreted to mean as soon as reasonably practicable in the circumstances. (The term "forthwith" is also used in Sections 13 and 15 for reporting discharges to the natural environment.)

The potential for "adverse effects" to be caused is essential for a release to be classified as a spill. The EPA definition of adverse effects ranges from impairment of any part of the natural environment, to the loss of enjoyment of the property, to discomfort. All of these concepts rely to some extent on the quantity of material spilled as well as its chemical, physical, and toxicological characteristics. Part X does not specifically address the possibility that small amounts of material may be spilled without causing an adverse effect. Nor does it provide minimum reportable quantities.

This lack of direction prompts discussions about hypothetical cases such as spilling a few litres of paint on bare ground inside a facility. Would this need to be reported as a spill on the basis that there is some small potential for vapour emissions or contamination of soil or ground water? A response frequently received from MOEE staff is that if there is contamination, it must be reported. The data recorded by the SAC during 1991 illustrate a growing trend to report small quantities of spilled materials. Approximately 20% of all reported spills with known volumes involved less than 10 litres (MOEE, 1993a).

Deciding how to handle small spills is difficult since unwanted results can occur just as easily from choosing to report very small spills as from choosing to report only spills of a certain volume or size. A company may report all spills and feel that it is being a good "corporate citizen"; however, the associated effort may tie up a large portion of the environmental staff's time and the company might gain a reputation of having frequent incidents, particularly if the number of spills is reported to the public without corresponding text about the volumes of material involved. Another unwanted outcome would be if the information is presented during a hearing or trial to illustrate deficiencies in the company's environmental performance. Conversely, a company that only reports what it feels are substantial spills may leave itself and its directors open to charges for failure to report.

The Duty to Respond

Section 93 of the EPA describes the **duty to respond (or act)**. This duty requires that the owner of the pollutant and the person having control of the pollutant shall do everything practicable to prevent, eliminate, and ameliorate adverse effects and to restore the environment. It is interpreted as consisting of three parts:

- stop the spill from continuing
- remove or render harmless the pollutant and everything that has been contaminated, and
- restore the natural environment to a state as if the spill did not occur

The duty to report and the component of the duty to respond that involves stopping the spill from continuing can conflict with one another. In an ideal world, sufficient personnel would be present to stop a spill from continuing and, at the same time, notify appropriate parties. Unfortunately, in many cases there are insufficient personnel to perform both tasks simultaneously.

It is usually during the first few minutes of a spill that the greatest mitigation may be performed such as turning off valves or laying down adsorbent material. Accordingly, the priority should be on performing short duration tasks, getting assistance from others, and notifying the MOEE. It is important to avoid the mentality that "If I did a little bit more, I would not have to report it."

Section 91 describes restoration of the natural environment as needing to include all forms of life, physical conditions, the natural environment, and things existing immediately before the spill that are affected or that may reasonably be expected to be affected by the pollutant. The phrase "do everything practicable" makes the scope of this duty somewhat vague, but acknowledges that limitations may exist when attempting to respond and restore the natural environment. To determine what is practicable, Section 91(3) indicates that consideration should be given to the technical, physical, and financial resources that are or can reasonably be made available.

The restoration or clean-up component of the duty to respond does not necessarily fall on the owner of the contaminated site; however, a purchaser of contaminates property becomes the "owner of the pollutant" and thereby becomes responsible for remediating a site contaminated by others. This type of undesirable outcome has prompted prospective buyers to perform environmental site assessments (see Section 5.4). It also has put pressure on property owners and potential vendors to perform assessments and remediate properties in advance of offering them for sale.

MOEE Responses to Spills

The MOEE is most likely to learn of a spill by receiving a report at the Spill Action Centre (see Section 12.4). MOEE staff sent to investigate will be interested in gathering information that can help characterize the spill event, determine the nature and extent of environmental damage, and evaluate the adequacy of the clean-up and restoration efforts. All findings, actions, and recommendations likely will be documented. Whether the documents are transferred to the Investigation and Enforcement Branch will depend on the circumstances surrounding the spill.

Sections 93 through 98 provide the MOEE with several tools for responding to spills. If responsible parties fail to clean up a spill site, Section 93 empowers the MOEE to initiate clean-up and to sue the responsible parties for the costs. Section 97 authorizes the Minister to order clean-up assistance from anyone considered necessary. Ordered persons must act with monetary questions being resolved later. Section 95 enables superior court judges to provide power of entry and the ability to commandeer equipment to anyone who has a duty to respond to a spill or clean-up.

Compensation and Distribution of Costs

Section 99 describes who is financially responsible for costs arising from spills. **Direct costs** include materials and equipment used to contain, retrieve, or dispose of the pollutant or contaminated materials, and the costs to restore the environment such as replacing damaged or destroyed vegetation. **Consequential damages** are those caused indirectly by a spill such as food spoiled by a disruption of electricity, the accommodation of temporarily displaced persons, and forced closures of businesses. Responsible parties are liable for all the direct costs associated with cleaning up a spill and any consequential damages that result from their fault or negligence during a spill or clean-up.

Sections 111 through 123 establish the Environmental Compensation Corporation (ECC) and spell out its powers and responsibilities. The ECC was established to compensate persons for loss or damage incurred as a direct result of the spill of a pollutant or neglect or fault in carrying out an order or direction under the Act.

The ECC may pay compensation to an owner of a pollutant or a person having control of a pollutant, if such individuals have had to pay compensation to spill victims but were not themselves at fault for the spill. The ECC does not replace the role of insurance companies, nor does it lessen the legal responsibilities of those involved in a spill.

Exempt Spills

Regulation 360 discusses various aspects of claiming compensation from the Crown and the ECC. Sections 18 through 22 of the regulation classify and exempt several types of spills. Some of these are exempted entirely from the requirements of Part X, while others are exempted only from the reporting provisions of Section 92:

- Class I spills are those from sewage works, water works, waste management systems, waste disposal sites, or activities involving pesticides for which a Certificate of Approval, order, licence, or permit has been issued and the spill does not contravene any other part of the EPA or any other statute, regulation, or by-law.
- Class II spills are planned and the consent of an MOEE director must be obtained before being carried out. The effects of Class II spills must be monitored. Class II spills are exempt from the requirements of Section 92 only.
- Class III spills involve 100 L or less of fuels, lubricants, or cooling liquids from vehicles that do not enter and are not likely to enter any surface water or water well. Class III spills are exempt from the requirements of Section 92 only and are not exempt from the notification requirements of the Highway Traffic Act.
- Class IV spills involve water from reservoirs formed by dams.
- Class V spills involve pollutants from fires, where the pollutants are products of combustion in quantities not greater than those normally found in 10 or fewer households.

In addition, Part X does not apply to the disposal of animal wastes in accordance with normal farming practices.

Revisions to Regulation 360 are scheduled for implementation in 1994. It is anticipated that the existing regulation will be replaced with three regulations to address the following issues:

1 - classification and exemption of spills
2 - limits of civil liabilities for farmers
3 - compensation from the ECC

12.2.2 Ontario Water Resources Act

The OWRA has similar notification requirements to those of the EPA. For example, Section 30(2) requires every person that discharges or causes or permits the discharge of any material of any kind, and such discharge is not in the normal course of events, or material of any kind escapes into any waters or on any shore or bank or into any place that may impair the quality of any waters, shall immediately notify the Minister.

An important difference between the EPA and OWRA notification requirements is the use of the term **may** in the OWRA versus **likely** in the EPA with respect to adverse effects or impairment. It is less difficult to prove that a contaminant may impair (the OWRA phrase) than it is to prove that a pollutant is likely to cause adverse effects (the EPA wording).

12.2.3 Gasoline Handling Act

The Gasoline Handling Act (GHA) addresses the storage, transportation, and distribution of gasoline and associated petroleum products. It is administered by the Ministry of Consumer and Commercial Relations (MCCR). The regulation made under the authority of the GHA is Regulation 521/93. Section 17 of the Regulation adopts the Gasoline Handling Code (GHC) which prescribes operational aspects of underground storage tank systems, above ground storage tank systems, bulk plants, private outlets, farm outlets, tank vehicles, and the storage of used oil. The descriptions of the various types of storage systems and outlets refer to subsection 8(39) of the GHC. In the event of a leak or spill, subsection 8(39) requires that the owner or operator of the facility or the driver of the tank vehicle shall take "immediate corrective action and shall":

- immediately notify the Fuels Safety Branch of the MCCR
- immediately notify the Chief Fire Official of any fire or explosion
- immediately notify the SAC of any leak or spill
- notify the local municipality of any leak, spill, fire, or explosion
- provide all information as requested by an MCCR director or inspector
- take all reasonable action to recover the escaped product.

12.3 FEDERAL LEGISLATION AND REGULATIONS

12.3.1 Canadian Environmental Protection Act

The Canadian Environmental Protection Act (CEPA) prohibits the release of toxic substances into the environment. Section 11 defines a substance as being toxic if it can have an immediate or long-term harmful effect on the environment, constitute a danger to the environment on which human life depends, or constitute a danger in Canada to human life or health.

Section 36 requires that a person who owns or has charge of a toxic substance listed in Schedule I of the CEPA immediately before its initial release or its likely initial release into the environment, or who causes or contributes to the initial release or increases the likelihood of the initial release must report the incident as soon as possible in the circumstances and make a reasonable effort to notify any member of the public who may be adversely affected by the release or likely release.

12.3.2 Transportation of Dangerous Goods Act

The Transportation of Dangerous Goods Act (TDGA) uses the term **dangerous occurrence** to describe events that include spills of dangerous goods or wastes regulated by the TDGA. Unlike provincial statutes, minimum quantities of materials are necessary to trigger the TDGA notification process. Table 12.1 presents the quantities or levels for which immediate reporting is required.

Part IX of the TDGA Regulations lists various reporting centres throughout Canada. The duty to report an occurrence applies to the person who has charge, management, or control of dangerous goods at the time he or she discovers or is advised of the occurrence. Section 9.13 of the TDGA Regulations requires that occurrences must be reported immediately to:

- the appropriate authority in the province in which the goods are located (in Ontario, this is the local police)
- the National Environmental Emergencies Centre (CANUTEC) when railway vehicles are involved
- the nearest Canadian Coast Guard Ship Safety Office and the regulatory authority of the nearest port, harbour, or wharf when a ship is involved
- the Regional Aviation Regulations Office of the Aviation Group of the Department of Transport if an aircraft is involved
- the Regional Aviation Regulations Office of the Aviation Group of the Department of Transport and the airport operator if an airport is involved
- the owner, lessee, or charterer if a road vehicle is involved
- the owner or the consignor of the dangerous goods

Section 9.14 of the TDGA Regulations requires the employer of a person who has charge, management, or control of dangerous goods involved in an occurrence shall file a written report within 30 days with the director general. The report must contain the information outlined in Form 2 as set out in Schedule IX of the TDGA Regulations. A written report also is required for several other types of events. These include the loss, theft, or misplacement of a consignment of product of certain classes of dangerous goods, and the discharge, emission, or escape of dangerous goods from any packaging or means of transport.

Schedule XII of the TDGA Regulations lists chemicals for which shipments must carry 24-hour emergency phone numbers.

Many dangerous occurrences also are classified as spills under Part X of the EPA and therefore carry requirements for reporting to several agencies.

12.4 ONTARIO SPILLS ACTION CENTRE

The MOEE operates the **Spills Action Centre** (SAC) which can be reached by dialling the following toll free number 24 hours a day:
1-800-268-6060
The SAC staff will determine whether the report is to be handled as a spill or as an environmental complaint. If it is a spill, the staff may ask for the following information:

- name and address
- telephone number/call back number
- circumstances of the spill
- material spilled (including chemical composition)
- source of spill
- quantity spilled
- weather conditions
- action being taken to clean up the spill
- involvement of other agencies

The SAC works closely with response agencies such as police, fire departments, the Canadian Coast Guard, and other reporting or information centres such as CANUTEC. SAC and CANUTEC can provide technical advice on emergency response and clean-ups.

All telephone conversations are recorded by SAC for future reference and potentially as a basis for prosecution. Upon receipt of the notification, SAC may take the following steps (MOE, 1988):

- contact suspected pollution source in an attempt to verify and resolve the problem
- contact local MOEE personnel to initiate the field response
- contact other agencies or potentially affected parties as needed such as police, fire a departments, ambulance, local municipalities, etc.
- notify senior MOEE management if the incident is considered serious and coordinate information flow to the public
- for a major incident, contact the Minister's office and convey orders or directions from the Minister where necessary
- maintain liaison with the agencies in charge of public safety in an emergency and co-ordinate the MOEE's supporting efforts
- provide information on chemicals and clean-up techniques

All occurrences reported to SAC are recorded on the computerized Occurrences Report Information System (ORIS). This system facilitates the tracking of occurrences and generating of summary statistics. The most recent summary of spills prepared by SAC concerns the year 1992 (MOEE, 1993a). The findings of that report include:

- A total of 5,014 spills were reported to SAC in 1992, down slightly from the 5,251 reported in 1991.
- Almost 59% of reported spills involved oils or fuels. Many of these occurred as a result of transportation accidents or leaks from storage facilities. Chemicals or chemical solutions accounted for approximately 15% of the spills, wastes, and wastewaters another 18%, and gaseous emissions about 6%. Other and unknown materials account for the remainder.
- About 28% of spills have confirmed environmental impacts. More than two-thirds of these involved soil contamination and the remainder involved pollution of surface waters. Another 32% of spills were recorded as having a potential to cause adverse effects.
- Approximately 45% of all spills were completely cleaned up, while 22% were partially remediated.
- Motor vehicles were the most common source of spills in 1991 accounting for about 28% of all spills. Spills from other modes of transportation were relatively infrequent. Spills from manufacturing and processing facilities accounted for about 19% of spills. Approximately 5% of spills occurred at service stations.
- The most frequently cited causes for spills in 1992 included container leaks, pipe/hose leaks, cooling system leaks, container overflows, storage tank leaks, and valve/fitting leaks or failures.

12.5 SPILL PREVENTION

Spill prevention is a cornerstone of environmental protection. Human error, whether in the form of improper procedures, lack of training, or poor engineering, has shown to be the cause of approximately 75% of all hazardous chemical spills (Shrives, 1987). Several steps can be taken to prevent spills of pollutants into the environment:

Chemical Handling Procedures – A first step in establishing chemical handling procedures may be to obtain copies of reference books on spill response such as *Environmental and Technical Information for Problem Spills (EnviroTIPS)* and the *Manual for Spills of Hazardous Materials* (Environment Canada, 1984a and 1984b). Both publications have been produced to assist in the design of countermeasures for spills and to assess their impact on the environment. There are EnviroTIPS manuals for more than 50 common and widely used hazardous compounds. The *Manual for Spills of Hazardous Materials* provides qualitative and quantitative information on 220 chemicals for those responding to, and planning for, spills of hazardous materials.

The Centre for Occupational Health and Safety (CCOHS) provides information on 27,000 substances as part on its "CCINFO disc" series. CCINFO databases include information on the physical and chemical properties of substances as well as the toxicological hazards they can pose. Listings of additional references may be obtained from the SAC and CANUTEC offices.

Process or System Modification – In the long run, modifications to processes may be the most cost-effective way to reduce or prevent spills. Modifications can eliminate the need to use certain substances, eliminate the ways the substances are handled, or eliminate the use of certain processes. An example of a system modification would be the use of recirculating cooling water as opposed to once-through cooling water. A leak of a chemical into the cooling water would stay within the system and provide an opportunity for corrective action before any of the chemical has been released to the environment.

Chemical Substitution – There is a growing trend towards replacing hazardous chemicals with non-hazardous chemicals. Wherever practical, chemicals that are spilled frequently or in large volumes should be substituted with products that pose lesser environmental concerns. Parameters that should be reviewed when assessing possible substitutes are toxicity (e.g. the concentration at which 50% of test organisms do not survive), persistence (the susceptability of the substance to degradation), and bioaccumulation (the ability of the substance to accumulate in humans and wildlife). For example, prior to selecting a hydraulic oil, data could be a collected concerning operational specifications, toxicity, and persistence, and costs (both purchase and disposal). If more than one product was able to meet the operational specifications, the next two criteria would be assessed with the goal of reducing the environmental impact of a potential spill.

Planned Maintenance – Equipment failure often contributes to spills whether directly or indirectly. The MOEE no longer entertains the defense of equipment failure if planned maintenance was not being carried out in a scheduled manner.

Back-up Equipment and Systems – Because many spills result from the failure of equipment, some form of back-up or redundancy in equipment and systems is being seen as the only way in which spills can be prevented. It also is looked upon by the MOEE as an integral part of spill prevention.

Containment – Berms, dykes, or storage ponds can be used to collect and treat released substances in controlled manners. Adequate containment can prevent releases from reaching the environment and thus prevent the release from being classified as a spill. Containment may allow a facility to continue to operate after a release occurs and thus avoid or reduce down-time.

Hazard Assessment – Hazardous operations (HAZOPS) assessment and fault tree analysis are two types of procedures frequently used to assess the appropriateness and effectiveness of equipment, procedures, and resources available to prevent and respond to releases, spills, and other types of upset conditions. These types of assessment can identify areas of potential vulnerability, deficiencies in design or scheduled maintenance, etc.

Employee Training – Regular updates of spill notification and response procedures as well as hazardous chemical handling, storage and disposal are important. At some facilities, "spill drills" analogous to fire drills are practised to ensure that all parties know their responsibilities and can carry them out in an effective manner.

12.6 EMERGENCY RESPONSE PLANS

12.6.1 Regulatory Requirements

The MOEE has no legal requirement for emergency response plans or spill contingency plans to be in place at facilities, although they are strongly encouraged. Section 18 of the EPA authorizes MOEE directors to order persons who own or manage an undertaking or property to prepare contingency plans when the director has reasonable and probable grounds for doing so.

For certain dangerous substances, specified in Schedule XII of the TDGA (such as infectious waste, explosives, certain gases and radioactive wastes) the generator or consignor of the waste must file an emergency response plan with the director general of the TDGA. Documents for each shipment of the dangerous goods must show the emergency response plan number and the telephone number for actuating the plan. The plan should allow for a qualified person to be dispatched to the accident to deal with the emergency.

12.6.2 Initial Response

It is the responsibility of the owner of the facility where the emergency has occurred or the owner of the material being released to initiate emergency response activities. The initial steps or activities of response plans typically focus on safety, stopping the spill from continuing, and notification. Accordingly, the sections of emergency plans that address initial response activities often include:

- maps showing evacuation route(s)
- maps indicating location of potential hazards accompanied by brief description of each
- descriptions of alarm systems and locations
- shutdown procedures and valves/switches locations

- contact information for individuals responsible for shutdown
- "call-out" procedures for employees and visitors
- locations of closest residences
- contact information for police, fire, MOEE, municipality, etc.

Contact information should be included for both internal and external parties. Names, titles, and telephone numbers (including home numbers for employees) should be available. It is essential that this portion of the response plan be updated frequently.

In the event of an off-site spill or a spill at a place with off-site effects, the initial response should include the immediate dispatching of a company representative to the site to ensure that all action is being taken to mitigate the effect of the spill and that the clean-up and restoration is being done properly and in compliance with MOEE and TDGA requirements.

Generic response plans have been prepared by several organizations. Two examples of publicly available booklets are those issued by the Canadian Manufacturers' Association (CMA, 1990) and the Canadian Standards Association (CSA, 1991).

12.6.3 Clean-up Procedures

Once the initial steps of an emergency response plan have been implemented, attention will turn to the tasks of containment, recovery, and clean-up. An emergency response plan should contain sections that address:

- classifying unscheduled releases or events
- determining suitable actions
- determining the types and amounts of equipment, supplies, and personnel required to implement the suitable actions require
- contact information for locating sources of equipment, supplies, and personnel, and
- environmental monitoring procedures

As noted in Section 12.2.1, releases to the environment must be classified on the basis of whether or not adverse effects are likely to occur or impairment. If adverse effects have occurred or are likely to occur, the release is classified as a spill, and the requirements of EPA Part X must be acted upon immediately. If the consensus is that the release is not a spill, internal procedures should be followed.

A large portion of the response plan may be devoted to describing various response options and the decision points for determining when specific options are suitable or necessary. The array of possible actions should reflect the substances involved, the types of events that can occur, the potential locations of spills, the locations of neighbours and sensitive environments, the ways that released materials may move in the environment, the types of adverse effects that could occur, the accessibility of the general area and specific sites of concern, and the proximity of potential sources of assistance.

Each type of action that might be taken to contain, recover, or clean up after a release will require specific types and amounts of equipment, supplies, and personnel to be implemented successfully. List of contractors, suppliers, and other potential sources of assistance should be kept and updated frequently. Some facilities have clean-up contractors on retainer to ensure a better response time. In addition, a list of registered haulers (see Chapter 4) should also be kept. It does little good to do a great clean-up job only to have the waste taken off-site by an unregistered hauler and face the possibility of receiving a violation notice.

Table 12.2 presents equipment which should be accessible to respond to spills. The list includes equipment to contain, recover, and clean up spilled material, monitoring equipment, protective and foul weather gear for workers, and various types of useful materials. Relatively simple items such as plywood sheets, rolls of heavy plastic, hay bales, empty drums, portable pumps, and generators have proven to be very useful in spill response. A totally encapsulated suit and self-contained breathing apparatus should be available for situations where there is the possibility of hazardous or unknown vapours.

The MOEE may require environmental monitoring of the area during and following clean-up. Monitoring will be needed to assess the types and extents of any adverse effects that have occurred, and to assist in identifying further remedial actions. The monitoring may include collection and chemical analysis of soil, surface water, ground water, air, aquatic organisms, etc. Short-term toxicity tests may be performed (see Chapter 13). Long-term monitoring efforts might investigate changes in the benthic community (bottom dwellers), levels in sediment and vegetation, bioaccumulation in aquatic organisms, residual toxicity, and contamination of food resources. It may be necessary and beneficial to obtain information about "background" or ambient conditions to determine whether adverse effects have truly occurred.

The final stage of emergency response is to create a positive paper trail of investigation into the spill, development of recommendations, and implementation of the recommendations be undertaken to eliminate or at least mitigate future spills. The "tallying" of spills with no further preventative action can undermine a company's claims of reasonable care or due diligence.

12.7 BEST MANAGEMENT PRACTICE PLANS

The term Best Management Practice (BMP) plan has been used by the MOEE for several years in the context of preventing damages to aquatic environments. A BMP plan is generally defined as the processes, procedures, actions, and activities used to prevent pollutants or hazardous substances from damaging the aquatic environment. The concept of BMP plans is included in the MOEE's Model Sewer-Use By-Law which, in turn, has been incorporated into many municipal sewer by-laws.

The MOEE requires BMP plans at industrial facilities as part of the Storm Water Management Plans component of the Municipal, Industrial, Strategy for Abatement (MISA) program for both direct and indirect dischargers (see Chapter 3). BMP plans, as defined by MISA, are used to control on-site spills, leaks, and runoff from raw materials storage and handling areas. In many instances, the first step towards developing a BMP is to create a BMP Committee to prepare the BMP plan and assist in its implementation, maintenance, and updating. Plant management is responsible and accountable for the plan's quality.

The activities and responsibilities of the BMP Committee should:
• identify toxic and hazardous materials to be addressed
• identify potential spill sources
• develop incident reporting procedures
• establish inspections and records procedures
• periodically review of BMP for possible changes
• co-ordinate incident notification, response, and clean-up procedures
• establish training programs for personnel, and
• assist in the interdepartmental co-ordination of plan implementation

Although the context for BMP plans is restricted to aquatic environments, the components of a BMP plan have many similarities to those described in Section 12.5. for spill prevention:

Risk Identification/Assessment – Risk assessment should be used to identify those parts of a plant that a BMP plan needs to address. All ancillary sources need to be examined to determine the potential risk of toxic pollutant or hazardous substances being discharged to receiving waters.

Materials Inventory – A listing all hazardous substances and toxic chemicals used, stored, or produced on-site should be prepared. Details of this inventory will be commensurate with quantities present and potential access to receiving waters.

Materials Compatibility – The BMP plan must provide procedures for ensuring that container materials are compatible with the toxic or hazardous substances to be stored, and with the equipment used to fill and move these materials.

Preventive Maintenance – A facility's equipment and systems should be tested from time to time to uncover conditions that could lead to malfunctions or failures. The elements of a preventative maintenance program include predetermined schedules for conducting the tests and inspections, written records of the test results, and written records of the corrective steps taken (such as adjustment, repair, or replacement). Existing preventative maintenance plans should be evaluated by qualified plant personnel to recommend any changes to bring it in line with other BMP requirements.

Record-Keeping – Several types of activities and conditions need to be recorded in a way that allows the information to be retrieved. Record-keeping systems need to capture information concerning preventative maintenance (as noted above), all unscheduled incidents, response(s), and the corrective actions taken. Record systems should be reviewed using written procedures at specified frequencies to ensure appropriate spill protection and procedures are in place.

Incident Reporting – A system needs to be in place to ensure that incidents such as spills, leaks, or other unusual releases are reported as required by various Acts and regulations. Such systems can help minimize the recurrence of incidents and expedite clean-up, as well as comply with legal requirements.

Employee Training – All employees need to understand the BMP plan. The program should emphasize plant processes and materials, safety hazards, discharge prevention practices, as well as proper and rapid response procedures. Information meetings should be held at least once a year to highlight individual responsibilities. In addition, any incidents, equipment programs, or changes to the BMP plan should be reviewed. Spill or environmental incident drills can be used to improve employees' reactions to situations and incidents. These drills, held at least semi-annually, must form a fundamental part of any training program.

Housekeeping – A clean, orderly work environment is a subtle but constant reminder of the need for a conscientious approach to environmental management at a facility. This can be accomplished by providing staff with periodic training in good housekeeping techniques examples of which include the neat and orderly storage of bags and drums of chemicals, placing materials such as scraps, cuttings, and packaging in proper containers, keeping the workplace floor clean, and ensuring that places have been designated for storing all of the raw and waste materials that are handled.

Security – The accidental or intentional entry to a facility resulting in sabotage, theft etc. can be prevented by installing a security system. Existing security systems should be detailed in the BMP plant along with any necessary improvements to ensure no toxic chemicals discharges from unauthorized entry.

12.8 MOEE SPILL PREVENTION STRATEGIES

In 1990, the MOEE developed its **Five Point Spill Prevention Strategy**. The MOEE has asked approximately 30 companies that are large and/or repeat sources of spills to prepare prevention and response work plans that contain the following components:

- Spill Risk Assessment should be based on a review of spill records and identify high-risk areas and causes of spills. This helps set priorities for corrective and preventative actions.
- Spill Detection involves a review of all the indicators that can signify a spill. Indicators can include detectors but also include routine procedures used to inspect and monitor various types of activities or functions.
- Spill Containment should look at options for preventing off-site impacts, mechanisms to store spilled materials on site, mechanisms to divert spilled materials to catchment areas, the use of sorbent materials, and options for treating and disposing spilled materials and spill collection materials.
- Spill Response Plans should provide quick response, identify types and locations of emergency response equipment, identify the notification procedures that should be followed, and refer to other sources of response information.
- Environmental Awareness Training needs to emphasize the responsibilities of individuals, departments, etc., the responses that might need to be taken, and the consequences of a spill (and possibly some types of response actions).

12.9 SHARING EMERGENCY RESPONSE INFORMATION

12.9.1 Provincial Assistance

The Province of Ontario has a contingency plan for spills of oils and other hazardous materials that is intended to be implemented when:

- the incident is beyond the capabilities of the party responsible
- the responsible party fails to respond
- the source of a major spill cannot be established easily, or
- upon request for assistance

The plan complements the Joint Canada-United States Marine Pollution Contingency Plan and the National Marine Emergency Plan (MOEE, 1993b). As part of MOEE efforts to foster spill readiness, various training films and reports are available from the SAC.

12.9.2 Trade Associations and Cooperatives

Several industrial associations and local industries have formed spill response groups to share resources and costs so that a cost-efficient and timely response capability can be achieved.

The **Transportation Emergency Assistance Plan** (TEAP) was developed by the Canadian Chemical Producers' Association as a Canada-wide emergency-wide response program. TEAP allows for companies to share resources by pooling data, equipment, and expertise. The TEAP program includes procedure manuals and training. There are sites across Canada which have response teams that are available 24 hours a day. In addition, there are numerous voluntary response centres.

The **Hamilton Harbour Spill Control Group** is an example of a co-operative venture undertaken by a collection of companies. It provides funding and assistance in the advent of a spill to the Hamilton Harbour. The group is coordinated by the Hamilton Harbour Commission.

12.9.3 The Role of the Community

A spill contingency plan should be developed with community involvement. The Canadian Chemical Producers' Association (CCPA) document entitled "Community Awareness and Emergency Response Code of Practice" outlines various forms that community involvement can take. It encourages each member to develop an emergency response plan which:

- identifies situations where company materials or processes can have an impact upon the a community in the event of an emergency
- is based upon emergency plan framework developed by site management to both address such emergency situations and to assist other authorities in emergency response planning for neighbouring industry and the community
- integrates the company's emergency response planning and organization with those of industrial neighbours and the community into a community emergency response plan
- is communicated regularly, in its key elements, to the community, and in a manner which recognized their right to know, to gain their co-operation and support, and
- requires active participation, co-operation and co-ordination by company people with local officials and the media during the planning and communication stages

Under the Emergency Planning Act of 1983, municipalities may develop emergency disaster plans which deal with large-scale emergencies and disasters. Most incidents, however, are not of a sufficient magnitude to require the implementation of an emergency disaster plan, and therefore, usually involve the traditional essential services such as fire departments, ambulance services, local police departments and, occasionally, the municipal public works department (Lesnicki, 1989).

Many municipalities have recognized that public works departments may play a more active role in responding to spills. Hence, municipal emergency response teams have been formed such as the Emergency Spill Response team of the Regional Municipality of Halton. Established in 1986, the team is comprised of regional staff from the Waste Management Division of the Public Works Department. The team receives additional training in spill response and has at its disposal a specially equipped van to deal with incidents (Lesnicki, 1989).

12.10 SUMMARY

Spill prevention is a critical component of environmental protection. Steps that should be undertaken include training, planned maintenance, back-up equipment, emergency procedures, environmental audits, containment, substitution of chemicals, and modification of processes/systems. Having a dynamic emergency response plan in place can be an essential element in demonstrating that reasonable care or due diligence is being taken.

In the event of a spill, individuals and companies are responsible for the prompt notification of the discharge to the MOEE, the municipality, the owner of the pollution, and the person who has control of the pollutant. In addition, Part X of the EPA requires the owner of a pollutant and the person having control of the pollution that is spilled to do everything practicable to prevent, eliminate, and ameliorate the adverse effects and to restore the natural environment.

REFERENCES

Canadian Chemical Producers' Association (CCPA). Not dated. *Responsible Care: A Total Commitment.*

Canadian Manufacturers' Association (CMA). 1990. *A Simplified Guide to Emergency Planning.*

Canadian Standards Association (CSA). 1991. *Emergency Planning for Industry.* CAN/CSA-Z731-M91.

Environment Canada. March 1984a. *Enviro-Technical Information for Environmental Spills: Toluene.* Environmental Protection Service.

Environment Canada. March 1984b. *Manual for Spills of Hazardous Materials.* Environmental Protection Service.

Lesnicki, V. 1989. "Handling Spills – Technical Issues." Presented at the Spills Response and Regulation Seminar, Toronto, 1 December.

Ontario Ministry of Environment and Energy (MOEE). November 1993a. *Spills Action Centre Summary Report of 1992 Spills.*

Ontario Ministry of Environment and Energy (MOEE). September 1993b. *Province of Ontario Contingency Plan for Spills of Oil and Other Hazardous Materials.*

Ontario Ministry of the Environment (MOE). 1988. *Spills – Response Program.* ISBN 0-7729-3210-7.

Shrives, J.S. May 1987. *Best Management Practices (BMPs) and Their Application to Ontario MISA Program.* Draft Version.

Table 12.1
QUANTITIES OR LEVELS FOR IMMEDIATE REPORTING UNDER TDGA

Class and Division	Quantities or Levels
1	all
2.1 and 2.2	≥ 100 L*
2.3 and 2.4	all
3	≥ 200 L
4	≥ 25 kg
5.1	≥ 50 kg or 50 L
5.2	≥ 1 kg or 1 L
6.1	≥ 5 kg or 5 L
6.2	all
7	any discharge or a radiation level exceeding 10 mSv/h at the package surface and 200 µSv/h at 1 m from the package surface
8	≥ 5 kg or 5 L
9.1	≥ 50 kg
9.2	≥ 1 kg
9.3	≥ 5 kg or 5 L

Note
* container capacity

Table 12.2
POTENTIAL EQUIPMENT FOR SPILL CONTAINMENT AND CLEAN-UP

- booms and oil skimming devices

- shovels and brooms

- pumps and vacuum equipment

- adsorbent materials

- neutralizers

- protective clothing such as respirators, gloves, etc.

- foul weather gear

- Material Safety Data Sheets (MSDS) for all chemicals used on-site

- portable air or water monitoring devices/kits

- sample bottles and sample buckets (i.e. for fish toxicity test)

- sand, earth, or vermiculite

- plywood sheets

13.0

The Role of
Toxicity Testing in
Environmental Management

13.1 BACKGROUND

Most environmental Acts include sections that prohibit releases of substances that can cause adverse environmental effects. The wording used in these acts often is somewhat vague. For example, some prohibit the release of "deleterious substances"; others prohibit the discharge of substances in "toxic amounts"; yet others prohibit releases that create "toxic conditions." The federal Fisheries Act has been used to convict persons for discharging a "toxic substance" based on the mere presence of the substance, while the amount of substance involved has been used to assess the level of damage and the extent of fines.

To give scientific meaning to the concept of toxicity, an extensive array of test methods have been developed that use many different test organisms and techniques for interpreting data. Much of this work has focused on aquatic environments and the characterizing of liquid effluents. As a result, the control of effluent toxicity has been incorporated into water quality regulations, orders, approvals, and guidelines for many types of commercial and industrial operations in Canada. Recently, advances have been made which likely will lead to terrestrial toxicity tests being incorporated into soil management policies and regulations.

13.2 TYPES OF TOXICITY TESTS

13.2.1 Acute Lethality Tests

The most common use of toxicity tests is to measure acute lethality of an effluent to an aquatic organism. This involves placing a species of fish or invertebrate into a series of containers each holding a different dilution of the effluent or toxicant to be evaluated. One of the containers — the control — contains only dilution water. The test organisms are observed at predetermined time intervals over a relatively short period (typically less than four days). The number of organisms that die in each of the dilutions provide the data used to estimate the dilution required for the effluent to be non-lethal. These tests are intended to quantify the overall toxicity of an effluent. They do not identify the substance(s) that cause the toxicity.

Several variations of the basis procedure have been developed to evaluate specific aspects of acute lethality. These variations can be described or categorized according to three characteristics: test duration, test method, and the organisms tested. The most commonly used test duration is 96 hours, but shorter (typically 24 or 48 hours) or longer durations are also used.

Test methods largely concern how the water-effluent dilutions are managed during a test. In **static** tests, the solutions are not renewed for the duration of the test. In **semi-static** or "static replacement" tests, the solutions are renewed once every 24 hours. In **continuous flow** (or "flow-through") tests, a device call a diluter is used that provides a continuous flow of effluent or toxicant dilution to the test containers. A fourth type of test, the **in situ** or "ambient water" bioassay test, requires cages to be set at different locations in the receiving water to develop an effluent dilution gradient.

The **rainbow trout** (*Salmo gairdneri*) has become the standard cool-water fish for freshwater pollution studies and research in aquatic toxicology. A large inventory of toxicological data has been assembled for this species over the last 20 years. Culturing of rainbow trout is well-established in Canada and many hatcheries will provide eggs or young fish of appropriate size and quality for toxicity test purposes. The fish must be certified as being free of specific pathogens by Fisheries and Oceans Canada (Environment Canada, 1989).

The other organism most frequently used in acute lethality tests is the **water flea** (*Daphnia magna*). It has a short life cycle capable of producing young at about two weeks of age and is relatively easy to culture in the laboratory. It is widely distributed in ponds and lakes of intermediate water hardness in Canada and the United States and has been found to be sensitive to a broad range of aquatic contaminants. Because of its small size (about the diameter of a large pencil head), tests using *Daphnia magna* require less than 1% of the volume of test solution required for trout. This greatly reduces the physical requirements for sampling and transporting of effluent samples. *Daphnia magna* are more sensitive and respond more rapidly to some toxicants than fish (Johnson and Finley, 1980) and are easily raised in the lab in large numbers.

Other freshwater species such as the Fathead minnow (*Pimphales promelas*) and bluegill sunfish (*Lepomis macrochirus*) have been used, but primarily in the United States to assess of warm-water environments. Other organisms, such as sea urchins, bivalves, and marine minnow species are used to evaluate marine environments.

Protocols for acute lethality tests using trout and daphnia were published by the MOEE in the mid-1980s and later used in the Municipal, Industrial Strategy for Abatement (MISA) program. (The essential elements of these protocols are summarized in Table 13.1.) At the time, they reflected protocols developed by Environment Canada, the U.S. Environmental Protection Agency (U.S. EPA), and American Society for Testing and Materials.

In the last couple of years, Environment Canada and the Department of Fisheries and Oceans have undertaken the Environmental Effects Monitoring (EEM) program to assess the adequacy of effluent regulations under the Fisheries Act and to achieve national uniformity in monitoring effects. Under the EEM program, monitoring requirements will be established for specific industrial sectors. The first of these have been developed for facilities regulated under the Pulp and Paper Effluent Regulations. These requirements, summarized in Table 13.2, illustrate the increasingly complex nature of toxicity testing as well as the need to assess the receiving environment and communities of aquatic organisms.

The **results of acute lethality tests** are expressed in terms of the concentration of the effluent estimated to cause the death of 50% of the test organisms. This is referred to as the 50% Lethal Concentration (or the LC_{50} value). The LC_{50} value and its 95% confidence limits can be calculated or determined graphically by plotting percentage mortality against effluent concentration. In the past, the term "median tolerance limit" (abbreviated as TL50 or TLm) often was used. It is synonymous with LC_{50}.

If no test organisms die after exposure to undiluted effluent, the result is reported as "non-lethal." If less than 50% of the test organisms die in undiluted effluent, the LC_{50} of the effluent is reported as greater than 100% (> 100%). If 50% or more organisms die in undiluted effluent, a statistically valid LC_{50} is calculated from the mortality data. Some jurisdictions also require that the 95% confidence limits be reported.

The highest concentration of a test substance in which no changes are observed is referred to as the no-observed-effect–concentration (NOEC).

LC_{50} data also can be used to calculate Toxic Unit (TU) values according to the equation:

$$TU = 100 \div LC_{50} \qquad (13.1)$$

This expression can be used to estimate the amount of dilution required to make the effluent non-lethal (LC_{50} >100%). For example, if an effluent has an LC_{50} of 5%, it has a TU value of 20 and requires a 19:1 dilution to become non-lethal. More toxic effluents have higher numbers of toxic units and require greater dilution than less toxic effluents.

The TU value can be used to express the "amount" of toxicity being discharged per unit of time as the Toxicity Emission Rate (TER) using the equation:

$$TER = TU \times Flow \tag{13.2}$$

The TER can be used to compare quantities of toxicity being discharged from different sewers within a single plant or to compare discharges among plants. The TER concept places equal weight on the toxicity and the flow of the effluent.

13.2.2 Acute Sublethal Tests

While most acute tests are directed toward observing lethal effects, sublethal effects such as organism immobilization and lethargy also may be observed and measured. For example, immobilization often is reported in tests with *Daphnia magna*. The numbers of immobilized organisms can be used to calculate the median effective concentration (EC_{50}) value in the same way that the LC_{50} is calculated.

Sublethal tests have been developed that use bacteria as the test organism. One of these assays, known as the "Microtox," has been used to evaluate various types of effluents. The test establishes an EC_{50} value on the basis of the amount of light produced by the luminescent bacterium *Photobacterium phosphoreum*. The test requires less than one hour to conduct and less than 5 mL of solution. The test has been reported to be less sensitive than tests that use rainbow trout or daphnia (McLeay and Associates Limited, 1987). Environment Canada has not included this test in aquatic environment monitoring, likely because of its lack of sensitivity.

13.2.3 Early Life Stage Sublethal Tests

Ultimately, it will be important to estimate the extent of sublethal effects that an effluent has in the receiving environment. Sublethal tests are required under the MISA program once a discharge is shown to be non-lethal during acute toxicity testing. Several sublethal tests are being used across Canada to estimate the extent of impact zones for discharges. The test organisms are exposed during sensitive stages of the life cycle. The types of effects that may be observed in sublethal tests include growth, reproduction, hatching, behaviour, and larval survival and development.

Several parameters can be used to express the results of chronic sublethal tests. The lowest concentration at which effects are observed is referred to as the LOEC. The geometric mean of the LOEC and the NOEC is referred to as the threshold effects concentrations (TEC). The data from sublethal tests can be analyzed statistically to determine the concentrations at which inhibition is observed in predetermined percentages of organisms. For example, the concentrations at which inhibition is observed in 25% is referred to as the IC_{25}. Confidence intervals can be assigned to IC values using procedures similar to those used to describe LC_{50} values.

Because of the duration and costs involved, sublethal toxicity tests are not used as frequently as acute tests to assess effluents. As shown in Table 13.2, the Pulp and Paper Effluent Regulations require sublethal testing of effluents four times per year.

The following are a few examples of sublethal toxicity tests (U.S. EPA, 1989):

Ceriodaphnia dubia **Survival and Growth**: Ten animals, each less than 24 hours old, are exposed to different concentrations, each animal being placed in a separate exposure vessel. Each surviving organism is transferred daily into a new test vessel with freshly prepared test solution and food suspension. Once the *C. dubia* has matured and produced young (on about the third day), only the adult is transferred to fresh effluent solution and fed. After seven days, the cumulative number of young produced per female are counted. The test is also conducted in a ten-fold replication. Results are expressed as the TEC, NOEC, LOEC, and the IC_{25} with its 95% confidence interval.

Daphnia sp. **Life-Cycle Toxicity Tests**: Using *Daphnia sp.* which are less than 24 hours old, 10 animals are exposed to different concentrations, each animal being placed in a separate exposure vessel. The test organisms are transferred into fresh test solutions and fed every day. Once the individual daphnids have matured and produced offspring (approximately 8 to 14 days), only the adults are transferred to a fresh test solution and fed. The remaining young are examined, counted, and recorded. After 21 days, all surviving first-generation daphnids are thoroughly examined, sacrificed, and weighed. The Chronic LC_{50}, daphnia growth, and reproduction are then evaluated statistically. This test is not yet used in any Canadian jurisdictions but is under consideration.

Fathead Minnow Larval Survival and Growth: Ten newly-hatched fathead minnow larvae are placed into each test vessel. The larvae are fed and after seven days of exposure are sacrificed and weighed. The test is conducted in a four-fold replication. The TEC, NOEC, LOEC, Chronic LC_{50}, and larval growth IC_{25} are estimated using statistical methods.

Fathead Minnow Embryo-Larval Survival and Teratogenicity: Fifteen eggs fertilized within 24 hours are removed from spawning substrates, washed, and placed in test vessels. The test solutions are renewed daily with freshly prepared concentrations. The number of surviving, dead, and deformed larvae are recorded over a seven-day period. Seven-day embryo and larvae LC_{50} values, TEC, NOEC, LOEC, IC_{25}, as well as teratogenicity endpoints are calculated using statistical methods.

To study marine environments, sea urchins, bivalves, and marine minnow species are being used for sublethal toxicity tests. In many instances, corroborative field studies and monitoring of indigenous species are required before the relevance of these tests are appreciated.

13.2.4 Terrestrial Toxicity

Efforts to improve methods used to assess soil quality are considering the potential for soil contaminants to affect terrestrial organisms. There is not yet a consensus at to which organisms should be evaluated, the test protocols that should be used, or how the results might be converted into environmental guidelines; however, all of these aspects are being investigated by organizations including the CCME, U.S. EPA, the International Organization for Standardization, and the Organization for Economic Cooperation and Development.

The deriving of criteria based on terrestrial toxicity likely will begin with identifying the organism(s) potentially at risk from the contamination. Ideally, the selected organism(s) should reflect important characteristics of the ecosystem, be sensitive to the contaminants of concern, and be relevant to the land uses of interest. The available information may limit the extent to which this can be realized.

Once the organism(s) have been identified, the way(s) in which contact occurs with contaminants can be evaluated. These pathways may include direct ingestion of soil, water, or other organisms, direct contact with soil, inhalation of air, or indirectly via the food chain. Direct contact and/or ingestion are likely to be the pathways of greatest concern for organisms such as soil bacteria, fungi, and earthworms. Food chain effects are likely to the pathways of most concern for animals at higher trophic levels that are consumers (i.e. herbivores and carnivores). For many species, the information needed to assess pathways is very limited. Numerous assumptions will be needed to estimate intake rates of soil, food items, water, or air, dermal contact rates, amount of time spent in contact with contaminated materials, bioavailability of contaminants from ingested material, etc.

The next step will be to compare the estimated extent of contact to the data from toxicity tests (typically conducted in the laboratory) or observations/measurements made in the field. Soil toxicity information is lacking for many contaminants. Generally, there is more information available for inorganic contaminants than organic contaminants. The largest information base involves terrestrial plants, while a growing area of study involves organisms such as earthworms and isopods (such as woodlice) that are constantly in contact with soil. Few studies have been conducted on birds, with many of the published accounts are limited to poultry or other game bird species. Relatively little information is available for mammals other than laboratory rodents. Some information is available for direct soil ingestion by grazing animals including cows and sheep.

The test protocols most commonly used and accepted are short-term (7 or 14 day) mortality tests for earthworms and a 5-day seed germination/root elongation test for plants. The results are expressed as LC_{50}, EC_{50}, IC_{25}, NOEC, and LOEC values analogous to those used for reporting the results of aquatic toxicity testing. Other tests are being developed that will evaluate end-points other than lethality. Long-term tests also are being developed that will last for at least one reproduction cycle (for soil invertebrates) or one growth cycle (for plants).

To determine soil quality criteria, toxicity test results for a contaminant will be used to create a distribution of concentrations at which effects occur. A point in that distribution, possibly divided by a safety factor, will be used to define a concentration below which adverse effects should be not occur. For example, the point corresponding to the 10th percentile (i.e. 90% of the effects happen at concentrations greater than the selected point) might be chosen. The magnitude of the safety factor will reflect the quality and quantity of toxicity data, with larger values being used when the data are limited or otherwise suspect. The value produced by dividing the selected point by the safety factor would then be used as one of the pieces of information used to establish a soil quality guideline or criterion.

The preceding discussion indicates that the assessment of soil and sediment toxicity is following much the same path as water quality toxicity assessment; however, several factors make soil and sediment toxicity assessment more complex and may slow the rate at which toxicity is incorporated into setting soil quality criteria. In water, the molecular and soluble fractions of contaminants can be measured directly and related to biological effects with relatively easily derived modifiers such as pH and hardness. In soils, the measured concentrations of contaminants are less important than the percentage that is biologically available, which is influenced by factors such as adsorption, absorption, chelation, and binding to organic compounds as well as the factors that are relevant for water.

These factors (and perhaps more) have made it difficult to draw correlations between measured concentrations of contaminants in soil and the effects observed in biological systems. These findings not only suggest that different approaches should be used to derive water and soil quality criteria, but also may point to limitations in other aspects of environmental management. For example, in Ontario (and in many other jurisdictions), the procedure used to determine if solid wastes are "registerable" or "leachate toxic" is to compare concentrations of contaminants in an acidic aqueous extract to drinking water objectives (see Section 4.2.2). While intended to protect human health by controlling the quality of ground water around disposal sites, the approach may not be protective of aquatic or terrestrial organisms. Given that aquatic biota demonstrate greater sensitivity to ambient contaminant concentrations than do humans, ground water quality judged acceptable for human exposure will not necessarily provide the same level of safety to other biota.

13.3 ONTARIO REQUIREMENTS

Several provincial acts use toxicity concepts to prohibit specific types of activities. For example, the Ontario Water Resources Act (Chapter 361, Section 16(1)) prohibits persons from discharging any material into any water that "may impair water quality." Section 14 of the Environmental Protection Act states that "no person shall discharge a contaminant or cause or permit the discharge of a contaminant into the natural environment that causes or may cause an adverse effect." Under the terms of the Canada-Ontario accord, Ontario has agreed to establish and enforce effluent toxicity testing requirements at least as stringent as federal requirements.

Acute lethality testing is a requirement of the Municipal, Industrial Strategy for Abatement (MISA) program (refer to Section 3.3 for additional information on MISA). Under the MISA program, most dischargers are required to perform acute toxicity testing using rainbow trout and *Daphnia magna*. By January 1996, MISA regulations will require that the effluents from pulp and paper mills, major mines and metal refineries, and petroleum refineries not exceed prescribed amounts of contaminants and that the effluents must not be lethal to more than 50% mortality in tests of trout and daphnia. A consistent record of acceptable lethality tests may result in chronic tests taking the place of acute lethality tests. Similar requirements for other industrial sectors are being developed.

To meet the lethality limits outlined under the MISA program, companies may elect to conduct a Toxicity Identification Evaluation/Toxicity Reduction Evaluation (TIE/TRE). A TIE/TRE approach is discussed in Section 13.5.

The document entitled *Water Management Goals, Policies, Objectives, and Implementation Procedures* (commonly referred to as the "Blue

Book") states that one of the overall goals of the MOEE is to ensure that surface waters are of a quality which is satisfactory for aquatic life (MOE, 1992). Policy 3 of that document addresses effluent regulations and indicates that bioassay tests may be required to identify discharges deleterious to aquatic organisms. Discharges which produce 96-hour LC_{50} values under static test conditions may require more rigorous biological testing to determine if additional treatment is needed to afford adequate protection to the environment. The testing may include biological responses other than mortality.

The Blue Book recognizes the concept of a mixing zone around a discharge point; however, mixing zones should not be rapidly lethal to important aquatic life or result in conditions which cause sudden fish kills or mortality of organisms passing through the mixing zone or create barriers to the migration of fish and aquatic life.

13.4 FEDERAL REQUIREMENTS

The federal government has incorporated aquatic toxicity testing into effluent regulations and guidelines for several commercial and industrial sectors. For metal mining (excluding gold), meat and poultry product plants, potato processors, and petroleum refineries, undiluted effluent must not be fatal to more than 50% of rainbow trout in a 96-hour, flow-through test. Since the promulgation of these regulations in the 1970s, relatively few flow-through tests have been conducted due to the excessive logistical demands of the protocol.

In 1992, the Department of Fisheries and Oceans promulgated the Pulp and Paper Effluent Regulations (SOR/92-269) under the Fisheries Act. Some of the key requirements of the regulations include monthly acute lethality testing using rainbow trout and *Daphnia magna*; *Daphnia* tests conducted in parallel with the trout tests that trigger additional trout tests when 50% mortality is exceeded; discharges must exhibit less than 50% mortality in trout tests after 31 December 1995; and the results of EEM program studies must be submitted by 01 April 1996 and every year thereafter. Facilities may elect to undertake TIE/TRE studies to eliminate lethality.

In that same year, Environment Canada and the Department of Fisheries and Oceans initiated the EEM program to assess the adequacy of effluent regulations under the Fisheries Act and to achieve national uniformity in monitoring effects. One part of the EEM program has been to standardize acute lethality and sublethal toxicity test methods for several test organisms including trout, *Daphnia*, fathead minnows, echinoderms, amphipods, sticklebacks, luminescent bacteria, and algae.

Another part of the EEM program is to describe in detail the monitoring requirements of the effluent regulations as they are prepared for specific industrial sectors. The first set of EEM requirements was prepared for the pulp and paper sector and is summarized in Table 13.2. The requirements are described in detail in an annex (Environment Canada and Department of Fisheries and Oceans, 1992) to a general EEM guidance document (Environment Canada and Department of Fisheries and Oceans, 1993). EEM requirements and annexes for other industrial sectors are in preparation.

13.5 DETERMINING THE CAUSES OF EFFLUENT TOXICITY

13.5.1 Conventional Approach

Traditionally, when an effluent is identified as toxic to aquatic organisms, a sample of the wastewater is analyzed for certain pollutants such as those in the MISA Analytical Test Groups of substances (ATGs) or the U.S. EPA priority pollutants. The concentration of each pollutant present in a sample subsequently is compared to toxicity data for the pollutant in the published literature or the rationales for the *Provincial Water Quality Objectives* and the surface water guidelines of Environment Canada (Figure 13.1). Unfortunately, determining the source of an effluent's toxicity rarely is so straightforward.

The first problem encountered is one of effluent variability. There is no way to determine whether the toxicity observed over time is consistently caused by a single pollutant or combination of pollutants or a number of different pollutants, each periodically being the cause of the toxicity. Experience has shown that the latter scenario occurs frequently. Further complicating the problem is that the variability in conventional effluent monitoring parameters may not coincide with variability in the effluent of the causative toxicant (Mount and Anderson-Carnahan, 1988).

A second limitation with the conventional approach is the assumption that only the ATGs or priority pollutants cause the toxicity. While some pollutants are regulated largely due to their toxicity to aquatic organism and/or a high frequency of occurrence in discharges, the ATGs or the priority pollutants list by no means represents the universe of toxic chemicals present in wastewater. Limiting the search to these compounds excludes other chemicals from consideration and limits the chances for successfully identifying the causative toxicant.

Another limitation is that the conventional analytical focus does not account for interactions between toxicants or the influence on toxicity under conditions commonly encountered in effluents such as extreme pH or high-dissolved-solids concentrations.

13.5.2 U.S. EPA Approach to Toxicant Identification

In the United States, the National Pollutant Discharge Elimination System (NPDES) includes toxicity testing requirements. Chemistry and toxicity data pertaining to the discharge are provided by the discharger, the U.S. EPA, and/or the state. The lowest one-week average flow that will likely occur once every 10 years is also provided. Depending upon the data, it is then decided if toxicity limits should be incorporated into the permit.

Where toxicity limits have been imposed, the in-stream concentration of the effluent in the receiving water must not exceed the lowest observable effect concentration of the most sensitive test species. For dischargers with greater than a 100:1 dilution at low flow, there must not be acute lethality at the end of the pipe (i.e. the LC_{50} must be greater than 100%). For dischargers with less than 100:1 dilution, the dischargers also must comply with a chronic toxicity limit and the effluent concentration which occurs at the edge of the mixing zone at low flow must not cause a chronic effect.

When a discharger is not in compliance, a step-wise investigative process termed a Toxicity Reduction Evaluation (TRE) can be used to determine the measures needed to maintain toxicity at an acceptable level. A key part of a TRE is the Toxicity Identification Evaluation (TIE). Procedures for performing TIEs have been developed by the U.S. EPA National Effluent Toxicity Assessment Centre (NETAC). The NETAC approach is divided into three phases (Burkhard and Ankley, 1989):

Phase I   –   identification of physical and chemical nature of toxicant(s)

Phase II –   identify toxicant(s)

Phase III –   confirm suspected toxicant(s)

Figure 13.2 shows the relationships of the NETAC approach to TIE with the overall TRE assessment.

Phase I of the TIE is used to characterize certain physical and chemical properties of the toxicant(s) using a series of relatively simple, low-cost chemical and biological analyses. Each test is designed to remove or render biologically unavailable a specific group of toxicants such as oxidants, cationic metals, volatile compounds, non-polar organic compounds and metal chelates (Mount and Anderson-Carnahan, 1988). Figure 13.3 presents the various Phase I tests.

The **oxidation reduction test** is designed to determine whether oxidants and other electrophiles are responsible for effluent toxicity. Examples of oxidants include chlorine, bromine, iodine, ozone, and chlorine dioxide. Sodium thiosulfate ($Na_2S_2O_3$) is added in varying ratios to produce reducing agent/total electrophiles solutions and thus reduce any toxicity due to the above compounds.

The **aeration test** is designed to determine whether the toxicants present are volatile. Sparging of samples using air or nitrogen gas is used to remove the volatile substances from solution. Examples of chemicals which may be detected using this method include benzene and hydrogen sulfide.

The **filtration test** involves passing samples of the test solution at three pH values (pH of 3, 7, and 11) through glass fibre filters. The test identifies which groups of compounds can be precipitated under acidic or alkaline conditions. Data from this test can help define treatment strategies.

The **pH adjustment test** is used to identify the presence of cationic and anionic toxicants. Changing the pH changes the ratio of ionized to unionized chemical species and since the later is the more toxic form, the toxicity of the solution will change as the pH is shifted.

In the **graduated pH test**, the pH of the effluent is adjusted within the tolerable range of 6.0 to 8.0 before retesting with aquatic organisms. This test is designed primarily to identify ammonia, hydrogen sulfide, and cyanide, but some ionizable pesticides and heavy metals also can be identified.

The **Solid Phase Extraction (SPE) test** is designed to determine the effluent toxicity caused by non-polar organic compounds and metal chelates. The effluent is passed through a small column, which removes non-polar organic compounds. Toxicity reduction suggests the presence of toxic organic compounds.

The **chelation test** is used to determine if the toxicity is caused by cationic toxicants such as heavy metals. Ethylenediaminetetraacetate ligand (EDTA) is a strong chelating (binding) agent that produces non-toxic complexes with many metals and can reduce the toxicity of solutions containing metal ions.

Aquatic organism toxicity tests, performed on the effluent prior to and after the individual characterization treatment, indicate the effectiveness of the treatment and thus provide information on the nature of the toxicant(s). By repeating the series of toxicity characterization tests using samples of a particular effluent collected over a period of time, these screening tests can provide valuable information on the variability associated with the type of compounds causing the toxicity (Mount and Anderson-Carnahan, 1988).

Phase II of the TIE is directed toward identifying toxicants. Various chemical fractionation techniques such as high-performance liquid chromatography, mass spectroscopy, and further SPE tests may be used. The results obtained in Phase I are used to select appropriate techniques for Phase II.

For each toxicant that is identified in Phase II, the published literature is searched for LC_{50} values or individual tests of that chemical may be conducted. Concentrations of the toxicant in effluent can be compared with the LC_{50} values. A list of suspected toxicants is then compiled.

Phase III of the TIE is used to confirm the suspected toxicants identified in Phase II. Techniques that can be used in Phase III include correlations, relative species sensitivity, spiking, and removal of one toxicant at a time from the effluent. In most instances, several tests are needed to confirm the toxicants. Research is continuing at the U.S. EPA and many other laboratories to refine this phase of the overall approach.

Once a TIE is completed, it may be necessary to enter the next step of a TRE which involves the selection and implementation of control methods. In some cases, it is possible that Phase I of the TIE can indicate which treatment methods should remove the causative toxicant(s) from the effluent. Bench-scale studies can be used to evaluate the feasibility of treating effluent toxicity on a large scale. The actual identity of the causative toxicant(s) may not be required; it is only necessary that enough information be available on the toxicant physical/chemical characteristics to predict which treatment options should be studied (Mount and Anderson-Carnahan, 1988). This is analogous to designing a treatment system to handle a specified biochemical oxygen demand (BOD) loading with little or no knowledge of the actual chemicals that comprise the BOD.

In other cases, Phases II and III may be needed to identify the toxicants. If a causative toxicant can be identified in an effluent, the next step of a TRE can be to track a toxicant back through the process line or effluent collection system to its source using chemical analysis (provided that it is not a by-product of other chemicals in the system). Once the source is identified, a source investigation can be conducted. The source control may be in the form of improved spill control, process modification, substitution of raw materials, pretreatment, and/or treatment.

13.6 SUMMARY

Toxicity testing is part of both provincial and federal regulations. The MOEE has described acute lethality toxicity tests using rainbow trout and *Daphnia magna* as part of the effluent monitoring required under the MISA program. New federal regulations include an extensive array of toxicity testing for pulp and paper mills. Requirements for other industrial sectors are being prepared.

Facilities that fail to achieve a non-lethal discharge may be required by provincial and/or federal regulations to perform studies such as a Toxicity Identification Evaluation/Toxicity Reduction Evaluation. A well-documented step-wise investigative process for toxicant identification has been documented by the U.S. EPA. The approach focuses first on identifying the physical and chemical nature of the toxicant(s), followed by the identification of the toxicant(s) and development of control alternatives. The approach may result in product substitution, process modifications and/or additional treatment.

Regulations under both the MISA program and Environment Canada's new national effluent regulations also require sublethal toxicity testing of effluents. The types of effects that may be observed in sublethal tests include growth and reproduction, and early life stage survival.

REFERENCES

Burkhard, L. P. and Ankley, G. T. 1989. "Identifying Toxicants: NETAC's Toxicity-based Approach." *Environmental Science and Technology*, 12(12):1438-43.

Craig, G., K. Flood, J. Lee, and M. Thomson. 1983. *Protocol to Determine the Acute Lethality of Liquid Effluents to Fish*. Aquatic Toxicity Unit, Quality Protection Section, Water Resources Branch.

Environment Canada. July 1990a. *Reference Method for Determining the Acute Lethality of Effluent to Rainbow Trout*. EPS 1/RM/13.

Environment Canada. July 1990b. *Reference Method for Determining the Acute Lethality of Effluent to Daphnia Magna*. EPS 1/RM/14.

Environment Canada. 1992a. *Technical Guidance Manual for Aquatic Environmental Effects Monitoring at Pulp and Paper Mills*. EPS 1/RM/.

Environment Canada. 1992b. *Chronic Toxicity Test Using the Cladoceran Ceriodaphnia dubia*. Conservation and Protection, Ottawa, Ontario. EPS 1/RM/21.

Environment Canada. 1992c. *Test of Larval Growth and Survival Using Fathead Minnows*. Conservation and Protection, Ottawa, Ontario. EPS 1/RM/22.

Environment Canada. 1992d. *Algal Growth Inhibition/Simulation Test Using Selenastrum capricornutum*. EPS 1/RM/.

Environment Canada. 1992e. *Early Life-Stage Test for Toxicity Using Salmonid Fish*. EPS 1/RM/.

Environment Canada and Department of Fisheries and Oceans. 1992. *Annex 1: Aquatic Environmental Effects Monitoring Requirements at Pulp and Paper Mills and Off-Site Treatment Facilities Regulated under the Pulp and Paper Regulations of the Fisheries Act*.

Environment Canada and Department of Fisheries and Oceans. 1993. *Technical Guidance Document for Aquatic Environmental Effects Monitoring Related to Federal Fisheries Act Requirements*. Version 1.0, April.

Environmental Protection Act (EPA). 1989. *Ontario Regulation 695/88 as amended to Ontario Regulation 533/89 under the Environmental Protection Act: Effluent Monitoring - General*. Schedule 4 - Toxicity Test Requirements.

Johnson, W.W., and M.T. Finley. 1980. *Handbook of Acute Toxicity of Chemicals to Fish and Aquatic Invertebrates*. U.S. Fish and Wildlife Service, Publication No. 137.

McLeay and Associates Limited. 1987. *Aquatic Toxicity of Pulp and Paper Mill Effluents: A Review*. Environment Canada report EPS 4/PF/1.

Mount, D.I., and L. Anderson-Carnahan. February 1988. *Methods for

Aquatic Organism Toxicity Reduction Evaluations; Phase I Toxicity Characterization Procedures, Second Draft - February 1988. U.S. Environmental Protection Agency.

Ontario Ministry of the Environment (MOE). October 1992. *Water Management Goals, Policies, Objectives, and Implementation Procedures.*

Poirier, D.G., G.F. Westlake, and S.G. Abernathy. 1988. *Daphnia magna Acute Lethality Toxicity Test Protocol.* Aquatic Toxicity Unit, Aquatic Biology Section, Water Resources Branch, MOE.

United States Environmental Protection Agency (U.S. EPA). February 1989. *Short-Term Method for Estimating the Chronic Toxicity of Effluents and Receiving Water to Fresh Water Organisms.* Second edition. U.S. EPA 600/4-89/001, February.

Table 13.1
MOEE PROTOCOLS FOR ACUTE LETHALITY TESTING

Test Organism: rainbow trout (Salmo Gairdneri)
- 96-hour duration
- individual fish should weigh between 0.5 and 5 g
- the longest fish should not be twice the length of the shortest fish
- 10 fish per test container
- maintain dissolved oxygen concentration of 7 mg/L
- pH between 5.0 and 9.0 (prefer 6.0 and 8.5)
- temperature 15 ± 1 °C
- dilution water must be capable of maintaining healthy fish stocks for at least 10 days
- fish should not be fed within 24-hour period prior to the test or during the test
- observations mandatory at 0.5, 1, 2, 4, 24 hours and every 24 hours thereafter (should be made as often as possible)
- five test concentrations (e.g. 100, 50, 25, 12.5 and 6.3%) and a control solution (100% dilution water)

Reference: Craig *et al.*, 1983

- six test concentrations (i.e. 10, 20, 30, 40, 65, 100%) and a control solution (100% dilution controls)

Reference: EPA, 1989 for MISA monitoring

Test Organism: water flea (*Daphnia magna*)
- 48-hour duration
- minimum of 10 organisms per chamber
- only used when water hardness is greater than 80 mg/L
- pH between 6.0 and 9.0 (prefer 6.5 and 8.5)
- temperature 20 ± 1 °C
- five test concentrations (e.g. 100, 50, 25, 12.5 and 6.3%) and a control solution (100% dilution water)
- observations mandatory at 1, 2, 4, 24, and 48 hours
- dissolved oxygen, pH, hardness, and conductivity must be measured immediately before and after the test is completed

Reference: Poirier *et al.*, 1988

Table 13.2
FEDERAL EEM PROGRAM TOXICITY TESTING REQUIREMENTS

Pre-design Requirements
- 96-hour Rainbow Trout lethality tests and 48-hour *Daphnia magna* lethality tests of the effluent as described in Environment Canada, 1990a and 1990b
- plus provide a description of the study area (or receiving environment), history of the mill and operations, and effluent quality characterization studies

First cycle EEM Requirements (for Freshwater Environments)
- quarterly fish early life stage development tests using Fathead minnow or a salmonid species if the Flathead minnow is not indigenous
- quarterly invertebrate reproduction tests using *Ceriodaphnia dubia*
- quarterly plant toxicity tests using *Selenastrum capricornutum* or *Lemma minor*
- plus surveys of adult fish and invertebrate community; tissue analysis for chlorinated dioxins and furans (for mills using chlorine bleaching), tissue tainting evaluations (where there is a history of tainting), chemical characterization of receiving water and sediment
- all test methods to be those described in Environment Canada, 1992a through 1992e
- extensive reporting requirements as described in Environment Canada and Department of Fisheries and Oceans, 1992
- other test species and procedures to be used for marine environments as described in Environment Canada and Department of Fisheries and Oceans, 1992

Subsequent cycle EEM Requirements
- first cycle results to be reviewed prior to defining requirements for subsequent cycles

New Mills
- required to complete the pre-design and first cycle requirements prior to start-up to establish baseline conditions against which future results will be assessed

Figure 13.1
CONVENTIONAL APPROACH TO IDENTIFYING EFFLUENT TOXICANTS

Step 1   Toxicity test of effluent

Step 2   Priority pollutant analysis

Step 3   Comparison of analysis results to literature values for aquatic organism toxicity

Step 4   Toxicant(s) identified—reduction, substitution and/or treatment of toxicant(s)
          Toxicant(s) not identified—perform additional monitoring of parameters, in terms of both frequency and number of parameters

---

Figure 13.2
FLOWCHART FOR TOXICITY REDUCTION EVALUATIONS

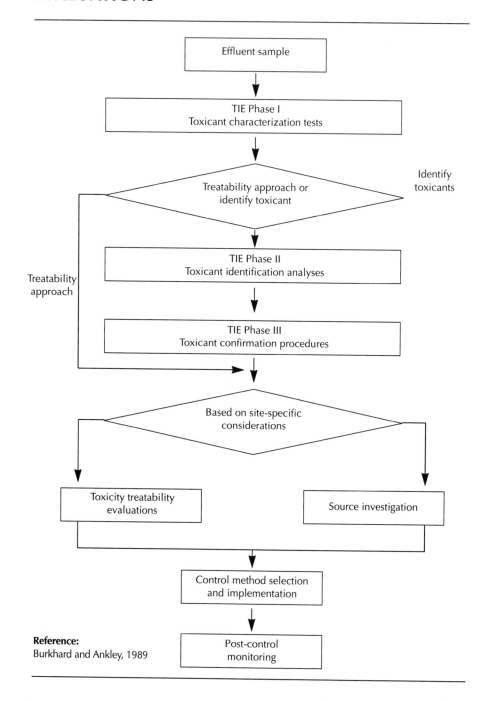

Reference:
Burkhard and Ankley, 1989

Figure 13.3
TOXICITY INVESTIGATION EVALUATIONS—
PHASE I TESTS

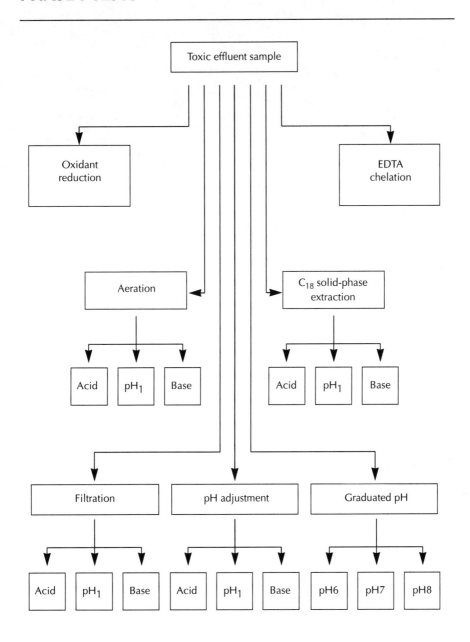

Reference: Burkhard and Ankley, 1989